Revolution and
Counterrevolution in China

Revolution and Counterrevolution in China

The Paradoxes of Chinese Struggle

Lin Chun

VERSO

London • New York

First published by Verso 2021
© Lin Chun 2021

1 3 5 7 9 10 8 6 4 2

Verso
UK: 6 Meard Street, London W1F 0EG
US: 20 Jay Street, Suite 1010, Brooklyn, NY 11201
versobooks.com

Verso is the imprint of New Left Books

ISBN-13: 978-1-78873-563-6
ISBN-13: 978-1-78873-564-3 (UK EBK)
ISBN-13: 978-1-78873-565-0 (US EBK)

British Library Cataloguing in Publication Data
A catalogue record for this book is available from the British Library

Library of Congress Cataloging-in-Publication Data
Library of Congress Control Number: 2021930373

Typeset in Minion by Biblichor Ltd, Edinburgh
Printed and bound by CPI Group (UK) Ltd, Croydon CR0 4YY

To the memory of Lin Xia – sister, friend, a pure soul, true communist; and to our romance with revolution growing up in red China

Contents

Preface

A century ago, in July 1921, thirteen people representing China's earliest communist groups – already working on promulgating the Marxist ideas and labour agitation in various provinces – gathered in Shanghai to hold their first national congress. The founding of the Chinese Communist Party (CCP), the revolution it led to victory twenty-eight years later and the social transformations it has steered since have all been nothing less than world-historical. Time and again the party has narrowly escaped extinction, only to build itself into the largest and most formidable revolutionary party in history – until undergoing a perceived normalization after thirty years in power. This book focuses on the continuing changes within the People's Republic and the unprecedented challenges it faces today, set against the historical and international parameters of global capitalism which are themselves evolving, ascribable to the intervening forces among others of the China factor. About Chinese development and its vast internal and external implications, I wish to ask *what, where, how* and *why*, in the awareness that there is no simple answer to any of these questions and history can never end. With an open mind, I appreciate sharing some preliminary clarifications in debating the nature and orientation of struggles in China.

I am deeply grateful to the friends and colleagues with whom I have had the good fortune to discuss relevant issues; many of their own works have also inspired and educated me. I owe them a huge intellectual debt. I have nevertheless decided not to name any individuals, so as to ensure that I am duly regarded as being solely responsible for my arguments. The only exceptions are John Merrick and my copyeditors at Verso. I have had a special feeling for Verso since my student days of researching the British New Left, and I am honoured to publish this book with it. John took the trouble to have my manuscript thoroughly edited, and his queries helped me to think and explain better. I am also exceedingly indebted to Duncan Ranslem and Natalie Hume for their further, meticulous editorial help. They too, of course, take no responsibility for my views or any stylistic errors remaining. Meanwhile, I have adapted passages from *China and Global Capitalism* (Palgrave, 2013) in Chapter 1 and from 'China's New Globalism' (in Leo Panitch and Greg Albo, eds, *The World Turned Upside Down? The Socialist Register*, Merlin Press, 2018) in Chapter 7. I thank these publishers and editors for their kind permission.

On this occasion of the CCP's centennial, the first thing to remember is that tens of millions of heroic men and women, mostly young, fought and died for the creation of a new China and a new world. Their precious lives should not be wasted. This is the pledge we all made as Young Pioneers. My late sister, to whose memory this book is dedicated, was serious about it all her life, as a pupil, peasant, student, scientist, researcher, technician and teacher (in that order), more serious than typical officials today. I miss singing with her our favourite revolutionary songs; the best we did was to duet 'On the Taihang Mountains' (a red base area 1937–49) and 'There's a Young Soldier . . .' (untitled with wartime Soviet lyrics).

Lin Chun
1 October 2020

PART ONE

Revolution and History; China and Global Capitalism

1

Awakening to the modern world

China is an ancient civilization, one of the oldest and longest surviving in human history. The origins of the Qin–Han state were being built at around the same time as the rise of Rome in the Western Hemisphere, from an amalgam of the Warring States and the conquest of Greek poleis respectively. Both China and Rome expanded into giant empires, comparable in scale, splendour and sophistication. The 'silk people' (as the Romans called the Chinese), and Da Qin (as the Chinese called the Romans), although having little actual knowledge of each other, conducted a flourishing trade, making exchanges across vast continental and maritime expanses and involving many other societies. Yet imperial China, influenced also by the earlier Arabic-Persian and Indus cultures, had no affinity with the military might and methods typical of its European counterpart. And their political genetics differed between the dominant ideas of *unity* in the former and of *autonomy* in the latter. In this sense, 'empire' – a term borrowed from the language of the Europeans – is the wrong label for China until a much later stage (it is used here only by convention, with due awareness of the mismatch). While the Roman Empire fell in the fifth century, China survived all the major premodern empires. The far-reaching imperial stretch, rooted in the basic social organism of official-gentry management, cultural magnetism and elastic inter-unit liaisons, is a factor in this longevity.

While republican Rome appears paradigmatic in Western history, ancient China is often believed to be a despotic outlier from 'normal' progress, to the extent that many of modern China's political traits are attributed to a deep dynastic past.[1] On this reading, China is either incapable of modernity, or has not yet learned to be adequately modern – tautologically so because of its unbroken traditional and territorial inheritance. Even the contemporary People's Republic of China (PRC) can be no more than 'a civilization pretending to be a nation-state'.[2] However, as economic and social historians have revealed, China has long been economically and culturally open, as typified in the cosmopolitanism of its high Tang-Song period. By the fifteenth to sixteenth centuries, it was the largest trader on the silver standard, contributing to the formation of the global capitalist system, and, for a few centuries, it was the richest nation in the world. Moreover, the twentieth-century Chinese revolutions made a world-historical difference for the country, the region and the global order, enacting the 'revolutionary break with the past' required as the entry ticket to modernity.[3]

The intensity of imperialist encroachment and anti-imperialist movements marked a revolutionary century in China under the influence of the Russian Revolution, constitutive of wider liberation struggles at the time. To situate China globally by way of clarifying its evolving interactions with the genesis and expansion of capitalism is not to find a fixed genealogical entity in a static international order, nor is it to measure the distance between a latecomer and some standardized modern projection. To track China's transformations as a nonlinear series of historical passages, both forwards and backwards, is to bypass the European imagination of the world epitomized by the capitalist totality. Yet capitalism encompasses the local and global contexts, at the same time catalysing China's industrial growth and social contestations, communist and post-communist transitions, and competing political and socioeconomic systems more broadly. It has been a process of uneven development, one filled with contradictions as well as opportunities.

1 Sunny Auyang, *The Dragon and the Eagle: The Rise and Fall of the Chinese and Roman Empires*, Cambridge MA: MIT Press, 2014: xxiv; Francis Fukuyama, *The Origins of Political Order: From Prehuman Times to the French Revolution*, New York: Farrar, Straus and Giroux, 2012, chs 6–9; Timothy Brook, 'Great States', *Journal of Asian Studies* 75:4, November 2016: 962–3.

2 Lucian Pye, 'Social Science Theories in Search of Chinese Realities', *China Quarterly* 132, December 1992: 1162.

3 Barrington Moore, *Social Origins of Dictatorship and Democracy: Lord and Peasant in the Making of the Modern World*, Boston, MA: Beacon, 1966: 431.

Marx and revolutions in Asia before Europe

Global–local interactions are always a two-way street, containing both possibilities and constraints. Because of the overriding and relentless power of capital, any sizeable national or regional society can be understood only in its position relative to the conditions of global capitalism. We therefore follow Marx's conception of world history, beginning with the epoch of capitalist global transformation, which for the first time connected hitherto disjointed economies and cultures through a chain of conquests by both heavy artillery and cheap commodities. Capitalism is thus an engine of modern global development, and one that requires a holistic approach from observers and critics. The epochal conditions shaped by capitalism's economic, political, military and ideological powers were colonial and imperialist from the outset. In turn, these conditions are so powerful that they become internal to local and initially resistant societies, disregarding the diverse identities, desires or contentions of a heterogeneous globe.

In *The Communist Manifesto*, Marx and Engels brilliantly construed the historical distinctions that mark the capitalist epoch. The need for endless accumulation forced the new bourgeois class to chase across the globe, in doing so constantly revolutionizing production while transforming any pre-capitalist relations found along the way. A world market then enabled integration as much as polarization, between rich and poor, dominating and subordinate, oppressor and oppressed peoples. These parallel processes saw both the production of imperialist monopoly super-profit for the colonizers and, for the colonized, the barbarity of invasion, extraction, looting, enslavement and genocide. The birth of modern industry was 'heralded by a great slaughter of the innocents', and processes of plunder and exploitation that Marx called 'the chief momenta of primitive accumulation', where trade and gunboat diplomacy were interchangeable. Theories of capitalism and imperialism differ on many matters, but they largely concur on this point of their generic symbiosis. Marx noted in particular how the Opium Wars allowed the British 'moneyocracy and oligarchy' to rob India and China, bankrupting their handicraft sectors and textile industries as well as their trading networks and socioeconomic fabrics. These wars fortified the 'supreme rule of capital', forcing 'a new and international division of labour' through an ever-intensified exhaustion of China's silver reserve and coastal de-(proto)industrialization.[4]

Marx initially had faith that the Western bourgeoisie would set about creating a world in its own image, a faith that was unshaken until the 1850s, an intense decade of watching events unfold in Asia. For a while he fell back on an earlier Eurocentric depiction of Oriental stagnation, finding no radical novelty in the Asian history's first 'revolutionary epoch' with the Taiping Rebellion in China (1850–64) or the Indian Mutiny (1857–58). Yet, profoundly repulsed by the savage suppression of these uprisings, what remained 'gratifying' for him was that any social upheaval in the Orient 'must have most profound consequences for civilization'. This was an optimism he was to stand by, asking, 'Can mankind fulfil its destiny without a fundamental revolution in the social state of Asia?'[5] Later in the 1870s, pondering the Narodnik thesis about Russian renewal, he came to see the feasibility of skipping capitalism in the prototypical case of the village *mir*, or peasant commune, that had inherited communal property on the one hand and growing individuality on the other. Being contemporaneous to the development of capitalism in the West, the Russian commune might 'appropriate its fruits without subjecting itself to its *modus operandi*'.[6] This was a real breakthrough in the Marxist conception of history. It doesn't matter conceptually if the *mir* had neither ancient roots nor a collective tradition (as more recent studies have found), if capitalist relations had already penetrated Russia in the late nineteenth century (as Marx feared and Lenin perceived), or if the opportunity for a revolutionary turn was lost (as the 1877 Russo-Turkish war ended with Russian victory). Marx's new vista of a backward East leading the way in a communist transition mattered. In the end, capitalism cannot be a sure path to, let alone the sole form of, modernity. He disclaimed any 'master key' in historical understanding, arguing against the dogma of an inevitable developmental stage for all societies.[7]

---

4 Karl Marx, *Capital I* (1867), London: Allen & Unwin, 1971: 453-4, 'Revolution in China and in Europe' (1853), *Collected Works of Marx and Engels (MECW) 12,* London: Lawrence & Wishart, 1978–2004: 96, 99.

5 Marx, 'Revolution in China and in Europe': 93, 98; 'The British Rule in India', *MECW 12*: 132.

6 Marx, 'Drafts of the Letter to Vera Zasulich' (1881), *MECW 24*: 352-6.

7 Lin Chun, 'Marx and Asia: The Shift of Marx's Conception of History', in Matt Vidal ed. *The Oxford Handbook on Karl Marx*, Oxford: Oxford University Press, 2018.

This far-sighted global perspective is neglected in Marx's dual legacy concerning non-European development, and is the more important side than the standard reading of his 'oriental despotism'. Conversely, it also shows how Asia was methodologically significant for Marx, allowing him to reach a nondeterministic conclusion. He wrote to a socialist friend in 1877 that the turbulence in Eurasia could be 'a new-turning point in European history', and that 'this time the revolution will begin in the East, hitherto the impregnable bastion and reserve army of counter-revolution.'[8] Now socialist revolution could happen first outside the capitalist heartland of Europe. This was prophetic, predicting the way that the twentieth century was to pan out, with revolutions occurring outside the global capitalist centre. Marx had gone through a whole series of ideas, from the Jewish, Irish and Polish liberations to peasant 'Chinese socialism' and a potential leap in Russia to communism. He was never a romantic, however, and harboured no illusion about the impediments of backwardness. Rather, he emphasized political will and revolutionary agency against a backdrop of complacent determinism.[9]

Class and nation: Imperialism, nationalism and uneven development

Marx's cases are exemplary of the thesis of uneven and combined development characteristic of an era of capitalist competition and inter-imperialist wars. Contrary to the usual perception of Marx tethering socialist revolution to the industrialized nations, he discussed unevenly developed production and its variously evolving social and legal relations, as well as literature and the arts. For him, 'the point is not the historic position of the economic relations in the succession of different forms of society. Even less is it their sequence [in Proudhon's muddy idea of historical movement].' The post-capitalist vision of Russia and related discussions were precisely about compressing stages for a rare simultaneity of the 'oldest',

---

8 Marx, 'To Friedrich Adolph Sorge', 27 September 1877, *MECW 24*: 278.
9 Marx, 'To Editor of the Otecestvenniye Zapisky', *MECW 24*: 199.

communal management, and the 'newest', transplanted technologies.[10] The word *compress* is perhaps better than *combine* here, as it captures both the dynamic process of temporal synchrony and the spatial unevenness of compressed temporalities. As history moves via series of punctuations, turns and contretemps, politics catalyses the present synthesis of past and future. Confined to its own structural yet transformable parameters, global capitalism is a historical and open system. This thesis was elaborated by Leon Trotsky in reflecting on the Russian Revolution, and by Mao Zedong in elucidating the Chinese Revolution. It remains central to Marxist inquiries and politics in our own times. One example is David Harvey's 'spatial fix', developed from Henri Lefebvre's production of space; another is Gunder Frank's or Giovanni Arrighi's Asian and Chinese resurgence.

In practice, the communist revolutionaries went further, identifying and exploring opportunities at the weakest link of imperialist chains. Revolutions could only be instigated at such weak links, making both political change in state power and economic catch-up possible. That is, socialist revolutions can take place not where capitalism succeeded but where it failed. As splendidly evidenced in modern history, capitalism is far from a developmental panacea available to all. It keeps banking on the resources and surplus value of mass production in the peripheries, tending to hinder development there, as has been demonstrated by unequal exchange and dependency theories. Moreover, early capitalism – under its population and land pressures in Europe – depended also on overseas ecological sustenance. Classical primitive accumulation hence buttressed a self-enhancing system of international exchange and division of labour.

Whereas the colonial-imperialist expansion of European nations took place on a colossal scale, similar methods are simply not viable for late developers. Pockets of successful late development, such as in post-war East Asia, were heavily contingent on the aid and markets the United States offered to its Cold War allies in the region. Such pockets could not alter the basic pattern of a polarizing global order. To clarify, therefore, causally it was not backwardness that aggravated colonization, nor did revolutions lead to underdevelopment. This factor

---

10 Marx, *Grundrisse*, trans. M. Nicolaus, Harmondsworth: Penguin, 1973: 107–11, 'Drafts of the Letter to Vera Zasulich', 'To Editor of the Otecestvenniye Zapisky'.

explains also why nationalist and socialist revolutions adhered to each other, as in China among others. Further still, the impressive rates of GDP augment that occurred in the 'tiger' economies and especially in the reformist Chinese economy, came at enormous human, social and environmental costs. The capitalist core backed by its industrial-military complex continues to source imperialist rent from the global South through the production and reproduction of polarization. The concentration, centralization and financialization of capital, and the domination, exploitation and sabotage of the capitalist peripheries by the system's core states, have hampered socially beneficial and ecologically sustainable growth.

The Chinese revolutionary Marxists learned about the logical function of capitalist global conquest from China's own encounter with Western and Japanese imperialism from the mid-nineteenth century onwards. The late Qing illusion of modernization through imitation of the West was shattered by the violent slicing of the country at the hands of rival imperialist powers. Their local pillars, initially recruited from the old regime based on patrimonial or 'feudal' landed interests and later from a newly formed class of compradors, were a by-product of semi-coloniality. The term 'feudalism' was borrowed from European and Japanese historiography to refer to an unproductive landlord economy tied to the ruling bureaucracy. Whether elements of a typical feudal system had ever developed in China was irrelevant. The pedantic charge that the word is a conceptual error for Chinese history, on the basis that the Qin unification in 221 BC had ended any feudal fragmentation, is beside the point. The term makes practical sense, insofar as it allows for revolutionary mobilization without implying any destined transition to capitalism in a linear social theory. What is at issue is that the prospect of a home-grown, strong and autonomous national capitalism, liberal or otherwise, was blocked by imperialism. It was not until after 1949 that China could rebuild itself by fashioning a socialist state for development.

The choice of the word 'rebuild' is deliberate. Economically, when China led the way in outputs and short and long-distance trade (of a commercial capitalist variant dominated by merchant-productive capital) in a disparate world economy, Europe was peripheral. China's economic decline after 1800 was profoundly political, in terms of both domestic state failure and effective foreign intervention. An influential argument in the Chinese Marxist historiography is that China had indigenously developed an 'incipient capitalism'. This is a politically charged counter-factual whose aim is to implicate imperialism for having fatally diverted China's supposedly natural course. Regardless of the methodological Eurocentrism or historical (im)plausibility of such a course, the point is that the ruthless hegemonic agenda of global capitalism is responsible for sinking a civilization of continental scope and unparalleled wealth. The social and governing crises in a partially colonized China were directly attributable to foreign destruction, of which the astronomical war reparations imposed by unequal treaties was only one example.

As archaeological evidence shows, the origins of Chinese civilization are to be found in the intricate interweaving of a variety of material cultures. Never a monolith, this country, its vast and fluid inner and outer frontiers often traversing the formal boundaries of internal lands and external vassals, has always comprised many paths and worlds. One consequence is an interactive history of gradual amalgamation or mutual construction between and among the natives of the Central Plain and other communities located near and far. Clusters of people with different linguistic, religious and other cultural identities intermingled, rather than being assimilated by any local majority. The prevailing perception of sinicization and a sinocentric regional order of a tributary empire is likely a myth, and quite a few lasting Chinese dynasties thrived under non-Han rulers in amalgamated cultures. Worth considering is rather the Marxist attempt to conceptualize a pre-capitalist tributary mode of production encompassing both the Asian states and European (and Japanese) feudal variants. Preceding the capitalist colonial relationship between metropolitans and colonies, such a conceptualization at least supersedes the false dichotomy of Occidental dynamism and Oriental impasse, accrediting the non-western regions their due of developmental vitality.[11]

Under violent pressure of world capitalist modernity, the sovereign constitution of a politically unified and social-culturally compound *zhonghua minzu* (Chinese nation), differed sharply from the European pattern, whereby singular national states emerged from ethnic cleansing

---

11 Samir Amin, *Class and Nation: Historically and in the Current Crisis*, New York: Monthly Review Press, 180: ch. 3; Jairus Banaji, *Theory as History: Essays on Modes of Production and Exploitation*, Chicago, IL: Haymarket Books, 2010: 23–40, 354–6.

and unification via warfare. The origin of the modern identity of China is therefore distinct from those polities of the Westphalian system. As long noted by Owen Lattimore among others, an agricultural society and its nomadic neighbours interacted through the ebb and flow of not only wars but also, and more often, peacemaking and incorporation.[12] The 'pacified empire', Max Weber observed, had rarely engaged overseas aggression due to its time-honoured, inward-looking worldview as well as its geographical barriers to expansionist impulse. He proposed a contrast between Chinese unified territories without 'armed peace' and a fragmented Europe, its 'varieties of booty capitalism' rivalling 'through war loans and commissions for war purposes'.[13] Incidentally, the crucial role of militarism and especially war finance in the making of capitalism logically anticipated the financialization of the present capitalist operation.

An obvious complication is that even though external expansion and military adventures did not characterize premodern China, neither was the 'empire' (as Asia's 'big states' were introduced to Europe) a paradise of harmony and justice before foreign intrusions. Such romanticization would recapitulate sinological otherness while betraying the modern struggle: if the empire was so harmless or even admirable, what could have explained China's great modern transformations? During many centuries of territorial and cultural integration which was more or less settled eventually,[14] impoverished and oppressed societies and groups did rebel, and countless conflicts eventually pressed for a revolutionary solution. With a critical edge, the influential new Qing history emphasizes intra-Asian imperialism and the need to decentre the Chinese configuration. This is valuable, provided we give due recognition to China's inward-looking tradition and largely reactive attitude towards border incursions and foreign encounters. The argument becomes superfluous or distracting, however, when we consider the modernizing force of revolutionary nationalism. The latter was itself built on the historical interpretation of a polity rooted in constantly reciprocated acculturations of diverse georegional and cultural identities, including

12 Owen Lattimore, *Inner Asian Frontiers of China* (1940), Boston, MA: Beacon, 1967.

13 Max Weber, *The Religion of China* (1915), trans. and ed. by Hans Gerth, New York: Free Press, 1964: 26, 103–4, 61–2.

14 Brook, 'Great States': 962–3.

those of 'weak and small nations' (in the communist terminology) as much as the multilineal Han majority. Facing an unprecedented crisis of what was warned in the liberal media as 'racial extinction' at the turn of the twentieth century, China in revolt could reinvent itself not as an empire posing as a nation but as an imminent modern state tempered by national liberation.

As the declining Qing state fell prey to the capitalist jungle and nationalist struggles arose, China became, so to speak, a 'class nation' in its global position. Foreign encounters deepened the country's politico-social crises while 'awakening' its people, as Lenin noted in a series of commentaries on Asia's first Republican revolution in 1911. Now under siege by rival imperialist forces, the globally recognizable 'class' status of China gave its resistance a coherent character. Such a character could not displace domestic class conflicts and local pillars of imperialism. But it did curtail localism fostered by the earlier provincial self-governing movement, and required a strategic and pliable class alliance in the anti-imperialist struggle which came to underpin the CCP's signature undertaking of a united front. It was this historical condition that compelled the Party to be defined as an innovative working-class organ-ization in a New Democratic Revolution with a socialist outlook. The exploited and oppressed status of a nation-in-formation buttressed a collective self-consciousness in the form of revolutionary nationalism. For Joseph Levenson, it was class-based 'communist cosmopolitanism' that tied the national peoples and 'the people' as an international class: 'As the Communists honoured both these "peoples", they could be nationalist and internationalist at the same time.'[15] In the words of Ernest Gellner (not referring to China), who was among those who argued that nationalism creates the nation rather than the other way round, 'only when a nation became a class . . . did it become politically conscious and activist' – 'a nation-for-itself'.[16] Such an image happens to capture the marvel of China redeeming itself from an old multicultural empire, and becoming a new political community and sovereign multi-national state while acquiring the self-awareness of its own 'class' location in a polarized international system.

---

15 Joseph Levenson, *Revolution and Cosmopolitanism: The Western Stage and the Chinese Stages*, Berkeley: University of California Press, 1971: 6–8.

16 Ernest Gellner, *Nations and Nationalism*, Oxford: Blackwell, 1983: 121 and ch. 9.

Contrary to the perceived incompatibility between nationalism and internationalism in Marxism, Marx and Engels defended proletarian nationalism in *The Communist Manifesto*. Even if theoretically 'working men have no country', for them 'the proletariat must first of all acquire political supremacy, must rise to be the leading class of the nation, must constitute itself as the nation . . . though not in the bourgeois sense of the word.' As Antonio Gramsci understood it, the point of departure must be national, yet 'the perspective is international and cannot be otherwise'.[17] In line with this Marxist proposition, national liberation as a popular aspiration was constructed into a rallying ideology in the Chinese revolutionary argument: national and class interests or national and social liberation fundamentally coincide in the Communist Revolution with the nationalism of oppressed peoples and proletarian internationalism. The conception of class nation in the capitalist spatial order of uneven and compressed development and international conflicts was unambiguously grasped by Li Dazhao, a founder of the CCP. He defined a China juxtaposing old and new as an oppressed proletarian nation which must engage global 'class struggle' against imperialist powers. Because of this class nationalism, revolution in China was 'of world significance'.[18] On the eve of the founding of the PRC and the occasion of the party's twenty-eighth anniversary, Mao recalled that 'the October revolution helped progressives in China, as throughout the world, to adopt the proletarian world outlook as the instrument for studying a nation's destiny and considering anew their own problems.' His conclusion was to follow the path of the Russians.[19]

Class and class struggle were therefore the basic analytical and strategic conceptions for China's domestic and foreign relations. They denote the Communist Revolution's dual historical mission of national and class liberation. Most importantly, the Chinese emancipation struggle had to integrate multilayered social and ethnic dimensions. The modern transformation of China did not entail any denial of its inherent multiplicities, based as they are on a diversity carved in the

17 Antonio Gramsci, *Selections from the Prison Notebooks*, ed. Quintin Hoare, trans. Geoffrey Nowell-Smith, New York: International Publishers, 2018: 240.

18 Li Dazhao, 'The Racial Question', *New Republic* 6, June 1924, 'Victory of the Commoners', *New Youth*, 5:5, 1918.

19 Mao Zedong, 'On the People's Democratic Dictatorship', *People's Daily*, 1 July 1949.

longue durée, combining elements from East and Inner Asia as well as the Eurasian West and South, into Oceania. These traditional diversities have only grown with the ever increasing intensity and extensity of communication and migration, contravening dichotomized East and West. Yet the absence of imperial breakdown renders China's modern identity an anomaly, a conceptual violation of the standard European perspective that considers *nation* as antithetical to *empire*. The temporal-spatial duality of the Chinese state baffles a modernity based on the nation-state model of capitalist development, even though the framework of unified market and government had been pursued much earlier, since the Qin–Han system. Remarkable 'modern' economic ideas, such as those recorded in the *Discourse of Salt and Iron* from the Western Han period (202–9 BC), influenced, among others, French Physiocracy two millennia later. The model, however, is parochial and obsolete, hypocritical as well, ignoring both the West's guilty record of racism, colonialism and imperialism, and the present catastrophes arising from imperialism's hijacking of the most powerful democracies. There is another problem. Even if the notion holds somewhat, that empire signifies premodernity and despotism while nation embraces progress and democracy, it is missing a vital distinction between and among states, as well as between nationalisms of different kinds, such as between oppressor nations' imperialism pretending to be in national interest and oppressed nations' liberation struggles. China, among other, tells a story about rejecting the capitalist nation-state model and aspiring to craft a people's power, proudly multinational and socialist. It cries for the local experiences, knowledge and yearning suppressed in the globally hegemonic narratives to be recognized and empowered.

Revolutionary modernity

The nation versus empire dichotomy peculiar to China has its roots in the complexities of modern sovereignty, especially how communist nationalism transformed bourgeois nationalism originated in Europe. To define a national citizenry and its plural societal identities, state sovereignty must first be achieved. Continuities between the Chinese dynastic and republican states in their shared demographic and geographic inheritances are superficial. Since uneven development entails anguish as much as potential 'privilege of backwardness', independent national development is premised on subjugated people breaking free of their shackles. That is, China could only become modern through a thorough social revolution, constructing a new nationalist agency and ultimately a sovereign people. Such a revolutionary rebirth would allow the country to be a sovereign equal in negotiating favourable trade terms and technological transfers from the advanced economies. However difficult, socialist modernization was thus conceived by the communist revolutionaries not only as an approach that was faster and fairer than capitalism, but also as the only viable option. In essence, the contrast between the revolutionary road and colonial modernity lies in the nations on the latter path being brought into history 'not as subjects but as objects of the transformative powers of capitalism'.[20] And that power often continues to exert its imperialist, racist and at times violently divisive influence. In nations on the former path, it was through revolutionary mobilizations from below that the common people attained subjectivity to make history themselves. In other words, the global position of a national or regional polity is determined not only by the epochal conditions but also by local abilities to modify these conditions, abilities that magnify during momentous events such as social revolutions.

One of the fallacies of Eurocentrism is its capitalist-centric ideology based on the Euro-modern experience. Long after its heyday, the modernization paradigm – now rebranded as globalization – remains a primary signifier and legitimating yardstick in ranking societies. The critiques of Eurocentrism are therefore ineffective when limited to an insistence on multilinearity or interculturality without repudiating the telos of capitalism. Yet too often in the postcolonial world, there is a correlation not between capitalism and development, but between capitalism and underdevelopment. It is precisely this effect that explains, again, the historical phenomenon of coherent nationalist and socialist revolutions arising to replace failed capitalism. Theoretically decoupling capitalism and modernity also means the pursuit of an alternative in the boundless post-capitalist horizon where social needs and human

---

20 Arif Dirlik, *After the Revolution: Waking to Global Capitalism*, Middletown, CT: Wesleyan University Press, 1994: 22; Lin Chun, *The Transformation of Chinese Socialism*, Durham, NC and London: Duke University Press, 2006: 52–7.

potentialities can be better fulfilled. A real connection can therefore be found between *socialism* and development, as exemplified by parts of the formal communist world that were originally backward before having undergone significant development. The extraordinary organizational capacity of the socialist state in China enabled one of the world's largest and poorest countries to be rapidly transformed. The state was committed to mobilizing human, material and financial resources as productive factors, centrally and locally, while promoting people's livelihoods. As far as industrialization is concerned, socialism demonstrated itself a startling shortcut: missteps notwithstanding, the communists in power were everywhere effective nation builders and modernizers.

Capital in the twenty-first century, however, increasingly concentrated and financialized, looks ever stronger, commodifying land, labour and lifeworlds across the globe. With its unprecedented boost of Chinese and other 'emerging' markets threatening to suck all forms of development into its own orbit, is capitalism in the end unavoidable? Has the validity of Eurocentric convictions in capitalist global modernity been vindicated by post-communist transitions? If revolutionary China and its socialist construction ever showed the world hope for a possible alternative, the present orientation of Chinese policies only sharpens these questions.

So far, modern China's trajectory might be categorized as having blended the models of revolution, modernization and globalization; or sequenced as late, socialist and post-socialist development. It continues to evolve and to entertain contradictory possibilities. Comparatively, the Maoist experiments resisted the Stalinist style of statist economic management and governance, and also differed sharply from the post-colonial 'dependent development' of peripheral capitalism. This path was unique despite communist China's affinities and ties with both the Eastern camp and the Third World. As market reforms have altered the national course since the opening of the Chinese economy, it is questionable whether China has now altogether lost its willingness and ability to challenge the global parameters. The earlier premise – of historical socialism 'stand[ing] guard over the process of articulation to ensure it does not result in the restoration of capitalism'[21] – seems no

---

21 Arif Dirlik, 'Postsocialism? Reflections on "Socialism with Chinese Characteristics"', in Arif Dirlik and Maurice Meisner, eds, *Marxism and the Chinese Experience*, Armonk, NY: M. E. Sharpe, 1989: 364.

longer to hold, but neither does the delusion of capitalist teleology. Signalling a deep defeatism, official reformers (as opposed to both their socialist and neoliberal critics) admit the unavoidability of capitalism – if not desirability – however thinly disguised. Even cultural conservatives give capitalism an easy pass by subscribing to a bogus apolitical sinocentric stance. In what Bruce Cumings sees as 'a new orientalist craze', the self-orientalizing narratives of traditionalism, nativism or hybridity function to authenticate provincial Euro-American assumptions that pretend to be universal.[22] Conformism is the order of the day.

National autonomy or global integration?

The development of capitalism since the 'long sixteenth century' (1350–1650) was driven by the relentless accumulation and monopoly building of the major capitalist powers. It created an ever freer movement of increasingly virtualized international capital, as predicted in the classic Marxist analysis of overaccumulation, financial capital and imperialism. These trends have fashioned a reckless casino economy increasingly severed from real production. In a post–Bretton Woods system, unequal fiscal capabilities in the absence of the gold standard along with the loss of international balance of payments have enabled (primarily) the US to enlarge and export its inflation, credit and deficit under the dollar hegemony. The 'new global financial architecture' facilitates easy transfer of liquid 'surplus fictitious capital' globally to wherever it can be most profitable, making contemporary crises predominantly financial.[23] In particular, the liberalization of global stock and money markets has led to surplus capital flowing into developing countries, mostly as short-term, speculative portfolio investments for quick returns. The opening of China's market began in conjunction with capitalist mutation and

---

22 Bruce Cumings, 'The "Rise of China"?' in Catherine Lynch, Robert Marks and Paul Pickowicz, eds, *Radicalism, Revolution, and Reform in Modern China: Essays in Honor of Maurice Meisner*, Lanham, MD: Lexington, 2011: 185. See also Daniel Vukovich, *China and Orientalism: Western Knowledge Production and the PRC*, London: Routledge, 2012.

23 David Harvey, *The Enigma of Capital and the Crises of Capitalism*, Oxford: Oxford University Press, 2010: 16, 30.

the onset of the neoliberal paradigm, resulting in a quick stimulus as well as heavy costs.

The limits of this opening up is nowhere more strikingly revealed than in the current US trade war with China. In April 2018, the US Department of Commerce suspended the supply of essential chips to Chinese technology company Zhongxing Telecommunication Equipment Corporation (ZTE), instantly paralysing its operation. Another tech giant and global leader in 5G, Huawei, faced the same sanction as well as others to its export markets. In June that year the Chinese government responded with 'special opening-up measures' to widen market access for foreign investment in twenty-two key fields, including finance, transportation, services, infrastructure, energy, resources and agriculture. These measures were swiftly put in place over the following weeks and months. No significant agreement between the two countries took place at the Asia-Pacific Economic Cooperation (APEC) meeting in November, or at the G20 summit right after. American blockages have persisted since, with steep import tariffs added to almost all Chinese goods. The American argument against the 'Balkanization of technology' defends its monopolies in the name of intellectual property rights, denying independent progress towards innovation and upgrading as an equal right among countries. Henry Paulson, former US Treasury secretary, threatened an 'economic iron curtain' unless China open its markets entirely and stop seeking technological transfers from joint ventures, which in 2019 is exactly the direction China began to take.[24]

Beijing duly released new 'special administrative measures for the access of foreign investment' in July 2018 to remove restrictions on foreign investors, along with an additional 'special negative list' applicable to China's free trade zones. It was followed by two more lists in 2019 and 2020, with steeper forfeiting.[25] On 5 November that year, Xi Jinping delivered a keynote speech at the opening ceremony of first China International Import Expo in Shanghai, emphatically encouraging foreign partners. The Expo showed, he remarked, 'an important decision made by China to pursue a new round of

---

24 Henry Paulson, Speech at the Bloomberg New Economy Forum, 7 November 2018.

25 The State Development and Reform Commission, 31 October 2018.

high-level opening-up' and widening market access; economic globalization is 'the wheel of history'. Not mentioned was the ambitious
'Made in China 2025' initiative announced in 2015, the aim of which
was to leap over technological thresholds in ten critical areas in order
to develop an autonomous national knowledge economy equipped
with mostly local-made components – an initiative that was the main
target of the US. China is also pushing ahead with opening its traditionally guarded financial and service sectors to include such key
social policy areas as education, healthcare and public utilities. On 16
October 2018, Premier Li Keqiang vowed that China would 'completely remove' constraints on the business of foreign banks, security
firms and asset management companies. A few weeks later he promised the IMF chief that China would soon grant foreign capital full
holdings in banking, bond, mutual fund, future market and insurance
industries. Financial reform had been on the agenda for some time,
but it had never reached the point where the question became how
China could accommodate the market volatility and risks that it had
previously sought to evade.

Most of these pledges were indeed implemented and more concessions were on the horizon. An influential government advisor provided
the justification that China has accomplished its historical mission of
catching up, and has thus entered a new stage of leaping 'from the
Listian to Smithian era of growth'. Protection of national firms, for one
thing, is no longer needed. Instead it is time to 'introduce more pressure
from foreign participation so as to boost Chinese industry's growth
dynamic and international competitiveness'.[26] Yet China emerged
humiliated again from the US trade truce in mid-October 2019, when
the US temporarily shelved – not removed – the threatened new tariffs
on 30 per cent of Chinese imports. In return Beijing agreed to increase
its annual purchase of American agricultural produce by more than
double, up to $50 billion, to keep Boeing orders at between $6 billion
and $20 billion, to begin completely opening its financial sector and
much else besides. Forgoing any leverage to retaliate, however limited –
by boycotting certain imports and exports, for example, or imposing
more restrictions and heavier taxes on US companies operating within
its borders – China has simply become too globalized to even be

26 Mei Xinyu, 'From Listian to Smithian Era', *Financial References*, 29 June 2019.

willing to imagine rebuilding its self-reliance. Washington also has the additional leverage of threatening to expose information about certain corrupt Chinese officials at will.

These vulnerabilities are predictable, not only because of the enormous disparity between the two powers but also due to China's transition from a strategic shallow integration to an opportunistic deep one. The former connotes the use of foreign capital, technologies and managerial skills as the means to advance an independent national economy, while the latter refers to the subordination of a national economy to the wholesale embrace of globalization dominated by the global capitalist powers. For decades, China has allowed the US to take advantage of its own growth model by exporting cheap goods for American consumption and holding colossal foreign reserves in US bonds. China's accession to the World Trade Organization (WTO) in 2001 accelerated this process. The US waged its latest commercial and financial attacks using a looter's rationale, with the aim of destroying China's industrial policy and independent technological upgrade capacity. Purely in terms of trade volume and GDP growth, China may indeed have benefited from its WTO membership; but one cost, among many, is China's increased dependency and vulnerability in the ongoing trade and tech war. The painful entry negotiations have already forced China to 'substantially open its market' in financial services.[27] According to a leading US negotiator, Charlene Barshefsky, promised concessions from China were 'broader actually than any World Trade Organization member has made'.[28] The PRC Supreme Court also pledged that in case of any inconsistency, domestic laws would comply with WTO statutes. Despite diversification effort and some decreases, China's trade surplus and foreign reserves are still mainly in dollars, financing American consumption and debt, to the detriment of Chinese interests in labour, market, environment and security.[29] It remains the

27 Lee Branstetter and Nicholas Lardy, 'China's Embrace of Globalization', in Loren Brandt and Thomas Rawski, eds, *China's Great Economic Transformation*, Cambridge: Cambridge University Press, 2008: 658.

28 Quoted in Leo Panitch and Sam Gindin, *The Making of Global Capitalism: The Political Economy of American Empire*, London: Verso, 2012: 293.

29 It was estimated that goods manufactured elsewhere and sold in the US at 'the China price' saved the average American $600 a year (Ted Fishman quoted in Richard Mertens, 'China on the Rise', *University of Chicago Magazine*, 98:6, 2006: 6).

case that 'Chinese economic dynamism is held hostage to US fiscal and monetary policy.'[30]

Despite some efforts in recent years, the overall situation remains that technology-intensive manufacturers and high-tech exports are either foreign invested and controlled, or dependent on foreign designs and monopolized technologies.[31] The preference for foreign over domestic companies was legally enshrined, to the extent that 'domestic and foreign capital effectively operated within different legal parameters' with 'the more favourable laws applied to foreign, not domestic capital.'[32] Worse still, the foreign architects of neoliberalism have been directly involved in the top-level designing of liberalization and privatization in China, as exemplified by *China 2030*, jointly issued by the central Developmental Research Center and the World Bank in 2012. *China Daily* approvingly reported that the 'World Bank urged China to revamp its financial system in a decisive, comprehensive and coordinated manner,' and to smash 'state monopolies', as though the Bank had overriding authority over Chinese policymaking.[33]

Making deep concessions, some of them unnecessary, for the WTO accord, China missed a golden opportunity to use its huge size and weight to gain concessions for itself in return, and thereby for the developing world at large, concerning such matters as economic security, capital control, and fair international trade. This compliance cut the space for national industrial policies, and allowed China's dependency on imports and foreign markets to endure. As Robert Wade foretold,

> the US would retain extraordinary provisions for tariffs to defend its domestic market against . . . Chinese imports, whereas China would concede to a brutally swift dismantling of protection for local farmers and manufacturers and vastly increased freedoms for foreign firms and financial services.[34]

---

30 David Harvey, *A Brief History of Neoliberalism*, Oxford: Oxford University Press, 2005: 142.

31 Peter Nolan, *Is China Buying the World?*, Cambridge: Polity, 2012: 84–94.

32 Panitch and Gindin, *The Making of Global Capitalism*: 296.

33 Xinhua News, *China Daily*, 28 February 2012.

34 Robert Wade, 'The Ringmaster of Doha', *New Left Review* 25, Jan/Feb 2004: 151.

In this, China has been losing its economic and financial sovereignty while witnessing an expansion of comprador capital and power. Its distorted national economy then suffers mutually reinforcing trends of foreign dependency and domestic demand deficiency, linked to intense labour exploitation, especially that of two generations of migrant workers. This in turn undermines the foundation of the socialist economy that had enabled China to develop rapidly while withstanding international antagonism and later also global and regional financial crises since the 1970s.

One of the lessons coming out of this experience is that state is a pivotal agent of globalization, and sufficient national autonomy and complete global integration are incompatible. It looks as though the China that broke free from its imperialist chains seventy years ago is now bowing to the system as a pathway to 'wealth and power'. Yet without socialism making sense inside China, with respect to the emancipation of labour and equality and justice in thawing social contentions, national pride changes meaning and loses weight. Decoupled from the socialist cause, any project of Chinese nationalism perceived as joining the club of great powers is bound to be delusive and chauvinistic in one form or another. It forsakes the denotation of China's century-long struggle for national liberation.

2

Revolutions and reforms

China's revolutionary twentieth century was preceded by popular revolts that had broken out since 1840, precipitated by the two Opium Wars. Armed rivalries among older and newer imperialist powers in Asia and other continents intensified in the late nineteenth century, eventually leading to the outbreak of the First World War in 1914, which in turn triggered the beginning of an age of socialist revolutions in Russia in 1917. In China, both the Republican Revolution of 1911 and the subsequent Communist Revolution of 1949 should be viewed in their indigenous origins as much as international catalysts of regional and global politics. In particular, the establishment of the world's first soviet power following Russia's revolutions since 1905 was a decisive influence on China as it emerged from the wreckage of failed late Qing reforms. Paradoxically, it was primarily a home-grown communist force in China's agrarian society that recast the peasantry in resistance against foreign powers and their local allies. A new country, aspiring to socialism, was born in a most unlikely place from a long fought revolutionary transformation.

Reforms are never very far from revolutions; and reform can either derail or foment revolution, depending on the circumstances. Contradictions have never ceased to dynamize Chinese struggle. The post-1949 anti-bureaucratic campaigns constituted a seamless 'continuous revolution' against the threats of decay and betrayal, both real and exaggerated, that culminated in the 1960s. The post-1978 reform curbed this revolutionary momentum, and after 1989 the state performed a radical shift to embrace neoliberalism. Looking at the history of the PRC then, we are left with a series of questions. Did China's twentieth-century revolutionary events constitute a single, integrated revolution, or a sequence of plural, categorically differentiated revolutions? Has the post-Mao transition been largely consistent, without radical ruptures? What is the relevance of questions concerning revolution, reform and counter-revolution? The meaning of the critical junctures of 1978 and 1989/92 are intelligible only in light of the significance of 1949.

The relationships between and among these distinct yet overlapping temporalities show that periodization is a politically conscious interpretative act, often with a hidden agenda for the future course of development. Our twofold task here is comprised as follows: first, to demonstrate how revolutions function as markers of history, so that non-revolutionary events and general historical movements can only be evaluated through their lens; and second, to explain why the epochal conditions of capitalism are vital for China's actual evolution and its ramifications as well as for their conceptualization. The politics of defining, sequencing or differentiating periods of time is part and parcel of the production of knowledge, narrative and history. The underlining argument, then, is that a revolution cannot rest, if only because of the constant presence of counterrevolution; and hence that a revolution's negation may yet itself be negated.

Revolutions as markers of history

Revolutions are markers of history. Social revolutions are, by definition, events that bring about fundamental changes in socioeconomic structures and political systems. They also change certain normative codes, expectations and cultural values, altering the direction of a society's development. Such an event is a dialectic opening that 'interrupts the law, the rules, the structure of the situation, and creates new possibility.'[1] Yet it can be extremely difficult for revolutionary strategists and actors to decide when a revolution should begin or end, or whether a further revolution is needed. It is harder still for them to effect change, as they most likely have no real control over the course of the revolution.

---

1 Alain Badiou, *Being and Event*, London: Bloomsbury, 2011.

China's long revolution in the short twentieth century has been massively and astutely explained, most recently by Wang Hui.[2] Yet questions remain. Even long after it seized power in China, did the Communist Revolution really end? Was not it fundamentally unfinished before it was abandoned, if we judge it by the goals it set for itself, of building a socialist economy and democracy? Did the early-1990s surge of privatization actually mark a revolutionary as opposed to a reformist turn, given its policy subordination to domestic and foreign capital? Revolutions, even if originally idealistic, also tend to degenerate when replaced by a new ruling order, one that begins to reinstate corruption and necessitate oppression. Bureaucratization and the great purge under Stalin 'justified' by the severity of external hostility amounted to a total perversion. Even Mao's Cultural Revolution ultimately undermined its own rationale. The question is therefore not only concerned with the fate of Chinese struggles but also that of the international communist movement as a whole, or whether any attempt at replacing capitalism with socialism is doomed to fail.

The standard literature on modern China, including that by most Chinese and foreign experts, correctly begins its chronology with the Opium Wars in the mid-nineteenth century. The traditional way of life in the Middle Kingdom had long since begun to crack, and the country fell into a mutually dependent semi-colonial and semi-feudal status (a characterization formally adopted by the CCP in 1928 in conjunction with the 'great social history debate' engaging concerned intellectuals into the 1930s). The horrendous vandalism of the imperialist civilization mongers caused local state involution, general urban decline and rural bankruptcy. Amid the disorder of landlessness, usury, bandit violence and widespread poverty, entrenched nexuses of autocrats and warlords expanded. Within this deepening crisis around the turn of the twentieth century, China's traditional social structure was collapsing. There emerged a comprador-bureaucratic class entangled with the ruling landlords, which grew side by side with a nascent national bourgeoisie and a class of industrial workers. Without subsequent popular struggles, therefore, the year 1840 would not have acquired its significance – it was Chinese resistance, not any foreign force, that inaugurated China's modern era. Mao was thus faithful to

2 Wang Hui, *The Short Twentieth Century: The Chinese Revolution and the Logic of Politics,* Hong Kong: Oxford University Press, 2015.

history in honouring China's revolutionary martyrs since 1840, as for example in the Monument to the People's Heroes in Beijing. Thus the revolutionary twentieth century 'was not an outcome but a producer of its pre-history', and also a precious source for twenty-first-century socialist endeavour and imagination.[3]

In 1850, Marx and Engels ventured a 'very paradoxical assertion' that 'the next uprising of the people of Europe . . . may depend more probably on what is now passing in the Celestial Empire' than any other events. As they said, 'it may well be that Chinese socialism is related to European socialism just as Chinese philosophy is related to Hegelian philosophy.'[4] That same year, the Taiping Heavenly Kingdom of Peace, under the guise of Christianity, was launched in a village in the far south of China with a programme of equal sharing of land and work. This peasant uprising, which was to sweep across the country over the next fourteen years, is often treated in Chinese communist theory as part of an old bourgeois democratic revolution in the East. Its resemblance to the classical Western revolutions was limited to the function of paving the way for capitalist development, which nevertheless could not be fulfilled in China due to imperialist blockages. Not only did Marx recognize the movement's complicated nationalism against both foreign invaders and an alien Manchu rule, but he also linked it to prospective anti-capitalist revolutions in the strongholds of capitalism. In 1858, referring to Taiping, he argued that 'the Chinese revolution will throw the spark into the overloaded mine of the present industrial system' to trigger political explosions.[5] In contradiction to his more dismissive assertions on revolts in China and India, and in a reversal of his thinking about a one-way transformative, globalizing capitalism, Marx made a liberated Asia conditional for European and universal emancipation. This was to be a prophetic statement, one that charted the passage of the revolutionary twentieth century.

Towards the last decades of the nineteenth century, China had fallen into a state of social and political devastation. The ailing dynastic state was deeply corrupt, internally fragmented and externally feeble. The conditions were ripe for a republican revolution, with nationalist

---

3 Wang Hui, 'Twentieth-Century China as an Object of Thinking: Spatial Revolution, Horizontal Time and Replacement Politics (I)', *Open Times* 5, 2018: 85.

4 'Review' (1850), *MECW 10*: 266–7.

5 Marx, 'History of the Opium Trade' (1858), *MECW 16*: 538.

organizations, such as Xingzhonghui (Revive China Society, 1894–1905) and Tongmenghui (Chinese Alliance, 1905–12), and dozens of trans-regional protests and uprisings. The last of these, in Wuchang, seized provincial power in October 1911. Many provinces followed suit by declaring independence from the Qing court, and the emperor abdicated. Republican China was proclaimed on the first day of 1912, with Sun Yat-sen (Zhongshan) acting as its provisional president. The new government was faced with the immediate problem of how to build a new state, and a series of formidable questions concerning sovereignty, republicanism, constitutionalism, and racial and territorial integrity. Compelled by the need to mount a pan-nationalist mobilization against foreign powers, the earlier anti-Manchu rhetoric had already been replaced with the commitment to a 'republic of five races' (Han, Hui, Mongo, Tibet and Manchu), but its actual state form required more federalist thinking. National liberation in China really involved reconfiguration of both its internal and external relations. On balance, the Republican Revolution was a national democratic one in a much fuller sense than the previous revolutionary or reformist attempts since 1840. It achieved a unique 'historical compromise' by incorporating different political and military forces across regimes and other boundaries.[6] The Western and Eurasian regional powers were also involved in negotiating the settlement.

The republicans succeeded in putting an end to an anachronistic polity but left fundamental social problems unresolved and failed to repel imperialist influences. Sun's ambition to combine political and social revolution did not materialize beyond the achievement of overthrowing the monarchy. The government was also dogged by constant skirmishes among competing warlords, each backed by his respective foreign master. At the same time, this limited revolution was pregnant with bolder possibilities. Sun proposed the 'three people's principles' of nationalism, socialism and democracy; he also called for 'equalizing the land and constraining capital', and for an alliance with Russia and with workers, peasants and all the world's 'bullied peoples' (*shouqu renmin*). These ideas integrated social and national liberation, and formed the basis of the first alliance between the nationalists and communists, who

---

6 Peter Zarrow, *China in War and Revolution: 1895–1949*, London: Routledge, 2005: ch. 2.

joined forces for the Northern Expedition (1926–28) to overpower warlords and collaborated on workers' education and organization. Lenin regarded Sun's social programme as 'bourgeois', but praised him enthusiastically for his proposal to unite the Chinese people with the 'toiling masses' globally. His final words on Asia were about the common struggle of the Russians, Indians and Chinese in the impending conflict 'between the counter-revolutionary imperialist West and the revolutionary nationalist East'.[7]

The Bolsheviks had not squandered the chance offered by imperialist war and its ensuing calamities. They struck at this weak link, turning war into revolution, and defeated the allied forces of White counterrevolution. Yet this occurred within an extremely difficult international environment, particularly following counterrevolutionary crackdowns in Germany and Hungary that had stamped out any promising European working-class movements. Lenin was intensely concerned about Soviet Russia's isolation, and set up the Third International to build revolution elsewhere: communism and internationalism were born twins. The Russian Revolution was key to the stimulation of communist revolution in China, and the Comintern played an important, though not necessarily positive, role in Chinese political events. There is a serious caveat here, however: the Marxism that inspired Mao's generation had to be sinicized and applied to a rural struggle. So-called mountain-valley Marxism eventually shed the impractical urban dogmas held by Moscow-trained theorists to produce an extremely hard yet victorious Chinese *land revolution*.

Among the array of fresh insights arriving on the Western winds in the giant country of the East – from anarchism to social Darwinism, Marxism to socialism – liberalism deserves special attention. On the one hand, the ferment of the liberal New Culture Movement around 1915 was looking for a modern renewal of Chinese society that would overcome its conservative traditionalism, feudal despotism and oppression of women. On the other, liberalism's power on Chinese soil was tainted by its associations with opium and cannons. After all, China's first encounter with liberalism came via imperialism. Yet the first generation of Chinese communist intellectuals were irresistibly liberal in the

---

7 V. I. Lenin, 'Better Fewer, but Better' (1923), *Lenin Collected Works 33*, Moscow: Progress Publishers, 1965: 501.

word's normative sense, not only in that they were fighters for social and national liberation, but also in their personal spirit, not least manifested in the prevalence of their belief in sexual equality and free love.

On 4 May 1919, students took to the streets to denounce Japanese demands on Chinese territories and other parts of the Treaty of Versailles that transferred the German concessions in Shandong to Japan. This outbreak of unrest was a landmark moment in the Chinese awakening to the defeat of republican nationalist sovereignty, and resonated with the Leninist principle of self-determination – as opposed to the hypocritical Wilsonianism characterized by imperialist powers making deals among themselves at the expense of other nations. In light of this, the May Fourth Movement was also profoundly cultural, not only echoing the call of New Culture to re-evaluate traditional ethics and greet science and democracy, but also embracing Marxism and radical mass politics. A first nationwide youth mobilization in China, it was part of the larger waves of anticolonial and anti-imperialist activism in the post-war realignment of international and regional orders, unseating capitalism as a global system.

What made the May Fourth Movement so different from its counterparts elsewhere was its anti-imperialist and anti-feudal stance: this was clarified only in its aftermath, above all in the formation of local communist groups which held their first national congress secretly in 1921. The founders of the Party were leading intellectuals, such as Chen Duxiu and Li Dazhao who ran the *New Youth* magazine among other publications and led debates of the day, bringing with them a generation of intellectual radicals. The May Fourth era was a high point, particularly with hindsight in the light of subsequent organization of workers and peasants, communist land struggle and people's war. It inspired later youth and student movements – from those of the 1930s and 1940s (as explained in Mao's 1939 speech 'The Orientation of the Youth Movement') to the send-down mobilization with a strong voluntary element in the late 1960s and 1970s, the demonstration of 5 April 1976, and Tiananmen Square 1989 – as well as being reimagined by them. Rather than viewing this iconoclastic episode in a linear chronological manner simply as having prepared the ground for 1921 and what came after, it makes sense to connect these events retrospectively: without *1921*, symbolic as well as actual, as the inception of the Communist Revolution and an entirely new political and military process, 1919 would lose its connotation as a precursor of something world historical. As Mao stipulated, after the May Fourth 'the political leader of China's bourgeois-democratic revolution was no longer the bourgeoisie but the proletariat ... [as] an awakened and independent political force.'[8] It was 1921 that signalled the turning point: what the old 'bourgeois' democratic revolution was unable to achieve had now been taken over by a new one, tasked not only with national independence but also with structural social change.

The New Democratic Revolution was forged under conditions of unimaginable hardship. It is particularly worth noting that the devoted participants, both men and women, were mostly very young. Their incredible idealism and heroism persisted against overwhelming odds – almost incomprehensible for historians of comparative revolutions. These odds included many grave mistakes made within the revolutionary camp: ferocious internal persecutions took place over a long and extremely dangerous period of fighting powerful counterrevolution. Purges, such as the 1930 Futian incident in Jiangxi and the 1935 Shanbei Sufan campaign, killed large numbers of comrades rather than enemies. The Chinese Trotskyists were suppressed both inside China and in the Soviet Union where an unknown number of CCP delegates and students on the Left Opposition were banished or executed.[9] Still, the epic Long March stands as a permanent testimony of loyalty and determination, and a symbol of an unparalleled revolution. Even many sceptics of the cause would not deny its appeal; as Joseph Esherick admitted, 'the determination, sacrifice, and commitment of individual communist revolutionaries – the subjective elements of the revolutionary dialectic – were both essential to the revolution's success and critical in shaping its nature.' Maurice Meisner, meanwhile, described the Chinese Communist Revolution as 'the most massive – and perhaps the most heroic – revolution in world history.'[10]

The year 1949 signified not the end of the revolution, but its continuation. The revolutionaries' ongoing task was to complete land reform and eliminate counterrevolution while embarking on a socialist

---

8 Mao Zedong, 'On New Democracy', *Selected Works of Mao Zedong 2*, Beijing: People's Publishing House, 1965: 348.

9 Gregor Benton, ed. *Prophets Unarmed: Chinese Trotskyists in Revolution, War, Jail, and the Return from Limbo*, Chicago: Haymarket Books, 2017: Introduction.

10 Joseph Esherick, 'Ten Theses on the Chinese Revolution', *Modern China* 21:1, July 1995: 59; Maurice Meisner, 'The Significance of the Chinese Revolution in World History', LSE Asian Research Working Papers 1, 1999: 1.

transformation. By 1956, China had nationalized its industries and formed agricultural cooperatives based on equal right to land. The nationalization of industry was preceded by a transitional stage of merging public and private enterprises: unlike the Soviet method, whereby industry was confiscated by the state, the government only took over the large bureaucratic capitalist sector, also introducing a scheme that paid private capitalists a fixed percentage of dividends in compensation. The Great Leap Forward campaign launched in 1958 reorganized rural collectives into larger communes. On the political and ideological front, a series of rectification campaigns, including 'anti-rightist' and 'socialist education' movements, heralded the launch of the Cultural Revolution in 1966. In foreign relations, China's initial policy of 'leaning to one side' of the Soviet Union ended in the late 1950s, while it continued to support national liberation and postcolonial developments. Amid the confusions and disruptions of postcolonial developments, China aided its socialist neighbours and communist guerrillas in Southeast Asia; assisted nationalists and socialists in the Arab world, Africa and Latin America; and stood in solidarity with the black and civil rights movements in the US. Proudly self-reliant, China created a precious space of autonomy for itself in an extremely treacherous geopolitical environment. The contradictions of the Chinese position in global politics on an anti-imperialist platform – both US-led imperialism and Soviet 'social imperialism' – were costly, but also disruptive for the narrow Cold War logic.

The significance of the Chinese Communist Revolution

The year 1949 may not have marked a total break with the past, but it did signify the start of a new era. It was no doubt a monumental marker of history, not only in China, but also globally. This doesn't mean that the Chinese Communist Revolution was destined to succeed without contingencies, nor can its grave errors and mammoth costs be ignored. Moreover, it is obviously the case that the revolution did not realize all its aspirations or stated goals – far from it in fact, and certain perversions were inescapable. Worse still, its failure to curb degeneration produced some results which ran counter to its original promises. The period after 1949 was turbulent, to put it mildly, and there were some catastrophic episodes. In a sense then, one can argue that the revolution remains forever unfinished. As Perry Anderson remarked, 'Revolutions . . . typically accomplish only twenty per cent of what they set out to achieve, at a cost of sixty per cent. But without them there is no leap of society in history.'[11] In the spirit of recognizing such leaps, we must defend the historicity and fundamental justice of the Chinese Communist Revolution, beginning with a brief summary of what it actually achieved. In the light of the current retreats blighting the PRC, each of the achievements detailed below appears even more precious.

First of all, China as an oppressed nation was liberated to preserve its integrity and independence. 'The Chinese people have stood up!' as Chairman Mao proclaimed at the opening Chinese People's Political Consultative Conference (CPPCC) right before the PRC founding ceremony of 1 October 1949. The revolution's greatest achievement was national unity and autonomy for China. To defeat an armed counterrevolution, the revolution had been forced to arm itself, and then defend its newly attained peace and freedom. Not only that, it also defended itself on the battlegrounds of Korea in the years immediately after the new state was founded, against American threats of invasions and open nuclear war. As Wang Hui has insisted, Mao's proclamation would have been unsustainable without the 1953 Korean Armistice Agreement, a true communist victory and Chinese moment.[12] China's brave decision to uphold its internationalist obligation by entering the Korean conflict was also a defence and consolidation of the new Chinese state against all odds. There was no magic about this stalemate imposed on the world's most powerful military forces, other than the indomitable will of the poorly equipped Chinese soldiers and commanders, along with their Korean comrades, and the unbroken support that reached them from the new communist homeland. The modernity of the PRC was fully affirmed in a sovereign, secular and socialist constitution, albeit with the intrinsic tensions typical of such a project. In this sense, China reached an equal footing among the modern nations long before the so-called rise of China credited to the market 'miracle'. Seventy years ago, it stood up and reshaped the balance of power, in Asia and beyond. Whatever China's more recent accomplishments may be, they are all predicated, or directly founded on, its revolutionary national liberation.

---

11 Perry Anderson, 'Lucio Magri', *New Left Review* 72, Nov/Dec 2011: 120.

12 Wang Hui, 'The Korean War in the Twentieth-Century Chinese Historical Perspective', *Beijing Cultural Review* 6, 2013: 78–100.

Second, the establishment of the PRC marked the construction of the sovereign people, a new collective subject achieved through social organization. A commitment to putting the people at the centre of the state is a definitive feature of a modern political community. Unlike most other anti-colonial movements in the Third World, the Communist Revolution in China was socially committed. It had engaged in a broad political alliance and waged a people's war, laying the foundation for the post-revolutionary regime as essentially a people's power. However abstract or abused it has been at times, the Chinese search for an effective form of democratic citizenship began with the revolution itself. The act of replacing a shapeless mass – a 'sheet of loose sand', as observed by Sun – with a constitutionally designated sovereign people as 'masters of society' was ground-breaking. Sophisticated organization in work and life, around urban work units, rural communes and residential communities, secured regime support or conformity at the grassroots level – the PRC has never been a police state dependent on general terror for its survival. These building-blocks of Chinese socialism functioned both to regulate and to protect citizens, who relied on their units for income, security and support. The system also enabled a significant degree of direct popular participation in political and public affairs as part of its everyday materiality. The steep decline in the number and character of work units in the marketplace today has undercut social cohesion and the sense of belonging to a community. Normatively, the will of the people was understood as the source and legitimacy of state power, however seriously distorted by bureaucratization, and more recently by marketization entailing degraded labour. Women's liberation was additionally prioritized in a state feminist project; not without its own pitfalls, the pursuit of gender equality required conscious female participation from below. Even anti-communist critics found it difficult to deny the benefits of removing the dregs of old patriarchal values and the creation of unprecedented spaces for women to pursue their self-realization.

Third, the revolution liberated previously hindered productive forces. It did so by establishing public ownership and management, as well as honouring and protecting the workforce. Within a few decades of self-reliant development after the Soviet Union withdrew aid in 1959, China succeeded not only in laying an industrial foundation for the national economy but in also fashioning a rudimentary yet inclusive social security and welfare system. It provided free or inexpensive public services in housing, schooling, transportation, healthcare and preventive medicine. Political upheavals did not stop decent annual growth between 1952 and 1978, with the industrial sector growing at a double-digit pace.[13] Although rural revitalization was impeded by urban bias, the quality of peasant life, despite restricted movement, was 'not merely improved but transformed', at least in the more well-to-do regions.[14] The commitment to meeting basic needs sustained public investment in human and physical infrastructure. Except for the extraordinary period of 1959–61, the population was mostly well fed, healthy and literate. According to the United Nations Human Development Index, new China led the Third World by a large margin in life expectancy (extended from somewhere between thirty-five and thirty-eight years in 1949 to around sixty-seven in 1980), basic education and reducing infant mortality. A 'public good regime' based on united labour was itself a causal factor for China outperforming other countries at a similar income level. As John Gurley commented at the twentieth anniversary of the PRC, these factors were 'so basic, so fundamentally important, that they completely dominate China's economic picture, even if one grants all of the erratic and irrational policies alleged by her numerous critics.'[15] 'Few events in world history', as Meisner contended, 'have done more to better the lives of more people.'[16]

Fourth, there is always a cultural dimension to revolutionary change, and particularly China's because it was of such great magnitude. The Communist Revolution ushered a political culture of collectivism and egalitarianism in social production, reproduction

---

13 The available numbers vary. See e.g. Mark Selden and Victor Lippit, *The Transition to Socialism in China*, Armonk, NY: M. E. Sharpe, 1982: 19–20; Barry Naughton, 'The Pattern and Legacy of Economic Growth in the Mao Era', in Kenneth Lieberthal, Joyce Kallgren, Roderick MacFarquhar and Frederic Wakeman, eds, *Perspectives on Modern China: Four Anniversaries*, Armonk, NY: M. E. Sharpe: 228–9; Samir Amin, *The Future of Maoism*, Delhi: Rainbow, 1998: 50–4. All these sources recognize notable growth in China before its market reform, including during the Cultural Revolution.

14 Chris Bramall, *In Praise of Maoist Economic Planning: Living Standards and Economic Development in Sichuan since 1931*, Oxford: Clarendon, 1993: 335.

15 John Gurley, 'Capitalist and Maoist Economic Development', in Edward Friedman and Mark Selden, eds, *America's Asia: Dissenting Essays on Asian-American Relations*, New York: Random House, 1969: 345.

16 Meisner, 'The Significance of the Chinese Revolution': 12.

and distribution. Above all, new China's fresh approach was in emancipating the exploited and marginalized from their old bondage, physically as much as mentally, thereby making *the people* the historical subject. While exploitation and domination along the lines of class, gender, ethnicity, region and sector were far from eliminated, they became things of the past, not only legally but also normatively and ideologically. Participatory mass campaigns were effective in fighting illiteracy and endemic diseases, in improving sanitation and in encouraging women to join the public workforce. Traditional values were re-examined to make way for socialist perceptions and aspirations. As the common masses were supposed to change the world while changing themselves, there emerged the challenge of how to make the new socialist person without resorting to totalitarian indoctrination. A solution was found in the Maoist notion of practising 'three great revolutions': class struggle, production and scientific experiment. New China was new because of the people's unparalleled mental status and engagement that stemmed from profound social and cultural transformations.

Fifth, it is worth emphasizing that the revolution achieved overall social stability and ethnic peace – a contrast with the later reversions that took place during the market reform. The PRC state presupposed cultural and institutional multiethnicity, and carried with it a sacred duty of equality, solidarity and unity. Focusing on the minority nationalities concentrated in the country's poorer hinterland, one of the first tasks people's China assigned itself was to redress the past wrongs of Han chauvinism. The revolution's sympathy for the 'weaker and smaller nations' and its intrinsic commitment to universal liberation were stipulated in the PRC laws and spelt out in its social policies. There was constitutional protection for the rights of minorities to self-rule, to use native languages and to preserve or reform local traditions, customs and religious beliefs. These socialist mandates found an innovative institutional expression in the semi-federal system of minority regional autonomy and preferential treatment. The central government also consistently invested in the autonomous regions, sustaining substantive infrastructural and aid projects. Despite a paternalistic overtone and unintended side-effects, the moral and political determination to reduce regional and ethnic disparities was unwavering.

Finally, the Communist Revolution in China was never merely a national event. It was always self-consciously part of the world revolution sparked by the storm of 1917. It was primarily anti-imperialist and anti-colonial, and developed within the geopolitical intricacies of the competition among superpowers for spheres of control. This is why the revolutionary creation of a socialist republic in China had such powerful regional and global impacts. The Chinese revolution rewrote the histories of Asia and the world, as well as China itself, by transforming its national destiny it furnished conditions for change elsewhere and provided a model for Third World development. This model challenged the supposedly universal paradigm of capitalist modernity, showing exploited and oppressed peoples how things might be turned around by daring popular struggles. The revolution's world-historical victory also thoroughly altered the dynamics of hegemonic geopolitics, and global power configurations and alignments. In contrast with the enduring poverty and conflict that reigned elsewhere in the capitalist peripheries, the Communist Revolution in China won peace, integrity and self-determination; it was able to consolidate its new state, recover from war and destruction, construct a strong national economy and improve general living standards. However, as a continuous political and discursive struggle, it has been tested and contested repeatedly.

The politics of periodization (i): revolutions

The unending assaults on great social revolutions – French, Russian, and Chinese alike – in a revisionist historiography have enjoyed reinforcement from the disintegration of the former Communist Bloc. Such discourse is not without valuable insights, but is unwilling or unable to acknowledge the long-standing liberal consensus across the political spectrum on the historical accomplishments of the Chinese revolution. Even if Barrington Moore's axiom about the necessity of a revolutionary break cannot always be taken literally, China exemplified the social advantages of revolutionary transformation for large, poor, agrarian, illiterate and patriarchal societies. Empirically and comparatively, as Theda Skocpol has explained, successful social revolutions give 'birth to nations whose power and autonomy markedly surpassed their own pre-revolutionary pasts and outstripped other countries in similar circumstances.'[17] As most historical and political sociologists concur, it was the synthesis of communism and nationalism, revolution and modernization, that succeeded in unifying and developing a country as massive, old and burdened by tradition as China.

An important stand of revisionist scholarship, led by a group of influential China experts in the US, argues for the 'collapse of the 1949 wall', or proposes a need to break the '1949 barrier', in a post-Cold War context of 'diminishing significance of 1949'. This understands the revolution less as a communist intervention than as a 'consensual Chinese agenda'.[18] The call to remove the received periodic divide between the republican and communist revolutions echoed the slogan 'farewell to revolution' that has been circulating inside China since the 1980s. To establish an undifferentiated temporal period between 1911 and 1949 is to erase, perhaps unintentionally, Jiang Jieshi's betrayal of the 'great revolution' of 1924–27, or the Guomindang (GMD) state's counterrevolutionary violence, including its 1930–34 military campaigns to teminate the red regimes in South China. Such periodization also re-evaluates the Republican era and stresses its nationalist and modern-ization credentials, and this in turn entails a more negative assessment of the Mao era than the former, generally sympathetic scholarly consen-sus. Within China's policy and academic circles it was further asked whether the abortion of the New Democracy of mixed economy, coali-tion government and national-popular culture – elaborated by Mao in 1940 and stipulated in the 1949 Common Programme as the PRC's provisional constitution – was not a regrettable misstep. Socialist adven-tures since the mid-1950s came under fire more severely than ever before, resembling the fiercest Cold War–style anti-communism.

There is also an orthodox Marxist narrative that dismisses the vital distinction between these two kinds of 'bourgeois' revolution and

---

17 Theda Skocpol, *State and Social Revolutions: A Comparative Analysis of France, Russia and China*, Cambridge: Cambridge University Press, 1979: 3.

18 Michel Oksenberg, 'The American Study of Modern China: Toward the Twenty-First Century', in David Shambaugh, ed., *American Studies of Contemporary China*, Armonk, NY: M. E. Sharpe, 1993: 315; Esherick, 'Ten Theses on the Chinese Revolu-tion': 41; Paul Cohen, 'Reflections on a Watershed Date: The 1949 Divide in Chinese History', in Jeffrey Wasserstrom, ed. *Twentieth-Century China: New Approaches*, New York: Routledge, 2003: 30–1.

thereby erases two distinct political temporalities in China. This is based on the notion that the revolution, because it was land-based, could not be proletarian and was not enacted by the working class. According to this positivist approach and rigid logic, the Chinese communists were in fact petty bourgeois, and their rural revolution was substandard. Coinciding with the post-communist intellectual turn, these theorists portray the market transition in China as a consolidation of the bourgeois revolution of 1949, and as a necessary stage before the right class agency can grow mature to take the next step in a prescribed sequence of evolutions. A more general conflation considers the CCP leadership to have long transformed themselves 'from nationalist revolutionaries into a bureaucratic ruling class.'[19] However, not only did the CCP have a well theorized self-identity as an ingenious working-class organization committed to communism, but China's class-like position in global capitalism also confirmed the dual nature of the communist revolution. Its ambition to pave the way for socialist rather than capitalist development in itself categorically distinguished the *new* bourgeois revolution from the old one. Underlining this ambition was the material indispensability of the Chinese working class, which was initially small yet politically vital and militant, and still much larger and stronger than the national bourgeoisie. The latter was weak and politically ambivalent due to semi-colonial conditions and the dominance of foreign capital which foreclosed any indigenous prospect of liberal capitalism. These points were best theorized in the works that Mao produced in wartime Yan'an, particularly *Chinese Revolution and the Chinese Communist Party* and *On New Democracy*. These constitute the most original Chinese contribution to Marxism, and are yet to be learned by our international Marxist critics.

In common to both liberal revisionist and orthodox Marxist approaches is a trivialization of the Chinese Communist Revolution. What is missing is the whole complex background of national and social crises that compelled a thoroughly revolutionary response in China. Global capitalist contradictions were unsolvable without peripheral cataclysms, as Marx already understood in the late nineteenth century. In

---

19 Neil Davidson, *How Revolutionary Were the Bourgeois Revolutions?*, Chicago, IL: Haymarket Books, 2012: 621; Neil Faulkner, *A Marxist History of the World: From Neanderthals to Neoliberals*, London: Pluto, 2013: 257.

contrast, the perspective of modernization as apolitical and function-
alist is a fallacy, portraying the CCP at best as merely an instrument of
modernity, and at worst as disastrously regressive. Such misconceptions neglect not only the revolution's social immensity and depth
but also the gulf between Maoist and post-Mao polities. They also
validate subsequent capitalist integration retrospectively, envisaging a
deformed Chinese version of Marxism undergoing an unskippable
stage of capitalist development. Moreover, this perception echoes the
familiar philistine questioning of Chinese modernity: has there really
been a modern breakthrough in China? Within the rubric of the
'modern', has China ever broken with the dark side of its past? Is communist rule not just another dynastic cycle of despotism and
bureaucracy with superficial regime alternations? Given its 'tyranny of
history' and 'history of tyranny', is not the liability so great that 'even a
historical event of such magnitude as a revolution appears to have
accomplished little more than scratch the surface of a society hard-
ened into immutability'?[20]

Returning to the '1949 wall' debate, it should be uncontroversial that
the 1911 revolution had no strategies or programmes comparable with
those that the Communist Revolution developed subsequently, despite
its ideology of republicanism and anti-imperialism. As a narrow political revolution it ended several thousand years of dynastic cycles but
failed to solve China's existential crises, either national or social. Yet, it
set sail the country's irreversible revolutionary century, being soon surpassed by the much greater revolution led by the CCP. The differences
between old and new bourgeois revolutions, and between the pre- and
post-1949 socioeconomic and political systems are categorical. To be
sure, some groundwork was attempted during the republican period,
from constitutionalism to women's rights and rural education. But the
regime, corrupt and repressive to the bone, refused to carry out land
redistribution (until after it had retreated to Taiwan where the GMD
had no landed interest) among other pressing social reforms. These
failings allowed its communist competitor to win over popular support
and national power. Seventy years later, even if the post-socialist conditions have become blurred, the biggest obstacle to 'deconstructing' the

---

20 W. J. F. Jenner, *The Tyranny of History: The Roots of China's Crisis*, London:
Penguin, 1992; Dirlik and Meisner, eds, *Marxism and the Chinese Experience*: 17.

epoch-making event of 1949 is still the popular perception of the PRC nurtured in its early decades, a lingering notion of 'society's normative infrastructure'.[21] The language that demarcates new from old China, or distinguishes between post-liberation and pre-liberation, is naturally and meaningfully kept in everyday Chinese.

When the essayist Hu Feng wrote in October 1949 that 'time has begun', he was among the many millions witnessing the history-making events of the revolution with joy and excitement, while the People's Liberation Army (PLA) was still sweeping to take control of the whole country. But social revolutions as historical markers can also be tragic and costly: they may betray themselves, devour their own children and breed counterrevolution from within. For eagle-eyed defenders such as the literary giant Lu Xun, however, 'in revolution there is blood, there is filth, and yet there is also new life'.[22] The essence of revolution is freedom, and the right to revolution is freedom's due.[23] The year 1949 marked China's ascent from its post-1840 position as one of the world's most wretched lands. It is necessary to appreciate this, along 'with an acute and painful awareness of all the horrors and crimes that accompanied the revolution'.[24] In comparing the communist Russian and Chinese revolutions, Perry Anderson was sound in his verdict: 'If the twentieth century was dominated, more than by any other single event, by the trajectory of the Russian Revolution, the twenty-first will be shaped by the outcome of the Chinese Revolution'.[25]

We can see in the debates around the meaning of 1949 a primary case of the politics of periodization or historical consciousness. Contemporary Chinese history has to be interrogated in its specific conditions of development and crisis, and politically designated timeframes mobilized to construct and consume information. Different lines of periodization speak for different outlooks, positions and interests, and

---

21 Ching Kwan Lee, *Against the Law: Labour Protests in China's Rustbell and Sunbell*, Berkeley: University of California Press, 2007: xi.

22 Lu Xun, *Complete Works of Lu Xun 10*, Beijing: People's Literature Press, 1981: 336.

23 Nicolas de Condorcet, quoted in Hannah Arendt, *On Revolution*, New York: Viking, 1963: 21; Costas Douzinas, 'Adikia: On Communism and Rights,' in Costas Douzinas and Slavoj Žižek, eds, *The Idea of Communism*, London: Verso, 2010: 92.

24 Meisner, 'The Significance of the Chinese Revolution': 12.

25 Perry Anderson, 'Two Revolutions: Rough Notes', *New Left Review* 61, January/February 2010: 59.

struggles over dates, events and sequences are indicative of conflicting ideas and ideologies. Within the contending grand narratives, revolutions are local events that have translocal or global significance. Great social revolutions define an age and its circumstantial conditionality, against which other historical elements can be contextualized and evaluated. In other words, they are the key links between and among temporal conjunctures in concretely politicized and variously globalized spaces. The post-1949 history of the PRC is essentially a continuous revolution, therefore, filled with numerous social, political and economic campaigns for a socialist project in advance of the market transition. As to the debated chronology of the 1960s in relation to the Cultural Revolution, it is largely inconsequential in the sense that China's relationship with the capitalist global structure did not fundamentally change until much later.

Market reform derailed

The difficulties and intrinsic contradictions of Chinese socialism provided a basis for the later reorientation. A direct stimulus here consisted of extensive grievances, especially among the old guard and intellectual elite, caused by the Cultural Revolution's excesses. The possibility of reorientation was opened up by Mao's passing in September 1976. Intense political struggle followed, with the Gang of Four arrested in October; Deng Xiaoping campaigned against the Mao loyalists and attempted to unify the party by 'liberating the mind' and 'seeking truth from facts'. A few months before, in April 1976, over a million people had spontaneously gathered in Tiananmen Square to protest what was seen as 'cultural despotism' by mourning the premier Zhou Enlai, who had died in January of that year. The reformers then rode the tide of discontent. The 1978 third plenary of the eleventh party congress resolved on 'reform and opening'. The intention at the time was articulated in terms of socialist self-adjustment in two directions: to unseal a closed domestic political-economic system and to end foreign blockages. The breakthrough towards the second goal was already made under Mao in 1971, when Beijing replaced Taipei as China's representative at the United Nations, a step towards normalizing Sino-US relations. Economic liberalization focused on rural decollectivization and managerial autonomy for urban enterprises while 'making use' of foreign capital, market and technologies for Chinese growth.

Crucially, what was endorsed at the plenary was reform within the bounds of socialism, set by the legitimacy of the Communist Revolution, even as Maoist mistakes helped drive reformist reactions. China then had to use trial and error to decide what to reform, as well as where and to what extent. The late 1970s was a critical time, when the impasse reached by the Cultural Revolution intersected with the 'normalization' of politics after that upheaval. With hindsight, it was perhaps a missed but momentous opportunity for political regeneration: China could have evolved on an entirely different course had other decisions been made at this juncture.

Beyond the separation of party and government functions and the elimination of lifetime tenure for leaders, at the top of the agenda was the need to achieve a 'highly civilized, highly democratic' socialism. A Democracy Wall appeared in Beijing and was emulated elsewhere; public optimism spread through both government outlets and popular channels. Honest reckoning with past mistakes prevailed, and there were serious proposals for socialist democracy and the rule of law. Voices for socialist democracy from within the party joined forces with those from the streets, 'as if two groups were calling to each other across an alpine valley.'[26] This window of political change soon closed, however, as Deng redefined socialism in merely economic terms: the goal was 'common prosperity' (from which his policies would deviate anyway), conditional on the party holding on to power. Yet without popular participation and the search for truly socialist reforms, the party was deprived of an opportunity for self-rejuvenation and for developing the constitutional architecture for a rational and democratic socialism.

Still, amid early signs of a neoliberal turn, the first reform decade of the 1980s can be readily separated from the next three, with the events of 1989 marking a turning point. Before then, the socialist mandate was debated and these discussions impacted many major decisions. Social commitment to solidarity and egalitarian goals had withstood new market forces to varying degrees. Radical measures were attempted, with an eye on any potential social turmoil. Price reforms that

---

26 Roger Garside, *Coming Alive: China After Mao*, London: Andre Deutsch, 1981: 324.

threatened hyperinflation and market panic, for example, had to be tempered by a dual-track price scheme, but the latter created loopholes for rent-seeking, initiating a power-money nexus that has since been enormously augmented by a bureaucratic market system. Discontent over official corruption, social insecurity and rising inequalities began to simmer, and eventually erupted in 1989, triggered by the death of the liberal-minded CCP general secretary Hu Yaobang, perceived as having been unfairly treated in an internal leadership struggle. Far from the common portrayal of the uprising as an anti-communist call for regime change or Western-style democracy, the students and fellow protesters of 1989 demanded a clean and accountable government true to the commitments made in 1949. The decision to send in tanks and troops to clear Tiananmen Square signified the collapse of the initial reformist consensus; state violence then paved the way for the neoliberal derailing of what could have been self-correcting socialist reform.

The second reform decade was kicked off by Deng's southern tour to reclaim China's first special economic zones (SEZs) in 1992, which transformed the initial international condemnation of China's policy into a sort of economic collaboration. In a series of speeches, Deng dictated a neoliberal turn that radicalized policies on market integration without politically endangering communist rule. This can be seen as a determined response to the dissolution of the USSR and the ensuing turbulences across the now disintegrating Eastern camp. Socialism was quietly replaced by a new developmentalist doctrine of growth at any cost. China began to pursue institutional capacity building, in pursuit of its 'economic miracle' that took place over the following two decades – notably pushing such policies as price liberalization, preferential treatment to foreign direct investment (FDI) and, above all, privatization of medium and small-sized state-owned enterprises (SOEs). The wave of privatization also involved once thriving, collectively run township and village enterprises (TVEs), from which local governments eager to receive FDI withdrew support. Tens of millions of workers were laid off from the state sector, and many millions more rural labourers 'lost collective farming and gained urban poverty'.[27] A transient population of rural migrants took mostly low-end manufacturing,

---

27 Zhun Xu, *From Commune to Capitalism: How China's Peasants Lost Collective Farming to Gain Urban Poverty*, New York: Monthly Review Press, 2018.

construction and service jobs in cities, without reliable protection. An antagonistic capital–labour relationship developed, and preserving a favourable environment for FDI and GDP became a state priority over industrial and social policies.

Meanwhile, the 1994 tax-sharing reform, part of a fiscal recentralization policy to reduce the budget deficit, relinquished a large portion of central government's financial responsibilities for local public expenditure. One result was that local governments had to respond with inadvertently rationalized levies on rural households. This predation, along with other serious problems, from soil and water pollution to unprofitable farming and land eviction, accumulated into what became known as a threefold crisis in the wellbeing of agriculture, peasant livelihood and rural welfare. Li Changping, a grassroots official working in a Hubei township, described the crisis in a letter to Premier Zhu Rongji in 2000 as one of 'peasant poverty, rural hardship and endangered agriculture'. Sure enough, these conditions inflamed the 'rightful resistance' that was mounting.[28] In the urban areas, too, as the government withdrew from many of its social obligations, the marketization of housing, education, healthcare and old age security significantly weakened the infrastructure of public welfare. The commodification of essential public goods and services – maintained in many capitalist countries as well as post-communist ones – is one of the more obvious signs of a degenerate 'socialist' reform. By the early years of the new millennium, with the development of what David Harvey posits as 'neoliberalism with Chinese characteristics', the failure of 'common prosperity' on the reform's own terms was self-evident.

The post-WTO third reform decade began promisingly with a 'pro-people' gesture aiming to rectify the hardships of the 1990s. Hu Jintao, the party general secretary, recommended a 'scientific conception of development' to address popular discontent over farmland loss, wage arrears, sweatshop conditions and surging inequality. The government stopped taxing agriculture, introduced farming subsidies and worked on integrated urban–rural social security. However, other major issues – such as the political deprivation of labour or growth that relying on production for the world market at the expense of Chinese workers, environment and resources – were left untouched. The Hu–Wen New

28 Kevin O'Brien, 'Rightful Resistance', *World Politics* 49:1, October 1996.

Deal in the end could do no more than damage control, such as managing the impact of the 2008 global financial meltdown. No new social contract was signed, nor was any self-repositioning of China in the global economy attempted.

The fourth reform decade, still unfolding, continues to emphasize *minsheng* or livelihood, promoting the rhetoric of 'the people's good life'. Xi Jinping came to power in 2012 and declared a 'new era'. His platform of anti-corruption has been popular; so has, in a promised social policy package, his campaign for 'accurately' identifying and assisting the poor. The implementation of the latter, however, is marred by bureaucratic formalism and fraud. Years of reform have generated spectacular energy and growth, transforming the lives of a very large population, which is no small feat. The pledge to eradicate absolute poverty by 2021 is perhaps controversial, not because of any shortage of financial capability, given China's current level of per-capita GDP, but because the distribution of national wealth is so unequal and the structural conditions for poverty are not changed. The certain means to achieve poverty eradication, such as free and universal public medicine and education, are not officially considered. Policy thinking has also failed to register that exploitative labour relations, marketization of public provision and a feeble social safety net are bound to keep reproducing poverty. In a baffling response not only to domestic quandaries but also to complex international obstacles, Xi's economic policies have so far only pushed China in a more neoliberal direction even than his predecessors managed, as though the resolution lies there. The Chinese economy is thus set on a path of perpetual dependence on foreign capital, markets and core technologies.

Meanwhile, the confidence in the people once celebrated in the mass line has now collapsed into fear. Heavy-handed repression has been extended from political dissent to silencing wider areas and groups. The authorities are so alert that ordinary discontent and behaviour have now pose a threat, from a factory strike to a religious ritual ceremony, from loosely grouped activists to individual petitioners. The methods of surveillance, censorship and general control are ever more hi-tech while the governmental goal of maintaining stability (*weiwen*) takes precedence, with a swelling budget to match. The Xi era has also been branded by its flagship Belt and Road Initiative (BRI) announced in 2013, entailing a massive outflow of Chinese FDI into resource-rich and geostrategically important countries and regions. Being the world's largest creditor (despite internal debts) is a measure of China's enormous wealth accumulated from exploiting labour and natural resources, as well as its vulnerability in a world dominated by US power and dollar hegemony. Needless to add that foreign policy is always a continuation of politics at home. There now exist striking contradictions between the idea of 'socialism' and its manifestation of 'Chinese characteristics', evident in China's formal statements (with a chimera of Maoist renascence) and actual policies, performative confidence and apparent insecurity, domestic hindrances and international adventures.

The politics of periodization (ii): reforms

The year 1978 marked the end of the 1949 revolution, which began to ferment in the New Culture movement of the late 1910s and closed around the events of 1976 transitional to the post-Mao era. It is then only through the lens of 1949, or through the communist revolution's original aspirations and commitments, that contentions over the reorientation of 1978 can be examined. The marker of the 'long 1949' stands as a normative gauge with which to measure the rights and wrongs of China's subsequent development and position in the world. If, on the scale of history, the outcome of the revolution is still in the future, the baseline was definitively drawn in 1949 – even though new society can never be sharply separated from the old. Just like the 1949 moment, the 1978 threshold cannot be dismissed with generic phrases such as 'one-party rule' or 'communist regime', given the wide variation in lived experiences and outcomes across time and space in the local, national and international communist systems. The mistake of applying these terms indiscriminately is immediately apparent in critical differences (amid similarities) in ideologies, policies, party–mass relations and so on, between both the pre- and post-1978 periods and the pre- and post-1989 periods. Periodization is precisely about making distinctions, and thereby producing a sense of historicity. To test it we must look to the major puzzles in Chinese modern history, not least the question of the CCP's staying power in a post-communist world.

The endurance of communist rule, which is baffling for many, is usually put down to a mix of economic development with trickledown effects in elevated living standards and reduced poverty, nationalist coagulation, state adaptability and two decades of a favourable international environment that resulted from China's diplomatic and market opening. This list raises the questions, however, as to how and why these factors are considered desirable. Any convincing explanation would have to confront the deeper, path-dependent causality: the lasting appeal and organizational capacity, albeit compromised, of a ruling party historically rooted in a popular indigenous revolution. This residual strength has so far worked, to the extent that cracks within the circle of political elites are largely held in check, resentments against local wrongs are contained from the centre, and governments at various levels feel an obligation to respond to social outcries, consultative deliberations and selected pressure groups. Protests arise mostly because of unmet expectations that the ostensibly socialist state still induces. That the protesters can hope to achieve anything is down to the fact that their demands are made on the rulers' own terms, which have maintained a people-oriented rhetoric as well as real pressure on legitimation. Explanations that overlook the lasting credentials of past struggles are meaningless.

In the same vein, such dividends could both sustain the regime and push it back to its origin in resisting the capitalist 'revolutionization' of the reform. In other words, defending and advancing the fundamental promises of 1949 would be the only way to prevent the fomentation of another revolution from below. It is impossible to defend 1949 by apologising for China's current position; and ultimately, it is the party's inner decay, the loss of its founding mission and vision, and its collusion with private capital and power that have done more damage than any outside force could. Meanwhile, of course, the question concerning regime durability becomes tricky as its communist identity trembles.

The need to acknowledge the continuities between the pre- and post-Mao period is motivated by several concerns. The stress on the positive legacies of Chinese socialism is based on the fundamentals that without national autonomy, a sovereign government and state infrastructural build-up, the spectacular growth customarily attributed simply to market opening would not have been possible. Nothing close could have been achieved had China not been an independent and liberated modern nation in the first place – not to mention the other side of the story, that every gain in the marketplace has been paid for by losses in the same measure. Moreover, as has been amply shown in numerous

empirical studies, successful reform policies often tap into their inherited sources of socialist modernization. From the national developmental
capacity of mobilizing productive factors to a high-quality workforce,
pre-reform preparations appeared as prerequisites for reform to pursue
its pledged agenda. Pinpointing an essential comparative advantage in
China's market transition, Carl Riskin noted that historical capitalism
'did not have to deal with a healthy, long-lived and literate population
steeped in powerfully egalitarian values.'[29]

Conceptually, it is important to clarify that, by definition, a socialist
reform would aim at correcting the deficiencies and wrongs of, while
not severing its connection with, the socialist experiments of the previous era. A wholesale departure from the socialist base violates the very
connotations of reform, and would be suicidal for the reformers. A
'revolution' in a post-revolutionary historical context can mean only
counterrevolution. Invoking the intervening variable of global capitalism, the PRC has evolved to alter the dynamics of international political
economy and power relations. By the same logic, taking the country
away from the system and entering it on a different path would be of
equal significance. The capitalist integration of China would be another
world historical defeat of the socialist experiment, following the collapse
of the Soviet bloc.

Other interpretations based on the continuity thesis serve mainly to
conceal post-reform's non- or anti-socialist policies, or to justify them
through a lineage of 'communist' legitimacy. Discontinuities between
the two eras, however, are also overwhelming. The year 1978 was indeed
a new beginning by the dialectics of revolution and reform. Two opposing lines of argument stand out here. Right wing ideologues against
socialism, implicitly endorsed from above without necessarily conform-
ing to the official assessment in the Central Committee's 1981 'Resolution
on certain questions in the history of our party since 1949', use Maoist
failures, both real and fabricated, to promote reform's radicalization.
Conversely, critics of reform regard the Communist Revolution as
rightly and necessarily encompassing both 1949 and 1966, hence insisting on the Dengist betrayal. Feeling vindicated by the emergence, since
the 1990s, of a super-rich oligarchy springing from or networked with
office holders, they believe that Mao had been proven right after all.

---

29 Carl Riskin, 'Behind the Silk Curtain', *Nation*, 10 November 1997: 14.

However, the denial of socialist intention in which the reformist promises were based is unconvincing, and cannot explain the broad accord within the reform project of the late 1970s. If the end of the Mao era signposted the closure of a revolutionary century, it was because changes were morally necessary and popularly desirable – the decision to enact self-readjustment without abandoning socialism was genuinely liberating. Rejecting oversimplified interpretations, China's post-1978 journey should be seen as undetermined, a matter of the politics of possibilities.

In light of all this, there is a pressing concern to periodize the course of Chinese reforms. Holding the 1949 benchmark constant, it would be impossible to accept any consistent genealogy of the 'forty years', as is generally taken for granted. In retrospect, what we see is a willing and almost uninterrupted march towards global integration since the 1990s, rather than a reluctant temporary strategic retreat from war communism analogous to the New Economic Policy (NEP) of Soviet Russia a century earlier. Any resemblance is superficial since state capitalism in the Soviet case was only instrumental for a proletarian state. In this sense, the demarcation of '1978' under the rubric of market transition is misleading without further periodization. If Chinese reform appeared synchronic with the neoliberal tide of globalization since the 1980s, wholesale integration did not begin to take shape until the 1990s, which was indicative of China redefining its relationship with global capital.

The year of 1989 was critical, riding on the wave of neoliberal solutions in the core capitalist countries. To define 1989 as a watershed moment is to recognize the first phase of reform as socialist, in contrast with the perversion of socialism that took place over subsequent decades. The conjuncture of 1989/92, with two years of relapse after the Tiananmen crisis, was marked by a redefinition of reform – hence the great irony: that the same factors which caused the protests in Beijing and other urban centres, notably the corruption and socioeconomic injuries and insecurities, returned afterwards, but on a much bigger scale. If it was the crisis of Chinese socialism that compelled and legitimized that reform, the making of capitalism with Chinese characteristics after the 'long 1980s' was marked by an accumulation of its own crises. The year 1992 was established as a landmark of neoliberalization, followed by deepening globalization, mass privatization, intensified polarization and mounting bureaucratization and corruption. All was ratified through a corresponding ideological re-articulation. If certain affinities with NEP or New Democracy were present before 1989, they soon vanished. The clarity of political logic in this trajectory, then, is that the immediate precursor for the events of 1989 is the reform initiative of 1978, which, in turn, can only be measured by the benchmark of 1949. Questions concerning the morals of communist revolution and the legitimacy of a rectifying reform can be answered only with reference to this sequential signification.

The mainstream periodization proposals rely on the two periods – thirty years before the reform and forty years after – not negating each other. Their primary assumption is authorized by Xi's criticism of 'historical nihilism' and the promotion of a linear narrative of China 'standing up' under Mao, 'getting rich' under Deng, and 'becoming powerful' under Xi. In a speech commemorating the fortieth anniversary of reform on 18 December 2018, he highlighted the 'three great milestones' of 1921, 1949 and 1978 without underscoring Mao's foundational contribution.[30] Going farther, some commentators inserted the republican period to present a modernization continuum throughout 1919, 1949 and 1978; farther still, an impossible yet influential synthesis that appealed to official ideology attempted to 'unify the three traditions' of Confucianism, socialism and market reform.[31] This last perspective, suggesting an uninterrupted civilization of 5,000 years, assumes incessant cultural and technological progress that is today reaching new heights. The blending of incompatible traditions in such teleological accounts of uniformity is just as wishful, especially at a time when bureaucratic and market forces join to tear society apart. These attitudes share the uncritical acceptance of a developmentalist premise in China's modern search for wealth and power, as though it is all about national rejuvenation rather than global capitalist sabotage.

It is unacceptable to conceal the turning point of 1989/92 as a way to legitimize – as the unavoidable price of development – what is illegitimate, measured against the intentions of 1949. Again the boundary drawn in 1949 remains alive in popular consciousness: old China

---

30 In the celebratory exhibition on forty years of market reform at the National Museum in Beijing, 'what was absent was the Revolution of 1949 and its iconic imagery ... There was no image of Mao ... his presence was negligible.' Vijay Prashad, 'China's Forty Years of Reform', Newsclick, 18 December 2018, newsclick.in/China-forty-years-reform.

31 Gan Yang, *Unify the Three Traditions*, Beijing: Sanlian, 2007.

signifies conflicts and poverty, injustice and hardship; while new China signifies a progressive and hopeful society in pursuit of equality and participation, errors and blunders notwithstanding. The fact that many phenomena of the old society have returned, from exploitation and patriarchy to corrupt and bullying officialdom, only reinforces these contrasts. The reluctance or refusal to appreciate the Communist Revolution in China also blocks the explication of the legitimacy crisis that has faced Chinese socialism since 1989, and is certainly not in the interest of the CCP itself. Precisely because of this, and since the party still lives off its past laurels amassed through revolutionary and socialist struggles, it has needed – for self-assurance as much as for persuasion – to downplay political and policy discontinuities between the pre- and post-reform periods. However, if the 'capitalist restoration' that Mao warned against is indeed happening, and if 'capitalist roaders' are actually gaining grounds, where is the claimed continuity, other than the rule by a party that is still nominally communist? One does not have to be 'ideological', as those claiming objectivity in defence of the status quo put it, to see that a gross undoing of the revolution has taken place in the ruthless accumulation of capital, along with all its predictable social and environmental consequences.

Political transformations through the landmarks of 1949, 1978 and 1989/92, along with their counter movements, have shaped modern China. Our periodization exercise suggests the following. First, China's twentieth century, long or short, must be viewed in light of the justifiable pride on the part of the protagonists in the country's liberation struggles. Second, while China has grown economically, it has degraded politically and culturally by losing the most valuable legacies of its revolutionary and socialist traditions – yet repudiations of revolution cannot be conclusive and may not be irreversible. Third, 1949 remains the touchstone or normative gauge of PRC history in terms of assessing its successes and failures, both of the Maoist and the reform periods, mediated by appraisals of China's evolving relationship with the capitalist global system that is itself historical. Only when understood neither as irresistible nor as the only imaginable horizon does the politics of periodization make any practical sense. It is clear then that the immediate evaluative reference for the events of 1989 is the initial reform programme of 1978; and in turn, 1978 can be assessed in light of the aspiration of 1949 – that is, to disregard the watershed of 1989/92 would be just another way to dismiss the signifi-cance of 1949.

Where the fourth reform decade, under Xi's extended term in office since 2012, is currently headed remains uncertain. So far not only have the post-1992 deviances from socialism remained in place, but the pushes for an ever more liberalized economy and an ever more controlled society also run counter to the rhetoric of socialism. As China's internal and external challenges mount to press for effective answers, however, its unilateral moves towards global integration are increasingly implausible. Only the advent of a socialist transformative politics from above and below can ensure the country's security and development. Such a politics could be precipitated by the unconcealed intent of the US to strangle a 'rising' China through trade, financial and any other means. The chances for another reorientation to reclaim the party and state are not all closed. In this light, whether 2012 or 2022 might eventually stand out as milestones will depend on whether the looming trend of labour and social movements and popular pressure can affect a leadership haunted by its own vows. It has indeed signalled a strong desire for socialist renewal, which, however, has yet to answer the question regarding how socialism should be interpreted. History remains open.

As a function of the conception and politics of history, and an act of organizing and framing non-linear time, periodization is both retro-spective and reflective by nature. Accounting for compressed and fluctuating or conflicting temporalities is political, if only because the past as historical time is always reconstructed by present understand-ings and future yearnings. Alongside social space as a means of control, spatially specific developments are defined and ranked, with time being 'the principal tool of power and domination'; hence 'it matters who owns time' as a prevailing dimension of social relations.[32] The practice of periodization and sequential inventions is itself a struggle for hegem-ony. As such, periodizing modern Chinese history is about discerning the nature of each of its crossroads, especially the present one, which is

---

32 Henri Lefebvre, *The Production of Space*, Oxford: Blackwell, 1974: 26; Zygmunt Bauman, *Liquid Modernity*, Cambridge: Polity, 2000: 9; Susan Buck-Morss, 'The Second Time as Farce . . . Historical Pragmatics and the Untimely Present', in Douzinas and Žižek, eds, *The Idea of Communism*: 68–9.

also part and parcel of mapping and interpreting the world. How might we narrate a global history of revolutions and counterrevolutions while transcending the positivist chronology of modernization? Ought we to ask questions concerning such handy labels as post-socialism, post-communism and indeed post-capitalism? The 'China moment', then and now, has been intrinsically global and can only be so grasped. This is not because a 'global China' exerts more impact on the world, but because capitalist transformation has been internalized by the Chinese identity. To reverse this process of internalization or disowning time, any conscious renovation of the country would require a reordering of what Fernand Braudel categorized plurally as 'structural temporalities'. The meta-histories, both Chinese and global, are still being written.

PART TWO

The Construction and Destruction of a Revolutionary State

3

From the rural margins

The CCP was indigenous, but also urban, intellectual and international in origin, while theoretically aware in its early days of the centrality of the peasant question in a country thoroughly agrarian. The bloodshed of the 1927 counterrevolutionary coup compelled the Communist Revolution to regroup and start from the beginning in the countryside. This revolution, due to its own historical circumstances, was strategically creative and substantially different from the earlier Russian example. As a resolute force for both national and social liberation, the CCP organized a united nationalist resistance as much as class struggle. Due to the involvement of rival imperialist powers characteristic of semi-colonial conditions and the ensuing fragmentation of counterrevolution, the party was always prepared to adjust its strategy according to changing domestic and international circumstances. The revolution was initiated in distant territories with great local variations. Coordinating these dispersed political and military units was perilous, but what was ultimately achieved was an organizational miracle. At one time, there were even two Central Committees – in Shanghai and Ruijin respectively; at other times, conflicting commands flowed from representatives of various headquarters, including the Comintern. Communications were repeatedly cut off during marches and battles. Nevertheless, the revolution mobilized across many regions, developed formidable military power, maintained deadly underground exertions in enemy areas and engaged in an ambitious cultural front of education, publishing, theatre and journalism in the face of the GMD White Terror.

It was guerrilla warfare and land redistribution at the village level that decided the outcome of revolution, giving the CCP 'a depth of social recitation the Russian party never acquired'.[1] The journey and victory rooted in the soil of rural China and a militarized party have left vital impressions on the PRC state and society. The significance of the Chinese revolution is associated not only with the now largely unused signifier of 'East' but also 'South' in the language of international development. As the plight of rural China today remains central to Chinese disorientation, and hence also its possible reorientation, the country's revolutionary transformation offers valuable lessons. 'Guerrilla style' flexible policy making is only one example of its contemporary relevance; there could be many others.[2] More fundamental stimuli might emerge from revisiting China's revolutionary trajectory of party building, mass line, people's war and rural organization.

How new was China's new bourgeois democratic revolution?

The enemies of the Communist Revolution were defined in the 1922 party programme as 'imperialism and feudalism', with 'bureaucratic-comprador capitalism' formally added in later. To remove these 'three great mountains' of foreign domination in collusion with domestic ruling and landed interests, the revolution had to be simultaneously national and social – though not yet socialist until the 1950s, as indicated in its 'minimum programme'. Because of China's semi-coloniality and the resulting absence of a strong national bourgeoisie capable of leading the revolution, a communist leadership was required to fulfil the task. National independence and 'land to the tiller' were already central to Sun's platform, but the old bourgeois revolution was far too narrow to achieve either. Yet as precisely the communists were now in charge, even a bourgeois revolution could not be stopped after its first goals were complete. The party's 'maximum programme' stipulated a prospective communist transition. The compression of variously 'bourgeois democratic' and

---

1 Anderson, 'Two Revolutions': 64.

2 Sebastian Heilmann and Elizabeth Perry, 'Embracing Uncertainty: Guerrilla Policy Style and Adaptive Governance in China,' in Heilmann and Perry, eds, *Mao's Invisible Hand: The Political Foundation s of Adaptive Governance in China*, Cambridge, MA: Harvard University Press, 2011: 1–29.

proletarian socialist phases was unorthodox. It was a conceptual lift from Marx who had hinted, without theorization, that nationalism and socialism could develop symbiotically from oppressed nations in rebellion.

Another distinctly new feature of the Chinese revolution was its rural-based strategic invention of 'encircling the cities from the countryside'. This did not contradict the CCP's communist identity. The party initially concentrated on urban organization while running short courses to train cadres and rural activists. Among the most legendary working-class acts of militancy under the CCP leadership in the 1920s were the Shanghai tobacco, machinery and textile workers' strikes; Beijing Changxindian railway workers' school and club; miners' movements at Anyuan (Hunan) and Kailuan (Hebei); rail strikes along the country's communications arteries; and a Hong Kong seamen's strike. Labour unionization, strikes, schools and magazines saw high political engagement across the regions, under the Chinese Trade Union Secretariat founded by the party in August 1921. The mass anti-imperialist May Thirtieth demonstrations in 1925 marked the party's first national showing. The Canton–Hong Kong strike of 1925–26, probably the longest in modern labour history, lasted over sixteen months. The last of the three armed workers' uprisings of 1926–27 in Shanghai was supported by a general strike of 800,000 workers. Were it not for the counterrevolution of 1927 that destroyed the first CCP–GMD alliance in a sea of blood, with the slaughter of tens of thousands of communists and their sympathizers, the Chinese revolution could have followed a different path altogether.

The communists did not surrender, but they had to re-evaluate the situation and reformulate their strategies. In the event, the party assembled its residual forces to launch the Nanchang uprising on 1 August in 1927 (the date has since become Army Day, celebrated annually in the PRC). The conjunction of dispersed troops from Nanchang and other uprisings gave birth to the first armed force of the CCP, the Worker-Peasant Revolutionary Army, under the banner of the axe and sickle. It was soon reassembled in the Jinggang Mountains and renamed the Red Army in January 1928, under the command of Zhu De and Mao Zedong. This marked a decisive retreat from the strongholds of counter-revolution but also a daring advance into the rural border regions, ultimately in order to seize the cities and state power. Since then, through valiant struggle the red bases were built and lost, then regained and enlarged. From Ruijin, the capital of the first Chinese Soviet Republic, to

Yan'an, the CCP's commanding base after the Long March, and from guerrilla and militia fighters to field armies throughout wars against invading Japanese and later US-equipped GMD troops, the communist forces gradually linked up their scattered bases into larger and more integrated territories. They were both the much needed rearguard of a prolonged people's war, and the material foundation for future national power.

In Mao's summary of the experience of the communist revolution in China, the three 'magic weapons' were party building, armed struggle and a united front. In practice these intertwined. Party building was paramount, especially under the circumstances, where a vanguard proletarian organization with a majority peasant membership was enacting a revolution in a predominantly rural setting. Hence the charge that the CCP was petty bourgeois in nature after 1927: it 'had effectively ceased to be a working-class party, since its entire urban membership base in that class had been destroyed, and had become instead a rural guerrilla organization based on the peasantry'.[3] This is factually one-sided and conceptually superficial. In fact, workers – urban as well as hired rural labour and artisans –continued to be a vigorous component of the Chinese Red Army and the party's underground network in the areas controlled by counterrevolution. Examples include the coal miners of Anyuan, who formed the backbone of Mao's troops at the 1927 Autumn Harvest Uprising, and the workers of Shanghai and other cities, who joined the communist networks, both urban and rural, in the surrounding regions. More to the point, given the impossibility of the dogmatic belief in establishing a socialist power at one stroke by overthrowing landowners as well as capitalists in China, it was prerequisite to find a non-urban centric strategy, despite the party's working-class self-identification.

In theory, what is missing from this critique of the Chinese Communist Revolution is China's proletarian-like position in an imperialist global system, and the new bourgeois revolution carrying within itself a socialist ambition. Class cannot be a positivist sociological category; instead it denotes political positions and attitudes dynamically related to specific historical conditions and political economy. Mao's answer was to prioritize political education in daily revolutionary practice, and to

---

3 Davidson, *How Revolutionary Were the Bourgeois Revolutions?*: 252.

involve not only new recruits, including peasants and intellectuals, but also, and emphatically, party veterans. 'The party ideology provided unity of goal, and its discipline gave it a vanguard of party cadres – ideological, ascetic, fairly uncorrupt – hotly debating the party line but then implementing it collectively.'[4] The petty bourgeois intellectuals drawn to the revolution, in particular, were required to temper themselves to become organic components of the proletariat through life-and-death battles and grassroots work. These locally specific class factors were what made it possible to educate and organize poor and middle peasants through their own activities, and to defend and expand the red bases. The principal method, implemented since the first days of the Chinese red army, of establishing a party branch in every company along with a democratic soldiers' committee went much further than the Soviet army system of political commissars.[5] The party's army was founded on loyalty, cohesion and discipline as well as 'subjective agency', and principles such as 'equality between officers and soldiers' and 'not taking a single needle or piece of thread from the masses'. 'Our party, our army' is still spoken as one word, and Mao's eloquence on these theoretical points has not been surpassed to this day.

The united front, the second magic weapon, was based on a worker–peasant alliance forged in an agrarian society. The party's class line was first formulated in Mao's 'Analysis of the Classes in Chinese Society' of 1925, before the revolution was forced to take its rural turn. He asserted that identifying friends and enemies was 'a question of the first importance of the revolution'; indeed, 'the basic reason why all previous revolutionary struggles in China achieved so little was their failure to unite with real friends in order to attack real enemies.'[6] Around workers and peasants, the wider alliance drew together progressive intellectuals and professionals, patriotic gentry and the industrial and commercial national bourgeoisie, and any other intermediates to be won over to the all-inclusive popular coalition. The party's nationality policy also reflected a united front open to minority elites, something that remained

---

4 Michael Mann, *The Sources of Social Power, Vol. 3: Global Empires and Revolution, 1890–1945*, Cambridge: Cambridge University Press, 2012: 409.

5 Mao, 'The Struggle in the Jinggang Mountains', 25 November 1928, *Selected Works* 1: 83; and 'The Democratic Movement in the Army', 30 January 1948, marxists.org/reference/archive/mao/selected-works/volume-4/mswv4_27.htm.

6 Mao, *Selected Works 1*: 3.

more or less in place until the early years of the PRC. While the GMD leaned towards colonial capitalism and reactionary landowners, the CCP appealed to the rural and urban poor and the widest possible range of social sections. For this reason, as with the anti-Fascist popular front formed globally during the Second World War, certain constraints were placed on class struggle in times of national crisis. For the sake of 'the national united front of resisting Japan', the Red Army submitted itself to realignment under the national government at great cost, and both Yan'an (the Eighth Route Army) and Yunling/Yancheng (the New Fourth Army) followed a flexible, pragmatic class line, relaxing communist land and rent policies to accommodate even an 'enlightened' gentry. China's primary global status as an oppressed nation fighting to liberate itself determined such a united front as the sole viable strategy. Mao's metaphor of 'the foolish old man removing the mountains' explained its mass base: the party must work tenaciously to 'touch God's heart', and 'our God is none other than the masses of the Chinese people.'[7]

The third weapon in Mao's theory was armed struggle: the heroic choice, made in August 1927, of 'answering armed counterrevolution with armed revolution'. No non-violent path was open to the communists, since their enemies were armed to the teeth. To counter the White Terror and its military campaigns of extinction, the revolution had to arm itself, though only poorly at first, when it relied on weapons seized in the battle. There is an obvious analogy here, in the difference between the violence of slavery and that of slaves shattering their shackles. Revolution was no dinner party; class struggles were brutal. Yet the people's war was not just another episode of revolt; it was a vital step in the revolution's most innovative strategy of enveloping the cities from the countryside. Mao made it clear in a 1929 party congress resolution in Gutian that 'the Chinese Red Army is an armed body for carrying out the political tasks of the revolution.' It fought 'in order to conduct propaganda among the masses, organize them, arm them, and help them to establish revolutionary political power. Without these objectives, fighting would lose its meaning and the Red Army the reason for its existence.'[8] Armed struggle and revolution were in symbiosis, and the

---

7 Mao, speech on 11 June 1945, *Selected Works* 3: 1102.

8 Mao, 'On Correcting Mistaken Ideas in the Party', December 1929, *Selected Works* 1: 86.

revolutionary war paralleled the process of new state formation. Under the CCP, which was also committed to international communism and anti-fascism, national liberation was inseparable from class and social liberation. 'This was ultimately a Marxian revolution,' as Michael Mann concludes his examination of various interpretations of the Chinese Communist Revolution.[9]

The short-sighted assumption that Chinese communist revolutionaries, with a generally petty bourgeois background, were unable to carry out a socialist transformation overlooks both the relevant theory and the historical evidence. It is incapable of registering the revolution's reach to the rural as well as urban masses, as well as the speed and success with which the communist modernizers nationalized industries and commerce, and collectivized agriculture in the 1950s. Missing from such orthodox views is the power of politics to redirect history in defiance of a prescribed sequence whereby capitalism must precede socialism. The clarification is necessary because similar misconceptions echo Cold War narratives, leading to implausible and politically dangerous assertions. In this perspective, Chinese socialism either never seriously existed or was simply a doomed and parenthetical episode. The failure to appreciate the meaningful distinction between the party lines or state policies of China's pre- and post-reform eras, for example, precludes even a minimal understanding of where China has been and evolving. Furthermore, it is worth noting that the petty bourgeoisie remains an important category in analysing class and social relations in a country where profound socioeconomic transformations have not required petty production to disappear. Indeed, even today a large proportion of the population comprises small landholders as cultivators and urban self-employed producers. Marx might be a bit unfair in his bitter polemics against European 'petty bourgeois socialisms', and these critiques are not all that relevant to the Chinese conditions of modern development.[10]

---

9 Mann, *The Sources of Social Power, Vol. 3*: 411.

10 Cui Zhiyuan introduces Roberto Unger's 'petty bourgeois radicalism' as a synthesis of Marxism, Proudhonism and Lasellism. See also Cui, 'Liberal Socialism and the Future of China: A Petty Bourgeois Manifesto' in Tian Yu Cao, ed., *The Chinese Model of Modern Development*, London: Routledge, 2009; Lin Chun, *China and Global Capitalism: Reflections on Marxism, History, and Contemporary Politics*, London: Palgrave: chs 6 and 7.

The land revolution and people's war

The people's war was essentially a land war. Traditionally, despite ancient calls for equal sharing and repeated imperial reforms to halt land concentration, local officials and landlords kept encroaching on petty farming through heavy rent, levies and conscript labour. Peasant revolts sparked by poverty, tyranny and landlessness were therefore endemic in historical China. This pattern of periodic social upheavals took a turn for the worse in the wake of foreign impingements, which devastated the Chinese countryside with bankruptcies, famines and conflicts. As documented by China's Marxist economists since the 1920s, imperialist interventions tended to ruin small farmers; this explains why anti-imperialist mobilization could be just as effective among a peasant population. Meanwhile, although very large land-holding was uncommon, especially in northern China, and peasant hardship was not solely attributable to unequal land ownership, structural landlordism (of both resident and absentee landlords) and its institutionalized local land regimes prolonged peasant deprivation. The old 'feudal' relations and newer ones of foreign capital and domestic comprador bureaucracy conjoined to intensify the country's national and social crises.[11] Alongside a struggling population of petty peasants, rural hired labour was growing. Agricultural workers became far more numerous, while being poorer and often more badly treated than urban waged labour. Far from being an unlikely soil for communist agitation, rural China began with a land war and continued by sustaining revolutionary advances.

During its Jiangxi period, the CCP passed two resolutions on the land and peasant questions in 1928, calling for the expropriation of the landlord class. The policy was implemented mainly through village assemblies and poor peasant associations, following the party slogan of 'enlarging the Soviet territory, deepening the land revolution and recruiting for the Red Army'. Support was also garnered from party-led

---

11 Chen Hansheng, a Marxist economist, and his team's field research in Wuxi, Jiangsu, 1929–33 offers an example. See Chen, 'Land Distribution in Wuxi and the Prospect of Capitalism', and Fan Shitao, 'Chen Hansheng and the National Central Academy's Rural Wuxi Economic Investigation', *China Economic History Research* 5, 2020: 165–92.

militias and mass organizations of women and youth, along with cross-section social networking. There was no opportunity to adjust and consolidate the redistribution of land, however, before Nanjing's (the capital of the GMD government) five rounds of 'extermination campaigns' forced the much smaller communist forces to flee in late 1934 and relocate to the north a year later. The main base, already suffering economic and mobilizational exhaustion, was lost, and the remaining Red Army fighters and peasant activists suffered horrific reprisals. While the long marchers and local communist forces formed the Eighth Route Army during the second CCP–GMD united front to resist Japan, the New Fourth Army, fighting behind enemy lines in the lower Yangzi areas, was trapped and nearly eliminated by the GMD in 1941.

The first stage of land revolution had to be suspended until after the war was over. The party's wartime policy was to subordinate class to national interests, substituting forcible land redistribution with rent and tax reduction. It was with the party's May fourth directive in 1946, and especially the monumental Outline Land Law promulgated in 1947 during the War of Liberation that the CCP resumed its agrarian programme centred in distributive land reform. Village by village, region by region, from older to newly liberated areas, hundreds of work teams were dispatched to engage the rural masses. The teams surveyed the land and arranged re-registrations, organized classes for illiterate men and women to learn to write and count, encouraged the poor to understand their exploitation and suffering in class and gender terms, and directed struggle meetings against hated landlords and local tyrants.

The nationwide land reform was the last stage of China's land revolution against a 'feudal economy' controlled by a parasitic landed class who expropriated agrarian surpluses and squandered them on unproductive uses, including the grasping of yet more land and the building of mansions. The reform aimed at equal land rights for all farming families and individuals of both sexes. Although the male-dominated household was not challenged, women did enjoy the same right to hold land in their own name. The redistribution of land was accompanied by that of farming tools and animals, as well as policies that aimed for the equalization of household income and tax burdens. The process was highly charged in its class designation and method of 'relying on the poor and landless, allying and stabilizing the intermediate, neutralizing rich peasants and targeting the landlords'. A lesson from the earlier experience in Jiangxi was to avoid ultra-radicalism that overtly expropriated landlords and rich peasants, which alienated the middle strata and damaged the reputation of the communist project. The party's July 1947 national land conference developed the policy of combining land reform with a united front, as well as protecting national industry and commerce.[12] Unnecessary violence still occurred, however, most seriously in northern Shanxi in 1947, a distortion of policy that was subsequently denounced as an error of 'leftist adventurism' and rectified.[13] Mao treated the problem as critical as about the fate of the revolution, and spoke to the local party workers and wrote articles and party directives in the midst of an intense civil war to recapitulate essential issues of land reform:

> thoroughgoing reform of the land system is a basic task of the Chinese revolution in its present stage. If we can solve the land problem universally and completely, we shall have obtained the most fundamental condition for the defeat of all our enemies.[14]

The sweeping land reform decisively changed the balance of power between the communist and nationalist forces in the war. Notwithstanding the strategies and tactics used by Mao and his comrades in the military, alongside other conditions from broadened base areas to preparations for urban engagement, it is significant that millions of those who had recently gained land joined the PLA and its logistic troops. What has become legendary is the scene of the winter 1948–49 of massive *fanshen* (liberated) peasants pushing wheelbarrows of donated food crisscrossing the expansive battleground of the Huaihai campaign to feed 'the army of their own sons and brothers'. As the ongoing land reform continued to consolidate the communist rear, at the frontlines division after division of the GMD forces defected to the

---

12 Mao, 'Speech at the Expanded Central Committee Meeting', 21 July 1947, *Selected Works* 4: 268.

13 The party held a series of meetings and issued a series of directives in late 1947 and early 1948 to correct ultraleftism. See Mao's speeches and articles in *Selected Works* 4: 1267–84, 1306–33.

14 Mao, 'The Present Situation and Our Tasks', 25 December 1947, *Selected Works* 4: 1251.

PLA for the same reason that the peasant-soldiers had chosen to fight for their land: the communist policy specified that they too were entitled to a piece of land, as well as debt cancellation. Another reason was the party's successful policy of implementing basic equality among army ranks, including former captives from the enemy, and strong political education. Of its long-term effects, however, not only did class identification during land reform endure, other class labels also gained a caste-like quality – the next two generations inherited their predestined family class background. That is another story, of political and social lives in China after 'class struggle' lost its material basis in the means of production.

As the PRC founded, the regime required consolidation and economic recovery, and a new Agrarian Reform Law and an instructive *Report on the Question of Land Reform* were issued in 1950. Industrial and commercial enterprises owned by landlords were excluded from confiscation, and the rich peasant economy was preserved. On entering the Korean War in October that year, China fortified the united front for the war effort. By the end of 1952, apart from the potentially contentious minority regions where landed elites were not targeted but neutralized, more than 300 million lower-poor and middle peasants, or nearly 90 per cent of the rural population, had obtained their fair share of the land. Parts of the pastoral and forest regions went through similar reforms. As mutual aid groups and cooperatives voluntarily emerged, the party also began to conceive a policy on agrarian cooperation. The peasants were to see their lives improve apace.

To summarize, 'equalizing land rights' – as one of the two pillars of Sun's republicanism, along with 'constraining capital' – could not be realised without a communist revolution on the land. As a vital act of redistributive justice that liberated the forces of production, it had the immediately beneficial effect of eliminating reactionary and parasitic landlordism, improving outputs and peasant living, and making possible transfers of the surplus previously held by landlords into investment in public, social and human infrastructures to become part of the local economies on which the military supplies also depended. In the end, land reform was also a political requisite both allowing the socialist regime and its power base to be ingrained in village life and underpinning national industrialization. Land reform brought about transformation in three key ways. First, it dismantled the landlord class, including its micro-infrastructure and various urban ties, and articulated genuine peasant needs and concerns. This in turn enhanced regime legitimacy and rooted authority in the trust, support and participation of the population at large. Second, the experiences of land struggle were a learning process for both participants and leadership. Without such a process of overcoming peasant conservatism and remaking the peasantry into a revolutionary agent, the revolution, even if it had succeeded in taking over the state machinery, would have been socially shallow. The empowerment of the country's subaltern classes in both their social status and political recognition was a huge achievement. Third, alongside this material achievement there was also a cultural dimension to land reform, which allowed people to shake off a deep attitude of submission and dependency. Revolution was necessary not only to overthrow the old world but also to bring the exploited and oppressed onto the path of freedom, as Frantz Fanon explained in line with Mao's conception of ideology and practice.

Solving China's age-old land problem while creating a revolutionary peasantry was one of the revolution's greatest achievements as well as a major Chinese contribution to Marxism. New China set up a model of revolutionary modernity defined by popular emancipation, national development and internationalist aid schemes. In contrast, the lack of thoroughgoing land reform elsewhere hindered socioeconomic progress, as is shown by the fact that China has subsequently done a great deal better than most developing countries in meeting basic needs, observing social justice and transforming the subordination of labour, women and other marginalized social and ethnic groups. This case, however diluted by the market forces in more recent decades, carries with it a universal message about the necessity of structural transformation to eradicate backward or reactionary powers. It is precisely China's land revolution that is a main target of the post–Cold War revisionist historiography that attempts to negate violent social revolutions in general and the Chinese Communist Revolutions in particular, fusing red scare and red hatred into a triumphant discourse of counter-revolution and capitalism. Such perspectives are influential but empty in light of abundant evidence to the contrary.

The regional path of state building

The land revolution was a systemic undertaking *en route* to the construction of communist national power. It required concerted and coordinated effort from the party and its foot soldiers, the border regional governments and the army and its mass work teams. Part of the effectiveness of this strategy also lay in the party's ability to gain the everyday discursive space among the poor peasantry. State building in the midst of military operations was unprecedented in its dual-power approach, as a '(local) state in the state'. The local regime of each revolutionary base acted as a 'counter-state, movable counter power' erected initially in discrete territories under communist control.[15] In the rural margins of provincial borders more distant from the centres of counterrevolution, the ruling power tended to be weaker. In the first red base at the mountainous boundary of Hunan and Jiangxi, the Red Army built itself a harsh but precious home. Later the Chinese Soviet Republic controlled dozens of county-level soviets in the macroregions bordering the provinces of Fujian, Zhejiang, Jiangxi and Hubei. Similarly, Yan'an, the communist counter-state headquarter, was located between Shaanxi, Gansu and Ningxia. The significance and expansion of these areas can be understood only in terms of the revolution's unique temporal-spatial conditions and of the country's political unevenness and socioeconomic disparities.

The key to understanding this political dynamic is 'uneven and compressed development', indicating both domestic conditions and competition between foreign powers over China. Both conditions helped to determine the local manoeuvrability of communist forces and the erection of bases. Thus, unlike Trotsky's explanation in *The History of the Russian Revolution*, the Chinese revolution was not about leaping over any intermediate developmental stage (as presented in the European paths), but about identifying and breaking weak links of the counterrevolution. Such links of the imperialist chain necessarily existed or could be catalysed, not only in the inter-state system but also within a given country, particularly one of such massive size and with so many

---

15 Tsou Tang, 'Interpreting the Revolution in China: Macrohistory and Micromechanisms', *Modern China* 26:2, 2000: 205–38.

internal cleavages as China. Not only was it geographically and geo-economically divided, it was also riven in terms of its jurisdictional power. In his analysis of how the red regime, completely encircled by counterrevolution, could survive, Mao highlighted semi coloniality and indirect imperialist rule. This produced two circumstances. The first was a localized agriculture (as opposed to a unified capitalist market) in which an impoverished rural population could be receptive to revolutionary agitation. The other was the formation of rival domestic agents of foreign imperialism, producing incessant clashes and splits within the country. The red forces then often had to endure privation and isolation, losing many battles in the protracted war, but they persisted and carved out the peripheries where the reach of the White Army was more limited. This situation gave rise to the brilliant idea of 'armed independent power of workers and peasants'. Such regional powers could sustain themselves by developing a self-sustaining economic and financial system, and local trade unions, peasant associations and other mass organizations, as well as by expanding the regular Red Army outside the people's militias. They could also count on an impending wave of revolution at the national level. In a critique of pessimism, Mao's analysis of the dual power was titled 'A Single Spark Can Start a Prairie Fire'. All these strategies, he stressed, required a holistic perspective and adherence to the party line.[16]

The party's 'mass line' maxim designated a two-way flow of information and views, and optimized its commitment and policies in the base areas. The articulation of popular interests and preferences through a continuous spiral – *from the masses* (solicitation and inputs) and *to the masses* (aggregation and outputs) – meant that every detail of people's daily needs and demands was attended to, and at the same time government accountability was improved through grassroots elections and supervision. Popular analogies for the cherished party–mass relations were fish in the water or seed in the soil. Such relations denoted the pathway, painstakingly tracked, for the party to furnish the conception and institutions of worker-peasant alliance core to its own united front, and to fortify the army and its morale. The foremost effect of the mass line and people's war was the formation of a new historical subject – the

---

16 Mao, 'Why Is It That Red Political Power Can Exist in China?', 5 October 1928, 'A Single Spark Can Start a Prairie Fire', 5 January 1930, *Selected Works 1*: 47–56, 97–108.

dynamic interactions between the party and its popular movements – which in turn remoulded the party vanguard itself.

The mass line also had a cultural face, as seen in the 'Yan'an way': ideological education, consciousness raising and 'literature and the arts for the people'. The party theorists systematically produced works in Marxism, history and economics. The revolutionary discourse of liberation and democracy both prepared the path for and helped to constitute the revolution. The Military and Political University of Resistance regularly sent its graduates to be core workers in other base areas. The Lu Xun Art School was a leader in creative writing and artwork involving folk music, peasant aesthetics and local dialects. These institutions attracted large numbers of urban youth from faraway places, nationally as well as among overseas Chinese. In 1938 Tian Jian, one of many communist poets then at the Shanxi-Hebei base area, wrote his characteristic composition 'If We Didn't Fight', which moved people across the country: 'If we didn't fight, / The enemy with his bayonet / Would kill us. / And pointing to our bones would say: / 'Look, / These were slaves.' These cultural pursuits symbolized an entirely fresh mood of freedom and democracy, in contrast with the deep corruption of Nanjing's power elites. The image of the communist Red Army went global through Edgar Snow's 1937 book *Red Star over China* and Agnes Smedley's biography of Zhu De, among other works of reportage and journalism. The novelty in party-, class- and state-building facilitated through the land revolution and unity of party, government and army eventually turned the world upside down.

The strategy of building the state from the rural peripheries before national victory had left some imprints on the eventual form of the PRC state. The primacy of the CCP and its overriding power shaped the prototype of a sophisticated, integrated, fully fledged edifice comprising party, state and army. This grew into a wholly new type of state that followed a distinct logic, quite different from that of the traditional bureaucratic state as well as the other communist powers. The Communist Party in China, unprecedented in size and social penetration, had never been a regular political party to start with, and traces of the quasi-military style of command, control and social management were present long after wartime mobilization. The status of the party chairman (later general secretary), being both the head of state and chair of the Central Commission for Military Affairs, is a typical illustration of this. Through a thoroughgoing social revolution, the party both relied on and cultivated positive feedback from the masses it had politically constructed and nurtured. The masses, in turn, were expected constantly to refresh the party, making it a modern revolutionary organization. As such, the CCP was simultaneously a vanguard and mass party: a 'super party', as distinguished from typical Leninist parties.[17] Its ordinary members were themselves constitutive of the revolutionary masses. Without such a party, the Chinese struggles against overwhelming odds would have no chance to win. These characteristics were also seeds of the future growth and mutation of the PRC state.

The revolutionary state: A contradiction in terms?

In July 1945, just a year before outbreak of the civil war, Mao had a conversation in a Yan'an cave with Huang Yanpei, then an esteemed educator and senior political consultant of the nationalist government sympathetic to the Communist Revolution. Huang asked if the CCP could escape the vicious circle in Chinese history, of popular rebel victories followed by degeneration. Mao answered: 'We've found a way, which is democracy: only with the people supervising the government, can the government dare not to slacken; only if everybody takes responsibility, will our work keep going through changes of personnel.'[18] He also made the same point in Xibaipo right before the Communists took national power; and then in Beijing as well, warning the party of the immensity of the challenge, including the 'sugar-coated bullets' of material enticements. The Chinese communists, armed with extensive local experiences of rural state building, were on the way to prove themselves unbeatable city and industrial managers and nation builders. They were acutely aware of the gravity of the challenge of the CCP becoming the ruling party.

However, finding a workable form of democracy turned out to be no less challenging under the circumstances. The Maoist state, which aimed to be continuously revolutionary against the threat of bureaucratization and perversion, was paradoxical. For one thing, regime consolidation in

---

17 Wang Hui, *The Short Twentieth Century*: ch. 4.
18 Huang Yanpei, *Returning from Yan'an*, Chongqing: Guoxun Books, 1945: 65.

the face of resistance and hostility from internal and external enemies demanded a continuation of certain revolutionary and indeed repressive methods. For another, order and stability were prerequisites for both social reconstruction and economic development. Both required the state to strengthen rather than relax its rule. The result was the institutionalization and materialization of national and popular sovereignty on the one hand, and bureaucratic domination and state coercion on the other, in a perpetually self-contradictory power.

Moreover, the post-1949 state was also in a specific sense the inheritor of the deep-seated pre-revolutionary tradition of the Qin–Han configuration since the third century BC: the Han state had been maintained for four hundred years the exceptionally effective governing structure established by the short-lived Qin regime. The 'king's land under heaven' was divided into military (*jun*) and administrative (*xian*) units, which were easily incorporated into the republican state many centuries later. The myriad, and complex meritocratic bureaucracy had developed through patrimony as well as a class-blind examination system. According to Francis Fukuyama and others, China thereby invented the 'modern state', as the Han state already 'had many if not all of the characteristics that Weber defined as quintessentially modern'. Its rational bureaucracy was later replicated elsewhere by almost all modern governments.[19] Imperial China had erudite laws and rules aided by a standardized written script, copper currency, set measurements of goods, networks of communication through land and water routes. Some of these mechanisms still functioned in both the revolutionary and reformist Chinese state of central and local governance. Far more important than imperial heritage, however, was the revolutionary origin of the PRC, from the party's supremacy to the intertwined party-government-army institutions. The PRC state was new for its ideological ambition, national purpose and grip on organizing society. Whether the mixed legacies of traditional and revolutionary pasts were an asset or burden, or indeed both, the communist state in China has been visibly strong in pursuing its formidable political and socioeconomic tasks. It was and still is a striking contrast with the many weak or 'failed' states of peripheral capitalism.

19 Francis Fukuyama, *The Origins of Political Order: From Prehuman Times to the French Revolution*, London: Profile, 2011: 125–6, 134–8.

What resources are available in a polity of such demographic and geographical scale that would offer organizational and institutional unity and control? The CCP followed the Leninist doctrine, as stated in the party constitution, of 'democratic centralism'. This principle required the subordination of the individual to the organization, of the minority to the majority, of lower to higher levels of leadership and of the whole party to its Central Committee. The right to dissent was theoretically protected, on the condition that any resolutions must be obeyed. The party hierarchy operated downward from the centre, normally the Politburo, reaching from the local branches down to the smallest work units. Its ideological and philosophical background notwithstanding, in the foreground the mass line as a political persuasion and working method was subject to the agenda of class struggle and party leadership. This is both theoretically and practically coherent. The perception of the mass line as either a condescending elite tool or a version of voluntarist populism misses the point. Meanwhile, the party's disciplinary organs inspected party members, especially those in positions of responsibility. Such concentrated power over major decisions, from political to budgetary, from allocation of resources to peace and war, also implied an ever growing layer of intermediate officials. Socialism thus looked, inevitably, statist in the conditions of internal scarcity and external hostility, even with the tireless anti-bureaucratic campaigns.

Yet neither party nor state has ever been monolithic. The PRC state has significant elements of institutional pluralism that should not be dismissed. Apart from its Youth League, the party throughout the revolution built up a significant outer circle of transmission belts of trade unions, women's associations and various professional, fraternal and religious societies. Above all, the mandate of the 1954 PRC Constitution of 'all power to the people' found its expression in the National People's Congresses (NPC), proclaimed the 'highest organ of state power'. Following the Election Law of 1953, the first nationwide grassroots election to the local people's congresses was held in 1954. An important yet largely unnoticed feature of NPC is that the people's deputies attend the annual conventions but otherwise stay on their regular jobs; they are not professional politicians. The legislature's Standing Committee works with the State Council, and oversees the Supreme People's Court and the Supreme People's Procuratorate which is a specific institutional creation of the communist states. The NPC's local equivalents are more ceremonial compared to the powerful local governments. Another inventive institution is the Chinese People's Political Consultative Conference (CPPCC), an advisory body made up of smaller, so-called democratic parties and individuals who were friends and allies of the revolution. Well before 1949, the CCP had conceived a unique state structure of what subsequently claimed to be a system of 'multiparty consultation and cooperation' for the PRC. In practice, the efficacy and functioning of these institutions have varied through time and across issues, and are contested. As for 'checks and balances', the Chinese approach is to define a socialist republic serving the people in opposition to a bourgeois state as the tool of its ruling class: instead of a formalistic and inefficient separation of power, it rationally observes a 'division of governing labour' among its branches of power.

In other words, just like the revolution itself, China's post-1949 landscape of state and politics could never simply be about achieving a communist monopoly. For one thing, inner party factions were entrenched from wartime regional or army division identities, such as rural military versus urban underground, or the First versus the Fourth Field Armies, and so on. These factions outlived a multilayered and protracted revolutionary trajectory, competing for loyalty, credit and status. But more importantly, a feature of the CCP was the 'line struggle' over fundamental strategies and policies – ten such struggles were recorded in the 1981 resolution on the party history, including those over the Great Leap Forward and the Cultural Revolution. This offers us yet another angle to understand how the Chinese communist state distinguished itself from the Soviet Union: as the outcome of an indigenous revolution with self-transformative peasant agency and its own novel path to power. In fact, the party's rural background was so prominent that tensions arose between peasant and intellectual cadres, and between sections of the newly formed political elite with different levels of education. Moreover, as the new state needed skilled administrators and technocrats, many old state functionaries were kept, often with no less responsibility or pay than before, and this helped to cause strain in the state bodies. Overall, however, the PRC state displayed unparalleled solidity and ability, thanks partly to the political education offered by the revolution itself.

There was also notable institutional competition within state departments, including between different provincial authorities and between central and local bodies. The idea that the communist state was uniformly centralized is a myth: instead, state bureaucracies weaved a matrix of centralized vertical (*tiao*) and decentralized horizontal (*kuai*) lines of authority, and decentralization had been a strong tendency. Since coastal–inland, urban–rural, majority–minority and other disparities can be politically sensitive, the administrative infrastructure of provincial power and ethnic-regional autonomy provided a vital bargaining space for local desires and initiatives. Among the implications is that local leadership quality varied greatly, making a substantial difference from place to place. The middle layer of bureaucrats and grassroots party workers, replacing a traditionally predatory and exploitative gentry-official class, negotiated between directives from above and demands from below, and the 'social intertexture' of the body politic contained some pre- as well as post-revolutionary voices.[20] Grievances over their jurisdiction, large and small, were often perceived as local failures and provoked some calls for central intervention to enhance local accountability. Since the 1980s, alongside traditional provincial power and its bargaining capacity, there has also been an expansion of subnational autonomy at the lower levels; this anticipated subsequent waves of recentralization every few years, as illustrated by the 1994 tax reform to restore state coffers.

Market disruption in the cycles of devolution or *fang* (loosening control) and *shou* (regaining control) complicated the policy process. Even in the latter cycle of recentralization, when the state reinforced unity and coordination, local governments had considerable leverage and were able to make locally beneficial decisions. Revealingly, they often turned themselves into business actors, as depicted in the 'local state corporatism' of officially entangled market, trade and finance elements.[21] This concept captures the ramifications of the uniquely collaborative ownership and control structure, especially the ones between county and township governments that enabled the TVEs. A pervasive decentralization of market opening, labour standards and fiscal power subsequently rendered the Chinese economy among the

---

20 Vivienne Shue, *The Reach of the State: Sketches of the Chinese Body Politic*, Stanford, CA: Stanford University Press, 1988.

21 Jean Oi, 'Fiscal Reform and the Economic Foundations of Local State Corporatism in China', *World Politics* 45:1, October 1992: 99–126.

most decentralized in the world. The central government's effort to curtail local obstruction of national policies has become more committed and intense, yet the structure is still viable as central and local actors mutually defend their respective autonomy. They must also learn to cope with foreign participation, not least in striving to share benefits while minimizing cost. These interactive and interdependent forces have neither played a zero-sum game nor resulted in centrifugal excesses. Rising labour costs and Sino-US trade tensions brought about change, and the self-contradictions of a state-sponsored marketization were much intensified by the political logic of liberalization and globalization. Local market deals have long been intercepted by global ones, oftentimes bypassing central rules and regulations.

A further complication for the PRC as a unitary multinational state is its ethno-regional composition and semi-federal arrangement. In nearly two-thirds of its territories, the categories *region* and *ethnicity* are broadly equivalent, sharing many temporal (initially 'primitive' and 'backward') and spatial (peripheral or frontier) identities. Most of these regions also featured mixed ethnic-religious groups. The PRC presupposed cultural and institutional multiethnicity within its constitutional and policy framework of unity, equality and social cohesion. Its 'subsystems within the political whole' negotiated their autonomous spaces through a national-local 'dual rule'.[22] Alongside the majority Han population, five provincial-level autonomous regions were established to be the titular homes of the largest-minority nationalities: the Zhuang, Hui, Uyghur (along with other Muslim communities ethnically connected with central Asia), Mongol and Tibetan (Zang). Also constructed were hundreds of autonomous municipalities, prefectures, counties and townships in both minority and non-minority regions. With the return of control of the territories of Hong Kong in 1997 and Macao in 1999, two special administrative regions were created. Retaining their socioeconomic systems under a chief executive nominated by the NPC and elected by a unique semi-democratic legislature, the special administrative regions are an experiment of yet another ingenious formula of one country, two systems.

In the end, even if the revolutionary state is a contradiction in terms, the Chinese experience has demonstrated at least the temporary

---

22 David Goodman, *Centre and Province in the PRC: Sichuan and Guizhou 1955–1965,* Cambridge: Cambridge University Press, 1986: 3 and ch 1.

historical viability of such a state, and along with it a continuous revolution. Both state and revolution have faltered due to political exhaustion rather than economic stagnation, an outcome that was also contingent on Mao's death to allow demobilization and restoration. Further reflecting on the much debated durability of the Chinese communist regime amid the overwhelming disintegration of the former Eastern Bloc, the state's rural roots have made a fundamental contribution. After all, it was in the countryside that the communists attained their mass bases and military strength, and where they accomplished an ideological and organizational feat never seen before. The party has triumphed in carrying out a land revolution, and then completed land redistribution, collectivization and decommunization; and it comes to waver between peasant re-cooperation and agricultural capitalization today. Rural China has remained stable throughout, despite localized unrest. Beyond other determinants or stimuli, domestic and international alike, this factor of rural engagement is critical, and rests also on the improved lives and life chances of agricultural and other rural populations. In retrospect, the state born in 1949 must still solve its inherent as well as acquired problems, firstly acute tensions between the ruling power and its self-destabilizing revolutionary propensities, and then as the reformers fled from this conundrum, they have only found themselves faced with some ever greater contradictions.

4

State capacity and the mutation of power

Flouting the many gloomy predictions offered before the communists came to power in China, not only did the PRC state survive, but it has also consolidated and even flourished. It did so amid a massive war with the US-led UN army in Korea, the ruins of civil wars and an economy wrecked by stalled production and extensive poverty, as well as both overt and covert sabotages. New China was also put under trade and diplomatic blockades by the capitalist world while the US State Department tried to figure who lost China. The striking governability of the young communist state was quickly vindicated by its effective management of economic recovery, social control, and military and logistical capacity building. The subsequent cooperation of agriculture and nationalization of industry, incorporating handicrafts and commerce into the public sector, went smoothly – astonishing given their daunting scale and speed.

While they lacked experience in running the world's most populous nation, the communists had benefited from previous practice in economic management within the border regions. The 'states in the state' ran local economies with their own productive, financial and currency systems. This helped the newly founded regime after the revolution to overcome a surprised and angry international bourgeoisie who were waiting for its collapse, not least for the terrible hyperinflation left over from the fleeing GMD. By utilizing land reforms to secure peasant support and increase essential supplies, the people's governments in Beijing, Shanghai and other urban centres were able to bring both prices and excessive cash circulation swiftly under control.[1] After all, the fresh system needed to be material in producing and delivering basic public goods – and new China's national development had remade the country in socioeconomic terms, transforming its position in the world.

The revolutionary state was born constantly fighting an uphill struggle, however. The party's campaigns for purification were necessitated by the circumstances of its own non-proletarian constituents as well as antagonistic infiltration from outside – and these could also slip into unwarranted internal purges. Class and line struggles often had an arbitrary element, with family backgrounds and ideological stances replacing economic identities, and provoking misunderstandings and victimization. Meanwhile, the hierarchy and privilege already present in the Yan'an period had been fortified through Soviet-style institutionalization during peacetime. Urban–rural segregation also became more salient among 'socialist inequalities' (between state and collective sector employees, permanent and temporary workers, genders, ranked statuses, and so on) – another contradiction in terms. Such paradoxes sprang up during both the consolidation and the liquidation of the revolutionary state. The mutation of communist power and the erosion of the appeal of socialism can be seen both as responsible for and as a consequence of certain calamitous policies, before and after market opening. But the post-socialist period was evidently also the result of the deliberate work of a capitalist 'peaceful evolution', as Mao described John Foster Dulles's strategy during the Cold War. The Maoist rectification peaked during the Cultural Revolution – something unthinkable in any 'rational' state – and ultimately ended in catastrophe. The question, then, is why this occurred, and whether it means the death of revolution as such.

Socialist planning and national development

At the heart of the communist Chinese state was the desire and goal to overcome the classical problems in the Leninist doctrine of 'socialism and backwardness', and the imperative of development was engraved deep into the project of Chinese socialism. Its clarity of purpose was

---

1 Wen Tiejun and Dong Xiaodan, *De-Dependency: China's Real Experience of Dissolving its First Economic Crisis*, Beijing: East Publisher, 2019.

forged by the transformative opening for an industrial revolution, whose foundations were laid under Mao. Yet, while developing its own path-dependent brand of socialism, new China also followed the Soviet Union in its central planning, restructuring of higher education and system of military ranks and grades. The Soviet aid programme, which was 'the biggest such program undertaken by any country anywhere,'[2] was essential at the initial stage of Chinese industrialization against the international embargo, allowing China the ability to fulfil its first five-year plan (1953–57). Labour and other resources were mobilized through full employment of men and women in urban areas, as well as in a phased yet hasty process of rural collectivization.

By 1976, China was the world's sixth-largest industrial power. Between 1950 and 1977, its industrial sector grew at an annual rate of 13.5 per cent, the fastest of major nations in that period, and eventually comprised around 70 per cent of its total economic output. Meanwhile, the national income increased at least fivefold, in turn boosting a population growth of nearly 400 million people, due to both prolonged life expectancy and a steep drop in infant mortality.[3] This was a largely self-reliant economy, something that also helped to stabilize the system of basic grain and food production and supply since the agricultural recovery of early 1960s. The socialist state was able to claim, for the first time since at least the late Qing period, that it had succeeded in feeding almost one-fourth of the world's population on merely 7 per cent of the globe's cultivable land at the time. These achievements were all won without the costs wrought by primitive accumulation, or what Marx referred to as 'capitalist tortures'. Economically, revolutionary modernity afforded China a shortcut unlike either classical capitalist development through expropriation of land and direct producers, colonial extraction and slavery, or Stalin's 'socialism in one country' involving violent rural destruction.

Only the degree, not the essence, of socialist development in China might be disputed. There was indeed a crucial problem, still to be tackled, of the revolution's unfinished project of liberty, equality and democracy, in place of subordination, hierarchy and bureaucracy. As an

---

2 Odd Arne Westad, *The Cold War: A World History*, New York: Basic Books, 2017: 237.

3 Maurice Meisner, *Mao's China and After: A History of the PRC*, New York: Free Press, 1986: 436–9.

epic popular struggle for freedom and prosperity, the revolution's failure to fulfil its promises must be seen not only as an unintended consequence of its path to power, but also in the context of the immense difficulties it faced. The odds against such socialist islands enduring in the capitalist high seas created an environment where internal and external adversaries were able to coerce certain means at the cost of socialist ends. As the Budapest School philosophers neatly put it, economic hardships alone in part rationalized a 'dictatorship over needs'.[4] One of the greatest tragedies of international communism was precisely the perpetuation of a supposedly temporary situation which compelled civil liberties to be sacrificed for security, and resources directed to heavy and military industries more than agriculture and consumer goods. The difference between socialism and statism could be paper-thin: even in the case of Chinese communists whose determination to hold on to popular participation endured, concessions were made that allowed statist, dictatorial and oppressive predispositions to prevail.

This magnitude of socioeconomic reorganization depended on a developmentally committed socialist state. Without getting into a scholarly debate over the validity of the notion of 'developmental state' in the context of China, what is at issue is the developmentalist logic of socialism pursued in economically backward countries. Even though it shared certain features with other developmental states in East Asia, characterized by an extraordinary degree of autonomy and capacity, the PRC state appeared yet more autonomous compared to both its own domestic society and other states, and yet more powerful in its ability to mobilize and coordinate the allocation of resources. The gist of the Chinese state socialist model was its independent policy agenda. In particular, economic transition in the early years of the PRC was dictated by the state's developmental and redistributive priorities. In a dialectical interplay, micromanagement and macro planning and regulations enhanced regime legitimacy and granted its decision makers essential moral confidence and practical authority. The latter, however, could obviously also be a grave hindrance without an institutionalized balancing mechanism.

---

4 Ferenc Feher, Agnes Heller and Gyorgy Markus, *Dictatorship Over Needs*, New York: St Martins, 1983.

Industrialization pursued right after the war in Korea rejected the standard capitalist methods of primitive accumulation; instead, it required a socialist rural transformation. This was initially controversial within the party, as the order of New Democracy and the fruits of land reform were still fresh, and were felt to need consolidation rather than change. As it happened, however, equal land holding could not by itself solve the problems of those who lacked necessary capital, tools, animals or labour to cultivate. In some places, poor peasants began to sell their newly acquired plots while the rich ones hired labour to work the extra land they bought, threatening a return to pre–land reform conditions. The obvious vulnerability of scattered and secluded petty farming was also real, especially in times of flood, drought or family difficulties. Alarmed by signs of polarization, and pressed to safeguard peasant livelihood and simultaneously to shore up industrialization, while also encouraged by previous spontaneous experiments with mutual aid and small cooperatives in the base areas, the party came to a negotiated consensus on socializing agriculture nationally. Mao was of the view that the gains of land reform could be preserved and expanded only by moving ahead with cooperation. Economically, agrarian surplus from cooperatives would also help local small industry to provide rural development with the cement, machines, electrics, farm tools and chemical fertilisers that it needed. Augmented agrarian productivity and output would then ensure national grain self-sufficiency and increase peasant purchasing power, hence financing industrialization. Politically, only by being organized could the peasant masses permanently escape poverty and income disparities, and ultimately overcome their petty-bourgeois vulnerabilities.

The cooperative movement, rather than progressing slowly and incrementally, proceeded hectically. Notable here was its voluntary character, 'with neither the violence nor the massive sabotage characteristic of Soviet collectivization', as noted by Mark Selden among others. It 'was carried out smoothly primarily because, unlike their Soviet predecessors, the Chinese had already established a network of state-controlled institutions in the countryside.'[5] The peasant agency nurtured by the

---

5 Mark Selden, 'Cooperation and Conflict: Cooperative and Collective Formation in China's Countryside', in Selden and Lippit, *The Transition to Socialism in China*: 85; Barry Naughton, 'The Pattern and Legacy of Economic Growth in the Mao Era', in

revolution made the difference. By 1958, smaller cooperatives had merged into much larger people's communes. Under communal management and the concentration of productive factors, the socialist principle of 'to each according to her labour' was practised within the everyday labour process and refined into a system of work points. These points were calculated through regular public appraisals among production team members. The communes also put in place collective rules and funds providing basic provisions and social relief for the needy in the form of a government-backed moral economy. In addition to private homesteads, small family plots had been retained precariously at various times and locations. In the wake of the failed Leap in 1958–59, day-to-day operation at the level of productive brigade (a cluster of villages) was transferred to the smaller unit of the village team. In light of that failure, even sympathetic observers asked if collectivization had not proceeded too hastily. In response, it is worth considering the long-term benefits of collective agriculture as a cornerstone of socialist industrialization in China, and the essential work done on soil and water infrastructure during that period, beyond the capability of individual households.

Despite serious shortcomings that gradually diminished incentives and productivity, the advantages of collective farming were evident. It saved farmland by minimizing waste on hedgerows, boundaries and unnecessarily repeated paths and water channels. Larger fields suited stronger mechanization. Collective cultivation facilitated rapid diffusion of new seed varieties for increased yields, such as China's own high-yielding hybrid rice. Communal management allowed the effective spread of locally produced fertilizers and green technologies in land use and crop planning. Apparently, only the collectives could mobilize human and other resources to take those large, productively desirable projects. Between 1952 and 1978 the area of irrigated land in China tripled, resulting in unprecedented land rearrangements and soil consolidation for more efficiency in grain and sideline production. Communal factories also mushroomed to absorb rural labour and boost cash income, laying the groundwork for subsequent TVEs. Broader mechanization had to be postponed, but China accomplished its own green revolution (with certain unforeseen environmental externalities). Particularly important was the unified government-communal

---

Lieberthal *et al.*, eds, *Perspectives on Modern China*: 230.

managerial system. As a novel institution, it enabled not only labour organization and accumulation for large infrastructural works and rural industries but also grassroots participatory self-governance. It was a 'mass mobilization mode of transformation' and proved in China to be a highly productive system.[6] Still, as officials above the brigade level were government appointees, the communes were overtly managed from above, restraining peasant rights and rural autonomy.

The system also worked against forces of polarization, and inequality was mitigated. The weak and honoured (families of revolutionary martyrs and servicemen, for example) were protected in communal settings. Promoting gender equality, the collectives brought women from the confines of housework into united and gainful labour, and funded community nurseries and dining facilities. Communal clinics, schools, cultural clubs and engagement in mass campaigns, such as those to eradicate illiteracy and epidemics, extended to remote villages. The World Health Organization among others praised China's 'barefoot doctors', equipped with basic training, simple toolkits and cheaply manufactured yet quality drugs of both Chinese (including Tibetan, Bai and other local) and Western origin, who maintained rural public health and engaged in preventive medicine. By a sober evaluation, collectiviz-ation in China was not premature but 'instead a necessary precondition for the development of a modern agricultural sector'.[7]

This acknowledgement is also negatively supported by what ensued in the wake of rural disorganization. After a few years of promising growth during the first half of the 1980s that can be attributed to a combination of human motivation and policy incentives – from raising the prices of farm produce to liberalizing output markets and improving access to inputs, the sector was hit by serious damage. During the 1990s there was considerable loss of farmland, in addition to tardy responses to soil pollution and desertification; land seizures, by private and public developers alike, had become rife. Unprofitable farming and dis-placement also resulted in land abandonment in a country hampered by severe land shortages. Massive outflow migration speeded the

---

6 Ashwani Saith, 'China and India: The Institutional Roots of Differential Perform-ance', *Development and Change* 39:5, 2008: 736–9.

7 Chris Bramall, *Chinese Economic Development*, London: Routledge, 2009: 214–19, 225–6.

commodification of both land and people. These problems caused the general waning of rural life and governance – it was a tragedy of uncommons. Meanwhile, intra-rural and urban–rural disparities grew as urbanization and industrial use and abuse of land continued, with palpable environmental impacts.

Undeniably, the Mao era was responsible for some disastrous policies; the question is whether, or to what extent, policy failures such as the Great Leap were correlated with some intrinsic defects of communal agriculture. The official verdict on the latter is open to debate. Rural development was indeed curtailed in order to secure urban supplies and price stability, partly through state monopoly over the purchase and marketing of essential agricultural goods – and the party's rural roots meant that it made these decisions with a sense of moral guilt. Although the intention had been to follow the proposals in Mao's 'On the Ten Major Relationships' (1956) in establishing sectoral equilibrium and balanced welfare across the board, and stimulating trade that would benefit the countryside, these targets proved to be unattainable. In the end, industrialization took a heavy toll and ultimately prevented the communes from achieving higher rates of surplus retention for their members. Urban bias in policymaking was a given, and was not disguised.

A caveat here is that the conventional assumption of 'price scissors', a principal tool of what the Soviet economist E. A. Preobrazhensky hypothesized as the socialist internal accumulation,[8] by which the peasantry was exploited through deflating values from agricultural sales as a result of unequal sectoral exchange, has been neither empirically nor statistically substantiated in China. Evidence and reliable data are still insufficient to draw conclusions. The central directive at the time was to raise prices for agricultural produce while lowering the price of industrial products for rural consumption: the Soviet mistake of forfeiting peasant interests was not to be repeated. In contrast to the urban Bolshevik revolution and subsequent forced collectivizations that led to agricultural collapse and rural wreckage, China's rural revolution created a much closer party-mass relationship. Urban-to-rural reallocation of resources and investments in finance, expertise, policy incentives

---

8 E. A. Preobrazhensky (1926), *The New Economics*, translated by Brian Pearce with an introduction by Alex Nove, Oxford: Clarendon Press, 1965: ch. 2.

for rural industries and other provisions amounted to a reverse scissors effect, countering the law of internal accumulation. However limited under severe developmental pressures both internally and externally, the worker–peasant alliance allowed socialist industrialization to be pursued in a different manner, not only in terms of capital but also of labour accumulation. Elements of urban bias were consistently offset, despite structural obstacles. In this view, China's dual economic structure based on collective land and organized labour had in effect protected the rural population from the proletarianization common to more typical modernization processes.[9] This structure also explains how the Mao era achieved its extraordinary investments of living labour and massive economic surplus into productive capital; these effects can all be attributed to the initial land revolution being emancipatory at the grassroots.

The episode of the Great Leap requires some explanation. By design, the leap, riding on an optimism brought about by a number of successes in reorganizing the national economy, aimed at higher productivity, faster industrialization, national self-sufficiency and improved living standards. Its ambition was to break the statist and bureaucratic model of socialism via a process of devolution so as to relieve local mass initiatives. As such it was a rational endeavour. Yet in an uncompromising response to outside pressures, the movement went too far, violating 'economic laws', in Mao's words. It set up wildly impractical targets, applied an unrealistic rate of grain requisition, permitted 'backyard furnaces' and free collective dining halls that wasted huge amounts of energy and resources, and misused labour so that important farming and harvest seasons were not properly served. Derailed by a fervent propaganda campaign, the normal bottom-up reporting system also collapsed. Leaders were unable to access the truth on the ground, and were misled by exaggerated numbers and other false information. This caused over-procurement and subsequently also a devastating famine as well as delayed disaster relief. A sort of infantile adventurism prevailed so strongly that even Mao's repeated interventions since September 1958 did not calm what he called the 'communist wind' (freely sharing

9 Lao Tian, 'Capital and Labour in the Mao Era', *Utopia*, 25 February 2013; 'Mao on Price Scissors 1956–57', *Utopia*, 19 November 2019; Hu Bangding, ed., *Prices in Contemporary China*, Beijing: Contemporary China Publishing House, 2009: ch. 16.

funds, goods and resources without payment or compensation) of 'petty-bourgeois fanaticism'.[10]

That the leap was an indefensible catastrophe is obvious. Nevertheless, these were the utopian years during which China upgraded its farmland as well as its irrigation and agrarian technological systems. Urban medical, educational and other expertise was also brought to the countryside, far and wide, to push for mass literacy, mass immunization and public health, women's participation, and self-governance in a democratic spirit against bureaucratization. Even a tragedy of famine cannot obliterate this side of the story. Although bureaucratic ranking and cadre privileges were treated as an unescapable 'bourgeois right' (to quote Marx's *Critique of the Gotha Programme*) in the transitional period on the path to communism, Mao's inclination was to trim them down in favour of egalitarian, localized and democratic measures. The usual attack on central planning for the Great Leap is mistaken: the problem was not to do with a rigid command economy, although some productive targets were indeed arbitrarily imposed; rather, it was a case of wilfully disregarding and disrupting the regular operations of a planned economy. The Central Planning Commission was marginalized, and brought back only later to end the chaos. Generally, China's command system, with a large collective sector, was much looser and more decentralized than its Soviet counterpart. Hence what is at issue is not socialist planning as such but how the policies could have gone so far and so wrong. The question is a daunting one, not least because politically, morally and economically the communist regime in China could not afford to betray the origin of its legitimacy and power in the countryside.

---

10 For over twenty letters, speeches and articles on this topic see *Writings of Mao Since 1949*, vol. 8, Beijing: Central Documents Press, 1993; Pang Xianzhi, et al. eds, *A Chronicle of Mao's Life: 1949–1976*, vols. 3 and 4, Beijing: Central Documents Press, 2013.

Can bureaucratization be countered? Mass line politics and economic democracy

Bureaucratization was a by-product of socialist modernization embattling a hostile environment of internal and external pressures. In *State and Revolution* and elsewhere, Lenin admitted in the first days of Bolshevik power that this was a fatal defect of socialism in an undeveloped country. Writing to comrade Grigori Sokolnikov, he predicted that 'communists have become bureaucrats. If anything will destroy us, it is this.'[11] The contingency of 'socialism and backwardness' created the conditions for a bureaucratic monopoly over jobs, goods and services as well as rewards and penalties in conditions of scarcity. Mikhail Bakunin's depiction of 'red bureaucracy' operated by 'state engineers' was accurate, as social stratification occurred between workers and planners, producers and distributors, citizens in the system of state payrolls and outsiders, and so on.[12] That is, even the proletariat could find themselves in a position of bureaucratic domination, and even a communist party could not rein in such a perversion without losing its own ideological and organizational authority and autonomy.

In China, this situation was intensified by the revolution's participatory tradition, the Maoist mass line politics and radical democracy. Even there, however, democratic and bureaucratic drives were in competition within the state system. As the main employers, central and local states took on managerial staff and service officers who were administratively ranked, with differential pay. They were counted as bureaucrats in status and statistics. In the collective sector a hierarchical army of cadres also existed. Bureaucratic expansion thus appeared an economic necessity, despite conflicting with the intentions of socialist socioeconomic organization. According to one account, the PRC had about 8 million state functionaries by 1958, compared with some 2 million ten years earlier under the GMD. The Qing empire filled at most 40,000 official posts. 'Presumably for good and sufficient reasons, the Chinese Communists after a long and bloody struggle replaced the

---

11 Lenin, 'Letter to G. Y. Sokolnikov', 22 February 1922, in *Lenin Collected Works 35*, Moscow: Progress Publishers, 1976: 549.

12 E. H. Carr, *The Bolshevik Revolution: 1917–1923*, vol. 1, London, Macmillan, 1950: 249–55.

bureaucratic apparatus of pre-modern China with their own version, some two hundred times larger.'[13]

The proliferation of bureaucracy in the PRC embodied the structural and ideological contradictions of Chinese socialism. It was rationalized by the need for the state to oversee accumulation and allocation. The revolution, in this sense, was indeed betrayed, as charged by the Trotsky-ists as well as by Maoists arguing for a continuation of the revolution. But there was no obvious and immediate alternative: after coming to power, socialist revolutions 'have everywhere been Weberian.'[14] One justification for such a big state was the need for socialist paternalism in the provision of public good, while patrimonial elements of patronage and clientelist favouritism were minimized by party discipline. As the Leninist states were 'legitimated and organized according to claims of a very high standard of virtue', for any wrong doing they found in 'their own ideological heritage . . . a source of trenchant criticism'.[15] All things considered, 'socialist China's bureaucrats have provided a quality of leadership in both revolution and economic development which, at its best, has been aggressively efficient and honest.'[16] In popular memory today, however romanticized, Mao's government was clean and much closer to the people.

What makes the Chinese experience so intriguing is the ruling party's attempt, unique in history, to curb a 'socialist bureaucracy'. If a rational bureaucracy is a virtuous marker of modernity in mainstream sociological thought, 'it is seen in Marxist theory as a principal histor-ical vice in any form and wholly incongruous with socialism, particularly in the Maoist variant of Marxism'.[17] Socialism was incom-patible with a passive society, after all; and the revolution's popular

13 Barrington Moore, *Authority and Inequality under Capitalism and Socialism*, Oxford: Clarendon, 1987: 79.

14 Bruce Cumings, 'Introduction', in Bulletin of Concerned Asian Scholars, ed., *China from Mao to Deng: The Politics and Economics of Socialist Development*, Armonk, NY: M. E. Sharpe, 1983: 6.

15 Barrett McCormick, *Political Reform in Post-Mao China: Democracy and Bureau-cracy in a Leninist State*, Berkeley: University of California Press, 1990: 196.

16 Richard Kraus, 'The Chinese State and Its Bureaucrats', in Victor Nee and David Mozingo, eds, *State and Society in Contemporary China*, Ithaca, NY: Cornell University Press, 1983: 133.

17 Maurice Meisner, 'The Wrong March: China Chooses Stalin's Way', *Prospective*, 26 October 1986: 258.

tradition must be carried forward in search of a non-bureaucratic path of development. The belief in the agency of common people and class liberation premised on party line and cadres is embedded in specific historical and contextual circumstances. There was a constant search for open channels to a new type of radical politics, in which the previously subordinated people would find unique impetus and acquire subjectivity.

Mao was ahead of his more conventional Marxist colleagues in his conviction that, by stifling human agency, the statist model deviated from socialism. He favoured a policy of 'walking on two legs' grounded in participation from all – both (heavy and light) industry and agriculture, coast and inland, centre and peripheries, cadres and masses, majority and minorities, communist and non-communist circles, and so on.[18] Opposing bureaucratization, one-sided material incentives and rigid divisions of labour, his countermeasures were derived from mass line thinking and the idea of economic democracy. In an April 1956 speech he summarized the idea in terms of social and individual empowerment as the basis of the party's 'general line of socialist construction', and developed from this a dazzling, high-minded and successful process of nationalization and cooperation. Its deceptive signal, however, hastened the launch of the leap two years later. In retrospect, again, it was not through following but rather by ignoring the general line that the experiment became reckless and fell through. Mao's analysis of why and how every positive element should and could be mobilized for personal realization and social attainment retains its validity and power.

The farthest China has arrived in this direction is in having sought industrial and workplace democracy. The eminent Angang Constitution, elaborated by Mao in 1960 and formalized in the party's 'seventy industrial clauses' of 1961, was based on a degree of shop-floor self-management by small workers' teams and factory staff, and relied on workers' congresses already in place. This arrangement, attempted in the Anshan Steelworks and other large state firms, introduced an egalitarian approach that encouraged workers, technicians and managers to work together by swapping and sharing roles. It promoted technological innovation, multi-skilled teamwork and communication

---

18 Mao, 'On the Ten Major Relationships' (1956), *People's Daily*, 26 December 1976.

across horizontal–vertical grids.[19] The experiment did not last, but it did pioneer a managerial revolution and opened the prospect of democratic management borrowing from post-Fordist efficacy and cooperative competition. It was also supposed to stimulate curiosity, learning and energy on the ground. The project, assuming public ownership and an institution of workers' assemblies, entailed participatory planning and budgeting, equal pay for equal work and the long goal of freely associated producers performing unalienated labour and sharing control over the means and surplus of production. Even more ambitious politically, Mao's critique of Stalin's political economy textbook pointed out that the right to managing entrepreneurial and state affairs alike – missing from the 1936 Soviet constitutional stipulation on workers' rights – should be labour's 'biggest and most fundamental right in a socialist system'.[20] Not interpreted in individualist terms of 'negative liberty', right is defined and defended here in line with radical democracy.

Another legacy of the Chinese socialist imaginary is known as the May Seventh Directive. Comprising a series of Mao's commentaries between 1958 and 1967, its relevance has not receded even long after the changes that China has witnessed since.[21] In 'preparation for attacks and natural disasters' (*beizhan beihuang*) by constructing Third Front industries in the hinterland, Mao envisioned Communal Socialism as a model of the self-reliant sectoral synthesis without the 'three great distinctions' between town and country, industry and agriculture, and mental and manual labour. The PLA as a 'great school' would lead the way in its wartime tradition of fulfilling political, cultural and productive tasks beyond military functions. Meanwhile, against the utopian agrarian socialism of petty production, the model advocated comprehensive self-management and a range of proposals whereby rural development would transform and liberate agricultural labour, and engage them in more advanced production and wider activities locally without displacement or forms of proletarianization.

---

19 Cui Zhiyuan, 'The Angang Constitution and Post-Fordism', *Dushu*, 3, 1996: 11–21.

20 Mao Zedong, *Remarks and Discussions by Mao Zedong on the Socialist Political Economy* (1959–60), Beijing: China Historical Society, 1998: 139–40.

21 Among these documents is a letter to Lin Biao dated 7 May 1966. See Pang Xianzhi and Jin Chongji, eds, *The Biography of Mao Zedong*, Hong Kong: Zhonghe, 2011: 107–8.

The educational revolution that anticipated and continued during the Cultural Revolution, moreover, was to advocate open-door lectures and classes for knowledge and theories to be applied and contested in productive, scientific and revolutionary practices. Echoing Marx's realm of freedom, the Maoist communes would nurture creative, integrative and alternating engagements for individuals and communities. Members would engage in varied work, debate politics, enjoy free time, and philosophize. Everyone would also shoulder certain managerial responsibilities. Inspired by the Paris Commune, Mao's multifunctioning communes and their members are simultaneously producers and consumers, workers and artists, learners and educators, politicians and militias. Such communes would be set up in and around each city and county; clusters of them would then form larger associations across the whole nation.

During the January Storm of 1967 the gigantic Shanghai Commune was declared, claiming support from the city's 2 million–strong industrial working class. Were it to have survived, there would be an opportunity for serious and extensive experiments along the lines of the May Seventh project. But the rebel power was soon found impractical and was quickly replaced by a more regular governing body, the revolutionary committee. Selected experienced officials who had been sacked were brought back to work with younger cultural revolutionaries and PLA representatives in a 'triple combination'. There was in the end no chance for any single power to alter party's primacy and monopoly.

Still, the idea of communal socialism, like that of the Paris Commune, was to be a monument for the future: in the words of Marx, at least there was to be found a political form alternative to the game of 'deciding once in three or six years which member of the ruling class was to misrepresent the people in Parliament', and a new system under which 'the economic emancipation of labour' could eventually be worked out.[22] What was overlooked in Mao's plan, however, was a horizontal perspective of inter-communal relationships across both work units and communes, and the unequal treatment between and among native members, newcomers and outsiders. The great urban–rural divide only underscored this historical limit. Yet the aspiration of democratic self-management or participatory decision making was key. Now,

22 Marx, *The Civil War in France* (1871), New York: International Publishers, 1968: 213.

precisely because the search for a socialist alternative seems to have been abandoned, it is worth remembering that a hallmark of Chinese socialism was once an active citizenry engaged in a high-intensity politics capable of imagining the future.

The paradoxes of 'continuous revolution': Democracy and dictatorship

The Maoist conception of 'continuing the revolution under the proletarian dictatorship' provided the ideological guideline of Chinese politics after the completion of 'socialist transformation of the national political economy', and acted as a precursor to the Cultural Revolution. Different from the Jacobin 'permanent' and Trotskyist 'uninterrupted' revolutions, *continuous* revolution was a revolution within the revolution, one that kept advancing to accomplish what was deemed unfinished from the preceding stages. In the same way as the 'revolutionary state', a continuous revolution under the ruling communist party was in itself contradictory. The Cultural Revolution had thus to bypass the party, yet it ended with resuming the party rule. Revolution could hardly continue when the revolutionaries were themselves in power.

A resolution at the eighth party congress of 1956 stated that the principal contradiction of Chinese society had become one between advanced productive relations and backward productive forces. Since 'large-scale class struggle is over', policy focus changed to prioritize the economy. Events in Poland and Hungary, however, propelled Mao to be more alert to inequalities, bureaucratization and the remnants of anti-communism inside China. In 1957, he revised the congress judgement to assert that instead the main contradiction was 'between the proletariat and bourgeoisie, socialist and capitalist roads'. During the initially confident Hundred Flowers Campaign – 'letting a hundred flowers blossom and a hundred schools of thought contend' – unexpectedly constructive criticisms turned into escalating demands for power sharing. The sincere invitation to speak out trapped critics as much as the party itself. The ensuing Anti-Rightist persecution plunged half a million party officials and intellectuals into disgrace and reprisals. Again, the Lushan Conference of 1959 reversed an anti-ultraleftist agenda, advocating the purge of 'rightist deviationism'. An intense run of political movements followed, including in 1964–65 for Socialist Education to rectify bureaucracy and corruption at the urban and rural grassroots. Rehearsing his 1962 reminder, 'never forget class struggle', Mao's catchphrase was 'taking class struggle as the key link'.[23]

Echoing Marx, who foresaw the return of 'all the muck of ages' and advised revolutionaries to be vigilant against counterrevolution while becoming 'fitted to found society anew', Mao wanted the Communist Party to be guarded from a bourgeoisie generated from within its own ranks.[24] In the winter of 1964–65, he responded to a report concerning cadre–worker relations at the Luoyang Tractor Factory that 'the class of bureaucrats is a class sharply opposed to the working class and poor and lower-middle peasants.' Ten years later, not reconciled, he insisted that after 1949,

> some party members didn't want to move forward, . . . now they're against revolution. Why? They've become big officials, they want to protect the interests of the big officials . . . and they are worse than the capitalists. You're making socialist revolution and yet you don't know where the bourgeoisie are. They're right inside the communist party.

And he continued, 'the capitalist roaders are still on the capitalist road.'[25] Mao's persistent position, despite a painful awareness of the Cultural Revolution's agonies, was that nothing less than a counterattack from the revolutionary masses could defeat the cadre-capitalists. His detection of a new class was no breakthrough, as Trotsky and Milovan Djilas among others had raised a similar issue. But Mao was the least fatalistic of the critical communists, and the only one who had the vision and nerve to retaliate by appealing directly to the masses. The conceptual underpinning of his approach was the theory of continuous revolution. During the transition from socialism to communism, thoroughgoing socialist revolution was necessary, for 'the struggle between socialism and capitalism will take a long time before it can be finally resolved.' He

23 Stuart Schram, *The Thought of Mao Tse-Tung*, Cambridge: Cambridge University Press, 1989: part 2; John Starr, *Continuing the Revolution: The Political Thought of Mao*, Princeton, NJ: Princeton University Press, 1979: ch. 5.

24 'The German Ideology', *MECW*, vol. 5: 52–3.

25 Central Party Research Office, *Writings of Mao since the Founding of the PRC*, vol. 11, Central Documents Press, 1996: 265–6, vol. 13, 1998: 487.

was thinking theoretically about revolution in the conditions of a proletarian dictatorship: Would the variety of class struggle concentrate on the regime? Who would be the target of such a revolution? How to implement it? And so on. The restoration of capitalism in the Soviet Union rendered the question of consolidating the proletarian power 'a new central concern; while the problem lies in the party itself'.[26] Toward the end of his life, Mao considered the nature of such a dictatorship – the oscillation between ruling and its egalitarian negation – yet to be clarified, 'otherwise socialism was almost inevitably doomed to evolve into a new capitalism.'[27] Mao's conceptualization of the socialist victory depending on an open struggle was tentative, but a unique theoretical contribution.

The Chinese communists initially called their regime a 'people's democratic dictatorship' (as in most countries of Eastern Europe) rather than a 'proletarian dictatorship'. This pointed to the party's popular front tradition, although it was formally interchangeable with that of the proletarian dictatorship in the run-up to the 'great proletarian cultural revolution'. While the people, regardless of internal class divisions, were supposed to rule collectively over their enemies, a class in the word's original sense would have lost its economic connotation after the old exploitative classes had been structurally eliminated. From the Maoist standpoint, however, the ideological influence of such classes lived on, as seen in anti-communism during the liberalization of the Hundred Flowers Campaign. Worse still, there had (re) emerged newer forms of 'socialist hierarchy', from urban–rural disparities and cadre–mass discrepancies to official privileges and intellectual elitism.

The danger of class designation with no corresponding material basis was the slip of class boundaries into a 'blood line' or an essentialized politics of discrimination against people stigmatized with undesirable labels contingent on the historical class identities of their parents or grandparents. Such a conceptual and political breakdown of economic class gave class struggle an arbitrary character and allowed widespread

---

26 *People's Daily*, 31 December 1964, 18 May 1976; Pang, ed., *A Chronicle of Mao's Life*, vol. 6: 23–5.

27 Alessandro Russo, 'The Sixties and Us,' in Alex Lee and Slavoj Zizek, eds, *The Idea of Communism 3*, London: Verso, 2016: 137–8, 143.

caste-like social injustice. It poisoned the red guards of the Cultural Revolution and left a stain of shame on the revolutionary 1960s. While the language of class served as a mechanism for mobilization, it also hampered the alignment of social forces politically identifiable only by categories which were simultaneously divisive. Mirroring class struggle was the inner-party line struggle between proletarian revolution and bourgeois counterrevolution. Mao's theorization of line struggle underscored the justifications for revolution to continue.

It was never a question for the Marxists in the East that the communist state would act as a class power. 'The proletariat needs state power,' Lenin explained, 'a centralized organization of force . . . both to crush the resistance of exploiters and to lead the enormous mass of the population . . . in the work of organizing a socialist economy.' The Bolshevik state also stood firm because it was buttressed by the popular masses around their self-governing local soviets. Engels was quoted twice in *State and Revolution* that 'so long as the proletariat still *needs* the state, it needs it not in the interests of freedom, but in the interests of the repression of its opponents.' Only when fully fledged civil liberties become possible, 'the state as such ceases to exist.' It was in view of this ultimate possibility that the Paris Commune for Marx was not a revolution against any form of state power but 'a revolution against the state itself'.[28] There was no such a thing as a free state: the period of 'revolutionary dictatorship of the proletariat' between capitalist and communist society would be instrumental in converting the state 'from an organ superimposed upon society into one completely subordinate to it'.[29] This was where Rosa Luxemburg's sense of tragedy lay: limited by its historical circumstances, soviet democracy was a vital question to be raised but not yet practically solvable.[30] The crux of this classic predicament is simply that elements of such a dictatorship are not contingent but 'necessary, if the revolution is not to get bogged down and come to grief'.[31] In theory this would only be a temporary transition from the

28 Lenin, 'State and Revolution' (1918), *Lenin Collected Works*, vol. 25, New York: International Publishers, 1932: chs 2 and 3.

29 Marx, *Critique of the Gotha Programme, Marx/Engels Selected Works*, vol. 3, Moscow: Progress Publisher, 1970: 13–30, part 4.

30 Rosa Luxemburg, *The Russian Revolution, and Leninism or Marxism?* Ann Arbor: University of Michigan Press, 1961: 80.

31 Louis Althusser, 'The Historic Significance of the 22nd Congress' [of the French

point of the old state machinery being smashed to the classless society, when the state would wither away. The state's goal 'is its own end', or 'the re-absorption of political society into civil society'.[32] The authorization of power by the revolution bestows a republican temporality of 'limited legitimacy'. Marxist republicanism takes such a dictatorship as the rule of a politically conscious working class, which constitutes the majority of the population.[33]

The 'people's democratic dictatorship' in the Chinese political vocabulary was used to postulate popular sovereignty through a state system designed to be democratic for the people but dictatorial towards their enemies. It was historically trialled throughout wartime Chinese soviets and the new PRC government. Referring to the early years of Soviet Russia, E. H. Carr was defensive: 'repressive though the dictatorship of the proletariat was, it was unique in being a dictatorship exercised by a majority over a minority; and this not only gave it its democratic character, but enormously simplified its working.'[34] The same might be said about China, where 'for all its brutality, intolerance, and violence', the communist regime had kept the moral high ground as a 'powerful, effective and honest dictatorship'.[35]

The plausibly normative framework of democratic dictatorship is nevertheless found institutionally wanting. How might it correctly operate without sliding into something else? What could be its functioning institutions where the people as a whole really do come to exercise power, without allowing the state to slip into a 'dictatorship *over* the proletariat?'[36] What we saw in the twentieth century was the persistence of presumably transitional regimes, as the ideational post-revolutionary transition becoming ever more unfeasible. In the century's course following 1917, then, the knowledge and interpretation of the monolingual creeds of the communist system became unquestionable. Independent critiques were smothered. Logically, no space could be left

Communist Party], in Étienne Balibar, *On the Dictatorship of the Proletariat*, London: New Left Books, 1977: 203.

32 Gramsci, *Selections from the Prison Notebooks*: 253.

33 Lea Ypi, 'Democratic Dictatorship: Political Legitimacy in Marxist Perspective', *European Journal of Philosophy*, 28:2, 2020: 277–91.

34 Carr, *The Bolshevik Revolution*: 248.

35 Jenner, *Tyranny of History*: 156, 160.

36 Giovanni Sartori, *Democratic Theory*, New York: Praeger, 1962: 428.

for organized dissent, including loyal opposition. If the party and state acted as the true and sole representative of the nation and people, what could legitimize any contention, let alone contender, for the power? 'On what ground could anyone in a socialist society claim to possess a *right* to oppose a government that was ruled by and governed in the interests of the working classes?'[37] This paradoxical situation of historical communism makes the Maoist breakthroughs all the more astounding.

The Maoist commitment to continuing the revolution was largely unconscious of the potential for identity-based discrimination or ideologically determined persecution. Mao's calls for recognizing the right to rebel and respecting a 'truth-holding minority' met with stubborn resistance. Even a mass movement as radical as the Cultural Revolution, which for a while paralysed the party and state system, ended up vindicating its very indispensability. Institutionally speaking, while the CCP always had some factional cleavages and the PRC government was substantially decentralized, the communist authority was subject to no external checks and did not escape a totalizing tendency. The Cold War model of totalitarianism, however, offers both too much and too little for understanding Chinese politics: too much because the regime was never close to a total power; too little because a system capable of continuous self-transformation cannot be accounted for. More useful would be a conception that allows us to identify both the possibilities and the constraints of the Chinese state, along with the ability to capture its trajectory riddled by dilemmas and contradictions. The alienation of the population from the party in very different ways before, during and after the Cultural Revolution tells a fascinating story about the convoluted development of communist rule in China.

Why did the Cultural Revolution fail?

The Cultural Revolution was officially referred to as ten years (1966–76) of 'turmoil' or 'catastrophe'. Despite various textbook revisions in recent years, that verdict has not fundamentally changed. Historians tend to be more accurate, limiting the duration of the movement to the three years

---

37 Robert Dahl, *Democracy, Liberty, and Equality*, Oslo: Norwegian University Press, 1986: 14–15.

between the party Central Committee's May 16 notification of 1966 which called for mass counterattacks on a new bourgeois class, to the ninth party congress in April 1969 that signalled restoration of order. The 1966 notification warned that 'once conditions are ripe', such a class 'will seize political power and turn the dictatorship of the proletariat into a dictatorship of the bourgeoisie'. After 1969, and especially after the downfall of Lin Biao in 1971, despite Mao's last strike in late 1975 criticizing Deng Xiaoping, normalization was under way and domestic and foreign policy changes began to look 'more like precursors of the reform'.[38]

There were both structural factors and contingent triggers for this singular event. The line struggle within the party leadership, rather than a mere power struggle at the top, was causal. So were the previously accumulated social tensions that had been stirred up by bureaucratic privilege, policy errors, forms of repression and material discontent. Otherwise, even with Mao's personal appeal, the rebellion would not have so quickly attracted so many people to the cause. China's relative international isolation also played a part. Beijing's acute security pressure was such that only by holding firm to its political and ideological stance domestically could 'revolutionary China' be strong enough to stand on its own feet. Here the blend of nationalist sentiment and socialist fervour was reinforced by a situation that resembled Lenin's mobilization in 1918, which, as depicted by Slavoj Žižek, 'succeeded because his appeal, while bypassing the party nomenclature, was understood at the level of revolutionary micropolitics'.[39]

The Cultural Revolution was indeed cultural in the sense that class struggle after 1956 could only be accented cultural and ideological, or politically performative. In 1965, Mao told the French minister of culture André Malraux that 'the thought, customs, and culture of proletarian China, which does not yet exist, must appear'.[40] That was a Marxist vow to transform peasant China into an industrial nation for socialism, all of which hinged on establishing a proletarian cultural power in an otherwise post-revolutionary society after 1949. With a keen sense of hegemony in creating socialist subjectivity, Mao advocated a spiritually

---

38 Richard Kraus, *The Cultural Revolution: A Very Short Introduction*, Oxford: Oxford University Press, 2012: 20, 83.

39 'Revolution Must Strike Twice', *London Review of Books*, 25 July 2002.

40 André Malraux, interview, marxists.org/reference/archive/mao/selected-works/volume-9/mswv9_50.htm.

uplifting revolution that would 'touch the soul' of every participant, and the whole nation. The concept of 'politics in command' upturned the schematic Marxism of base and superstructure, making education, the cultural products and media the forefront of ideological struggle to 'destroy the old and establish the new'.

The Cultural Revolution was immediately proceeded by a series of rectification campaigns against 'poisoning weeds' in historiography, literature, theatre and films, newspapers, aesthetic critiques and so on, implicating individual producers as well as leaders at the propaganda and cultural front. Mao demanded that workers, peasants and soldiers must 'occupy the superstructural spheres' and replace 'emperors, ministers and generals' with commoners in history as well as on the stages of performing arts. He also called for regular folk to teach themselves to become managers and philosophers.[41] The 'red August' of 1966 was a month-long spontaneous terror aiming to destroy 'the four olds' or relics of traditional society: customs, culture, habits and ideas that were deemed feudal or bourgeois, and meant to be followed by a more sober period of 'struggle-criticism-transformation'. In striking contrast with Leninist vanguardism, the culture of the Cultural Revolution had a strong air of popular spontaneity and idealistic voluntarism. And the Maoist cultural politics penetrated in Chinese economic and social lives in general. Among household icons were Zhang Side and Lei Feng – model soldiers in 'serving the people', Daqing (an oilfield in Heilongjiang) and Dazhai (a village commune in Shanxi) – model productive units in constructing socialism, and such modern operas as the *Red Lantern* and *Shajiabang* or the ballet the *Red Detachment of Women*, among others, as model cultural products of sublime revolutionary determination and heroism.

The Cultural Revolution was thus also ingeniously revolutionary in its intentions, theories and methods. It was intended to enable 'the dark side of our work to be exposed openly, completely, and from bottom up', which Mao considered the only way to counter bureaucratization and revisionism.[42] It also forced the hierarchical apparatus of the party's

---

41 For Mao's relevant speeches and writings here and below, see Michael Schoenhals, *China's Cultural Revolution, 1966–1969: Not a Dinner Party*, Armonk, NY: M. E. Sharpe, 1996.

42 Mao, 'A Passage from Conversation with the Albanian Comrades', 8 February 1967, *Writings Since 1949*, vol. 12, 1998: 220.

state to open up to popular scrutiny. The guiding slogan of 'opposing revisionism' (internationally) and 'preventing revisionism' (domestically) was popularized; yet too often the primary motivation of the movement – to prevent communism from corroding – is overlooked. This motivation was evident not so much in public statements as in the assaults on bureaucracy, privilege and the capitalist roaders, as well as in the practical logic of mobilization from below. After 'bourgeois' conservative work teams were dispatched to the rebelling campuses, which Mao saw as a deliberate distortion of the intention to target power holders rather than rebels, in early August he published his own big-character poster 'Bombarding the Headquarters' in support of student organizations. When he criticized the Ministry of Culture, managed by 'dead mummies', or the 'urban lords' at the Ministry of Health, his concerns were over the hollowing out of revolution visible in the lack of cultural and medical resources in poor rural regions. It was true that Mao never attained complete consensus among the leadership, and turned his back on those he now regarded as 'figures like Khrushchev'. But the fact remained that he did not need such a drastic mass movement to fortify his unsurpassed authority; the political crisis in the mid-1960s was intricate, but it was no mystery or conspiracy.

The invention of the Cultural Revolution foregrounded ideology and politics, and was thus a seemingly idealistic intervention seeking to transform the superstructure. Nevertheless, it was materially grounded in the agency of self-organized groups of workers, students, professionals and other citizens, prompted by the motto 'justice of rebellion'. If one of the universal human rights is the right to resistance, it was a moral, if not legal, right in the millennial Chinese tradition, even without the language of natural right (as in *Mencius*). Modern Maoism reinstituted the notion, not only as a right but also as a duty, accented in labour's right to political and economic management. During the Cultural Revolution, the fact that real workers and peasants took positions in the central and local governments, the NPC and many cultural and educational institutions was radically inventive and a vindication of that principle.

The method of the Cultural Revolution was known as 'grand democracy', and conceived as an unlimited open public space for the 'big four': 'speaking out freely, airing views fully, writing big-character posters and engaging big debates'. Mao had been consistent in his opposition to bureaucratization and in his support for mass revolt. In a November 1956 central committee meeting, he put it bluntly:

> You are afraid of the masses taking to the streets, I am not, even if hundreds of thousands should do so . . . There are people who seem to think that now that state power has been won they can take it easy and act like tyrants. The masses will oppose such people, . . . which I will welcome because I think it will serve them right. Moreover, sometimes the only way to solve a problem is to fight.[43]

It was extraordinary that these words were spoken right after the uprisings in Poland and Hungary. More generally, to the defenders of 'law and order', or those who place their trust in representative democracy, such a promotion of mass freedom may seem irrational. But, in revolutionary China at the time, it was received with popular excitement, at least initially; although mass chaos was denounced after the tide turned, this lived experience was mentally and socially redemptive for many people. Ultimately though, the revolution went awry, along with its most inspiring promises. As its negative and repressive aspects expanded – from vicious abuses and unwarranted persecution to sectarian violence and daily disorder – doubts arose. Independent criticisms developed, as exemplified by Yu Luoke's courageous challenge to the bloodline theory and the lucid exposition of the need of democratic legality by Li Yizhe (the penname of a group of three people). By the mid-1970s, alienation and opposition had become widespread, and the April 1976 protest in Beijing, Nanjing and other cities signalled a popular will to change.

Why then did the Cultural Revolution and, along with it, high Maoism fail? It is necessary to note in the background that the retreat began earlier, as visible as since the name of Shanghai Commune had to be abandoned in 1967 under the enormous pressure of rational 'normality'. No later than the summer of 1968, when workers – their self-organized groupings fractured – were sent to stop violence in universities, the Red Guards in effect became illegitimate. Mao kept his reflective moderation, but never admitted that fears of an imminent capitalist restoration (as though China had ever been capitalist), with the capitalist roaders hidden behind communist power, were probably unfounded. In other words,

43 *Selected Works of Mao*, vol. 5, Beijing: People's Publisher, 1977: 324.

this revolution in search of a yet-to-be-configured foe was premature. Ultimately, the Cultural Revolution was waged too early, against an enemy more imagined than real. The label of such roaders would sound much more presciently only today, after decades of post–Cultural Revolution development. Misguided by such fears, the revolution confused the two kinds of contradictions delineated in Mao's own 'On the Correct Handling of the Contradictions among the People' (1957): divisions among the people; and conflicts between the people and their enemies. As a result, the wrong people were attacked for the wrong reasons, and the basic rights of individual citizens were violated amid the revolutionary disorder. This was a categorical, unforgivable error, since the friend–enemy antithesis is a political *sine qua non* for any revolution. In the end, if the fundamentals of the system were to stay, even an authentically rightful mass movement of anti-bureaucracy would have no chance to transform the power structure without undermining its own legitimacy. As such, Mao's political and ideological determinism was also negated by a formidable organizational dilemma: insofar as communist rule remained indispensable, self-organized mass movement autonomous of the party and state would be inadvertently but fatally self-destructive. Unlike the desire for 'red and expert' typified by tensions between revolution and modernization, ideology was not necessarily pitted against authority, discipline and expertise.

Second, the revolution's mass agents were baffled by a conceptually confounding class politics; they became bitterly divided, as much through 'civil wars' in factories as by campuses armed with weapons seized from local garrisons. Discrepancies between objective class realities and subjective class identities, and between sociological and ideological class designations, were illustrated by the symbolic unity that coexisted with factional infighting. If class labels were materially baseless, and if the movement was focused on state bureaucracy, then class and political struggles became disjointed, and so too did politics and discourse. The Maoist theory did not cohere around these incongruities. As workers' propaganda teams occupied the 'superstructural' institutions, the cleavages of workers between rebel and moderate or conservative factions outspread. The rural population was less mobilized, yet mobilized nonetheless, and at times engaged in violence. Unlike Lenin, who had no illusion about working-class immunity to bourgeois influence and insisted on correct class consciousness injected by a vanguard party, Mao had faith in popular self-education. A Maoist axiom popularized in the Cultural Revolution was that the masses must educate and liberate themselves. But factionalism was a perversion, and also an indication of revolution losing its designated targets. Still, Mao was also a Leninist in his conviction in the centrality of the party and its line struggle. These sheer contradictions explain how the Cultural Revolution was doomed.

The third factor was the method of Grand Democracy (*daminzhu*). It fractured participants, incited disputes and conflicts, and produced victims. The near absence of legal procedures led to the mistreatment of innocent cadres, intellectuals and people who were simply from the wrong family background. Many of the accused and persecuted were in fact among the most conscientious supporters of the regime. As the country was thrust into lawlessness, with fanatical mini-regimes of mass dictatorship, the judicial system was discarded or malfunctioned, and public struggle meetings – of denouncement, random detentions and beatings, personal humiliation, even death and suicide – were instigated. It was not without good reason that incivility and cruelty became the movement's most memorable features. Any pre-existing institutional defects were not corrected but exacerbated. While grand democracy led to an unprecedented level of participation, it also disregarded the party's traditional mass line infrastructure and democratic centralism. If mobilizational democracy, in the Chinese lexicon, makes any sense for a newly fermenting social experience after wartime revolutionary mobilization, the fact that it came at the expense of constitutionalism and basic legal protections and liberties points to a general issue of 'mobilization without emancipation'.[44] But we could also ask the reverse: can emancipation be achieved without mobilization from below? The question concerning inventive institutions of autonomous participation is yet to be answered.

As the party and state were put in jeopardy, the rebels appeared to be more destructive than constructive. Mao was absorbed by anarchism when he was young and searching for ideas; his thought later developed into the epitome of the radical wing of May Fourth liberalism. Without

---

44 This phrase is borrowed from Maxine Molyneux, 'Mobilization without Emancipation: Women's Interests, the State and Revolution in Nicaragua', *Feminist Studies* 11:2, 1985: 227–54.

those formative influences alongside his communist conviction, he would not so seamlessly have combined in himself the contradictory roles of number one rebel against bureaucracy and supreme leader of that very bureaucratic state. He fought the party machine he meant to rescue. Mao's personality cult is unquestionably a crucial factor in explaining the Cultural Revolution as well as its downfall. The concept of 'totalism' in Tsou Tang's analysis, as opposed to totalitarianism, is useful in that it separates social relations from the nature and methods of a ruling order; it emphasizes the historically and ideologically legitimating constraints on the communist regime, as both a moral and physical authority. Such constraints make reforms unilaterally initiated from above conceivable. By disentangling state–society relations from the rigid perception of an all-encompassing totalitarian state, the effects of real dilemmas and possibilities can be taken into account.[45] Inner-party dissent, for example, was suppressed not merely by discipline or punishment. The dissenters, highly placed officials and rank and file alike, often felt that they must follow Mao, who was larger in person and farther sighted than others, or else they should keep silent as 'a matter of both nationalistic pride and socialistic dedication'.[46] Mao's supreme reverence, built up through a most arduous social revolution, became unchallengeable. More fundamentally, the regime had grown not only out of the barrel of a gun, but also from the moral confidence of millions in the party holding it, who held the gun, and many also the pen. 'If the Cultural Revolution came close to destroying that political inheritance, it was nevertheless strangely shaped, and in the end constrained, by it too.'[47]

Revolutionary legacies

The true defender of socialist legacies is no apologist. The politics of debating Chinese socialism is never about going back to the past; rather, it is about historicizing, interrogating and clarifying the lessons of the past to be learned now. China's continuous revolution, historically

---

45 Tsou, 'Interpreting the Revolution in China'.

46 Edward Friedman, 'Maoism, Titoism, Stalinism: Some Origins and Consequences of the Maoist Theory of the Socialist Transition', in Selden and Lippit, *The Transition to Socialism in China*: 204–5.

47 Anderson, 'Two Revolutions': 69.

contextualized, would come out in a different light from the mainstream post-Mao narrative sustained by an unholy alliance of the ruling and intellectual elites. Yet those who make entirely negative evaluations of Maoist policies are hard pressed to explain how these policies could have been so popular. The concept of manipulation explains little: alongside much destruction and tragedy, the radical phase of Chinese socialism also saw explosions of collective and individual agency and a deepening social commitment to egalitarian values and participatory politics. The political campaigning and victimization in China are not comparable to Stalin's great purge. For all its faults and horrors, the subsequently vilified grand democracy of the Cultural Revolution originated in a democratic revolt against bureaucratization as the vehicle of line struggle. Personal experience may differ, generating diverse emotions and judgements on these events, but the liberty, as well as the tyranny of revolution, should equally be acknowledged.

It is then politically and culturally significant that, unlike most authoritarian regimes, 'the Maoist state chose instead to rule by activating society. It wanted believers, not subjects.'[48] The passing of this intense politics of equality and participation should serve as a reminder of the intrinsic virtue of an equal and active citizenship, and how not to trivialize democracy. This democratic upsurge offers a powerful contrast to the political apathy and cynicism that characterize today's fervently consumerist Chinese society. The fetishism of, or submission to, not only official power but also market dictation may be seen as the greatest harm ever inflicted on national and regional cultures. Observing the Cultural Revolution from afar, Ralph Miliband noted in 1968 that the issue of decentralization was tackled 'for the first time in the annals of Marxism' by the Chinese, who were 'the only ones to have really tried to respond in practice, and in theorizing their practice, to the "challenge of elitism" . . . at the vital core of the whole socialist project'. This was an important insight, although he was later repulsed by the absurdities and damages of the movement and accurately predicted its demise through demaoization.[49] Experimenting with a form of democratic socialism,

---

48 Marc Blecher, *China Against the Tide: Restructuring through Revolution, Radicalism and Reform*, London: Pinter, 1997: 220.

49 Quoted in Michael Newman, *Ralph Miliband and the Politics of the New Left*, London: Merlin, 2002: 230–1.

even if it was ultimately unsuccessful, could inform future struggles for a polity that is superior to those formal democracies hollowed out by the power of money, technocracy and vested interest. There were independent liberals who could see the value here. Roderick MacFarquhar regarded the Cultural Revolution as an experiment that opened a path towards a more equal and more democratic future for China.[50] In a different intellectual genre, the Chinese project carried a universal message for advanced democracies as well. Mançur Olson was intrigued by the Maoist rationale: The capitalist 'corporate-bargaining state' would be just as much in need of periodic upheavals to clean up the prejudiced 'distributional coalitions' monopolizing resources. Maoism was Jeffersonian in believing that the tree of liberty must be refreshed from time to time with its natural manure of blood.

Seeing the Leninist party as anachronistic and its transcendence in a 'partyless politics' of liberation, Alain Badiou has read the Cultural Revolution as the last revolution, an irreplaceable historical trial by means of mass action, or 'the last significant political sequence that is still internal to the party-state'. Even in its very impasse, this movement 'bears witness to the impossibility truly and globally to free politics from the framework of the party-state that imprisons it'.[51] The revolution saturated that embattled medium of power, and as such it failed. Paradoxically, for Mao, with Marx, 'the state is not the communist solution, but only a new context for that revolution'.[52] But there was also the problem of depoliticization, something that had already begun with false political divisions when the intended revolution was replaced by infighting. Into the post–Cultural Revolution era, once the proletarian self-identity was stripped from the CCP, a class party representing a class power and clutching a class ideology, it became statized, or indistinguishable from government administration. Wang Hui depicts a process of erosion whereby the party shifts from leadership of the

---

50 Roderick MacFarquhar, 'The Impact of the Cultural Revolution on Reform Era Political Culture,' in Tian Yu Cao, Xueping Zhong and Kebin Liao, eds, *Culture and Social Transformations in Reform Era China*, Leiden and Boston: Brill, 2010: 344–5, 350–3.

51 Alain Badiou, 'The Cultural Revolution: The Last Revolution?', *Positions* 13:3, 2005: 482, 506–7.

52 Miri Davidson, 'Alain Badiou: "Mao Thinks in an Almost Infinite Way"', VersoBlog, 16 May 2016, versobooks.com/blogs/2033-alain-badiou-mao-thinks-in-an-almost-infinite-way.

revolutionary masses to acting as ruler and relying on a bureaucratic machine.[53] The results – social disorientation and reversed power relations – are now clear for all to see. An effective means for post-Mao leaderships to maintain control over a now 'depoliticized communist party' (yet another contradiction in terms) was to quiet any dissent, especially from the left. This of course cannot but be highly political: if a partyless politics is still illusory, a state-party (*pace* the party-state) would be a soulless power in and for itself. Either way, the CCP's distinguished tradition of theoretical struggle and cultural politics has been lost.

Socioeconomically, Maoist policies, however adventurous they were at times, were not only the blunders commonly referenced but also prompted great upsurges of production with an eye towards curbing regional, sectoral, ethnic and gender inequalities. As Richard Kraus noted, there was a time when 'China's self-reliance joined an ideological puritanism to restrict individual consumption for the sake of public investment'; thus Deng 'inherited an economy free of debt to foreign countries' among other advantages – from a reliable labour force to a high domestic savings rate. Kraus put it candidly: 'diminishing the contributions of the revolutionaries who dragged their nation into the modern world, ended illiteracy, combated chronic disease, and laid the infrastructure for industrialization is perverse.'[54] This side of the story can be appreciated by looking into the mirror of the present situation. In a country many times richer than before, tens of millions of rural children are still spatially separated from their parents, who work in low-paid and often precarious jobs in faraway cities. Following rounds of market-driven reforms, high schools, universities and hospitals have become ever more unaffordable for the poor and vulnerable. Workers have returned to a status of subjugation, where obeying their bosses makes comradeship in the socialist factories (hierarchies notwithstanding) a distant memory. The rich and powerful mostly live in a different world from the common people. As the big pot and iron rice bowl have long been discarded, greed, insecurity and polarization have become acceptable in the name of efficiency and development. Gone are the

---

53 Wang Hui, 'The Crisis of Representativeness and Post-Party Politics', *Modern China* 40:2, 2014: 214–39.

54 Kraus, *The Cultural Revolution*: 63–83, 98–9.

aspirations to needs over profits, equality over hierarchy, self-reliance over dependency, and much else. Maoism, after all, represented a 'historically unique effort to keep the socialist values and institutions of the revolution from being overwhelmed by the imperatives of modern industrialism'.[55] It has been defeated.

Considering its global significance, Badiou recalled that 'thousands and thousands of militants from all over' identified themselves with Maoism during the 'red years': 'We think that the fundamental experience for pursuing communist politics is the Cultural Revolution and not the Soviet state.' The Global 1968 of anti–Vietnam war protests, anti-capitalism and anti-imperialism engaged a radical intelligentsia globally, as well as workers and civil rights fighters in the capitalist core countries. National liberation movements across the Third World chanted the names of Mao, Ho Chi Minh and Che Guevara. The end of the 'long 1960s', including the failure of the Chinese Cultural Revolution, marked the closure of a revolutionary century, as much the passing of its ideology. An alternative politics of equality is yet to be invented. But, in contrast to the recently renewed interest in global Maoism, in China the Cultural Revolution is treated as a 'muted heritage' due to political and ideological quandaries.[56] Any revolution, whether or not it is accomplished, encounters counterrevolution. If it was still 'too early' to evaluate the French Revolution nearly 200 years later, as Zhou Enlai allegedly claimed, then any conclusive verdict on the Chinese Cultural Revolution, condemnation or otherwise, would surely be too hasty.

From a historical perspective, the dark side of the Chinese communist endeavour was due to its unparalleled footpath running up against enemies who were overwhelmingly powerful and brutal. The PRC, confronted with daunting geopolitical adversities, had to keep a quasi–war economy and in the end the continuous revolution undermined the consolidation of the new state itself. The structural and relational position of China in a capitalist epoch explains many of the restrictions on its policy options. The Cultural Revolution has been depicted as an

---

55 Maurice Meisner, 'The Deradicalization of Chinese Socialism', in Dirlik and Meisner, eds, *Marxism and the Chinese Experience*, Armonk, NY: M. E. Sharpe, 1989: 352.

56 Davidson, 'Alain Badiou'; Badiou, 'The Cultural Revolution': 481; Wang Hui, 'Global 1968 Reconstructed in the Short Century', *Crisis and Critique* 5:2, 2018: 185.

anti-modern project that gave 'China's modernization both its unique and its universal character', and otherwise as 'ultra-modern' or 'post-modern', in the sense of post-bourgeois social experimentation (rather than fragmented politics), of which the contention is to do with rationality.[57] The novelty of the revolution is precisely where it hit its limit: an impasse appeared in believing that the masses could 'exercise an ultimate self-determination within the existing social order'.[58] Yet can a socialist state afford an anti-bureaucratic revolution? Was not such a revolution hopeless and hence reckless from the beginning? If it was clearly self-regenerating for the system, then ordinary people's right and capacity to control their own destiny would be normatively laudable. But is the contradiction intrinsic to a transitional process unsurmountable in the first instance, in which the people must create socialism while remaking themselves, so as to eventually expel the ruling class, old and new?

While Mao bypassed hierarchical power, revolutionary mass democracy was not independent of his authority. The theoretical legacies of continuous revolution are thus filled with contradictions. First, the scale of Maoist hegemony surpassed any kind of 'totalitarian democracy' to resemble a 'secular religion' beyond the imagination of even the most romantic revolutionary phase in history.[59] Second, the blending of Jacobin, Marxian and Chinese communist politics in the Cultural Revolution ushered both conceptual tensions and operational strains: between revolutionary radicalism and ruling conservatism, ideological fundamentalism and situational pragmatism, centralist vanguardism and spontaneous voluntarism, top-down mobilization and bottom-up participation, and so on. Third, people's democracy in general and grand democracy in particular were susceptible to voluntarism and blind populism. Even at their best functioning moments they could endure what François Furet depicted as a polity of absolutism.[60] In Maoist theory, these dialectical binaries would interact and dissolve through

---

57 Stephen Andors, *China's Industrial Revolution: Politics, Planning, and Management, 1949 to the Present*, London: Robertson, 1977: 23.

58 Perry Anderson, 'The Antinomies of Antonio Gramsci', *New Left Review* 1:100, November/December 1976: 39–40.

59 Jacob Talmon, *The Origins of Totalitarian Democracy*, New York: Secker and Warburg, 1952: Introduction.

60 François Furet, 'Democracy and Utopia', *Journal of Democracy* 9:1, 1998: 65–79.

such mechanisms as ongoing education for educators and constant criticism and self-criticism. How the party learned from grassroots peasant leaders about how to proceed with rural cooperation in the 1950s was one telling example.[61] Yet the relationship between the working class and its vanguard, or among masses, party and leadership, remained conceptually obscure and imperfect in practice.

In light of the replacement of popular sovereignty with pure power and what is hailed today as 'top-level designing' (*dingceng sheji*), the continuous revolution was an episode of advancing radical democracy in the history of the PRC. It was also remarkably foresighted in its attempts to impede degeneration. The fact that Chinese socialism had committed itself to the people – not only their welfare but also their political citizenship – should be its invaluable inheritance. This desire to transcend not only capitalism but also statism in a higher realm of socialist modernity and civilization may have been utopian at the time. But its glorification and empowerment of the people stand in sharp contrast to the present party guideline that focuses on the material wellbeing of the population as a grace of the state.

The historical logic of victorious revolutionaries split between those who are satisfied and those who are not, knowing that they must keep going if only to safeguard what the revolution has achieved,[62] was repeated in China – in the Chinese Communist Revolution and then its post-1949 continuation. The latter climaxed in the Cultural Revolution against the erosion of both Russian and Chinese revolutions. Revolution must strike twice, because the old world cannot be dismantled by a single stroke. Without further action, the revolution would abort or reverse. One lesson that we can take from Chinese revolutionary socialism, then, is that even a second strike is no guarantee; its own corrosion could still undo the first. That is, a continuous revolution would be an open contour, given that the eventual evaporation of the state (as the ultimate barrier to classlessness and freedom) depends on the wisdom and strength of the proletarian state. Mao's 'second Machiavellian moment' was thus

---

61 Mao wrote a brief editorial for each of the reports on peasant initiatives in three volumes of *The Socialist Tide in Rural China*, Beijing: People's Publishing House, 1955.

62 Friedrich Engels, 'Preface to Marx's "Class Struggle in France"' (1895), in Robert Turker, ed., *The Marx and Engels Reader*, New York: Norton, 1978: 51.

infertile, but his 'revolutionary materialism' was future oriented and created a new horizon of politics.[63]

The revenge of bureaucracy

Market reforms in China required the partial repudiation of the revolution's long-held beliefs and policies – partial because the regime needed to maintain communist legitimacy. Deradicalization began with the seemingly counter-ideological campaign of what was known as 'liberating the mind'. The official verdict, reached in 1981, was that Mao was 70 per cent right and 30 per cent wrong. The reorientation was highly ideological, even with a pragmatic, 'end-of-ideology' appearance. It was effective because the excesses of the Cultural Revolution had inflicted deep wounds, resentments and disillusionments, helping to catalyse totally negative feelings or political cynicism. This trend was also official in the purge of those who were now regarded as ultra-leftists, including reading groups of independent young thinkers, but especially the 'three kinds of people' who had been rebel activists during mass mobilization. The reformers were preoccupied by a fear of the return of mass upheavals, and thus sought to totally delegitimize the Cultural Revolution signalling disorder and abnormality. As the instinct of bureaucrats prevailed, the once popular desire for democracy to beat bureaucracy slipped away. Characteristically, the vibrant, nationwide discussions of 'democracy and legality' in the late 1970s were part of negating revolutionary style mass politics, paying little attention to the successful communist tradition of mass line democracy, let alone the ambition of labour participating in economic and political management.

The corrective policy was biased towards the rehabilitation and compensation of mistreated officials and intellectuals. The families of certain party leaders began to exploit legal loopholes in order to enrich themselves. Business opportunities boosted bureaucracy in a transitional economy that fused marketization with bureaucratic networks. If the PRC state had created a bureaucratized social system before market opening by virtue of its sole responsibility for economic growth and social organization, even a storm as devastating as the Cultural

---

63 To borrow from Louis Althusser, *Machiavelli and Us*, London: Verso, 1999: 84, 120.

Revolution had no chance to break it. If that revolution's ideology was incoherent in seeking to find capitalist roaders without private capital, the coming of age of a peculiar normal politics brought back battered cadres with greater power and privilege, and this time with private property as well. Chen Yun, a top party elder whose 'bird cage' analogy for limited market reform was influential even if overridden by events, instructed the party's organizational department to put 'our own children' into positions responsible for long-term regime security.[64] He did not expect though that personal wealth could accumulate that would in the next few decades stun the country and the world. The entitlement to rule became a new ruling-class consciousness among the descendants of a red aristocracy, however unthinkable in the Mao era.

After the transitional long 1980s, in which reform was still reformist, as though the party's 1956 resolution resonated, a politically conscious tendency within the CCP gathered momentum to part with the socialist tradition. Without formally renouncing its ideology, the party redefined its rule as an end in itself. The political and technocratic elites would soon allow some of their offices and positions to be profitable, and state assets to change hands openly or secretly, via legal or illegal means. The collusion of public power and private capital became routine in the 1990s. The initial mandate for a socialist market transition broke down, as the hybrid monster of bureaucratic capitalism took shape.[65] A new class materialized at long last, a distinct species, not like the incipient 'inner-party bourgeoisie' Mao had warned against, but rather a *déjà vu* of the bureaucratic-capitalist class of the GMD kleptocracy before 1949. The phenomenon also differed from the common post-communist nomenklatura or the making of Russian oligarchs. It is notable that privatization in China, although widespread and thorough, remains officially unspoken, as though it has never been a legitimate policy.

Somewhere along the way, it became a commonplace that the party, government and military cadres could disregard morality and discipline in pursuit of personal gain. A deeply entrenched culture of Chinese officialdom, deplored in a continuous revolution, returned to rot state,

---

64 Chen Yun, speech of 2 July 1981 and letter to Deng Xiaoping on 28 September 1982, reprinted in Zhang Shu, ed., *Collected Documents of Party History* 6, Beijing: China Museum of Revolution, 2015.

65 Maurice Meisner, *The Deng Xiaoping Era: An Inquiry into the Fate of Chinese Socialism*, New York: Hill and Wang, 1996: ch. 11.

army and society. The forceful anti-graft campaigns in recent years have been selectively used as a tool of power struggle; and they have left the root cause of corruption – the fusion of bureaucracy with private capital – intact. Even the party's own disciplinary and inspection agencies have been seriously infected with corruption. Bribery and patronage matter in appointments and promotions, as was shockingly exposed in some of the worst cases. Since not many people have been honest or brave enough to disobey the hidden rules of the official world, the party no longer possesses its traditional magic weapons of party building and self-rectification.

This development has rendered the Cultural Revolution doubly tragic. Not only did it miss the target while discrediting itself, it also brought about exactly what it meant to prevent. Before long, its monumental failure was confirmed by a horrendous revenge of bureaucracy with its macro and micro apparatus, old and new, at a time when another cultural revolution was a sheer impossibility. Any resistance to the new class was banished as not only unviable but also insane in an atmosphere of money fetishization and status worship. As the acceleration of an ever growing bureaucratic capitalist class came to the fore, Mao, too far ahead of his time, seemed belatedly vindicated. He avowed defeat while foreseeing the Dengist inverse, discerning the same capitalist roaders in the 1975 campaign of 'counterattack on the rightist reversion', nine years after the Cultural Revolution was formally launched. He did not anticipate, however, how a radically leftist movement could breed an ultra-rightist drift, and how the party would become an instrument of private capital. Today, in addition to lucrative privileges reserved for the acting and retired high officials, society is burdened by an ever expanding number – as many as 60 to 80 million – of power holders and administrators, many with a black box of larger networks. Capitalism is apparently no less bureaucratic. The paradox of a revolution within the state was then disentangled: the end of the former reaffirmed the unbending logic of the latter. While the Cultural Revolution intended to revive China's popular revolutionary tradition, the reform was a paradigmatic change to elitist pragmatism, solely embracing modernization.

The fact that Chinese revolutionary socialism has neither succeeded in overcoming bureaucracy nor in institutionalizing worker power does not lessen the value or feasibility of these goals. Mao was alert to the dark alternative, repeatedly bringing up the scenario of 'a nation-wide counterrevolutionary restoration, when the Marxist party becomes a revisionist or fascist one, and the whole of China changes its colour'.[66] However theatrical the term fascism may sound, it is a sombre warning against aligning bureaucratic and big private capital dictating state corporatism and expansionist nationalism. After all, the communist labour politics and the party mechanisms of supervision from below are bygone. The 'mass line' briefly picked up by Xi was abruptly dropped from the party rhetoric when a trace of the Maoist ethos seemingly reappeared, as in Chongqing.[67] An obvious sign of the distance between the rulers and the ruled is that the post-socialist state has so far refused even to require its officials to disclose personal income and assets, as is routine in capitalist democracies. This is not just about adding another item to the party discipline or state legislation, but about the nature of the state defined by its class character and relationship with the people it has promised to serve.

---

66 Mao, 'The Editorial Note on "Khrushchev's Phony Communism and Its World Historical Lessons"', *People's Daily*, 14 July 1964, 'Speech at the Extended Central Work Conference', 30 January 1962, *Writings since 1949*, vol. 10, 1996: 24–5.

67 Zhao Yuezhi, 'The Struggle for Socialism in China: The Bo Xilai Saga and Beyond', *Monthly Review*, 64:5, October 2012: 1–17.

PART THREE

The Neoliberal Adaptation

5

Counterrevolution and political economy

Revolution and modernization were parallel processes in the first three decades of the PRC. Not even the Cultural Revolution could afford to disrupt the economy, instead aiming to 'engage revolution while promoting production'. Economic development, compelled by the mission to overcome backwardness, was also seen as being consistent with the communist concept of transcending the fetters of capitalism in order to achieve higher productivity and freedom. In this, China accomplished what amounted to a socialist industrial revolution in a short space of time, turning itself from an agrarian society into a comprehensively industrial one well before market reforms.[1] This was achieved with neither colonial outlets for ecological relief and resource extraction nor internal accumulation through the expropriation of the peasantry that featured in Stalin's Soviet Union. This fact is often hidden in Deng's new order, supported by the now hegemonic neoliberal discourse which welcomed what it presented as a return to normality from the madness of the Mao era. That era was 'so hopelessly insane' that market reform 'in its return to the ideologically prescribed normal stream, appears as a return to sanity'.[2]

---

1 Wang Shaoguang, 'SOEs and Industrialization: 1949–2019', Guangming Topics, 3 April 2019, topics.gmw.cn/2019-04/03/content_32712941.htm.

2 Dirlik and Meisner, 'Introduction' to Dirlik and Meisner, eds, *Marxism and the Chinese Experience*: 16–18.

What remains unchanged though is the decisive role of the state in the economy. The present PRC state is different from the model of the developmental state capable of democratization, as well as the model of 'market Leninism' that is temporarily able to a socialist state and a capitalist market. This situation continues to disappoint modernization theorists and the like. But at issue is how a neoliberal counter-revolution has overturned much of what China's socialist reformers initially intended, following Lenin's advice that keeping the proletarian state in control of the dominant industries was the guarantee of success of the NEP. The confidence that negative market forces would be restricted and manageable within the socialist moral and institutional bounds in China has ultimately proved misplaced. Yet the opening of the market and facilitation of private entrepreneurship should not necessarily lead to the problems of growing economic dependency or the eroded public and collective sectors that will be analysed here. Rather, this outcome is the responsibility of the party, a party that has allowed the submersion of its ideology and organization by the increasingly bureaucratic capitalist-class position of the state. What we have is a twenty-first-century spectacle of a communist regime deter-mined to stay in power by pushing growth at all costs. A global China turns out to be global capitalism's lifeline, and capital's last conquest on a continental scale. In light of this, China's neoliberal adaptation is part of the neoliberalism that David Harvey depicted as a counter-revolutionary political project. Whether any self-correcting effort in China can work without a systemic breakdown would depend on whether its political economy has gone far enough to be thoroughly locked into the structural intricacies of capitalist development and crises.

Decollectivization: The counterfactual of 'double-level management'

In China's revolutionary and development trajectories, the connotation of 'agrarian' is never limited to 'rural'. In the policy lexicon, it is always linked to, or embedded in, the concepts of (central and local) govern-ment, capital and labour accumulation, sectoral equilibrium, migration and urbanization, and so on. The agrarian question has always been at the heart of popular concern and thus strategically critical, politically as much as developmentally. This also explains why, since the land reform that eradicated landlordism and its infrastructure, collectivization and decollectivization have twice transformed rural China without touching the foundation of equal land rights.

The reorganization of the economy and society following the earlier land reform replaced petty farming with agricultural socialization, first with cooperatives and later with people's communes. These moves were considered not only politically necessary for regime consolidation but also economically beneficial for the peasant population. Collectively concentrating rural productive factors helped to secure both primary resources and a vast market for industrialization, with collective farming functioning as a moral economy of basic needs. Notwithstanding its many problems, such as residential control, rigid planning, over-extraction and injured incentives, the arrangement enabled China to optimize its land under an extremely tight ratio of people to land – 'so much so that it is fair to say that China uses its available land far more productively than any other large-scale agricultural producer on the planet.'[3] Ultimately, rural collectives did not separate the producers from their means of production.

The wave of market reform started with the rural decollectivization of the late 1970s. Communal land was re-divided on an equal per capita basis, along with a carefully laid out policy of 'double-level management' in 1980, depicting both the household and collective managerial levels. The purpose was to incentivize the peasants in a production quota–based contract system known as family responsibility, and to connect it with a reserved collective layer of organization and protection. More generally, given the conditions of severe land shortage and hence the relative importance of land productivity over labour productivity, management at both levels could optimize the use and improvement of factors of production. Such optimization included the integration of scattered parcels of land for more efficient irrigation, machine deployment and soil treatment; management also mediated between and among government, market and farmers along with services of production, consumption and (re)distribution. The system was designed with institutional and legal support: a directly elected village committee, and

3 Bramall, *Chinese Economic Development*: 231.

collectively owned village land. Village-level management was supposed to include land assignment and any common land; public properties and funds, such as communal reserves for aiding the needy; and coordination of irrigation, electricity use and any other shared facilities. This dual system would, it was hoped, create a favourable loop of individual–collective interactions. To break with the communal era, however, the emphasis was placed on separation over unity. Dissent and resistance from collectives that had been run successfully were ignored. The immediate results were largely positive, as the substitution effect of raised prices for farm produce, together with the liberalization of output markets and better access to inputs, markedly improved performance until the mid-1980s. The shift also served to alleviate some of the worst poverty, something that astonished the world by bettering the lives of hundreds of millions in the poorer rural regions.

Yet double-level management soon by and large collapsed, leaving village committees struggling for minimal maintenance. A single layer of atomized households was deprived of collective sustenance, as seen in the decline of public utilities and facilities from schools and clinics to village roads, bridges and sanitation. The gains of family responsibility were offset by the looming difficulties of rural disorganization. Market drivers led to rising production costs and falling product prices. This served to disincentivize farmers from growing staple crops, with the grave potential consequence of national food insecurity. Further drawbacks included land waste from parcelization, idling, the inefficient (repetitive) application of pesticide and fertilizer leading to soil degradation and environmental damage, obstacles to sharing water and other common resources, the shortage of collectively accumulated and allocated funds for public services and disaster relief, constraints on machine use and technological diffusion, waning infrastructure and much else. These amounted to a general relapse, away from an economy of both scope and scale. The fragmentation of farmland (and forests, fisheries, etc.) and communities also saw revived class polarization and old society values, holding back social development. A situation in which defenceless farmers were confronted with natural disasters, market downturns or personal and family difficulties resembled the one that had given rise to the first cooperative movement. The evaporation of a nearly universal public health network, rudimentary as it was, exemplified this loss.

Fiscal reforms have forced county governments to be mostly self-reliant in public spending since the mid-1990s, with far-reaching consequences. In response, local officials reallocated the burden by inventing fees and levies on individual villages and households. Although widespread rural unrest ebbed after these levies were removed in the mid-2000s, at the same time as the removal of agricultural taxes and the increase in rural subsidies, the financial burden on local governments for the running of schools and other public services grew. It was not until late 2019 that the centre would again reform its revenue system, to lessen pressures on local debts and liquidity. The rural crisis only became more pronounced with unprofitable farming and the deterioration of soil quality among other eco-social conditions. Education and healthcare were also thorny issues. Rates of school enrolment fell, especially among girls, and most families could not afford to send their children to high school. The children of migrant workers, even those lucky enough to be taken to the cities with their parents, experienced difficulties with admission and the teaching quality in informal schools. Market-oriented medical reforms went from failure to failure. The poor remained poor, or became poorer still due to illness, and, tragically, many gave up on trying to access expensive treatments for curable diseases.

The plight of migrant workers was a key variable in this equation. As rural issues – not least migration, poverty and rundown communities – were intimately bound up with those of industrial and urban expansion, using the words *rural, peasant* or *agrarian* to describe one aspect of the threefold or triple crisis is not even accurate. Without proper settlement in either place, rural-to-city migration is a suspended existence for migrant workers, even though urban growth is dependent on their labour.[4] The most successful elements of the national campaigns for Constructing the New Socialist Countryside and Rural Revitalization were in providing China's vast rural expanses with electricity and internet coverage in addition to running water. Yet the rising practice of turning farmland and rural homesteads into construction land for sale by local governments violates peasants' right to collective property, and is a source of mass unrest. These problems are not solely rural or local; their

---

4 Biao Xiang, 'Hundreds of Millions in Suspension', *Transitions: Journal of Transient Migration* 1:1, 2017: 3–5.

solution would require further planning and coordination. As national policies continue to weaken smallholders, such coordinated efforts are limited. The triple crisis, then, signalled more general challenges still, raising issues that the whole global South is facing: the scramble for land, food insecurity, a massive drain of rural people and other resources and depressed livelihoods.

Imagine, then, how things could have been different if double-level management was insisted on after its first implementation in the early 1980s. It may have both invigorated and protected the farming households while mitigating their limitations and vulnerabilities. What was systematically argued in the 1950s, and still holds true today, is the need for minimal social protection. A degree of collective coordination could also have augmented peasant productive capacities and their ability to integrate with the market by optimizing efficiency in the use of land, labour and capital. Even without team leaders assigning daily tasks as in the past, such coordination would have far surpassed the reach of individual farmers in maintaining and strengthening agrarian infrastructures. In a commodified agriculture, without such institutionalized collective backing, farmers and villages have little bargaining leverage in dealing with the powerful market actors of urban and foreign agro-capital.

The demise of labour-absorbing TVEs through bankruptcy or privatization in the 1990s is telling. The collectively run enterprises provided jobs, cash income and developmental opportunities to many rural communities. Gone too was the whole prospect of rural onsite industrialization that offered a less costly path to growth. The dissolution of the communes, then, helped to create the massive, yet superficially formed, so-called surplus rural labour, and hence an ostensible or hidden urban 'reserve army'. Remittances from waged work began to make up the bulk of rural income, amid appalling conditions for migrant workers, their broken families and dilapidated villages. Agriculture itself has suffered. Accession to the WTO had greatly widened China's trading opportunities, but also plunged small cultivators into hopeless competition with big capital and cheap imports. Chinese soybean producers were the first victims, followed by cotton producers and textile exporters among others, with an immediately weakened market position.[5]

---

5 Yan Hairong, Chen Yiyuan and Ku Hok Bun, 'China's Soybean Crisis: The Logic of Modernization and Its Discontents', *Journal of Peasant Studies* 43:2, 2016: 373–95.

The 2006 removal of agrarian taxes rendered township governments (equivalent to the commune in administrative ranking) superfluous, giving them powers neither to extract nor to budget. Meanwhile, many lower-tier party branches and government offices were undermined by vote rigging, kin-based mobilization and the bribing of upper-level officials that occurred in village elections, pushing self-interested actors, mostly the super rich or even mafia into these positions. Such disintegration is one consequence of peasant atomization. At stake is the diminished subjectivity and managerial autonomy of the farming population. A single level management saw disparate labour and separate living depriving individuals and households of their collective potential for organized agency and self-government. Fuller exercise of peasants' social rights and entitlements to land, public services and fair, efficient communal decisions would require the recognition that both natives and fellow labour from in-migration – rather than external investors, agricultural or otherwise – should make local rules and govern local affairs. Here lies an additional organizational rationale for collective mediation through double-level management: to optimize state–peasant interaction and feedback loops, for example by allocating anti-poverty funds or running training programmes. The existing village committees, however, are barely backed by actual collective economy and power, hence incompetent in fulfilling these tasks. Worse, corrupt and predatory village heads can find ways to make land and other deals with external capital without consent by common villagers.

The fact that disorganization comprehensively weakened peasant and rural capacities forced some policy reconsideration, and a new consensus surfaced. Cooperation – in terms of inputs and outputs, supply and marketing, financing and services – was expected to uplift a weak sector in a market economy, providing platforms for information and collaboration among villagers. Government support for specialized and multifunctional cooperatives was stipulated in a 2007 law that aimed to promote intra-village collaboration, an attempt to favour larger farms with stronger bargaining power. Subsequently, emphasis was placed on an 'eco-conscious revitalization of rural China' by way of cooperatively 'standardizing' production.[6] By early 2018, over 2 million

---

6 Xi Jinping, speech at the annual rural work conference, 23 December 2013, Xinhuanet.

such cooperatives, involving nearly half of all rural families, were report-ed.[7] While the policy is biased in favour of supporting 'new-type agrarian managerial subjects' and has resulted in many private dragonhead enterprises branding themselves as cooperatives, the idea of reorganiza-tion from below leaned towards the recovery of a collective layer of communally employed land, capital and labour. Such a layer, by virtue of being collective, would strengthen the position of rural households against the fake co-ops that took state subsidies at the expense of farmers' thin profit margin.

There has been an upsurge of successful models, not necessarily con-firming the official version of agricultural modernization: the Tangyue (Guizhou) incorporation of village governance of land and co-ops; Puhan's Comprehensive Agrarian Association (of forty-three villages in Shanxi) which organizes production and public matters; Haotang's (Henan) experiment, with communal banks of land and forest to enhance collective accumulation and welfare; and Yantai's (Shandong) grass-roots party branch leadership of cooperatives that promotes fairness by holding large shareholders at bay. A number of surviving people's com-munes are also doing well. Alongside the famed Liuzhuang, Nanjie and other villages in Henan and the Zhoujiazhuang Commune of six villages in Hebei, a comparatively industrialized collective economy is expanding in rural areas. Production at the Gacuo township on the Tibetan plateau responds mainly to local demands, keeps a collectively accrued medical relief fund for all and takes special care of its precious pastoral environment. Other examples of cooperative shareholding and collective management in both rich and poor regions similarly demon-strate how a 'collective dividend' can still be enjoyed.[8]

These examples of new collectivism, departing from both government controlled communes and disorganized households, vary greatly, but they have common features. First, their collective economy is sustained

---

7 Liao Yue, 'How Village Co-ops are Remapping China's Rural Communities', Sixth Tone, 12 September 2019.

8 Wang Hongjia, 'Tangyue Road', *People's Literature* 1, 2017: 169–94; Lv Xinyu, 'Eco-nomic Poverty Alleviation Cannot Sustain Alone without Social Construction', shiwuzq.com/portal.php?mod=view&aid=1196, June 2017; Xie Xiaoqing, 'The Road of Zhou Village', *Economic Herald* 10, 2017; Ding Ling, Qi Lixia and Yan Hairong, 'The Gacuo Commune on the Snowy Plateau', October 2018, shiwuzq.org/portal.php?mod=view&aid=1687.

by unified land owning and managing. The farming households voluntarily submit land arrangements and readjustments to the collective authority (which is legally binding). Second, they are unities of both economic and social management, with layered cooperatives overseeing the operation of capital, funds, microcredit and other shared resources and activities. Third, such cooperatives adhere to the principle of equality in security, so that every member is looked after regardless of ability to contribute. Fourth, they practise democratic self-governance through participatory assemblies and the collective selection and supervision of leaders. A fundamental constraint on their further development, however, is the environment of a globalizing national economy and the powerful market forces of separating economic and social-political spheres towards privatization. The degeneration of Huaxi in Jiangsu from a model of wealthy socialist commune into a family-run, debt ridden conglomerate is only one example. The issues around rural collectives continue to be heavily contested: whether petty production under resumed double-level management can overcome the difficulties it faces or must be scaled up for capitalization cum modernization; and whether local needs and consumption can blossom in an expanding market of the commodified land and other essential sources of subsistence. The one thing that is for certain is that rural reorganization in China cannot simply resume traditional and closed forms; instead, it has to be a modern reinvention, linked to the post-capitalist imagery of an alternative modernity. Freely associated direct producers cannot accept an isolated or self-contained existence, but are tied to a socialized and technologically advanced mode of production. In a similar way to the May Seventh vision noted in the previous chapter, experimental communal socialism is clearly distinguished from old agrarian socialist fantasies.

The argument so far is that double-level management could prove to be superior to both old communal and newer family contract systems at a time of market transition. It could have nurtured a stronger rural development and healthier national growth pattern than the present one, benefiting both rural and urban Chinese while reducing the pains and sacrifices of workers, society and nature. The outflows of essential rural productive factors devastated the resource commons. If the resurgence of rural organization, amounting to a counter-current to privatization and commodification, tells us anything, it is how China missed a chance, already in hand at the beginning of the long 1980s, to pursue a more people-centred (as opposed to growth-centred) and socio-environmentally sustainable development. This set a precedent for the path of reform to radicalize in the 1990s. Giving up on double-level management was a precursor of forsaking revolutionary and socialist achievements, and prescribed a pattern of developmentalist policy thinking and making as a work of state–capital alliance.

'Earthbound China': The land question and urban illusion

A precondition for successful rural reorganization is the collective ownership and management of land. In fact, much of what China has achieved, including during the period of market reforms, can be attributed to its public land system. In addition to national territories and resources, this is a two-tiered system of government control on behalf of the whole people (*quanmin*) over urban land and the prerogative requisition of rural land for public purposes, with collective farmland (and woodland, pastures, etc.) shared by all rural residents as equal-use right holders. This system was founded on a thoroughgoing land reform; and the elimination of the domination of an exploitative and unproductive landlord class is commonly regarded as prerequisite for development.[9] China's public land has been an engine of growth, not least because industrialization and urbanization have been anchored by its free or low-cost use of land throughout the periods of central planning and market transition. One example is how the TVEs relied on pre-existing communal factories, as well as freely available communal land. Their other privileges, from abundant labour supply and easy credit to tax graces, were also due to the collective land regime. For better or worse, the rapid urbanization in China, too, would have been impossible without heavily subsidized land provision by the local governments.

While this regime has withstood the rural transformations remarkably well, market pressures are mounting, pressing for the commodification of land. The land question, thought to have been resolved once and for all, has returned to haunt China. Although the family contract system was

---

9 Lin Chun, 'Rethinking Land Reform in China and India' in Mahmood Mamdani, ed., *The Land Question: Capitalism, Socialism, and the Market*, Kampala: MISR 5, 2015.

not a resumption of private petty farming, dissolving communes structurally altered not only the countryside but also the national political economy. In addition to class differentiation and polarization, waves of outward migration deprived villages of labour while creating a large semi-proletarianized class of peasant workers. Urban expansion also saw a sizeable segment of new landlords living on the proceeds of land compensation and rent from the construction on their private homesteads of accommodation for migrants – known as 'urban villages', often within or at the fringes of rapidly expanding cities. Meanwhile, forced eviction by local officials and private developers alike became rife, as profits and debt repayments tied to bidding on land value appreciation overheated the real estate industry, which came to function like a financial market. The belief that modernization equates to urbanization prevailed among policy makers. In a convenient coincidence there were also tangible rewards, such as cadre promotion and cash returns – into government coffers and often personal pockets. The National Ministry of Land and Resources reported that land transfer revenue grew more than 27 per cent annually between 1998 and 2019. The degree of fiscal dependency of local governments on land auction and transfers is such that many of them would count half of their income on managing the land market.

Land financing, a government fiscal strategy riding on a highly speculative land market, employed a hybrid method: expropriating state land through direct allocation or paid transfers, and approving rural construction land for compensated acquisition. Local government as land broker created shadow banking vehicles to handle land deals, and for years endured resistance, at times violent. In a grey area, corrupt officials colluded with realtors to profit from trading the use rights of state land (including acquired rural construction land). But as local governments acting as market players also mortgaged land for loans, government debts piled up.[10] State monopoly in land supply also had the side effect of inflating land, and hence housing, prices. From a state-led modernization point of view, the risk was worth taking. Between 1990 and 2018, the total government income from land was more than three trillion yuan.

---

10 According to Huang Xiaohu, vice chairman of the China Society of Land Studies, in 2017 local government debt was 22 per cent of national GDP or 180 per cent of local revenue including income from land transfers, and it continued to grow ('Urbanization, Urban Development and Land Financing', Microeconomic Information, 25 May 2018, macrochina.com.cn/zhtg/20180525114794.shtml.

Huang Qifan, who oversaw both the erection of new Pudong district in Shanghai, a project 'unimaginable in a private land system', and a giant urban build-up in Chongqing, has clarified how land-banking works; Chongqing's experimental 'land voucher' scheme also aided a fiscal equilibrium of land supply, use, rent and revenue without farmland loss of any compatible scale or tax hype.[11] Such a system 'explains why China's public infrastructure is far better than it is in India, Russia and even many developed countries'.[12] This model of state engaging land capitalization for public projects, a novel form of socializing capital, is largely exhausted due to its rising costs and debt implications.

Following the 2013 delineation of 'three separated rights' derivable from ownership, contract and management of land to 'strengthen the protection of property rights', previously non-tradable rights were relaxed. The State Council's 2014 directive confirmed that 'the peasants have the right to occupy, use, profit from, circulate and mortgage their contracted land'; and the policy of 'clarifying and consolidating' this right should be soon completed by ministries, banks and regulatory bodies working together with officials at the grassroots. This effort to commodify land, designed to ease land transfer, was effective. By 2019, over one-third of China's farmland had been 'circulated', as out-migrated 'peasant workers' sub-leased their land to other villagers or returned it to the village, which could then lease it to outsiders or agricultural companies (this was previously illegal). This development involved nearly 90 million acres of farmland and 72 million farming households, with about 7 million acres given over for construction as opposed to farming.[13] The government promised that the 1983 land contract system would stay effective, with an extension of at least another thirty years. Since the word 'permanent', which initially appeared in a 2008 draft document, was too sensitive given the legal and political prohibition on private land, alternative language – 'long

---

11 Huang Qifan, interview in *China Business*, 5 March 2013. See also *China Review News*, 5 May 2012; Zhiyuan Cui, 'Partial Intimations of the Coming Whole: The Chongqing Experiment in Light of the Theories of Henry George, James Mead and Antonio Gramsci', *Modern China* 37:6, 2011: 646–60.

12 Cui Zhiyuan, 'A Socialist Land System with Chinese Characteristics', *Caijing Daily*, 14 July 2008.

13 Data from the Ministry of Agriculture and Rural Affairs, in Han Changfu, *People's Daily*, 28 September 2019.

term without change' – was officially adopted in 2015.[14] Chinese policy articulation can sometimes be deliberately vague, hence the seemingly insecure land ownership. It is the credible functions of evolving policies more than fixed institutions that have shaped development outcomes in China.[15]

Still trying to avoid wholesale land commodification, China formally holds onto a bifurcated land ownership structure. The current policy enforcing land titling, or consolidating rights (*quequan*), is seen by many as a form of quasi-privatization. For permitting such a right to be indefinite and tradable is a form of *de facto* ownership and makes it harder to distinguish collective from private rights. After the 2017 liberalization of farmland use restrictions, at the end of 2019, to simplify transactions through a unified land market, more than a dozen large municipalities were to pilot an experimental direct market entry of rural construction land without state approval and requisition. New generations are ever more likely to grow up landless and without a homestead. Even if only the use right is traded, collective authority over land is eroded or empty. The 2020 revised Land Administrative Law and its April additional specifications have granted provincial governments discretion of liberalizing the factor market, so as to further ease conversion of farmland to construction land. This is consistent with an infrastructure-driven growth pattern, but would worsen land dispossession to jeopardize staple grain self-sufficiency as a national policy, among other detriments.

While village authorities formally retain the rights for the allocation, regulation and leasing of collective land, these have continued to shrink. If the contractual relationship between the use right lessor and lessee has little to do with the preference of the collective holder, represented by the relegated village committees who have minimal management power, then the structure of shared ownership is effectively hollowed out. In many places land allocation has not been readjusted for many years, failing to account for marriages, births and deaths, or other shifts in the settled population. As a result, younger people increasingly

14 Chen Xiwen (former deputy leader of the Central Rural Work Group), 'The Relationship between the Peasantry and Land', 7 June 2017.

15 Peter Ho, *Unmaking China's Development: The Function and Credibility of Institutions*, Cambridge: Cambridge University Press, 2017.

grow up without a title of their own. Fixed land contracts that do not respond to change hence serve to make land use less equal and exclude newcomers. There are other obvious functions which require collective efforts, such as fairly and rationally managing common resources and reclaiming wasted or abused farmland. A good example is the relocation in the Ningxia Hui autonomous region. While many in Pingluo county migrated to work in cities, leaving their houses and land behind, others from Xihaigu, an area plagued for years by drought and abject poverty, needed a new home. The local government, with central government arranging financial and expert aid from the coastal east, brokered a deal for resettlement. While people from Xihaigu settled in the villages of Pingluo, with due recognition of membership and land rights, the migrants who left Pingluo received compensation and urban registration wherever they now lived. Without government planning and collective collaboration, such arrangements would not have been possible. Regardless, given the trend for new generations to leave the land, and with many young people never having farmed nor intending to do so, and as the collective power over land has diminished without substantial regulatory control or lease income, large areas of farmland are left uncultivated. The phenomenal land abandonment clashes harshly with the ongoing shortage of land.

At issue here, however, is not only microeconomic strategy and the reform of urban planning, jobs and residential registration (*hukou*) to grant migrants settlement with equal entitlements to public provisions. It is also, above all, whether there are other viable options, notably organized petty farming. Despite government expropriation and private corporate seizure of land, more generally the unique Chinese disjunction between displacement and dispossession – where migrant workers retain their land rights, however dispossessed otherwise – has largely enabled the country to avoid mass landlessness. In reflecting on internal migration it is necessary to broaden the focus beyond the human-social cost that migrant workers endure, especially their second-class citizen status in cities. For the once seemingly boundless supply of cheap labour, the country relied on the workers' remaining land as a last recourse and means of subsistence: the two-tiered productive structure allowed migrant urban workers to be paid below the cost of their reproduction, based as it was on their rural land being tended by family members or sub-lessees for produce or rents. Such workers could return to farming at times of need. The land thus served as a social safety velvet and pressure valve,[16] whereby the post-socialist system could tap into a socialist reserve of equal land rights. If global industrialization no longer requires rural sourcing and the classical agrarian question of capital is therefore indeed superseded, China has proved to be an exception.[17]

To this extent, the much maligned *hukou* system actually protects rural residents and acts as a barrier to the complete capitalist transformation of land. The reason many migrant workers are reluctant to give up on their rural *hukou* is precisely because it is bound up with land titling. Arguing against putting limits on liberalization of land management and trade, the advocates for privatization imagine that comprehensively opening investment opportunities to urban capital would prompt both agricultural modernization and urbanization. Peddling the new institutionalist doctrine that clarity of absolute property rights is the panacea for all ills, they believe that the popularly resented problems of forced demolition and unfair compensation from land seizure would then disappear. From the moral high ground, they fight land grabbing to demand a fair share of urban development for land-losing farmers – a superficially appealing argument. Land privatization cannot be the solution, however, since it can neither secure contracted land rights nor prevent the misuse of land.

Although privatization could not possibly restore pre-1949 conditions, it could result in severe polarization and rural and urban poverty, with the poor forced to mortgage or sell land under debt or other burdens. In a unified land market in which urban and rural land would be 'treated equally in both right and price' with no regard for rent differentials, as argued by liberal economists, accelerating privatization could be predictable, concentrating land in the hands of a new landed class, real estate gamblers, agro-capitalists and multinationals. Exploitative productive relations have already taken major strides. If a large agrarian proletariat is not yet in sight, even those who are not hired by

16 He Xuefeng, 'New Rural Construction and the Chinese Path', *Chinese Sociology and Anthropology* 39:4, 2007: 26–38.

17 Henry Bernstein, 'Is There an Agrarian Question in the Twenty-First Century?', *Canadian Journal of Development Studies*, 27:4, 2006: 449–60.

private capital are inevitably subordinated to an increasingly capitalistic order. More than autonomous cultivators, post-communal peasants are increasingly providers of land and labour in an ongoing capitalist transformation of agrarian management from above or below.

Private land ownership and free land trading could also further deplete the most fertile land via the obliteration of any effective public power to curtail waste, parcelization and private concentration or other adversary acquisitions, trades, renting and subleasing of land. This will have huge geosocial implications on grain production and food security for a population as large as the Chinese. Rushed urbanization has already put a massive strain on land supply. The raising of land values turned farmland into development zones, attracting speculative capital and debt finance, and destabilizing the national fiscal and spatial groundwork of macroplanning. Although the formal policy is in favour of smaller cities and towns over mega-metropolises, any de-agrarianization still banks on the land. China's agricultural land stock has already shown a steady downward curve since 1996, due to industrial zoning, mining, infrastructure and real estate. The nation's arable land has been diminishing at a speed of 24,000 hectares annually. The government's red line – 1.8 billion *mu* (or 120 million hectares) ring-fenced for staple crops and food production – is oftentimes ignored, threatening a food crisis given the limited international grain market and its sensitivity to demand fluctuation. China is already the world's largest grain importer. Official reports show that China's grain self-sufficiency steadily declined below 90 per cent in 2012, a sharp fall from the heyday of full self-reliance. As the trend continues, it imported 3.66 million tonnes of corn and 3.35 million tonnes of wheat from January to June, 2020. 'The import surge has increased expectations that China will fully use up its corn and wheat quotas for the year for the first time'.[18] As the state's staple grain stocks have consistently decreased, quantitatively as much as qualitatively, one of the policy catchphrases reinvented for 2020 is 'cherish food against waste'.

---

18 Speech by Han Jun, vice director of State Council Development Research Centre, at the China County Level Development Forum in Beijing, 29 January 2012, genetics. cas.cn/kxcb/kpwz/201303/t20130315_3794386.html; Hallie Gu, Tony Munroe, China's H1 grain imports spike, on path to use up annual quotas, Reuters, 24 July 2020, reuters. com/article/china-grains-imports-quotas/chinas-h1-grain-imports-spike-on-path-to-use-up-annual-quotas-idUSL3N2EV0TR.

Land enclosure by commercial agro-capital targeting high-value produce, or even more profitable de-agranized businesses (such as so-called ecological tourism), has also reduced staple crops. Privatization can neither block land concessions nor scale up grain production if policy merely follows market logic rather than curbing it. It is therefore a policy contradiction that state subsidies go to land holders, along with large transfer rent to the big holders, rather than to actual cultivators – these two categories do not overlap beyond the case of small farming households. In recent times, transnational capital has flooded into Chinese corporate agriculture, through upstream, downstream and supply channels, capturing the largest stake of profit. In the more financialized sectors, multinationals led by Monsanto, DuPont and others found in China an ideal investment environment. Foreign shares in Chinese corn, wheat, rice, soybeans and vegetable markets have steadily risen. Genetically modified (GM) seeds have taken over certain staple crops, destroying locally sustained, diverse seed varieties, natural and hybrid alike, including China's star breed known as super rice. A self-interested comprador bureaucracy yields to monopoly foreign capital to issue permits on GM products and seeds, including converting local varieties without rigorous scrutiny; native agriculture – with its producers, consumers and markets – is under great threat. The Ministry of Agriculture even has a timetable to commercialize the production of GM corn and soybeans in 2020. There is no way for land privatization to redress such catastrophic misdeeds.

Yet this quasi-privatization has cut still deeper into farming households and communities, serving to reinforce policies, peddled by foreign agribusinesses and domestic urban investors alike, aimed at modernization understood as commercial agriculture based on large scale private farms. Paired with urbanization, the process has seen the progressive concentration of arable land into the possession of capitalized big farmers and private entrepreneurs and developers. Given the still central position of subsistence farming and structurally lagging provision of urban jobs, however, this modernization option is not particularly viable. The original collective land system should be preserved for a sustainable household economy. Collective land and equal contract rights provide direct producers with a secure basis to resist 'domination, exploitation and dispossession by outside capital'.[19] Petty farming should find a future in a new kind of modern agriculture compatible with small holders. China's experiences encompassing communal socialism and rural reorganization can be just as advantageous as the celebrated East Asian model. The latter features farmers' associations, production and marketing cooperatives, and governmental financial and technological services, contributing to capitalist industrialization 'without a transition to agrarian capitalism as happened, in different ways, in the English, Prussian and American paths'.[20] In a State Council news conference on 1 March 2019, Beijing confirmed its new directive on 'organically connecting small farming households and modern agricultural development', recognizing the enduring foundational importance of such households as the majority of China's farming population.

Privatization also hinders the rational planning and management of land use in response to the already huge eco-environmental challenges faced by China, and globally. Decollectivization has disabled such pressing needs as soil improvement, irrigation and other infrastructural upgrading, as well as the dissemination of energy-saving technologies and conservation of the natural biodiversity of seeds, crops and wild plants. This argument by no means contradicts the point made earlier on household farming in an organized eco-agriculture, which does not in itself entail any intensive application of industrial methods and supplies. If the global developmentalist impasse is ever to be overcome, marginal petty production is indeed no answer; but neither is capitalist transformation. The hard environmental constraints require the coordinated treatment of polluted land, water and food. Chemicalization, for example, is a vicious cycle, with ever more input needed to compensate for downward productivity, to the detriment of nutritional value and taste. China saw at least 10 per cent of its farmland contaminated with heavy metals and cadmium, from the overuse of chemical fertilizers and pesticides.[21]

---

19 Qian Forrest Zhang and John Donaldson, 'The Rise of Agrarian Capitalism with Chinese Characteristics: Agricultural Modernization, Agribusiness and Collective Land Rights', *China Journal* 60, July 2008: 25–47, at 26, 44, and 'China's Agrarian Reform and the Privatization of Land: A Contrarian View', *Journal of Contemporary China*, 22: 80, 2012: 255–72.

20 Henry Bernstein, *Class Dynamics of Agrarian Change*, Sterling, VA: Kumarian Press, 2010: 30.

21 China's use of chemical fertilizers rose from 8.84 million tons in 1978 to 58.38 million tons in 2012: two and half to three times more than the global average of unit

As farmland is engulfed by factories, construction sites and urban sprawl, urban living doubles per capita energy consumption and the resulting carbon emissions. Having surpassed the US in consuming non-renewable energy in the year 2010, China is now the world's top polluter and emitter. Again, privatization of land can only worsen the situation.

As outlined before, the trend of privatizing land and agriculture under the twofold policy objective of urbanization and agrarian modernization is misconceived. It is still incomplete because of constitutional and legal obstacles the PRC inherited from its revolutionary and socialist origin. Amending the relevant clauses and laws is not simple, but the party has managed to go far enough in exploiting legal ambiguities. Overriding article 63 of the Land Management Law (1998) by which collective land cannot be let, transferred or rented out, the Rural Land Contract Law (2002) highlighted 'long-term and guaranteed' use right. Article 184 of the Property Law (2007) prohibited land mortgaging, but many villages and local banks have nevertheless encouraged private purchases of rural housing and homesteads. Private business claiming legal rights over collective land is widespread. The latest central directive issued in September 2020 stresses that government income from leasing land should be used to help finance rural revitalization. Yet when local states act as real estate agents to financialize the land, policy distortion is inevitable. The method of village mergers – moving villagers to large compounds of high rises, for example – is not only disruptive to farm-related labour but also devastates the domestic poultry production upon which rural living relies. If theoretically consistent, consolidating land rights should be about the consolidation of collective ownership and equal use rights. The *quequan* project, however, has brought China ever closer to land privatization. Worth noting, nevertheless, is that one delicate distinction remains: long before the modern 'bundle of rights' theory, historical China observed the duality of *ownership* (bottom) and *use* (surface) rights in land, or shared and unshared rights. Rural reorganization is not achievable if private property is regarded as absolute or even sacred, as in the libertarian thinking popular among China's own influential economists.

At stake in all of this, and in the state's moves to remove the legal hurdles that would prevent land privatization, is an agrarian population

---

consumption. See Tom Philpott, '6 Mind-Boggling Facts about Farms in China', *Atlantic Cities*, 21 August 2013.

of around 570 million, living in 3.17 million villages – a large part of the world's remaining peasantry. China remains 'earthbound' in the late sociologist Fei Xiaotong's seamless depiction, even as he disliked the word and preferred an unbound future for the country. Following the global crash in 2008 that hit the country's export manufacturing sector badly, 25 million migrant workers returned to their home villages. In 2019–20, the Covid-19 crisis showed once more how rural China provides such a crucial source of safety with its land rights structure still in place. An urban China with stable employment and a market supply of food for its majority population is still impossible to bring about. Capital and energy-intensive agriculture under private monopolies can neither augment unit output nor provide higher-quality products in current Chinese conditions. Indeed, capitalist industrial and urban cent-rism is incapable of ever providing decent living in the peripheries, as has been shown by finance capital's onslaught against land and labourers in the global South. To defend the hard-won public and collective land, and the people who still live on it, is to seek a reordering of the relationships among state, capital, labour, community and nature, in which a modern, need-driven economy of organic agriculture can prosper. Policies can be adjusted towards such an economy by investing in the human capital of direct producers, raising prices of home-grown produces, restricting imports and indeed buying into the local subsidiar-ies of agro-multinationals to reverse foreign control.

If a land market is to exist in a future socialist market economy as part of public finance, land holders cannot be private and trading must be publicly regulated for public gains. Meanwhile, sticking to the normative principle of land to the tiller, in due time anyone who has resettled and no longer tills should trade her land right for urban status. After all, the pro-ducer or actual user of land is the agent of agrarian change. According to John Stuart Mill's contention that land value has nothing to do with own-ership without labour, and Henry George's observations on socializing land and de-privatizing rent, ownership matters only as regards potential earnings from the added value of labour. In essence then, 'it is rent rather than land that must belong to the public'.[22] Sun Zhongshan – under

---

22 Zhang Luxiong, *Land to the Tiller: The Reality and Logic of China's Farmland System*, Beijing: China University or Political Science and Law Press, 2012: 32–3, 66–70; Liu Haibo, 'Rent Sharing: The Core of the Land System,' *South Reviews*, 30 December 2013.

George's influence and reiterating Kang Youwei's idea in *The Great Harmony* that 'all land will be publicly owned and operated' – proposed a unified land tax based solely on differential rents. As a single source of government revenue, such a system would minimize cost, reward labour, prevent private monopoly and eliminate speculation.[23] The reluctance of present-day Chinese policy makers to introduce progressive taxes on land, property, inheritance and other land-generated incomes is a result not so much of technical hurdles as resistance from vested interest.

China's collective land system is not just about equal sharing, however, but also about the collective resources and power on which the security and prosperity of individual right holders depend. In November 2016, eighteen rural cadres in Jinyun, Zhejiang signed an open plea 'to all rural grassroots cadres and masses', criticizing the *quequan* policy, which they saw as 'throwing open the door to private agro-capital and, by deceit or force, taking over and cordoning off the land'. Their fear echoed grassroots discontent about a wave of 'new enclosure'. This call to strengthen collective ownership, peasant agency and local autonomy in land use then prompted a group of concerned scholars to make a similar appeal. 'In the modern agriculture,' they argued, 'a collectively unified management is irreplaceable, as it guards the bottom line of rural security.'[24] Such a sector would enable petty family farming to endure, renew and thrive; and reverse the trend of de-grainization by corporate capital. A formal proposal drawing from these pleas was submitted to the CPPCC in March 2017. The struggle continues.

The logic and perils of privatization: State sector transformed

On the urban front (which also includes state functional and public service units), industrial restructuring began in the 1980s with a similar idea of contract responsibility. Among the best-known local experiments were Sichuan's separation of administration and management, and

---

23 Sun Zhongshan, 'Appeal to Li Hongzhang', June 1894, and 'Speech to the Journalist Parliamentarians', 9 June 1912, *The Complete Works of Sun*, vol. 2, Beijing: People's Publishing House, 2015: 628–30; Zhao Shude, *A History of China's Land System*, Taipei: Sanmin Press, 1988: ch. 7.

24 'A proposal by eighteen rural cadres in Zhejiang', People's Food Sovereignty, 8 November 2016, shiwuzq.com/portal.php?mod=view&aid=941.

Guizhou's licensing of private shareholdings in state firms. The goal was to achieve entrepreneurial autonomy in a competitive market. Following the 1985 dual-track price reform that immediately cut down state sector earnings, SOEs were set to shift away from government budget allocation while taking full responsibility for profits and losses on interest-bearing bank loans. During the same year, the State Restructuring Commission began to sketch a 'modern enterprise system' as 'a common legal framework in which any ownership form could operate, potentially creating a level playing field for competition.'[25] The first comprehensive company law was enacted in 1994 to guide the reorganization of non-performing SOEs. Converted SOEs, as corporations adaptive to market conditions, had legal options to diversify their shares in a hybrid ownership as well as to file for bankruptcy. The government's 1995 strategy of 'grabbing the big and releasing the small' was quickly overridden by frantic private takeovers to include medium and even large-sized enterprises as well. And not only loss-making but also profitable SOEs were sold off, often at knockdown prices, frequently to their managers or other insiders. At the turn of the century, the outcomes of this systemic change, or *gaizhi*, were so huge that it was commonly seen as a big bang, Chinese-style.

The provincial and sub-provincial governments were directly involved in dividing the family assets with a green light from the centre. By brokering deals, officials could enrich themselves, as could former SOE managers and cronies, through acquiring ownership. This was a form of bureaucratic revenge and a first step in bureaucratizing capitalism, with a prominent showing of princelings. Especially striking about the Chinese case of post-communist nomenclature privatization is that, although it was flaunted as a socialist reform, it did not even pretend to be 'fair' (as in Russia). Of course, SOEs by themselves are not necessarily socialist – but the differences between China's state sector before and after *gaizhi* were categorical.

As the budget constraints of fiscal federalism were tightened on regional governments after 1994, the latter were also incentivized to sell assets in order to enhance their financial position. Yet the agency cost was high, as privatized SOEs could be robbed as a *fait accompli* by their new owners through liquidation without liability. Some, for example, began with accounting fraud or filing bankruptcy by transferring funds and equipment away, and then underreporting fixed assets before or after the cheap sale to evade any settlement payments. The buyers, often connected to government officials, were treated so generously that they were not required to pay for anything beyond the (much undervalued) fixed assets. In many cases, they were not liable for any debt or compensational expenses, as public funds were made ready for the subsidization of private transfers. By keeping as little as 30 per cent of the existing workers in some sort of labour contract, they could win for the new owner a tax exemption certificate for three years. Similarly, some foreign investors began to buy partial stocks of Chinese SOEs and turned them into joint ventures, then deliberately made losses by unnecessarily importing expensive materials, hence artificially lowering their values for a cheaper final takeover – quite the model of 'self-embezzlement'.[26] Management buy-outs (MBO) as well as buy-ins by an instantaneous 'rogue bourgeoisie' could even be free: the buyer needed to pay nothing, but instead to obtain a state bank loan as a backdoor favour, or mortgage the firm in question (or its future earnings) through a mediating trust company. Since local cadres were evaluated on economic performance focusing on market integration and foreign invesment, what else could be expected but a race to get rid of burdensome SOEs?

Unacknowledged as privatization, this was in fact a looting process. It went further and faster in dismantling China's gigantic state sector than the more orderly programmes in most other transitional economies. With the huge stripping of state assets and public wealth, massive layoffs ensued. Between 1996 and 2004, the number of SOEs in a stock of roughly 135,000 dropped by 90.1 per cent. In 2006, the official media announced that *gaizhi* at the provincial level had 'entered its final stage' after the county-level SOEs were virtually eliminated. The state sector's share of industrial GDP shrunk to a quarter by the second half of 2007, as officially reported.[27] Above all, the main economic entities changed: by 2018 roughly non-state firms accounted for 72.3 per cent in investment and 80.9 per cent in exports, making up 82.9 per cent of total

---

26 Gao Liang, 'From Reform to Reflection', *Economic Watch*, 15 May 2007; George Akerlof and Paul Romer, 'Looting: The Economic Underworld of Bankruptcy for Profit', Brookings Papers on Economic Activity, 2, 1993.

27 *People's Daily*, 17 July 2006; Wang Jian, 'Macro Regulation Must be Transformed', *Hong Kong Dispatch*, 13 October 2007: 6.

industrial output.[28] This onward march of private transformation was so formidable that seemingly nothing could stand in the way. The 2004 nationwide debate over the MBO of Guangdong Kelon Electrical Holding Co. was briefly a belated wakeup call – but to no avail, and its guilty CEO was even rehabilitated in 2019. According to the statistician Zhao Huaquan, who has studied how public ownership collapsed between 2003 and 2010 as the Chinese economy doubled in size, its non-public components (domestic and foreign) grew 2.3 times while state and collective ones decreased from 57 per cent to 26.9 per cent. In 2010, except for agriculture and a few protected industries, public economic domination disappeared. Of the total assets across sixteen strategic industrial sectors, state capital made up 35 per cent, with no more than 23 per cent under government control. The non-public sector was comprised of self-employed small businesses at 2.2 per cent, private-owned enterprises (POEs) at 45.7 per cent, and foreign or joint ventures at 25.1 per cent.[29] A decade later, these numbers only got worse.

Not only did privatization by and large fail to achieve its claimed objectives of efficiency, productivity and upgrading, but it also weakened China's general economic position and independence. Aside from substantial losses of state assets and public property and growing macroeconomic imbalance, there was the inequitable distribution of the costs and benefits of reform. Chasing quick profits, fraud and corruption became routine: account books were falsified, bribes paid to fake quality standards, taxes evaded and debt collection unleashed. Scandals of poisoned food products and counterfeit drugs discredited the food and pharmaceutical industries for the first time in the PRC, causing social panic. Industrial accidents skyrocketed. Data from both state agencies and the International Labour Organization (ILO) in 2006 and 2007 showed that the death toll in China's privatized mines was the highest in the world. China also had more annual deaths per capita from occupational diseases and other work-related casualties across industries than any other country.[30] The curve has since trended down from that peak,

28 Liu Jiejiao and Xu Xiaoxin, 'Innovation and Prospect of State Firms in the Forty Years of Reform,' *Research on Financial and Economic Issues* 8, 2018: 3–11.

29 Zhao Huaquan, 'A Quantitative Analysis and Evaluation of the Mainstay Status of Public Ownership', *Contemporary Economic Research* 3, 2012: 41–8.

30 *China's Work Safety Yearbook 2012*, Beijing: China Coal Industry Press, 2013;

but the situation is still alarming. Not only did ownership change offer no cure for real problems, but privatization may also have been China's worst policy option judged by the most basic human value.[31]

Private restructuring also led to the commodification of labour and antagonistic capital–labour relations. Tens of millions of workers, approximately 40 per cent of the SOE workforce, were sacked from the drastically shrinking state sector. They were denied any voice in the decisions guiding a process that was devastating their lives. Many received little or no compensation or social security. With the demise of SOEs built by generations of dedicated workers, labour's political and social recognition also diminished, along with much of their trust and confidence in public institutions. Echoes of the old society re-emerged: insecure jobs, sweatshop conditions, urban poverty and swelling inequalities within and without industries.

The question, then, is how could all this be allowed to happen? How could decades of scrupulously accumulated labour and investment be so easily robbed? The substantial privatization of China's industries – in light of their remarkable size and solidity following the success of the first five-year plan – looked globally unprecedented in terms of speed and thoroughness. Analysis shows that the fate of SOEs is contingent on the national developmental strategy under a specific state ideology: nothing is 'natural' or inevitable. The transition from a command to market economy was a real challenge, but there is no reason why SOEs should not flourish in the socially regulated, socialized and eventually socialist market that the reformers initially sought to create. It is causally notable that many flaws of SOEs deemed to justify *gaizhi* came to be true only after they were targeted for transformation. Public ownership in itself did not cause SOEs to fail – privatization did.

Of course, to measure SOEs merely by their market value, without considering their vital national and social functions, is to demean them. A downward spiral began in the 1990s when cash flow and government support evaporated. In 1996, the sector posted net losses, and even nominally profitable firms began to 'teeter on the brink of insolvency', 'consuming

---

Ann Herbert and team, 'National Profile Report on Occupational Safety and Health in China', Geneva: ILO, 2012.

31 John Hassard, Jackie Sheehan, Meixiang Zhou, Jane Terpstra-Tong and Jonathan Morris, *China's State Enterprise Reform: From Marx to the Market*, London: Routledge, 2007: 4.

a monumental amount of investment capital and amassing extraordinary liabilities.[32] The existence of loss-making firms draining state revenues suggested that privatization was a rational response. However, beneath the surface there were other forces at work. Economic liberalization and deregulation were the global trend by which China gave up its autonomous industrial policy. The conditions of competition were also grossly unfavourable to SOEs. The effect of volatile energy prices and raw materials in the international market, coupled with a surprisingly anti-protectionist pricing system at home, added up. State preference and subsidies for foreign capital hurt native entrepreneurship across many sectors. The receding government commitment deprived SOEs of their priority on the national agenda. This was most harmfully seen in the heavy machinery, high-end machine tools, and certain public infrastructural industries with longer cycles of (or no) capital return and hence a competitive disadvantage.

Additionally, many state firms still carried out social service functions by running educational and care facilities while looking after their current, redundant and retired workers with costly welfare programmes; such firms could not make layoffs freely, for instance, as they were bound by old rules around job and lifetime security. Pressed from all sides, some also split and entered into mergers, losing their most profitable segments to joint ventures and retaining only dated equipment and the weaker parts of the workforce.[33] On top of everything, SOEs were 'constrained by their obligation to support the government's overriding priority of social and political stability.'[34] That is, the (socialist) state sector, austerely tormented by the (neoliberalized) state itself, continued to shoulder indispensable national economic duties while bearing much of the cost of transition. This lack of a level playing field created victims, not, as widely believed, of private companies, but of overburdened SOEs. The plight of the latter was a striking contrast to those private investors and foreign corporations that received preferential treatment. The superstition that SOEs are intrinsically

---

32 Wang Yong, 'Key State Firms Set to Revive', *China Daily*, 15 September 1997; Edward Steinfeld, *Forging Reform in China*, Cambridge: Cambridge University Press, 2008: 18.

33 Peter Nolan and Wang Xiaoqiang, 'Beyond Privatization: Institutional Innovation and Growth in China's Large State-Owned Enterprises', *World Development*, 27:1, 1999: 185.

34 John Hassard, Jonathan Morris and Jackie Sheehan, 'The Elusive Market: Privatization, Politics and State-Enterprise Reform in China', *British Journal of Management* 13, 2002: 222.

defective was deliberately propagated in such metaphors as rotten apples or popsicles to be urgently consumed.[35]

Today, China still lives with lasting consequences from the neoliberalized 1990s. The traditional stronghold of heavy industry in the north-east, for example, has lost a large slice of its population as a result of radical downsizing, which continues to hinder local economic regeneration. Already in 2007, according to the All-China Federation of Industry and Commerce, more than 5.5 million companies (or about 80 per cent of the national total) were private or *minying* (non-state) in different shareholding systems. These make up over 70 per cent of urban employment.[36] By 2017, of the approximately 113,000 surviving SOEs, or a little over 5 per cent of all minimally sizable enterprises, ninety-seven were under the central State-Owned Assets Supervision and Administration Commission (SASAC) established in 2003; others were overseen by the agency's provincial and municipal offices. Among them, tens of thousands were deemed 'zombies' – a term Xi Jinping did not hesitate to copy – to be cleared up by 2020. The Commission's 2006 guidelines specified a dozen key sectors where 'state-owned assets should expand in volume and be optimized in structure': full control over power, oil, natural gas, petrochemicals, telecommunications and armaments; a controlling stake in coal, aviation and shipping; and a heavy SOE presence in machinery, automobiles, information technology, construction, iron and steel, and non-ferrous metals.[37] A decade later, a mockery had been made of this list. Most had 'corporatized', or absorbed private and foreign partnerships. By the end of the 2010s, the entry bars were set so low for domestic and foreign private capital, euphemized as 'social capital' – even for the sectors in the first group of national monopoly – that little was left for a genuinely state sector. The 2020–22 action plan for SOE reform specifically targets the rail, oil, gas and electricity industries.

It is in fact difficult to define the different types of ownership structure in the contemporary Chinese economy. Undergoing a joint-stock

---

35 Lang Xianping summaries seven ways of acquiring SOEs cheaply in a case analysis of Kelon, 'The Carnival of Green Cool in a Feast of State Sector Retreat and Private Sector Advance', Xinlang Finance and Economy, 16 August 2004, finance.sina.com. cn/t/20040816/1202951523.shtml.

36 'Public Opinions' column, *People's Daily*, 19 November 2007.

37 Xinhua News, *People's Daily*, 19 December 2006, english.people.com.cn.

reform, SOEs are said to be those with majority state shares but otherwise owned by diversified shareholders. SASAC solely oversees and controls state capital rather than assets or micromanagement, acting like a portfolio investor, and not even necessarily the majority shareholder, in an array of firms. Impressed by the 'jungle of ownership' in China, Branko Milanovic has noted the blurred distinction 'between state-owned, purely privately-owned and a myriad of ownership arrangements in-between (state-owned corporation raising private capital on the stock-exchange, communal property mixed with private property, state firms with foreign private participation etc.)'. Chinese official statistics simply cannot catch the numerous forms and 'different rights of ownership from ability to dispose and sell the assets to usufruct only'.[38] SOEs increasingly operate through opaque holding entities with labyrinthine structures. Corporations as 'empires' also own subsidiaries, or subsidiaries of subsidiaries, and consist of a 'large web of patronage and business opportunity'.[39] Despite this chaotic picture, and calculated according to the minimal threshold of majority shareholding, nominal state assets were reported in 2018 as 178.7 trillion yuan ($2.63 trillion) with a profit of 3.4 trillion yuan. SOEs' profit margin on net assets has been around 8 per cent since 2008, and provided 60 million jobs in 2019. Hao Peng, director of SASAC, announced in November 2019 that 70 per cent of central SOEs are 'mixed ownership', and that state sector reform has reached the stage of 'capitalizing assets and pluralizing equity shares'.[40] SOEs are recognized as being strong in the field of research and development (R&D), and they lead in executing and financing the national Going Out strategy. Of the 111 Chinese industrial and banking companies that made it into the Fortune Global 500 in 2018 (up from sixty-three in 2012), 80 per cent were state owned or controlled.

To streamline SOEs, and regroup those that are centrally supervised into globally competitive conglomerates, is to complete corporatization and marketization, well in line with the tendency towards concentration

---

38 Branko Milanovic, 'Will Bourgeoisie ever Rule the Chinese State?', globalinequality, 6 March 2018, glineq.blogspot.com/2018/03/will-bourgeoisie-ever-rule-chinese-state.html.

39 Shaun Breslin, 'Government–Industry Relations in China: A Review of the Art of the State', Warwick University CSGR Working Papers 272, 2010.

40 Ning Gaoning, CEO of state-owned Sinochem, speech given at Qinghua University, 4 April 2019, article.xuexi.cn/html/121159985250029237022.html.

and centralization that is intrinsic to capitalist development. Given the notion of socializing SOE shares while separating the functions of owning and managing, Chinese terminology that equates 'social' with non-state and even 'private' capital could potentially advance the post-capitalist socialization of production on a conceptual level. Until then, however, such policy ambiguities are misleading or erroneous. A socialist production programme would see macroplanning under which enterprises fulfil their social obligations and 'commanding heights' industries are publicly controlled and protected. Socialist property relations would also see politically and legally enhanced industrial policies. The claim that China's basic economic system is socialist is highly dubious, if SOEs no longer dominate the economy and receive no state subsidies (which are now reserved for specific industries and R&D projects, regardless of ownership); the dramatically reduced state sector aims to maximize capital rather than serve the whole people in whose name it operates; and 'competitive neutrality' of market rules is sought between domestic and foreign capital, SOEs and POEs, all without sovereign self-promotion.[41] In any case, there is no evidence for the complaint that the private sector has been suppressed under Xi's rein. Nothing close to de-privatization or renationalization is happening; isolated and often temporary incidents in recent years of SOE acquisition or repurchasing were to bail out firms dying from ruptured cash flows. To the contrary, he has emphasized that 'our country's private sector should only grow stronger', and repeated the assurance that 'private enterprises and entrepreneurs belong to our own family.'[42] The environment for the private economy is all the more charitable, even privileged, to the extent that following the policy preference, a handful of criminally charged private CEOs have been acquitted.

---

41 Zhang Mao, bureau director of state administration for market regulation, 'Creating Sufficient Market Space for Minying Enterprises to Develop', Xinhuanet, 5 November 2018; Xiao Yaqing, director of SASAC, addresses the Central SOE International Cooperation Forum, Beijing, 6 November 2018.

42 Xi Jinping, speech in Hebei, 25 January 2017, via Caixin Video and Audio, and speech at Central Party School, Hebei, 21 January 2019, via Xinhua News; People's Daily, 2 November 2018.

Asymmetrical globalization: The dependency trap

International capital has aggressively participated in China's privatization. Much of foreign direct investment was channeled to acquire
SOEs, taking large shares of state banks as well. According to the UN
Trade and Development Conference's *Global Investment Report* 2006,
in 2001 less than 5 per cent of FDI in China was spent on local mergers
and acquisitions. In the first half of 2004 it rose to 63.6 per cent, and
then in the first six months of 2006 jumped a further 71 per cent from
the previous year, growing twelvefold between 2003 and 2006. China's
first five years in the WTO saw an inflow FDI worth $260 billion, as
Motorola, General Motors and General Electrics among others strode
into the Chinese market.[43] Indeed, foreign buyers sought out privatizing and privatized state firms, gaining controlling shares and power
over management, technologies and profits in several industries. Some
flagship SOEs were also compelled to move into merger negotiations.
The excessive influx of short-run, speculative capital to the local
money, equity, future, estate and insurance markets exposed and
exploited the weaknesses of China's regulatory infrastructure. A petition to the NPC in March 2006 signed by 170 concerned officials and
scholars warned against the trend: by 2005, value-added profits had
been ceded to foreign capital amounting to more than about 70 per
cent of China's electrical and information sectors and 90 per cent of its
auto industry (both production and market), as well as 80 per cent of
managerial decisions on its machinery and petrochemical industries.
In 2009, majority foreign shares extended to most Chinese industrial
leaders outside the monopoly sector, taking 55 per cent of China's
foreign trade volume and 85 per cent of its high-tech products. By
2010, foreign-dominated sectors had exceeded the state sector in assets
by 13 per cent.[44]

---

43 *Chinese Economy Weekly*, 25 July 2006; Yu Yongding, *Guangming Daily*, 31
August 2006.

44 Petition to the NPC, 'Strengthening Autonomy and Innovation in the Mainstay
Industries, Preventing Economic Colonization', March 2006. See also Gao Liang,
'Warning Against Multinationals Seizing the Opportunity of SOE Reforms To Control
China's Backbone Enterprises in the Machine Manufacturing Industry', 23 December
2005, cuhk.edu.hk; Zhao Huaquan, 'A Quantitative Analysis'.

More astounding still, in the sense that China had exported capital (and become a net exporter of capital since 2014), Chinese firms were bought mainly with China's own money. With accumulated overseas assets of about $2.9 trillion in 2008, China had a surplus outward FDI over inward FDI of $1.5 trillion, once its external debt of $1.4 trillion had been subtracted. In exchange for its investment amounting to several hundred billion dollars in real economic terms, China received something virtual – mostly in low-interest dollar bonds. This was an economy already burdened with investment fever and inflation, caused by the oversupply of local currency from funds outstanding for foreign exchange. Unequal market opening and privileged FDI also saw competitive pricing of China's exports and oftentimes monopoly pricing of its imports. Trade surpluses then constantly depreciated the yuan against the dollar. This is a case of highly unequal exchange: a relatively poor country subsidizing far richer ones – 'the greatest financial innovation of globalization in the twenty-first century'.[45] Critics have noted the wider implications: China's cheap exports of goods and natural resources combined with foreign reserves, mainly in US bonds, have allowed the US government to make easy loans to its own companies for variously acquiring high-end Chinese firms. Not only submitting itself to the financial superpower but directly aiding it, China has taken 'a suicidal model of economic development'.[46]

The controversial bid in 2005 by the US-based Carlyle Group to take over Xugong Construction Machinery Company (XCMG), China's largest construction equipment maker, is one dismal example of this phenomenon. The Carlyle funds were drawn from the global dollar credit markets, into which China contributed about $1 trillion; as was noted at the time, 'in effect Carlyle is buying a Chinese state-owned corporation with Chinese money'.[47] The deal fell through amid public anger. But other similar deals involving large and healthy SOEs went through: SEM in Shandong was partly sold to the US company

45 Huang Shudong, 'The Greatest Financial Innovation of the US Is To Buy China for Free', Utopia, 8 January 2019, wyzxwk.com/Article/jingji/2019/01/398001.html.

46 Jia Genliang, 'A Comment on Perez's Technological Revolution, Financial Crisis and Systemic Transformation', Economic Theory and Economic Management 2, 2009: 5–11.

47 Zuo Dapei, 'It is Wrong to Reform Xugong and Let Foreign Capital Control It', Sina Finance, 7 August 2006, finance.sina.com.cn; Henry Liu, Asia Times, 21 August 2006; Yu Yongding, 'China's Double Surplus: Origins and Counter Policy', Xinhua Digests 24, 2006: 48–50.

Caterpillar; Shenyang Zaoyan Machinery to Atlas Copco of Sweden; Jiamusi Agricultural Machinery, China's only plant capable of producing combine harvesters, to the US John Deere; Jinxi Chemistry Machinery, along with its indigenous core turbine technology, to the German Siemens. The list goes on. In 2006, the Heilongjiang provincial government sold off Jixi and Jiamusi Coal Machineries, along with one-third of China's shearer market and half of its tunnel-boring machine market, to International Mining Machinery Holdings, a US company that had come into existence simply in order to acquire these companies.[48] These advanced SOEs had all been moved from central to provincial management prior to foreign acquisition at prices that were often much lower than market value. In several cases local states even offered preferential conditions, leaving to the Chinese parent company all the liabilities including the compensation of dismissed workers and the repayment or restructuring of 'non-performing loans'. China's colossal loss is not only about assets and technologies but also the established national industrial chains, standards, brands, organizational and technological capacities, and markets. Other enterprises were affected by broken productive linkages and fragmented trades. The round of foreign acquisitions in the first decade of the new millennium were so precise in targets that they amounted to 'an objective identification of the most foundational advantages and best assets of China's equipment industry'.[49]

China has abandoned the goal of self-reliance and followed the model of using foreign investment and cheap domestic labour to produce for export at the low end of the global value chain, beginning with SEZs in the 1980s. This model was fortified during China's all-out and lengthy efforts at negotiating with the Americans and Europeans, initially in 1986 for entry to the GATT (General Agreement on Tariffs and Trade), and ultimately for WTO membership. Despite small modifications, the pattern has continued as an after-effect of the Chinese overcommitment to the rich nations' trade terms. Some of these terms, from almost unconditional market access to unilateral anti-dumping laws, were specific to China. While indigenization of technology was a commonplace for late developers, China found itself locked into a perpetual handicap: its

---

48 Jia, 'A Comment on Perez's Technological Revolution'.
49 Guo Liyan and Lu Feng, 'Self-Strengthening or Self-Harming: In-Depth Issues on Foreign Acquisition of China's Backbone Enterprises', *International Economic Review*, 2006: 6.

tariffs reduced from an average of 43 per cent in the 1990s to 9.7 per cent after WTO accession, compared to 27 per cent in Brazil, 31 per cent in Argentina, 32 per cent in India and 37 per cent in Indonesia.[50] By 2019, the rate was down to under 4 per cent or zero on selected imports. With a foreign trade dependency ratio of over 65 per cent at its peak, grossly uneconomical foreign mergers, and transnational corporations exploiting Chinese workers and resources to profit from producing for the world market, not only was the Chinese economy vastly more open and hence more vulnerable than most developing nations, it was also behind in building up its own fleet of world-beating companies.[51]

Missing out on opportunities to rectify and rebalance, China was trapped in artificial path dependency with increasing returns, particularly given the WTO's status as a post–Cold War hegemonic institution of neoliberal global capitalism. China in WTO did see limited industrial innovations alongside technological assimilations. Some self-protective manoeuvring for local markets was also in place as an effort to adjust the national growth model. But these fell far short of reversing the displacing effects of FDI or of a determined reassertion of independence through R&D to indigenize technology, redirect growth and negotiate fairer terms of trade and market integration. Albeit with arguable exceptions in a few areas, such as green energy, mobile internet, and the biomedical, space and AI industries, Chinese designers and manufacturers depend on, yet are often embargoed from importing, foreign core technologies, ranging from semiconductor chips to digital machine tools. Foreign and joint venture manufacturers also dominate most advanced production lines and the most profitable markets in China.[52]

Forty years after trying the strategies of 'exchanging market for technology' and 'participating in the international division of labour', and having made deep concessions before and after WTO accession, China is more, not less, technologically dependent. It has practically given up on demanding technological transfers on foreign investment.

---

50 Panitch and Gindin, *Making of Global Capitalism*: 293.

51 Martin Wolf, 'China Should Risk Bolder Trials', *Financial Times*, 6 June 2006.

52 Yuan Yang and Lucy Hornby, 'China Raises Alarm over its Dependency on Imported Chips', *Financial Times*, 18 July 2018; Sean Kenji Starrs, 'Can China Unmake the American Making of Global Capitalism?' in Leo Panitch and Gregory Albo, eds, *The Socialist Register 2019: A World Turned Upside Down*, London: Merlin Press, 2018: 186–95.

Its policies have favoured integration rather than autonomy. Among those who argued for China to not join the WTO, Peter Nolan explained that the membership would mean agreeing to 'dismantle almost the entire range of mechanism that had formed the core of its industrial policy' and that exposing its large tech companies would deprive China of opportunities to build national champions. It would become a mere subcontractor to the highly concentrated transnationals in control of global supply and value chains.[53]

The illusions of technological transfer-based high-tech ascendancy overlook the reality not only of absolute right to intellectual property but also of the absolute power of a unipolar global order against any perceived competitor. The prevailing economic doctrines in China, however, oppose import substitution and technological autonomy while valuing cheap labour, quick duplication and export as a comparative advantage. This doctrine partly explains the earlier trade booms, but not much else. The best criticisms are from empirical evidence, as seen in the current US trade blockages and tariffs since June 2018, implemented and threatened alike. In April 2019, ZTE was instantly paralysed and Huawei badly hit by the US-led sanctions on their supply chains (mainly chips) and their overseas markets. In a conciliatory gesture, the Chinese government in June announced 'special opening-up measures' to widen market access for foreign investment in twenty-two formerly protected fields. While the Huawei debacle is still unfolding and more Chinese tech companies could be similarly targeted, the dangers of an ideology favouring global interdependence and integration are already laid bare as a structural weakness in China's high-end technologies sector. The filing of bankruptcy by Shenyang Machine Tool Group in July 2019 and the suspension of its promising i5 system also shows how unfavourable has become the economic ecology for any attempt at self-reliance. The so-called industrialist critics (*gongyedang*) inside China have advocated an alternative economic ideology by updating the mercantilist theories of Friedrich List or Alexander Gerschenkron, with little policy impact.

Earlier in 2013, co-authoring *China 2030* with the World Bank, Chinese policy think tankers set the goals of 'breaking up state

---

53 Peter Nolan, *China and the Global Business Revolution*, London: Palgrave Macmillan, 2001: 864–5.

monopolies', lowering entry barriers and reducing the state sector to no more than 10 per cent of the national economy. Chapter 3, on 'structural reforms', targeted petroleum, chemicals and electricity among other industries to be privatized. Chapter 7 commended the radical relaxation of government control over the capital market. The highlighted 'anti-monopoly' method against SOEs was uncannily said to securitize China's national wealth by liberalizing its fiscal and banking systems towards 'internationalization'. This document, known as the Zoellick Report (after Robert B. Zoellick, World Bank president 2007–12), set the tone of mainstream Chinese attitudes towards foreign pressure on domestic reforms. The discourse – including such statements as 'what is demanded of us coincides precisely with what we ought and want to do anyway', or 'changes at home can be achieved by positively accepting foreign imposition [*daobi*]' – has since prevailed all the way to the unfolding US trade war against China.[54] The US has been able to win as the Chinese have in effect surrendered without a fight – phase one deals regarding US monitoring were wide-ranging and set to be legally binding (with NPC approval). There was no officially published Chinese version (while the English version was put online by the White House) before China signed it in January 2020, apparently to avoid domestic backlash in a country historically familiar with unequal treaties. As though this is not humiliating enough, the war is essentially over what Marx called 'fictitious capital'. China's risk on the road to financial integration is ever greater after steep concessions made since 2018.

The ambitious plan of *Made in China 2025* for greater independence in cutting-edge technologies, a policy that any sovereign country should have the right to pursue (and permitted by the 1995 Agreement on Trade-Related Investment Measures), was quietly shelved to satisfy American hardliners in early 2019. Having ceded from demanding technological transfers on foreign investment without its own comprehensive upgrading, China let its manufacturing remain dependent on the foreign supply of high-tech parts even as it gradually climbed up the value chain. This deficit in sovereign determination and control over the

---

54 Among many examples, see Li Daokui, director of Qinghua University's Center for China in the World Economy, 'Revitalizing Reform and Opening', Qinghua University, 23 June 2019, pit.ifeng.com/c/7nlLcLNqfk8; and Lo Jiwei, former Finance Minister, who attacked industrial policy generally and technological autonomy as empty talk and 'a waste of taxpayers' money', *South China Morning Post*, 7 March 2019.

national economy precludes success. Chinese lawmakers also quickly completed a series of legal procedures to ban their own enterprises from 'forcing' foreign investors to license technological spillovers. China's economic autonomy is solely reliant on its now shaky capital controls in a crisis-ridden global market.

Since 2005, the Chinese financial sector has been undergoing an institutionalization of new stock exchanges and capital restructuring of the largest state banks through public offerings. The latter was preceded by the participation of such foreign oligopolies as Goldman Sachs, UBS, City Bank and the Bank of America. The inroads made by such foreign short-term investments alone impedes the fiscal security of the nation and its small producers and traders. Capital flight, including the new rich (who often find ways to evade regulations) transferring wealth abroad, has become frenzied.[55] In July 2018, the five state-owned commercial banks and the other twelve shareholding banks were ordered to support 'marketization and legalization' through expanding their 'debt-to-equity' programmes of absorbing private and foreign 'social capital'. The latter, still unsatisfied, demanded China remove its capital account control altogether. One of the accusations was that the yuan's exchange rate and interest rates were manipulated, as though other central banks didn't do the same to their own currencies. Given that using fiscal tools to manage economic and monetary policies is the right of any sovereign state, the Chinese government needs to gradually adopt a more flexible currency exchange regime. Samir Amin among others advised China to shun the global financial system under the dollar hegemony prerogative of the US Treasury and Federal Reserve – the US state – in light of regional and global financial turmoil since the late 1990s.[56] The PRC State Council announced in January 2019, however, that China would nevertheless 'open its capital account steadily and in an orderly fashion', to be implemented with immediate effects.

Over many years, and at a heavy cost for its workers, resources and environment, China laboured on behalf of foreign consumption by

55 In the first half of 2019, China's hidden capital flight reached to $131 billion or more. Bloomberg News, 'China's Hidden Capital Flight Surges to Record High', 11 October 2019, bloomberg.com/news/articles/2019-10-11/china-hidden-capital-flight-at -a-record-in-2019-iif-says.

56 'Samir Amin (May 2018) – Financial Globalization: Should China Move In?', Defend Democracy Press, 14 August 2018, defenddemocracy.press/22137-2.

producing massive, and massively underpriced, goods. The largest chunk of profits was taken away, leaving Chinese workers on meagre wages and domestic companies in a race to the bottom.[57] Firms with a slim profit margin were practically unable to contribute to social insurance for their workers in the sunbelt industrial hubs. The contrast between Apple's astronomical profits and its Chinese subcontractors' thin margins, especially the miseries of the young workers assembling iPhones at high speed and precision, is notorious. The share of 1.2 million Chinese workers in the 2012 profit report on Apple iPhones was 1.8 per cent, an accepted imperialist super-exploitation for super-profit and rent. Operating more than forty complexes in nineteen provinces in China, Foxconn has a profit rate of about 7 per cent, mainly as a result of suppression of labour cost and local governments' favouring treatment measures, have permitted Apple to take up to 90 per cent of the global smartphone industry's profit.[58] A 'comparative advantage' in neoclassical economics is misread to justify suppression of labour cost and unequal global division of labour, and becomes a fatal disadvantage: 'cheap labour' is not only a symbol of exploitation and degradation in itself, but also a stain on the 'socialist market economy' embracing it. Foreign extraction depends on local state collaboration. The true advantage, instead, is the superior quality of China's workforce; it is this that has underpinned the spectacular 'Chinese speed' of growth. One example of domestic resource depletion and pollution, meanwhile, is rare earth. Strategic ignorance on this precious mineral deposit allowed fierce competition among private mining companies for export, which led to a 30–40 per cent drop in its unit price in the international market between 1990 and 2005. Despite having taken such a toll, China is still excluded from both the pricing and field technologies of the production and processing of rare earth.[59] These are the symptoms of an untypical 'resource curse'.

57 John Smith, *Imperialism in the Twenty-First Century*, New York: Monthly Review Press, 2016: 21.

58 Joint University Student Investigation Team, 'Foxconn, Have You Righted Your Wrongs?', *References*, Beijing Huayan Research 11, 18 March 2014; Jenny Chan, Mark Selden and Pun Ngai, *Dying for an iPhone: Apple, Foxconn, and the Lives of China's Workers*, Chicago: Haymarket Books, 2020: 18–20, 36–43; Huang Zongzhi, 'In Search of Market Economy Development Path without Stock Market Hegemony', *Rural China Studies* (Guilin: Guangxi Normal University Press) 16, 2020: 1–24.

59 Ku Shu, 'China Must Take Initiative in the "War Over Rare Earth"', Kunlunce Research Academy, 23 May 2019.

China's remaining public land and capital controls, both fragile, are the last defences of its independence or distinction from global capitalist integration, since capitalism was originated in transforming land into a commodity and immensely boosted by financialization. Although the word *privatization* is still somewhat illegitimate in the Chinese lexicon, due to formal ideological constraint and popular dissent, the approach of self-reliance that empowered new China to develop while withstanding international antagonism has been thoroughly discredited by the influential globalization ideology. Addressing the Boao Forum for Asia in April 2018, President Xi confirmed the agenda of more comprehensive economic liberalization: China would 'significantly expand market access' by stepping up imports and further opening its financial market and service industries; raising foreign equity limits in securities, insurers and banks; and lowering auto tariffs, easing restrictions on foreign ownership and enforcing intellectual property rights.[60] This commitment has since been stated again and again, despite the stark contradiction between an open China with numerous forms of foreign operations on the one hand, and the ferocious scrutiny and widespread rejection of Chinese attempts to join or acquire Western corporations on the other. China's financial system and Security Law have been reformed, and there are already foreign-owned banks, trusts, securities, futures and asset management firms operating in China. The *Southern Weekend* headline on the 2020 national day of the PRC, that 'Wall Street has moved into China' was to be expected. Such asymmetries only reconfirm the main thrust of the old theories of dependency and unequal exchange concerning the developmental imperative of national sovereignty, economic security and surplus retention in an age of perpetual imperialism.

Neoliberalizing the state

Neoliberal globalization, however, cannot go anywhere without its agents, nation-states. Its gains and losses are also largely determined by local manoeuvres. China's policy overhaul is an ambiguous case, as

60 Xi Jinping, speech at Boao Forum for Asia, April 2018, uscnpm.org/blog/2018/04/11/transcript-president-xi-addresses-2018-boao-forum-asia-hainan.

significant elements of both adaptation and resistance can be identified. But it is also a crystal-clear example of the way that neoliberal
developmentalism can be efficiently enacted by a post-socialist state.
This is so not only positively, because of centralized power and its
mobilizing efficiency of human and physical resources, but also negatively, as an essentially capitalist transition requiring dictatorship in a
society that possessed resilient socialist legacies. The PRC state, neoliberal and post-socialist *par excellence*, is bound by inertia of
legitimacy and capacity, as it pursues a self-negating transformation.
Thus unlike many other countries, neoliberalism is not structurally
hardwired into the Chinese state, which is why a process that has
inflicted so much discontent and so many conflicts has not encountered concerted mass protests strong enough to pose any real threat to
state power. That is, the existing, dual-faced institutions are still largely
regarded as capable for transmitting popular demands into pressures
on policymaking. In February 2012, for example, a 'people's proposal'
to the annual NPC convention was circulated on the internet. Among
other things, it demanded that 'the personal and family wealth of all
officials be publicized and their source clarified'; 'the losses of public
asset during *gaizhi* be thoroughly traced' and retracted; and 'firms
practising wage arrears, using unpaid student labour and maintaining
illegal working conditions' be closed down. Such events are rarely
reported in the media.

Under state directives and imposition, privatization in China has
involved central and local governments as well as private and foreign
capital. The problem with the project did not, therefore, as some believe,
lie in the lack of independent expert assessment or regulatory auditing
for irregularities. China's current position results from a series of political decisions and statecraft following an intricate logic of post-communist
transition. Some real planning, however messy, is at work in this, even if
a disjunction is observable between a state that seems to be retreating
from the economy and its boundless reach in dictating a rural 'separation of the three rights' on land, as well as urban restructuring of the
state sector. Provincial and sub-provincial governments play a critical
role, as most strikingly seen in the industrial disintegration of the north-
east. In Jilin, it was reported as an achievement that 99.6 per cent of
SOEs had completed *gaizhi* by the end of 2005; Liaoning followed suit,
then Heilongjiang vowed 90 per cent starting and 70 per cent finishing

rates for 2006. In that year, the National Development and Reform Commission's assessment found that the restructuring was insufficiently thoroughgoing and must be pressed forward concerning three issues: the factor markets of capital and land; the banking system; and what was considered an 'overconcentration of state capital and dominance of state shares' across industries.

Likewise, China's dependency trap is rooted in state engineering – above all in its preferential policies toward foreign investors – contrary to the East Asian experience of phasing out foreign dependency via industrial policies. In a widely open China, foreign capital has consistently enjoyed privileges in land use and tax concessions while taxation was more rigorously applied to Chinese firms. Government regulators are reluctant to enforce conditions on foreign investment from technological diffusion to long-term commitment. At least prior to 2008 – but also after in many places – foreign investors were subject to lower corporate tax bases and rates, distorting market competition in which domestic firms, SOEs and POEs alike, were plainly disadvantaged. The average taxes for domestic firms were easily double those of foreign ones. Despite a nominal rate of 33 per cent on business earnings, for years foreign firms paid only about 15 per cent after various tax waivers and breaks. Domestic small businesses faced both difficulties in borrowing from state banks and fierce competition among one another. They were at times granted some reduced or fixed-term tax exemptions, but never treated equally. SOEs often comprised a third class. Concerning 'the tax system, subsidies, trade regulations, and access to finance' in China, laws were more favourable to foreign capital. The incentives were so faulty that 'double offshore' Chinese capital registered as 'foreign' by making a 'round-trip' abroad and back in the guise of FDI via Hong Kong or the Caribbean: 'apart from accumulated effects over years of their higher taxes and suffering from other discriminative policies, SOE lossmaking . . . has nothing to do with their ownership.'[61] Again there was no failure by this sector as such; only the political artwork of an FDI-friendly state.

---

61 Panitch and Gindin, *Making of Global Capitalism*: 296; Zuo Dapei, *No More Selling Out: Exposing the Myth of Reforming SOEs*, Beijing: China Financial and Economic Publisher, 2006: section 2.

In fact, the SASAC is itself a central player in dismantling the state sector. The Commission's central office has called time and again for an acceleration of SOE 'structural readjustment' and for a withdrawal of state capital from all those considered 'non-key' sectors. The German acquisition of the state-owned LYC Group, China's biggest bearing manufacturer, was facilitated by the municipal SASAC of the city of Luoyang in 2006, despite strong opposition led by the National Association of the Bearing Industry. In the same year, the provincial SASAC in Shandong turned a blind eye to the transfer of 91.6 per cent of the large and well-run Luneng Group's stock to mysterious private holders who paid only a tiny fraction of the company's net worth. Luneng was then jointly bought back by the public sector two years later, in the process losing at least 70 billion yuan of public money. This was a case of the post-Cultural Revolution bureaucratic bourgeoisie not even needing to be explicitly unlawful.[62] The obscure affairs about HNA Group may never come to light, but one fact is unmistakable: an original SOE with a huge input of state capital from the Guangdong Development Bank has not only been completely privatized even without having gone through a process of buying, but it has also moved abroad, magically transformed for tax purposes into a US-based charity foundation. These highly complex transactions involved many secret deals, often with no publicly traceable information. There was also the two-step procedure of privatization implicating government insiders, first through the creation of fake employee shareholdings, and then by moving abroad the majority or entirety of the shares now held by private individuals. Experiments with genuine workers' shareholdings were discussed in a State Council document in 2016 and elsewhere, but as yet they have remained negligible.

The 'mixed ownership reform' (*hungai*) is currently a national campaign. Li Rongrong, then chairman of SASAC, restated in March 2017 that this policy was to be implemented through asset management companies, diversification of SOE equities and pooling private capital with state capital. The government pledged to make 'substantial progress', especially in the electricity, petroleum, natural gas, railways, civil aviation, telecommunications, finance and defence industries.[63] As *hungai* has been accelerated since the 2017 nineteenth party congress, in

---

62 Li Qiyan and Wang Xiaobing, 'Who's Luneng?', *Caijing Magazine* 176, 8 January 2007.
63 Xinhua News, *China Daily*, 10 March 2017.

April 2019, Gree Electric Appliances, the biggest SOE in Zhuhai, Guangdong, announced that it would sell its state shares, a majority holding
worth more than 40 billion yuan, to repair its ownership structure. The
heavy machining manufacturer XCMG, already resumed as a SOE by
heavy state reinvestment, was set to receive $2.26 billion from foreign
investors in exchange for a total of 46 per cent stockholding by the end of
2020, reducing state-controlled capital to just 25 per cent.[64] The SASAC
clarified late in the year that its approach of managing the capital of solely
state-owned or majority state-controlled companies is not applicable to
newer entities during and after *hungai*, including Chinese FDI abroad. In
September 2020, Vice Premier Liu He recapitulated the task of 'mergers
and restructures of state and private enterprises', with SEOs' 'special role'
of protecting social welfare and national economic security in a challenging time. He appeared unaware of the obvious inconsistency between
these high expectations and the policy that has pushed China's once
glorious state sector well on the way to obscurity.

If profit maximization for shareholders is both legitimized and
uncurbed, SOEs will no longer be accountable either to the state or to
the whole people. Indeed, their ownership structure has been increasingly infused by foreign capital and their earnings distributed as bonuses
and dividends, not to mention as salaries to highly paid managers who,
by the way, are ranked by bureaucratic grades. The very nature of the
state sector and the state itself becomes questionable, since the sector
founded on the state capital of the socialist accumulation, including
what the revolution gained from 'expropriating the expropriators', has
been transformed not merely by privatization but by a definitively
changed state in its direction of resource allocation and investment
decisions upon appropriating SOE surpluses. Meanwhile, financial
institutional reforms have encouraged not only shadow banking and
other high-return yet risky innovations, but they have also allowed state
banks to make lavish profits as the real economy has struggled with
funding and liquidity. Such practices belie the public function of state
banks – their very *raison d'être*.[65] If private interests can grow so

---

64 For Xugong, see CCMA, info.cncma.org/2015/12/07110531261.shtml; and Gree,
Kunlun Research Institute, mp.weixin.qq.com/s/z3hd0Pb6KwQuqx7p_281dw.

65 Robert Wade, 'A New Global Financial Architecture?', *New Left Review* 46, July/
August 2007: 127.

entwined with the nominally socialist state, the latter is their best guarantor or, rather, hostage. Neoliberalization in China is not confined to the economy; it is also transforming the state in a mutually entwined process.

Throughout rural and urban China, both de facto and explicit privatization have been 'accomplished not by the dismantling of state power, but by a program to reconstitute it.'[66] The PRC state, tied variously to private and foreign capital, demonstrates once again how a neoliberal capitalist project is not only far from any form of anti-state, but indeed requires state articulation and imposition. A powerful state is needed for the local adaptation of global neoliberalization, something that bridges the assumed gap between state intervention and market liberalization. The common view – that the Chinese state continues to be interventionist – may not be wrong but it is certainly imprecise: it omits the vital element of the exact nature of this newly reinvented state. From local governments being 'entrepreneurial agents' fostering private business with land and capital, to 'China Inc.', a state that holds vast control levers 'to play out in huge swaths of the economy',[67] state and market in China are not separable, let alone mutually antagonistic. State-led privatization, financial opening or marketization of public utilities and services speaks volumes.

Historically, in the Marxist analysis, the role of the capitalist state is inherent in the genesis and expansion of capital. This insight is widely shared. As Fernand Braudel postulated, it has always been the case that 'capitalism only triumphs when it becomes identified with the state, when it is the state'; Karl Polanyi put it just as sharply, claiming, against the 'stark utopia' of a self-regulating market, that 'laissez-faire was planned.'[68] What makes China exceptional is not that its state is interventionist in distorting the market, but how its market distortions have hijacked the state. Foreign and private capital that have acquired SOEs,

---

66 Dali Yang, *Remaking the Chinese Leviathan: Market Transition and the Politics of Governance in China*, Stanford, CA: Stanford University Press, 2004: 108.

67 Mark Wu, 'The "China, Inc." Challenge to Global Trade Governance', *Harvard International Law Journal* 57, 2016: 1001–63.

68 Fernand Braudel, *Afterthoughts on Material Civilization and Capitalism*, Baltimore, MD: Johns Hopkins University Press, 1977: 64; Karl Polanyi, *The Great Transformation: The Political and Economic Origins of Our Time*, Boston, MA: Beacon, 2001: 141.

not by following but by breaking or ignoring normal market rules, is an example. Capitalism with Chinese characteristics, neither laissez-faire nor Keynesian, neither state capitalism nor a capitalist state, retains 'duality between economic and political power and between central state direction and local party autonomy'.[69] It binds the state and market together to the extent that any contradiction between the logic of political authority and the logic of market can be smoothed over. Post-socialist conditions then add to this bureaucratic neoliberal reign a corporatist character. Such a state proves indispensable for a globalizing 'mixed economy'. What we then see is that bureaucracy and neoliberalism are compatible with one another through the assimilative neoliberalization of the Chinese state, in which the political class feels the need to appease both its own people and global rule-makers.

This point is more than the developmental state's 'governing the market',[70] or that neoliberalism depends on state power to form its policies. It rather posits that the Chinese state is required, by neoliberal globalization, to create a national economy in a country as uneven – as geoeconomically vast and sociopolitically diverse – as China's. Economic neoliberalism does not reject political repression; the neoliberals depend on state endorsement and in certain sections they are the state. Again, rural *quequan* and urban *gaizhi* and *hungai* do not describe something that has perished naturally or simply become obsolete; they are politically imposed strategies, however experimental and scrappy. As the epitome of a dualism of state socialist legacies and neoliberal capitalist novelties, the bureaucratized, neoliberalized and corporatized Chinese state, if consolidated, can be world-shaking. Globally, neoliberalism may have declined after 2008, but capitalism has not – and in China it still is running its course. There is never a Hayekian 'spontaneous' market transition. It was wishful thinking on Giovanni Arrighi's part to see the 'Chinese miracle' as exemplary of 'Smithian growth', past and present.[71] Meanwhile, even though it was never a monolith, the PRC state is now ever more fractured, reflecting the divisions within the party,

69 Michael Mann, *The Sources of Social Power. Vol. 4: Globalization, 1945–2011*, Cambridge: Cambridge University Press, 2013: 234.

70 Robert Wade, *Governing the Market: Economic Theory and the Role of Government in East Asian Industrialization*, Princeton, NJ: Princeton University Press, 1990.

71 Giovanni Arrighi, *Adam Smith in Beijing: Lineages of the Twenty-First Century*, London: Verso, 2007: 329.

divisions that have repercussions for the regime's power base. Its post-socialist component still guards state power ideologically and organizationally, buttressing as much as defying its profoundly transformed socioeconomic institutions.

6

The remaking of class and social relations

The restructuring of the Chinese economy has simultaneously been a process of reshaping both its productive relations and social relations, amounting to what William Hinton described as a 'great reversal' of the Communist Revolution.[1] The state has played a pivotal role while also redefining itself with a shifting support base. Still ruled by a Communist Party, the reformist state shows a strong capacity to adapt, cultivating and incorporating a new economic elite. But at the same time, it is also seriously engaged in anti-poverty and other *minsheng* (people's welfare) projects so as to maintain legitimation and stability. With its fully geared 'ideological state apparatus', the state's power has relied on an iron-fist approach to organized dissent. The result is a unique form of government, with the corporatist character of a mingled bureaucratic neoliberalism being facilitated as much as constrained by a post-socialism entailing the socialist legacies. These tensions of the double-path dependency between pre-reform socialist experiments and post-reform capitalist integration are striking. The latter is no longer tentative or politically hidden behind ideological euphemism, as it has been internalized in the mainstream Chinese consciousness. Yet certain values of China's revolutionary century remain remarkably powerful, not so much because they are unchanged in constitutional

---

1 William Hinton, *The Great Reversal: The Privatization of China, 1978–1989*, New York: Monthly Review Press, 1990.

terms or retained in the party rhetoric, but because they are a legitimate weapon of resistance. As a language of protest, socialism is more
meaningful for class and social movements and hence central to a
sensitive discursive struggle.

These changes and disjunctions have created fresh spaces for political realignments, as well as new possibilities and challenges for class
politics and class consciousness. E. P. Thompson famously argued that
class experiences and identities are not fixed at the point of production
or distribution, but are formed and transformed through class struggle.
This is not only a socioeconomic but also a cultural process, reflecting
the sorrows and aspirations of shared lives. Beyond class, negotiations
between and among identities and their articulations are constant at
both individual and collective levels. In a globalizing political economy
like China's, the relationship between labour and capital is influenced
by the relationships between (central and local) state and labour and
those between state and capital, including foreign capital. All must be
understood against the background of an unevenly evolving system of
global capitalism in which China is a weighty and growing participant.
The evolving Chinese positioning in globalization is above all also
critical to the country's own mutating class, regional, sectoral, ethnic
and gender structures and relations. 'Class' is politically too sensitive to
be mentioned in the official rhetoric, but not only does it remain
analytically indispensable but it is also destined to return in an impending transformative politics.

From the politics of recognition to a muted class language

The Chinese Communist Revolution was not only about class liberation but was also a national populist movement. It mobilized the
population across class, gender and ethnicity, and particularly around
the multi-class peasantry. Along the way, a sovereign people or *renmin*
emerged through mass line, people's war and united front politics,
transforming what were once the passive objects of history into its
subjective agents. In this, the collective identity of *renmin* is more than
what in the common understanding as a totalizing national people
formed through the political articulation of popular will. It is, like
class, not pre-given, but created to be the historical subject. Hence, the

conceptual subtlety of the people's revolutionary rebirth is that 'class' (understood not as a static designation but as a dynamic political process) is not displaced. Rather, it is core to the communist theorization, fully embraced as the key link among Mao's best-known political contentions. The vast and variously constituted masses in revolutionary China were identified through class and class alliance in accordance with concrete historical situations.

Class then, as in Göran Therborn's words, offered a 'compass of orientation' aimed 'towards the classes of the toiling people, the exploited, oppressed and disadvantaged in all their variety'.[2] Unlike contemporary populism on the left and right alike, which draws a demarcation between directional elites and the spontaneous masses, in the Chinese socialist vocabulary class was the foundation of the people. Generic signifiers – such as the people, the labouring people and the revolutionary masses – were far from abstract or empty, therefore, but were themselves founded in class and used as class markers. The fact that such iconic phrases as *people's sovereignty* and *working-class leadership* have risen and fallen synchronously since 1949 vindicates their mutual connotations. Indeed, the socialist project, as Walter Benjamin saw it, was 'to turn the mass into a class'. Marx's conception, more specifically, was to organize 'the proletariat into a class' through class struggle and revolutionary parties.[3] Chinese revolutionary socialism demonstrated this possibility, as the communist party ideologically and practically integrated these political categories.

Linguistically, the term 'people' or *min* in traditional Chinese carries the meaning of a disregarded populace and the justice of their latent power and resistance. Whereas in English the word 'mass' conjures up the loss of individuality in an indistinct crowd, the mass line in revolutionary China meant to amplify the worth of individuals as a collective subject. In its origins of revolutionary empowerment, the dynamic synthesis was what Gramsci identified as the *modern prince* and *subaltern*, as well as the *popolo-nazione*. The class-substance of the *Chinese*

---

2 Göran Therborn, 'Class in the Twenty-First Century', *New Left Review* 78, November/ December, 2012: 26, 29; and 'New Masses?', *New Left Review* 85, January/February, 2014.

3 Eli Zaretsky, 'To Turn the Mass into a Class', *London Review of Books*, 20 December 2019; Leo Panitch, 'The Two Revolutionary Classes of the *Manifesto*', in Terrell Carver and James Farr, eds, *The Cambridge Companion to the Communist Manifesto*, Cambridge: Cambridge University Press, 2015: 127–9.

people was constructed through the sovereignty of people and their new state, with a threefold reason: The referents of composite-class signifiers were historically derived from the dual-natured communist revolution of broad common struggles; the revolution's united front was predominantly powered by the popular classes around a worker-peasant alliance; and China as an oppressed nation striving for liberation acquired a class-like status and consciousness in world politics. The whole constellation of these conceptual constructions thus signifies class and class power. In the Chinese context, this same line runs through thinking about gender in relation to women's liberation, and nationality in relation to ethnic equality. Further still, 'the subaltern classes by definition, are not unified and cannot unite until they are able to become a "State".'[4] Thus the revolutionary creation of the PRC led not to a body politic of 'multitude: the name of the poor,'[5] but sovereignty of liberated labouring classes, the name of the people. The universality of such a subjectivity follows the logic of Marx's proletariat, which can only emancipate itself by emancipating all.

The discursive construction of class has to be materialist in its economic underpinning. The opening passage of Mao's 1925 class analysis remains a classic. There, Mao asked, 'Who are our enemies? Who are our friends? This is the foremost question for the revolution.' He went on to delineate rural and urban class divisions and their implications in an ongoing revolutionary upheaval. A correct revolutionary strategy depended on such a class analysis evolving with the changing socioeconomic conditions and political opportunities, locally, nationally and internationally. The centrality of the distinction between friend and enemy and its accompanying complexities bypassed many of the revolution's critics who dismissed the class character of the CCP, and consequently the authenticity and immensity of its revolutionary and socialist undertakings. This is also where ideological construction and destruction throughout Chinese revolutions and reforms can be gauged. Perhaps the greatest difficulty for any socialist transformative politics in China today is that this distinction remains unclarified.

---

4 Gramsci, *Selections from the Prison Notebooks*: 52.

5 Michael Hardt and Antonio Negri, *Commonwealth*, Cambridge, MA: Harvard University Press, 2011: 39.

While *the people* was defined both positively, as constituting multiple classes, and negatively, against their enemies, the exploitative classes had ceased to exist in China's economic reality by 1956, following land reform and the socialist transformation. With the elimination of landlordism and capitalism, the old class labels would no longer reflect any class position regarding the means and relations of production. The only ownership forms remaining were the 'whole people' and collectives. Yet the previously affixed economic class categories continued to determine social and political statuses. Discrimination against people with the wrong class background emerged, along with other social disparities. Mao called for the resumption of class struggle after 1956, and carried it out at the ideological level right through to the Cultural Revolution; some devastating experiences of this phase prompted the subsequent deradicalization after 1976 that renounced class struggle once and for all. Meanwhile, real and perceived material necessities made the turn to a market economy appealing. The irony, however, is that market reforms partially restored pre-revolutionary class systems while also producing new ones, thereby fostering the inequalities and injustice that reaffirmed the earlier Maoist perspective. Above all, the abandonment of the foundational communist idea of the dignity and wellbeing of labour caused a deep post-socialist crisis in an otherwise straitjacketed labour movement.

Looking at the historical loss of a particular politics of recognition can be instructive. In the initial phase, as 'low wages, full employment' in pursuit of industrialization depressed consumption, the general material shortage was effectively compensated for, not only with a rudimentary social security system but also with a beaming ideology that sanctified the glory and agency of labour. Peasants and workers, especially industrial workers, enjoyed political esteem and social prestige, to the extent that they were tasked with 're-educating' intellectuals in the factories and fields. The shift to the dominance of market values, therefore, could not be a mere economic matter. Along with material deprivation, the mental and psychological implications of the shift could be just as shattering, as in the case of SOE workers who had taken pride in their work-related identities and relied on their work unit networks for daily support. The strong sense of socio-political entitlements among labour was rooted in a social revolution with a labour-centred worldview. With privatization, 'China's workers have lost their world,' lamented Marc Blecher; 'a class that was so well treated, mighty, confident and active in the recent past now essentially rolled over or, better, allowed itself to be rolled over.'[6]

The rationale for replacing the socialist social contract between state and labour was established by refusing class language and politics. Privatization inevitably redefined that contract, along with its basis in a once socialist moral economy. The positivist chimera of the modern normality of social stratification subsumed class discourse in order to obscure class relations, producing a collective amnesia as capitalist development tore society apart. As the noise, or silence, about class affected everyday infra-politics, the exercise of power could be traced in the changing glossary of political terms. Adopting the Weberian terminology of 'strata' in ideology and communication was a tacit negation of the socialist past, as well as a frontal rejection of the labour movement. The labouring classes, hitherto the backbone of the communist regime, were put into 'vulnerable social groups' both in the official press and in public perception. The severity of reinstated class relations of domination and exploitation was then 'legitimized' in a 'theory' adopted into the party constitution in 2002. Henceforward the CCP was to represent all classes, directly negating the working-class vanguard. The problem is that even if the language was muted, the underlying realities showed through. Discursive remedies, from 'harmonious society' to 'the Chinese dream', only signposted inequalities and disharmonies, and hence the ruling order's fear and its crisis of ideology. The way that government at all levels muffled criticism and clamped down on protests amounts to a titanic act of violence on labour, both physical and symbolic, dismantling socialist class power. This dispossession of the cognitive and organizational capacity of workers has helped ensure the lack of a more conscious counter-hegemonic struggle.

The leap from excessive class ideology in the context of a basically egalitarian society and the subsequent stifling of such politics with the onset of class polarization and conflict is one of the great ironies of Chinese communism in power. Initially, a highly subjective conception of 'class differentiation based on political and cultural capital' was

---

6 Marc Blecher, 'Hegemony and Workers' Politics in China', *China Quarterly* 170, 2002: 283, 287.

applied to achieve class levelling.[7] But as family background was ossified in class categorization, this became confused with a misguided
'class struggle' of arbitrary persecutions. Later the term 'class' became
taboo in an officially sanctioned interpretation of development, where
anything reminiscent of radical egalitarianism must be disavowed. To
depoliticize the (re)adaption of global capitalist relations in the name of
reform is to make a U-turn from class war waged by revolution to
counterrevolutionary moves of overturning the original socialist
commitment. The paradoxes here are readily seen in the estranged
relationship between state and labour, amid the ascent of a capital-serv-
ing political elite as well as a politically conformist middle class.

The post–Cultural Revolution class realignment and re-bureaucrati-
zation happened precisely when any discourse around class was shut
down, a chilling reminder of the Maoist vigilance against the formation
of a new class internal to the party. As political advantage and economic fortune colluded in the crooked market of privatization, there
was a fusion of public power and private money that had never been
predicted in the theory of Cultural Revolution. As noted, the blending
of bureaucracy and private and foreign capital eroded the state protection of strategic sectors as much as it damaged the autonomy and
capacity of the state itself. A segment of princelings managed to leverage their background capital to amass vast wealth in the most profitable
areas, particularly energy, utilities, pharmaceuticals and real estate;
some also gained management and regulatory positions of responsibility in the financial and other sectors. Clearly distinguishable from the
socialist state capital of traditional SOEs, the managers of the giant
restructured state companies were treated like capitalist CEOs and
earned many times more than regular workers. An unprecedented class
has taken shape, with its own powerful political entrepreneurs and
technocratic experts. Additionally, since these wealthy notables are
overrepresented in legislative and consultative bodies and even sit in
various government offices, they have bifurcated the state.

Closely linked to these capitalist bureaucrats is a layer of compradors
mediating between official rentiers and international capital through

---

7 Joel Andreas, following Pierre Bourdieu's class theory possibly influenced by Mao,
in *Rise of the Red Engineers: The Cultural Revolution and the Origins of China's New
Class*, Stanford, CA: Stanford University Press, 2009: 262.

licensing, brokerage, commercial and legal advice, and delivery of favours, in exchange for financial and other returns. Here, the state system's symbiosis with business did not resemble the post-revolutionary degeneration symbolized by the capitalist roaders. Rather, entangled private desires and pursuits were institutionalized to form a re-emerging bureaucratic-comprador interest, with intellectual and media circles tending to be complacent. The embezzlement of public wealth into private possession often followed hidden rules so that no laws were directly broken. An indication of such counter-revolutionary mutations is the inuring of rent-seeking, which has facilitated the concentration of wealth and power. According to reports by the International Consortium of Investigative Journalists, the Chinese political and corporate elites have used offshore companies to store their fortunes secretly, while an estimated $1–4 trillion in untraced assets was moved out of China in the first decade of the twenty-first century.[8] Once again, as Mao warned, the decay of socialism will hardly lead to bourgeois democracy, but more likely to a capitalist-fascist dictatorship.

The only exception of the official class denial is the growth of a middle class, which is celebrated as a manifestation of modernity and prosperity with a stabilizing promise, thus compromising or even negating the politically charged meaning of class itself. Benefiting from the opening of markets, most self-identified members of this class are politically conservative, including a celebrated 'global class' of cosmopolitan professionals and technocrats with market skills and transnational links. This phenomenon provides one explanation for the transition being an 'abnormal' one, without the expected democratization. Conceptually, the middle class is elusive, with fuzzy boundaries and 'contradictory class locations'.[9] In the Chinese context, the label is even more obscure. By one estimation, which used a crude definition of the Chinese middle class as those at least earning at least $5.5 a day, it comprised more than 300 million people in 2020. Whatever its size and temper, whether of alienation or distaste, this alleged middle class is clearly too dependent on the existing order from which it benefits to

---

8 Oliver Campbell, 'Report Exposes Chinese Elite's Offshore Tax Havens,' World Socialist Web Site, 30 January 2014, wsws.org/en/articles/2014/01/30/virg-j30.html.

9 Erik Olin Wright, *The Debate on Classes*, London: Verso, 1989: 4–6, 24–8.

be a dissenting force, particularly so long as it continues to be immersed in consumerist culture. Its structure of feelings is divorced from that of the poor. In one typical example from 2014, a supposedly sympathetic television anchor lectured a group of young migrants in Beijing: 'Do not use the word "exploitation" so easily, and learn to be thankful to your bosses who give you jobs.' The largely middle-class audience applauded approvingly, leaving the workers who were trying to expose a tiny bit of their misery in tears. The aspiration to a middle-class life-style is not even relevant to the struggles experienced by lower-class labour, regardless of the illusion of social mobility.

A more interesting question here – developing the classical riddle over the nature of a salaried bourgeoisie of lower-level managers, white-collar petty-bourgeois wage labour and self-employed or free-lance and piecework earners – is whether the new brain workers and digital labourers in the growing technology and service sectors will constitute an independent class in the future. Global financial capital has increasingly operated through a techno-economic paradigm of intelligence-based and networked economy made possible by revolu-tionary advances in information and communication technologies, including automation, digitization and artificial intelligence. These advances are transfiguring class trends in China too, destabilizing everything from macroeconomic policies to household budgeting, and fashioning youth cultures from fervent consumption to internet addic-tion. So-called cognitive capitalism engages a biopolitical and cyberproductive workforce in 'immaterial labour' that simultaneously undercuts and enriches capital's ability of accumulating profits and rents. As labour processes diversify, knowledge workers gain more autonomy and discretion, particularly those who are younger and better trained, being more capable of innovation and more conscious of self-realization. Exploitation and domination also take some inventive forms, accommodating more decentralized, horizontal labour coordin-ation. Productive flexibility entails unprecedented freedom for both capital and labour.

Notwithstanding the conceptual issues of an ever more complex division of labour and class differentiation, a pressing question is the class nature of intellectual labour. Is the issue a shrinking or even dying working class, or is it rather its enormous expansion? Is there a cultural proletariat as opposed to a cultural bourgeoisie in the realm of cultural production and circulation? Should not the working classes – plural – incorporate the vast majority of a heterogeneous working population defined not by wage labour but by the structural relationships of a capitalist mode of production which assumes a variety and often a mixture of forms? A recent debate in China revealed a '996' pattern of office workers in private industry – at least twelve hours a day and six days a week of frantic working, many without secure employment and fringe benefits or a stable income. Such workers are unsure of their class identity, admitting that they are unable to afford the consumer capacity of what is usually ascribed to the middle class. While they are still better off than the majority of China's blue workforce, they too lack autonomy and security. The knowledge economy obviously cannot develop fully within such dysfunctional capitalist labour–capital relations. An alternative framework is yet to crystallize.

Workers' subalternization and their organizational dilemma

Marx's two-class theory has been newly vindicated during China's export-oriented industrial growth, powered by a massively expanded army of workers, including those in the state sector as well as by two generations of rural migrants. The National Statistics Bureau (NSB) reported that by the end of 2018 the largest share of the urban workforce comprised rural migrants numbering 288 million, or about 37 per cent of the total national workforce. Previously protected SOE workers concentrated in PRC's industrial hubs – machinery in the north-east, oil production in the north-west and Third Front industries in the south-east – were hit hard by privatization and its long and painful aftermath. With the dismissal of around 50 million workers from state and collectively owned enterprises between 1997 and 2002, the system of socialist planning over production, consumption and distribution was instantly broken. Many workers were thus caught in limbo, losing not only the iron rice bowl but also their dignity and any input concerning investment and surplus allocation. Joel Andreas documented the 'two conversions' legalized by the 1994 company law and 1995 labour law on marketizing companies and labour respectively. China's largely private manufacturing-for-export sector then 'perfected a high turnover employment model featuring low wages, extreme labour intensity, and highly coercive discipline'.[10] Industrialization was severed from working-class politics and economic democracy.

The downsizing of the state sector was accompanied by the equally drastic growth of the private economy. The rural dwellers who had been driven off the land mostly moved into private factories of the coastal sunbelt as low-skilled assembly workers. *Dagong*, literally 'selling labour', was how they described their unprotected lives featuring social exclusion and personal and family hardship. Since the 1980s, in the semi-sweatshop conditions marked by long hours, meagre pay, unpaid overtime, unhealthy night shifts and other workplace hazards, fines and physical punishments have become widespread. Private capital operates cheaply by ignoring the minimal labour, safety and environmental regulations that exist. Utterly degrading conditions, including restricted dormitory living and routine abuse by bullying shop-floor managers, led to a shocking string of suicides at various campuses of Foxconn, Apple's largest supplier, around 2010. This 'one-dimensional' dystopia saw the factory swallowing up its workers 'body and soul', depriving their labour of beauty, dignity or any meaning at all.[11]

In the background was the fall of the first-generation socialist working class, or 'the dusk of an entire social world, together with all the hopes and ideals that created it'.[12] While wages have advanced in recent years, job insecurity due to incomplete or fake contracts and a boss culture in which workers garner little respect have remained rampant. An increasingly high-tech labour regime has led to a series of abuses and negative consequences: line managers in Foxconn factories using stopwatches and computerized devices to monitor workers in order to maximize the prescribed quota within the required timeframe; delivery platforms automating work assignments causing spikes in traffic accidents; or sanitation workers being forced to wear a GPS device that raises an alarm if they are still for twenty minutes. Under capital's watchful eye furnished also by a variety of algorithm software, the crudest form of surveillance capitalism thrives. So while recent rises in

---

10 Joel Andreas, *Disenfranchised: The Rise and Fall of Industrial Citizenship*, Oxford: Oxford University Press, 2019: 193, 198.

11 Ban Wang, 'Dignity of Labour', in Christian Sorace, Ivan Franceschini and Nicholas Loubere, eds, *Afterlives of Chinese Communism*, Canberra and London: ANU and Verso, 2019: 73.

12 Lü Xinyu, 'Ruins of the Future', *New Left Review* 31, January/February 2005: 126.

Chinese labour costs may have lessened the downward pressure on jobs and wages globally, they have not reversed China's depressed labour standards. Meanwhile, labour-intensive foreign companies are leaving, inadvertently deindustrializing the Chinese economy.

Despite the supposedly levelling effects of the labour market, conditions and experiences differ between public and private firms, domestic and foreign companies, formal and informal sectors, contracted, sub-contracted and dispatched jobs, and so on. Given the brutally competitive export market, small business owners have found themselves squeezed by loan and liquidity issues by policies biased to favour big and foreign capital. Wholly or partially missing employer contributions to pensions and other legally required social security funds has become common. Institutional, regional, sectoral and residential barriers have continued to divide workers. The commodification of labour has also led to the informalization and casualization of employment, forming a huge and still swelling pseudo-class, a precariat of intermediaries and agency workers.[13] According to Philip Huang, contracted full-time labour was less than 10 per cent of China's formal economy workforce in the early 2010s, accounting for only 16.8 per cent of national employment.[14] Young migrants have become more inclined to engage in flexible services than factory jobs; the very rapid spread of online platforms and gig workers, from Didi (Uber) drivers and outsourced *waimai xiaoge* (delivery boys) to hourly hired carers and sub-subcontracted repair or renovation day labourers, has only strengthened the trend. The stated policy goal of reducing informality and outsourcing, meanwhile, has yet to be legislated and implemented. The changed social contract between labour and a deformed 'workers' state' helps to explain the subalternization of labour as a necessary part of the capitalist class and accumulation process.

One dilemma faced by workers is the legalization of labour rights. The 2008 labour contract law, revised since the 1994 law, achieved some protective measures for workers as well as the mystification of their rights. Yet in essence this was a landmark ruling by a government that

13 Eli Friedman and Ching Kwan Lee, 'Remaking the World of Chinese Labour: A 30-Year Retrospective', *British Journal of Industrial Relations*, 48:3, 2010: 510–16.

14 Philip Huang, 'Misleading Chinese Legal and Statistical Categories: Labor, Individual Entities, and Private Enterprises', *Modern China* 39:4, 2013: 347–79.

refused to back labour on political and moral grounds beyond legisla-tion. Industrial relations have since been moved into the 'objective' legal domain, where they are seen as a straightforward matter of judicial process rather than social justice. The fact that atomized workers must seek arbitration through the apolitical path of litigation and lawsuits indicates the loss of state as an institutionalized class power. With formal legality replacing the state representation of working-class inter-ests – or the legal state usurping the workers' state – individual plaintiffs and court rulings have no means to challenge management, given the sheer imbalance of power between capital and labour. Since the legal approach is essentially individualistic, it limits the expression of class will and action. Ideational legal formalism is thus a typical instance of depoliticization, with labour law functioning as a legitimate excuse for the dissolution of the state's commitments and obligations. Here, iso-lated legal redresses can be no substitute. Moreover, the whole judicial and penal system is useless for the masses of precarious job holders who do not even have the papers to go to the court. As late as 2013, 82 per cent of China's 40 million construction workers had not signed any contract with their multilayered bosses.[15] The situation has not improved much since. Legal appeals were dismissed on the basis that without an official contract any right could not be proven to be granted. Corruption of the legal system by money and power only made things worse for the weak.

At the same time that labour legislation was leaving the domination of capital intact, privatization led to the disorganization of workers. The All-China Federation of Trade Unions (ACFTU) – a corporatist arm of both state and society – has undergone various reforms, but has suffered an inevitable political decline. Legally mandated by the 1992 Trade Union Law (revised in 2001 and 2009), all workplaces with twenty-five or more employees must have a union branch of 'voluntarily associated workers', and their assemblies should periodically vote for their union representatives. The law even compelled Walmart, among other multi-nationals operating in China, to comply. However, such unions are not workers' own, and not only because they hold few democratic elections

---

15 Pun Ngai and Wuqiong Wenqian, 'The China Dream of a Contract: Investigation in the Situation of Labour Contract for Construction Workers in 2013', *References*, 20 February 2014.

and barely advance workers' demands and class consciousness. They are largely decorative, designed to serve a state that is only formally assumed to represent the fundamental interests of the working class, and are not tasked to lead a labour movement but rather pressured to prevent and restrain unrest. Many millions of the mobile workers scattered in the informal economy are not even nominally unionized. Under the reform policy of keeping a 'good business environment' for foreign capital, 'unions are weak at the enterprise level and are therefore unable to overcome endemic collusion between capital and local governments.'[16]

Would independent unionization be an option? So far, any such organization has been blocked, not only by the legalized monopoly of the official unions and police suppression, but also by labour's own ambivalence. Despite frequent protests and strikes through the 2010s, workers were trapped in a remarkable post-socialist dilemma, torn between demanding state backing, however distant it may have seemed, and attempting an alternative, unpromising and potentially costly path. To opt for independent organization is to give consent to regime neutrality, or to relinquish what the state had promised and was indeed constitutionally and legally bound to offer. This reluctance to let go what should be in the nature of a socialist state – the political power and socioeconomic wellbeing of its workforce – blurred despair and hope. It was the inheritance from a more labour-centred past, alongside the continuing state monopoly of both policy and symbolic spheres, that created this paradoxical and confusing situation and still impedes the articulation of any programme for organized labour to regain power. Besides, even if collective bargaining were to be achieved, it might merely facilitate reforms rather than reverse the current exploitative and oppressive productive and social relations. Legal and organizational rationalization in today's China only denotes workers' loss of a partisan state for the workers. This loss of 'sacred labour' – a century-old motto – represents an aggregate defeat of the Chinese working class and leaves behind the magnificent history of workers' struggle, sacrifice and triumph.

---

16 Eli Freidman, *Insurgency Trap: Labour Politics in Postsocialist China*, Ithaca, NY: Cornell University Press, 2014: 5.

The unmaking of a revolutionary and collective peasantry

Having discussed China's peasant revolution and collective land in previous chapters, we must address the question of how the internally
heterogeneous peasantry, made a generic class category as the protagonist
of the communist project, has collapsed into a segment of discrete
farmers. This is perhaps an even greater retreat for Chinese socialism
than the workers' disorientation, given that revolutionary rural mobilization and organization – in defiance of European Marxist theory – had
managed to remake a 'petty bourgeoisie' into conscious communist
followers. If the Third World revolutions have all more or less transformed their agrarian populations, the CCP is still unique in having
continued its land revolution to pursue agricultural planning and com-
munization just as sweepingly. Indeed, for socialism to survive, its
own primitive accumulation must be done internally through reforms to
agriculture and the organization of the peasantry. The twentieth century
saw China's rural masses as the builders of socialism, rising from the
margins to change the world. In this, the Chinese conceptualization
and practice of class alliance and class struggle has complicated the
standard Marxian law of industrial proletarianization. Nowhere else is
the contrast more striking than in the gap between this indigenous
revolutionary agency and the conventional image of peasant conservatism and passivity. Premised on communist leadership, the collective
identity of peasantry, allied with the working class, cannot be considered
premodern or pre-political. It is constructed as a political category.

Moreover, the CCP's rural strategy was based on a class line, of which
political education was a central element. The party was aware of 'the
serious problem' of educating the peasantry from the outset, given its
predominantly rural origin.[17] This was attempted through the creation
of a political space for peasant participation, organization and socialization. 'Peaceful land redistribution' from above was rejected for political
reasons. The peasants had to shake off their old mentality, their 'spontaneous tendency towards capitalism' (in Lenin's analysis), and indeed the
whole old world around them, by their own movement of class struggle.
The party then engaged itself in peasant struggles both institutionally
and discursively. Institutionally, throughout state building before and

17 Mao, 'On the People's Democratic Dictatorship' (1949), *Selected Works Vol. IV*: 419.

after 1949, peasant activists and leaders, without becoming professional bureaucrats, had been absorbed into the party, tiers of government, and central and local legislature bodies, bringing their intimate knowledge about the needs and voices from the grassroots. This was an inventive form of democracy, thoroughly lost today.

Discursively, the peasant masses were enabled by the communist articulation of their suffering, resistance and demands. 'Subalterns' in China could speak 'in a vocabulary provided by the state in the process of revolution', and they understood it as their own.[18] This was empowering, however limited or homogenizing that vocabulary might be. 'Speaking bitterness', commonly practised during land reforms, exemplified the efficacy of the party's effort at consciousness raising. It taught the labouring masses a fundamental truth, also nearly and astonishingly lost today, about the value of their hard labour, phrased in the simple question 'who has fed whom?' – was it the landlords who had offered their tenants and hired labourers a means of living, or was it rather the other way around, that they lived off the backs of the poor peasants? Something similar was discussed among factory workers, in terms of jobs and wages. The peasant masses, learning to transcend their material and cultural limitations, were set to accomplish a great mental and affective self-transformation through political education and participation – subjectivity and emancipation depend on the oppressed classes to gain the ability to speak for themselves.

The peasant question is important in the Marxist tradition, and was discussed by Engels and Lenin among others. Gramsci's appreciation of the political weight of the peasantry and semi-proletarian masses came independently of the Chinese experience; the latter went much farther. He argued, in line with the late Marx, that the 'proletarian act' did not have to be lone and violent, if only because the agricultural proletariat was 'familiar with the traditional forms of communal communism', and hence 'prepared for the change to a new form of society'.[19] Instead of crushing backward rurality, revolution in China was to lift it onto an advancing new path through political struggle and education. Mao's 1927

---

18 Gail Hershatter, 'The Subaltern Talks Back: Reflections on Subaltern Theory and Chinese History', *Positions* 1:1, 1993: 107–8.

19 Antonio Gramsci, 'Workers and Peasants' (1918–19), in Gramsci, *Political Writings, 1910–1920*, ed. Quintin Hoare, trans. John Mathews, London: Lawrence and Wishart, 1977: 29.

report from Hunan offers a vivid example. There he described how the needed class consciousness was within the reach:

> The gods? Worship them by all means. But if you had only Lord Guan and the Goddess of Mercy and no peasant association, could you have overthrown the local tyrants and evil gentry? You have worshipped them for centuries, and they have not overthrown a single one of the local tyrants and evil gentry for you!

But the change was possible: 'Now you want to have your rent reduced. Let me ask how will you go about it? Will you believe in the gods or the peasant association?'[20] The poor and lower-middle peasants, taking the wavering middle peasants along with them, were the mainstay of the revolutionary cadres and soldiers. Throughout revolutionary socialization from 'new democracy' to 'socialist transformation', China's rural masses had proven themselves – and ought to be duly recognized as – the subject, not the object, of history.

How could such a momentous feat be undone? Major moves in recent years to reorganize village collectives – as a distant echo, if not a heroic elegy – received limited government support, while the powerful counterforces of agro-capitalism continue to mount assaults. Is it that modernization has finally arrived, as decollectivization has repositioned China's rural population? This colossal reversion in the Chinese countryside – both the purchase and the undoing of class politics – complicates the increasingly plastic, ever changing identity of a population floating across sectors and regions. Will this mean that the 'last' peasantry will disappear under conditions of global modernity? Having its origins in the commodification of land and people, alongside colonial violence and the subordination of country to city, peasant nations to industrial ones and East to West (as sketched in *The Communist Manifesto*), capitalism is targeting the earth's last remaining common land and communities. Radical thinkers declare that 'the figure of the peasant has throughout the world faded', and that the 'death of the peasantry' is cutting us off 'forever from the world of the past'.[21]

---

20 Mao, *Report on an Investigation of the Peasant Movement in Hunan*, Beijing: Foreign Language Press, 1965: 35.

21 Michael Hardt and Antonio Negri, *Multitude: War and Democracy in the Age of*

Yet, in looking at China and the global South more generally, not only does small farming still feature in the lives of nearly half the world population, but it is also a necessity for food security and a geo-ecological imperative.

There is an irony in the desire to capitalize agriculture in China, as the process will squeeze out and drain the rural source of cheap labour that capitalist accumulation has relied upon, while destroying communal social ties of a likely more humanely connected and environmentally sustainable character. The corporate offensive under a state policy that favours 'new agrarian subjects' has displaced peasants, who were thus consigned to hardship in the name of industrialization and urbanization, processes that proceeded at pace on the backs of migrant labour. According to the official reports, less than 30 per cent of China's workforce is engaged in agriculture today, down from over 70 per cent in 1978. Rural families' non-farming income has exceeded and outpaced earnings from farming, while average urban income is still around three times higher. Increasing off-farm rural labour and the casualization of migrant workers render any sharp separation between the rural and urban empirically and analytically untenable. Again in both cognitive and policy terms, agrarian issues cannot be insulated or independently solvable: they are imbricated with urban challenges, and need to be dealt with in an integral macro-perspective, as in the Chinese socialist tradition.

If the peasant question is simultaneously about migration, rural surplus labour is at the heart of the issue. TVEs had once absorbed a large portion of rural labour, delaying what later became the largest migration in human history. This episode revealed a causal linkage between decollectivization and an augmented labour surplus in rural China. Although underemployment certainly existed in a system of labour accumulation in the collective era, it was quite unlike today's debt-financed land acquisition and investments of the more recent run of hysterical capital accumulation. The meaning of *surplus* requires scrutiny, as do its outlets. The amount of labour freed from the land depends on how the rural economy operates – the intensification and diversification of agricultural production and processing, as well as

Empire, London: Penguin, 2005: 120; Eric Hobsbawm, *The Age of Extremes*, London: Penguin, 1994: 289.

industrial, service and socio-cultural developments. The issue of labour being made artificially redundant was thoroughly tackled by the cooperative movement, for example. Mao contended in 1955, by way of commenting on a series of local reports describing how idle hands had been transformed on-site into useful labour, that cooperation would liberate the masses with 'unlimited creative power'. They could channel their energies by organizing themselves across all spheres and branches of 'a more intensive and extensive production', while initiating many projects to improve their own wellbeing.[22] This prospect has vanished, along with the communes and ephemeral double-level management.

Although the formal retention of collective land and equal land rights has curbed the process of dispossession, it is rural reform that is the root cause of migrant workers being paid below the living wage. This trick – 'displacement without dispossession' – is unique among the various global types of 'accumulation by dispossession'.[23] China's avoidance of large scale direct dispossession of farmers, and hence of the formation of a visible reserve army in urban slums, or of the tribulations of landlessness, is the secret of the cheap labour that is the stigma attached to products made in China. A discrepancy between the displacement of most migrant workers and the retention of their land rights entails their basic protection against dispossession. Such incomplete labour commodification or semi-proletarianization is attributable to the way land functions as a source of subsistence and security. Accounting for a large share of the cost of labour reproduction, this function is at the root of China's reputed competitive advantage – the socialist legacy's enormous concealed contribution to continued capitalist growth. Various coercive mechanisms are at work, however, which deprive rural labour of viable options. The 'forceful expulsion' of those seeking work away from home is a result of 'the suppression of alternative (indigenous) forms of production and consumption'.[24] Disincentivized by unprofitable farming and locally deficient off-farm opportunities, they have no 'alternative to selling labour'; this interpretation, associated

22 Mao, 'Comment on "Surplus Labour Found a Way Out"', *The Socialist High Tide in the Chinese Countryside II*, Beijing: People's Publishing House, 1956: 578.

23 Henry Bernstein, 'Some Reflections on Agrarian Change in China', *Journal of Agrarian Change* 15:3, 2015: 19.

24 David Harvey, *Spaces of Global Capitalism: A Theory of Uneven Geographical Development*, London and New York: Verso, 2019: 43–4, and Harvey, *The Enigma of Capital*: 189–93.

with diversified livelihood strategies through migration, is stronger than the prevailing model of the 'Lewis turning point'.[25]

Can the labour accumulation system be repaired in post-collective conditions, then? If petty farming is still both necessary and desirable, what is its implication on the now fragmented peasant identity and outflow migration? Concerning smallholders, many economic historians agree that family management suits intensive labour due to the sector's crop cycles and eco-climate dependency. As legend has it, unlike colonial empires that relied on extractions and transferring costs overseas, the Chinese invented smart policies many centuries ago to secure fiscal stability and grain reserves for disaster relief through price mechanisms and balancing harvest variations.[26] The Soviet agrarian economist Alexander Chayanov researched how households preferred the 'self-exploitation' of the flexible division of labour, as well as preferring ethically rational distribution over profit maximization. Peasants 'organized cooperatively as an independent class' would be superior to other forms of agricultural organization.[27] Intimate mutuality among kin was considered far better than hired labour, measured by incentives, efficiency and tenacity: it could contain the diminishment of arable land and augment yields. Missing from Chayanov's argument, however, is the counter-story about the vulnerability of isolated petty economies.

In today's China, under severe pressures of land (and water) shortage and pollution, a cooperative economy of scope (as opposed to scale) would be optimal for a vertically integrated agriculture. Such a petty-bourgeois system of sort, of both market dynamism and social equity, would stimulate the advantage of joining market, state and farms together while mitigating their respective rigidities and weaknesses.[28] There could be an element of exaggeration in commercial horticultural,

25 Hao Qi and Zhonglin Li, 'Giovanni Arrighi in Beijing: Rethinking the Transformation of the Labour Supply in Rural China during the Reform Era', Political Economy Research Institute Working Paper Series, University of Massachusetts Amherst, February 2018.

26 Peter Nolan, 'The CPC and the Ancien Régime', New Left Review 115, January/February 2019: 22–3.

27 Alexander Chayanov (1930), quoted in Bernstein, Class Dynamics: 60.

28 Philip Huang, 'China's Hidden Agricultural Revolution, 1980–2010, in Historical and Comparative Perspective', Modern China 42:4, 2016: 107–114, and 'China's New-Age Small Farms and Their Vertical Integration: Agribusiness or Co-ops?', Modern China 37:2, 2011: 124–8.

poultry and fish farming in view of the changed food pattern of the Chinese population, although by one account small added-value farming now accounts for two-thirds of China's agricultural output value and one-third of its total farmland.[29] Regardless, the starting point of higher unit output or land productivity applies more generally. Even staple grain production in China would benefit from sophisticated planning and labour in multicrops, intercropping, fallow and crop rotation, plotting corners, edges, hills and vales, selecting and preserving seeds, and expanding green fertilizers and pesticides. The conservation of natural biodiversity and the eco-biosphere of an organic agro-system in a closed loop of inputs and outputs would also be labour intensive; so would land reclamation and scaling, reforestation, infrastructural works of soil, water, transportation and much else. Abundant rural labour could then be reorganized into a unique advantage of human capital for a reconciled eco-productive order.

The changing mode of accumulation and the development of factor markets in rural China has hastened the demise of the peasantry as a collective class. Even if the 'middle farmers', or the middle stratum of the farming population, have emerged with their heterogeneous origins as a pillar of contemporary agricultural labour in China, most are still small farmers. Their reorganization is the hope for rural revitalization. Besieged by the external capital of agro-investors, developers and financiers, rural China is undergoing another round of differentiation: agrarian capitalists engaging land procurement and hired labour; petty commodity producers struggling with shrinking market opportunities and mounting market volatilities less inimical to larger agribusinesses; dual-track households with long-term or seasonal absentees working whatever remains of their land, supplemented by remittances from off-farm employment; landless wage workers among the sporadically jobless poor; and petty cultivators on the brink of losing an independent livelihood.[30] All of these are fluid and conceptually plastic. Fieldwork has shown how households become subject to penetration by capital from above and below, moving continually towards commercialized

29 Huang Zongzhi, 'The Dual Governance of State and Village Community', *Open Times* 2, 2019: 28.

30 Qian Forrest Zhang, 'Class Differentiation in Rural China: Dynamics of Accumulation, Commodification and State Intervention', *Journal of Agrarian Change* 15:3, 2015, doi.org/10.1111/joac.12120; He Xuefeng, 'Who are the Peasants?', *Economic Herald* 3, 2013.

agriculture and away from self-subsistence. Even those who till and live on their own land are not free from structural capitalist relations. 'The existence of small family production neither sufficiently demonstrates non-capitalist development of agriculture nor represents an alternative to capitalism.'[31] The structurally reshaped labour regimes mediated by government and private capital define or redefine class positions, and sometimes the contentious peasant–state relationship.

The peasantry as a political figure is dismissed by some theorists of both Marxist and liberal persuasions who choose to forget the modern Chinese experience of social transformations. The collective peasant category, not to be confused with the simple reference to occupation denoted by 'farmers', have been stripped of their class identity, leading to the current plight of the unorganized rural masses. The resurgence in exploitative, superstitious, patriarchal and other old society values and forces have reordered village lives and undermined rural China's position in the national economy. Despite a formal policy of land redivision by equal use rights, for example, the male head of the household is more likely to control titles and inheritance. Henry Bernstein reminds us of the faulty agrarian populist image of peasants as 'a unitary and homogeneous, as well as virtuous and threatened, category', and of 'petty bourgeois socialism' in Marx's critique as a 'half echo of the past and half menace of the future'.[32] A vital distinction between pre-capitalist utopian agrarian socialism and a modern socialist agriculture is economic organization – rural cooperation needs government and social support in both policy and financial terms, beyond peasant spontaneity. The Chinese communists were Marxist enough to reject an agrarian socialism of a 'reactionary, backward and regressive nature'.[33] Behind the private land accumulation and labour commodification that have demobilized a distinguished peasant agency is the changed party line – a situation of 'peasants without the party' (*pace* Lucien Bianco). When the revitalization of the countryside is perceived as a task to be completed by large capitalist stakeholders, the real, autonomous managerial subjects are disregarded. Although

---

31 Yan Hairong and Chen Yiyuan, 'Agrarian Capitalization without Capitalism? Capitalist Dynamics from Above and Below in China', *Journal of Agrarian Change* 15:3, 2015: 366–91.

32 Bernstein, 'Some Reflections': 61, 45.

33 Mao, 'Letter to Qin Bangxian', 31 August 1944, *Selected Letters of Mao*, Beijing: People's Publishing House, 1983: 237–9.

party branches remain everywhere and villages are formally designated to be self-governed through villagers' assemblies, elections and committees (the 1987 Organic Law), rural governance lacks the intrinsic dynamism characteristic of the communal period.

Ultimately, if a disorganized simple commodity agriculture has no future as it faces capitalist destruction, and if eco-environmental constraints are hard on industrializing agriculture, then the only rational and modern way out is a socialist agriculture connected with socialist industries. Such an alternative would encompass upgraded industrialization, rural reorganization, and integrated social development, overcoming both the rural–urban divide sustained by the earlier internal accumulation, and its capitalist reconfiguration that sets development of the two sectors on a collision course. China's geopolitical challenges today should help policy thinking and promote a spatial strategy to prioritize the countryside. China has a hidden advantage here, in that the local spaces now being invaded by capitalist and globalized circuits were once thoroughly organized commons, from which two historical lessons can be learned. First, only a socialized national economy can incorporate the two sectors away from wasteful and toxic urban standardization while achieving sectoral equilibrium and fair exchanges. Second, direct producers' free cooperation can overcome insulated petty production, and find a locally suitable manner and degree of land concentration, machine use and application of technology under associational management. The process would also feature a renewed subject formation, resonating with, as much as transcending, a past of revolutionary mobilization and collective farming.

Contested identity, equality and autonomy: The spatial politics of citizenship

The multifaceted imperial heritage is as much a blessing as a curse for the PRC, which more or less acquired the Qing geographic and demographic configurations (though considerably diminished since the heyday of Qing expansion). This has left the country many long-drawn border issues with its neighbours, of which some are still unsettled and a few conflict-prone. A clearer cut with the past by renouncing all the unequal treaties signed under the old regimes, whether China was a victim (apparently in the majority cases) or beneficiary, could have simplified the problem. But the fact that China itself fell prey to modern imperialist subjugation necessitated revolutionary nationalism, which continued to dominate Chinese national and geopolitical thinking after 1949. Since the 2010s, however, the mutation has entered an excursion towards national capitalism, in which any self-critical reflection is blocked, along with a parallel, most worrisome alteration in the country's internal ethnic relations. Here the general background is that having skipped the 'normal' breakdown of empire common to the Eurasian trajectories, China's immense unevenness and diversity, among the Han majority (91 per cent) and the other fifty-five officially recognized minority 'nationalities', remain overriding national features. The rough coincidence of China's ethnic and regional borders, where territorial and sociological makeups often overlap, is also conspicuous. Large parts of poorer interior and frontier hinterland are nevertheless rich in natural endowment that could give any disparity an ethnic appearance exploitable in a contentious identity politics.

Historically, domination and subordination divided rulers and subjects, although imperial rulers of Han and non-Han origin alike also used a sophisticated blend of methods to manage diversities. Their strategies were variously configured but essentially about incorporation more than conquest, engaging endless amalgamation (*ronghe*) or mutual absorption rather than majority assimilation (*tonghua*). This persisted through an intensely interactive period of state formation among peoples and cultures in China. As a political construct, the Han identification was a plural amalgamation of local dialects and customs. Nevertheless, inequality was intrinsic to such empires, and an imperial legacy was the deep distrust not only on the part of the Han towards the ruling Mongol or Manchu aristocracy, but also between predatory local regimes, mostly in the hands of Han officials, and their oppressed subjects comprising multi ethnic-religious communities. The state of semi-coloniality only exacerbated such mistrust and conflicts.

The 1911 revolution quickly abandoned its anti-Manchu position, and proclaimed China the first multinational republic of Asia. Going further, the Communist Revolution then followed Marx's conviction that no nation can be free as long as it oppressed other nations. The revolution aimed at national liberation, not only from Western and Japanese imperialism but also from a chauvinist Ancien Régime at home. This twofold commitment laid the constitutional foundation for the future PRC. One

of the party's 'ten great demands' published in 1928 was to 'unify China
and recognize ... [minority] national self-determination'. In 1931, the
Jiangxi Soviet emulated the USSR in pledging the non-Han populations'
'right to determine for themselves' whether they wished to establish their
own state, join the socialist Chinese union or form a self-governing unit
inside the union. Rallying their forces from diverse ethnicities on the rural
margins, the communists themselves were from various regional-cultural
groups. The Red Army passed through Tibetan, Yi, Hui, Mongo and other
minority regions during and after the Long March, and established revolutionary bases in Buddhist and Muslim areas, such as Mongolia and the
Tibetan segments of Gansu and Ningxia. Mao told Edgar Snow in 1939
that on the victory of revolution, 'Tibet, Mongolia, Burma, Indo-China
and Korea' would be autonomous republics voluntarily attached to, or
detached from, a Chinese confederation. In 1945 the party formally envisioned a democratic 'federal republic based on the free union of all
nationalities'.[34]

In power, however, pushed by international blockades and in fear of
national disintegration, the party retreated from its Leninist principle of
fully fledged self-determination and shifted position on the minority right
to secede. Instead, the 'weaker and smaller nations' were to be uplifted in
a socialist society of equal and democratic citizenship achievable through
ethnic-regional autonomy and preferential treatment. The 1954 constitution proclaimed a 'unitary multinational state created jointly by the people
of all its nationalities', in which 'the national autonomous areas are inalien-
able parts of the PRC'. Secession was prohibited. This change is often
taken out of context, or mistaken for desertion of the party's position on
equality and solidarity among nationalities. Yet the socialist aspiration
continued to be about cherishing cultural diversity and universal liberation rather than just managing it. Critiques of this policy miss the fact that
the establishment of a common national identity reborn from shared
struggles was a primary achievement of the revolution. The multinational
reconstitution of a sovereign *state-nation* of the PRC is indeed exemplary
of 'we the people' ascending from great social revolutions to overturn
oppression and divide. By the socialist mandate, and prerequisite by

---

34 Relevant original documents are collected in Conrad Brandt, Benjamin I.
Schwartz and John King Fairbank, eds, *A Documentary History of Chinese Communism*,
New York: Atheneum, 1967.

national unity and integrity, Article 4 of the Constitution declares: 'All
nationalities in the People's Republic are equal. The state protects the
lawful rights and interests of the minority nationalities and upholds and
develops a relationship of equality, unity and mutual assistance.' This is
then a case of universalist revolutionary modernity in contrast with
passive and divisive colonial modernity. National liberation in China
involved participation from diverse nationalities, and the revolution did
not seek to create a homogenizing nation-state with any dominant nationality but rather declared sovereignty on behalf of the diversely constituted
people as a whole.

One of the first tasks that new China assigned itself was to redress past
injustice against its minorities. Central and local governments dispatched
hundreds of work teams to carry out a painstaking identification
programme to delineate ethnic and/or religious identities of groups and
individuals. This project, intended to right past wrongs and liberate the
'weak and small nations', differed categorically from the colonial tech-
nique of divide and rule. The universalist conception of socialism was the
guideline of the process. Whether or not the project had gone too far, it
did succeed in preserving some nearly extinct languages as well as other
cultural inheritances. It also acted as a foundation for the implementation
of affirmative action policies, from easier access and more generous provision of financial assistance in production and welfare to lower entry
scores for university admission and exemption from strict family planning. Preferential policies were so effective that they 'encouraged Han
people to marry into or otherwise seek to join these [minority] nationalities'. Between 1982 and 1990 alone, the Hui population grew by 19 per
cent. By 2005, Tibetans in the Tibetan Autonomous Region (TAR) had
grown 11.3 per cent. The Uyghur population had increased from 3.74
million in 1955 to more than ten million as reported in the National
Census 2000. These rates of population growth are much higher than the
national average between 5 per cent and 6 per cent in the same period.[35]

---

35 Vincent Goossaert and David Palmer, *The Religious Question in Modern China*,
Chicago: University of Chicago Press, 2011: 375; Ma Rong, *Social Development and
Ethnic Relations in Chinese Minority Regions*, Beijing: Social Science Academic Publisher,
2012: 68; Thomas Heberer, 'Some Considerations on China's Minorities: Conflict or
Conciliation', Duisburg Working Papers on East Asian Studies 31, 2000: 3; Li Jianxin and
Chang Qingling, 'Current Situation and Change in the Demography of Xinjiang's Main
Nationalities', *Northwestern Journal of Ethnology*, 3, 2015: 21–36.

Nationally, the minority population rose from 6.1 per cent in 1953 to about 9 per cent in 1995. A few smaller groups tripled in size.

During the 1950s and 1960s, province-level minority administrations were established under the Autonomous Law. These were supplemented by lower-layer autonomous municipalities, prefectures, counties and townships in other provinces: constitutionally and legally, such jurisdictions were overseen by local people's congresses with the right and power to exercise autonomy and enact locally appropriate regulations and policies. This quasi-federalism was an institutional innovation, designed with great care. Premier Zhou Enlai in 1957 judiciously explained why institutional mechanisms would embrace – while also transcending – nationality and territoriality, with ethnically intermingled populations and regionally uneven development, including villages and families of mixed identities within culturally specific communities. Xinjiang was and still is home to more than forty ethnic-religious groups, for example. There could be no exclusive homeland for any single group other than Tibet, and many more Tibetans still reside in the surrounding provinces. Such conditions neither required nor permitted solely ethnically or territorially defined, and therefore obstructive, boundaries. They rather compelled as well as enabled political and economic coordination among local units in a dual administrative structure of region and ethnicity, so that the less developed could catch up. Zhou also stressed the need to counter unrelenting external attempts to undermine the new communist regime by manipulating ethnic and religious cleavages.[36] After all, the Chinese revolution determined the post-revolutionary state's steadfast insistence on national independence and integrity. Yet, in an unfortunate twist, Zhou's warning anticipated some of China's worst domestic regional and geopolitical mistakes decades later.

Thanks to this semi-federal arrangement in defiance of the outmoded nation-state framework, socialist China avoided for the most part the colonial consequences of imposed borders, arbitrary partitioning and ethnic cleansing that so commonly result in lost homelands, broken lives and split loyalties. To reduce regional disparities, Beijing also consistently invested in upgrading the infrastructure of minority areas using

---

36 Zhou Enlai, 'On a Few Questions Concerning Our Nationality Policy', in *Selected Writings of Zhou Enlai*, Beijing: People's Publishing House, 1984. See also Wang Hui, *The Politics of Imagining Asia*, Cambridge MA: Harvard University Press, 2011: ch. 4.

large-scale transfers of funds, technologies, public service facilities and expertise from wealthier provinces. The long practiced 'sister' liaison between specific coastal and poorer locations to build tech-industrial zones, create manufacturing jobs and carry out social aid programmes remains common. Notwithstanding a degree of paternalism and an inevitable gulf between objectives and outcomes, 'internal peripheralization' has not occurred. Despite setbacks, autonomous regions have made substantial progress, as is clear from human development measurements and intergroup synchronization; and although its ideology on ethnic relations has been watered down, the PRC survived the global wave of cultural nationalism and those tragic and violent turns from the breakup of communist federations along ethnic-national and religious lines. The fact that China still stands unified in a post-communist world expresses the depth and authenticity of its revolution. In other words, the weakness of religious radicalism and ethnic violence is attributable not mostly to oppression but rather to the lasting power of socialist persuasion. Although the latter is ever more fragile, it was not until the 2008 Lhasa and 2009 Urumqi riots that a policy crisis became obvious in west China.

Old socialist paternalism, new capitalist developmentalism and harsh campaigns against separatist tendencies have all had an impact. However, the relentless accumulation of capital combined with resurgent jingoism from the Han majority has generated social as well as ethnic polarization in the reform era. Some everyday activities have been criminalized by a Han-based cultural code, a counterproductive policy that violates the regime's own mandate. Equally damaging are the proactive or over-reactive, violent crackdowns that generate a vicious circle of revenge. On the other hand, observers who focus on oppressive control mistakenly imagine that the PRC has never achieved ethnic peace. Some also believe that this is a flaw common to all communist regimes, as though the communist federations had not impressively united different nationalities side by side for sustained periods of time, in stark contrast to the tragic repercussions of their dissolution. This view fails to account for the evolving attitudes of key minority groups in China before and after the reforms, and, misled by the feeble assumption that the PRC state is a 'quasi-colonial' power stuck in an antagonistic relationship with its national minorities, it obscures the origins of the present crisis.

Regarding the 'Tibet question', the importance of external causal factors – namely colonial interventions in the region followed by the effects of the Cold War – are now well recorded. Details have come to light about the British invasion of and manoeuvring in the Himalayan region before the communist takeover in China, and the subsequent training and arming of Tibetan rebels by the CIA. The region is still geopolitically sensitive today, as is demonstrated by the Sino-Indian border disputes and skirmishes. The Seventeen Point Agreement signed in 1951 by the PRC central government and the representatives of Tibetan elite (despite some internal fractures between Yadong and Lhasa Kashags) was both ground-breaking and a necessary component of the revolution's victory. The young Dalai telegraphed Mao in October to confirm his personal support while collaborating with the PLA. He went to Beijing in 1954 to attend the first National Congress and met with Mao. Fondly remembering the occasion, he recalled the meeting in his autobiography, *My Land and My People*. As recently as 2012, he praised his 'very good relationship' with Mao, likening it to the one between a loving son and father, and spoke of his attraction to 'the Marxist idea' of equality.[37] He also understood why the initial communist 'democratic reform' against Tibetan feudalism was popular among former serfs, whose homes were often decorated with the twin portraits of Mao and the Dalai. It is the 1951 agreement, rather than any historical claim on either side, that has confirmed the status of Tibet as under the PRC's jurisdiction, and which delegitimizes attempts at independence.

For years, the Dalai Lama was under US pressure to leave Tibet and publicly disavow Chinese sovereignty over Tibet; things eventually turned sour in 1959 when outside forces gathered and forced him to flee.[38] The land reform initially avoided Tibet zones in order to accommodate local elites (while reform in neighbouring provinces nevertheless caused panic among Tibetan landlords), but was then brought in to abolish large private landholdings as well as the theocratic system of serfdom. Beijing's pragmatic approach, which had alternated between united front and class

---

37 Interview with Andrew Marr, BBC, 24 June 2012, bbc.com/news/av/uk-politics-18568716; 'Mao was like a father to me, says the Dalai Lama', *The Hindu*, 29 June 2012.

38 A 1951 telegram from Washington reads, 'Your Holiness will understand, of course, that the readiness of the United States to render you the assistance and support outlined above is conditional upon your departure from Tibet, upon your public disavowal of [the Seventeen Point] agreements . . .', Melvyn Goldstein, *A History of Modern Tibet, Vol. 2. The Calm Before the Storm: 1951–1955*, Berkeley, CA: University of California Press, 2007: 232.

struggle, or 'ethno-elitist' and 'ethno-populist', shifted towards the latter.[39] For the Tibetan poor, even if class struggle from below had formerly been restricted, the liberation was indeed liberating. Yet the wounds of 1959 still cast a dark shadow because the beloved Dalai Lama, supreme spiritual leader of Tibetan Buddhism (descended from the Gelugpa lineage), was denounced, causing a head-on collision with local sentiment. A hefty element of coercion was fused into otherwise valid social reforms, and the situation was complicated by the fact that half of the 6 million Tibetans resided outside the TAR. This problem of greater Tibet has been an obstacle in many rounds of ultimately fruitless negotiations between Beijing and Dharamsala. Beijing's loss of collaboration with the Dalai may also lead to a far more perilous situation, as his successor will likely demand independence rather than autonomy, and could resort to force.

The growing tensions in the Xinjiang Uyghur Autonomous Region (XUAR) cannot be shielded from external influences either. These have included both direct and indirect interventions from the Soviet Union in the 1960s, as well as agitations from Central Asia linked to the renewed movement for 'East Turkestan independence' since the 1990s, along with political Islam. Already suffering massive geopolitical aftereffects following the demise of Soviet bloc, the region was later hit by the global 'war on terror' orchestrated by the US. Beijing reframed its security concerns accordingly, in a prevailing liberal discourse of differentiating between 'good' and 'bad' Muslims, while conflating ethnic and religious identities. This prompted surging lobbies in the major democracies under their typical double standard, by Free Tibet and the World Uyghur Congress among others. Fierce information and propaganda wars continue between a defensive PRC and its growing critics. Further internationalisation of these domestic problems in the Information Age is not only an outcome of local antagonisms but also a causal factor in their proliferation.

The fundamental cause, however, must be domestic, as external influences effect only through internal stimuli, catalysts and triggers. The central puzzle here is how tensions can have mounted to such an extent with no formal change in either ideology or institutions. The fact that no constitutional amendment since 1978 has touched Article 4 on minority rights, mutual assistance and equal citizenship, nor has any established

---

39 Justin Jacob, *Xinjiang and the Modern Chinese State*, Seattle, WA: University of Washington Press, 2016: ch. 1.

pro-minority legal clause been removed, only sharpens the question. To answer it, one must understand what has changed in terms of social commitment, and which state institutions or policies have become malfunctioning. One issue is obviously the loss of the substance of formal provisions, but this doesn't explain the inception of the crisis. It is possible to draw two immediate conclusions, however: first, any abuse of stipulated provisions is straightforwardly unconstitutional and illegal; and second, if socialism underlined past successes, however limited, then its erosion must be responsible for the present impasse.

To identify internal causal factors, the first thing to note is the significant inflow of mainly Han (and Hui) settlers to minority regions and its wide socioeconomic and cultural consequences. If it is true that an invasive market produced these effects during the first two reform decades through the free movement of capital and labour, in the absence of deliberate state promotion of Han migration to undermine local cultural demographics (notwithstanding the conversion of army units into the Xinjiang Production and Construction Corps to reclaim wasteland in the 1950s), then it is also the case that the encouragement of such movement subsequently became an implicit policy. Nationally, as noted already, the spatial ramifications of market transition have been nowhere more visible than in the massive rural-to-urban migration. But the ethnically specific westward pattern, in contrast with the major trends towards eastern metropolises and south-east industrial sunbelts, can be far more disruptive, and fears about redrawing their familiar demographic and cultural landscapes inflamed locals. Between 1990 and 2000 in the TAR, the proportion of Han Chinese rose from 3.68 per cent to 5.9 per cent of the population, which did 'not point to any mass influx of Han'.[40] The figure has since stabilized at around 6 per cent, but since new settlers have tended to concentrate in Lhasa the city's ethnic constitution has visibly changed.

In Xinjiang the non-Muslim population has expanded apace, amid turbulences like the 2009 riot when hundreds of people, mostly Han, were killed or injured in Ürümqi (this had been precipitated by a murder involving two Uyghur victims in a Guangdong factory). Southern XUAR

40 Colin Mackerras, 'Tibetans, Uyghurs, and Multinational "China"', in P. H. Gries and Stanley Rosen, eds, *Chinese Politics: State, Society and the Market*, London and New York: Routledge, 2010: 233.

saw more discord, including competition over land use, as strife over religion was exacerbated by poverty and despair. Not only had the antipathy between Uyghur and Han communities intensified, but their physical segregation in separate residential quarters was also a problem. In place after place, cross-boundary communications became bitter and prone to violent outbreaks. The tightened labour market was affected particularly badly: without the quota system that had been functional in the past, discrimination against minority job seekers occurred not only in private but also in the state sector. A typical example, described in a news report, comes from the Kashgar Prefecture, where Uyghurs make up nearly 90 per cent of the population, but half the posts advertised on the government's civil service recruitment website were open only to Mandarin speakers. Government vacancies, let alone responsible positions, are regularly filled by people brought in from non-local pools. Local workers can even be barred from the gas and oil industries, unable to profit from the natural resources of their land. What began with market spontaneity has since mutated into institutionalized social exclusion.

Internal Han migration is connected to a cultural politics of the threatened loss of traditions and identities. This has given rise to a perceived 'cultural genocide', caused as much by the horror of commercialization as by ethnic homogenization. In Xinjiang, especially since 2016, local policies have appeared not a rebuttal of the charge. The first test is the foundational promise of 'freedom [for the minorities] to develop their spoken and written languages, to preserve or reform their traditions, customs and religious beliefs' (a statutory clause in Common Programme 1949, Article 53). Linguistic nativization and bilingual or multilingual communication were regional requisites in the public arena, from schools and offices to courtrooms and broadcasting. Until the 1980s, 'great efforts were made to bring education to all the minority areas, and in some cases this meant first of all creating a written language which could serve as the basis for education.'[41]

Since market opening, an inadvertent result of reducing language barriers to job opportunities has been a compromised native language education. Many bilingual programmes deteriorated into mandatory

---

41 Peter Ferdinand, *Communist Regimes in Comparative Perspective: The Evolution of the Soviet, Chinese and Yugoslav Systems*, London: Harvester Wheatsheaf, 1991: 241–2.

Mandarin. There was even a local, likely unofficial drive to outlaw aspects of Uyghur culture and to erase the Uyghur language from the entire regional system, as though a non-Han mother tongue could in itself be unpatriotic. On 8 October 2017, Kashi University in South Xinjiang published a proposal claiming to be from its faculty and calling for its students to set an example by using the 'nationally standard language': 'Let us use Putonghua alone for communication within and without class-rooms, in society, life, and among kin and friends.' It additionally urged, 'if you find anyone among your fellow teachers or students not using it, correct them!'[42] This call is again straightforwardly unconstitutional; it invades the private sphere, and violates the basic cultural rights of 12 million Turkic Uyghur speakers, along with 3 million others speaking other minority languages. It is also bound to fail: minority languages continue to be written and spoken throughout the regional communities today. Still, a visitor reported that in Xinjiang's state-run Xinhua book-stores, the shelves were half empty: 'In each store I visited, the only Uyghur-language book was a copy of Xi Jinping's *The Governance of China*.'[43] This is a real sign of the desertification, if not the extinction, of once thriving, legally protected minority cultures. Younger generations' ignorance of a rich Uyghur literature deeply worries the community and its desperate yet silenced intellectuals. Tibetan is now a subject of study rather than a language of instruction in Tibetan schools. Since 2018, the original bilingual programme in Kazakh schools, which held most classes in the Kazakh language, has been phased out. In the summer of 2020, protests and boycotts erupted in areas of Inner Mongolia when the regional decision to replace Mongol with Mandarin in half of school classes was announced – yet the so-called bilingual education model two has gone ahead anyway. All this is in sharp contrast with the former socialist commitment to linguistic diversity, when the legendary cultural troupe Ulaan möchir (Red Twig) travelled to entertain Mongolian herders in far-flung corners of the grassland, and when linguists, musicians, writers, artists and film projectionists studied traditional folklore in local dialects across diverse minority regions. 'Multilingual acts of

---

42 Professors of Kashgar University, 'To All of Our Faculty and Students: A Proposal of Striving to Set an Example of Using State Common Language', 8 October 2017.

43 Christian Shepherd, 'Fear and Oppression in Xinjiang: China's War on Uyghur Culture', *Financial Times*, 13 September 2019.

nation-building and socialist political education belonged to the same "imagined community" of the People's Republic.'[44]

Religion is an equally vital contention. In Tibet, any open expression of loyalty to the Dalai Lama is prohibited, although private Buddhist practice is mostly unrestricted. In Xinjiang established rules and codes have collapsed into extreme forms of religious policing, including the selective banning of beards, scarves, other Islamic symbols and Ramadan rites. In some places Muslim communities were forced to hand in prayer mats and 'terrorist items' such as knives, flammable objects and other items deemed suspicious. Punishments for non-compliance included not only detention and self-criticism sessions but also passport confiscation, fines and exclusion from social benefits. Certain editions of the Quran were seized during campaigns against 'illegal' publications and religious teaching. Such blanket restrictions on daily life angered even moderates and non-believers. Officials of Han origin have also been sent periodically to live in Uyghur, Kazakh and Kyrgyz homes, with the goal of 'improving harmony'. This intrusion is especially offensive for conservatives because of its infringement of the Islamic code around female segregation. In addition to these restrictions on religious freedom, unchecked 'great Han chauvinism' – criticized as a 'greater danger' than minority ethnic nationalism in Mao's 1956 treatise – also returned to demonize Uyghurs and fellow Xinjiangers. Discrimination, which frequently occurs during the processes of hiring and licensing, hotel and airport check-ins, and other social encounters at home and away, has left a lasting psychological wound on a proud people. Mao's Marxist approach was to see the national question as essentially one of class, with ethnic estrangements subordinated to class conflicts under reactionary rulers.[45] This approach took political-economic rather than cultural identity as the basis of equality. The new policy of 'sinicizing religions', however, is both politically and culturally chauvinist, as well as being illegal.

The 1984 Law on Ethnic Regional Autonomy reaffirmed that ethnic minorities should be 'masters over their own affairs'. The minority regions did recover from the excesses of the cultural revolution. The following super-liberal period, however, dramatically reduced the scope of local

---

44 Christian Sorace, 'Undoing Lenin: On the Recent Changes to China's Ethnic Policy', *Made in China* 5:2, 2020, doi.org/10.22459/MIC.05.02.2020.

45 This pertains to the sixth relationship, in Mao, 'On the Ten Major Relationships'.

governments, to the extent that a large number of public servants resigned and ventured into business, and many Han cadres were recalled from areas where they had lived and worked for decades. In Tibet, Xinjiang and Inner Mongolia, public funds were allocated to numerous mosques and temples, which were often lavishly built or refurbished – an 'overcorrection', in the view of many non-Han locals, as these funds may have been better spent on schools, libraries and hospitals. Instead, the state poured investment into cultural buildings that ultimately helped re-ethnicization and religious revival. Meanwhile, a retreat from secular socialism precipitated a general post-socialist 'spiritual crisis' and led to a rise of religion across traditionally atheist zones, drawing tens of millions to follow Christianity, Catholicism and the more orthodox sects of Buddhism. The synchronicity of religious movements and market expansion is no paradox: a booming industry of 'religion for profit' has developed, encompassing temple and church management, spiritual tourism and so on. Money and market values have come to permeate religious beliefs, artefacts and rituals.

Intensified ethnic and religious strains also have their origins in socioeconomic conditions, and the capitalist transition must take its fair share of responsibility. Like the rest of China, markets have brought with them inequality and the commodification of the lifeworld, in addition to, or in the guise of, ethnic-regional disparities. Not only are such effects amplified in the minority regions that have an ethnically specific appearance, but they go deeper still, exposing the horrifying prospect of commercial homogeneity, and hence a culturally and eco-environmentally destroyed homeland. The developmentalist push towards resettlement, inequality, the marginalization of local languages and cultures, corruption of religion and so on cannot be compensated by tangible economic benefits such as 'universal' living standards. Ürümqi is now one of China's most polluted municipalities. The exploration of Xinjiang's natural resources without substantial sharing of the benefits with the virtually disfranchised locals through investment or productive and distributive decisions reinforces these resentments. The central government's gigantic Developing the West project, established in the 1990s and now part of the BRI, has poured national largesse into poorer multiethnic regions. It has the potential to achieve the legitimate goals of local economic gains, strengthened inter-communal ties and frontier security in western China. The project is ethnically sensitive, however.

Although economic inequalities are by no means ethnically specific in the marketplace – for example, research finds that at least in Tibet, ethnic background is by and large not directly correlated with income prior to 2008, market pathologies impact the minority most seriously.[46] Power disparities between bosses and workers, or higher and lower-ranking officials, do map onto ethnicity, with more powerful positions being overwhelmingly occupied by Han people. Contentious identity politics is both a source and a result of ethnicizing difference, or essentializing ethnicity, in interpreting social and communal inequalities. The belief that economic growth can reverse local grievances and even provide a solution to culturally and religiously specific conflicts is profoundly mistaken: growth as such is not necessarily appealing to local communities, and hearts and minds cannot be bought. When *minsheng* provisions are used in tandem with force, the whole project is tainted.

In the demographic, cultural and socioeconomic contexts discussed earlier, another factor in explaining elevated ethnic contentions is the issue of autonomy as such in the designated autonomous regions. Concerning minority power and political representation, by law 70 per cent of regional and lower-level administrators should be from local ethnic groups, to ensure independent authority over their own regional affairs. In reality, minority groups have had a significant presence in the local state sector, including government offices and the police force. But they have increasingly been outnumbered by Han cadres and officers, and shed from more critical positions, such as party secretary. In late 2020, Inner Mongolia had completed an administrative reform, resulting in an overwhelming majority of Han cadres taking important posts in the regional government, including director of its Nationality Affairs Commission.[47]

More subtly, the aggregate changes of recent years have demoralized the previously tailored self-esteem and social status of non-Han party members as well as mass supporters of the communist regime. Just as seriously, the minority populations are also underrepresented in the national legislative and governmental agencies, especially in leading posts. The lack of democratic exchange between Beijing, with its regional appointees, and local representatives has produced a situation of

---

46 Ben Hillman, 'Rethinking China's Tibet Policy', *China-Pacific Journal: Japan Focus* 6:6, 2008.

47 Xinhua News, *Inner Mongolia Daily*, 13 November 2020.

dwindling mutual trust. Allegedly weak local civic identification with the Chinese nation rationalizes hardline handling of incidents of discontent.[48] As many decisions are made without local participation and consent, hence a missing feedback loop during implementation, no mechanism of timely corrective adjustment exists. This failure in political representation for minorities could lead to a futile push for Han-centred assimilation, countering the long-standing communist commitment. While market-induced power devolution and pluralization of economic geography could be more responsive to locally articulated preferences, the trend has bypassed large areas of supposedly autonomous regions. Control over associational activism and the internet and social media is especially tight. The constitutional autonomy of TAR and XUAR is virtually disregarded.

The final cause to be highlighted is the state oppression and social coercion supposedly justified by the exaggerated threat of the 'three evils': terrorism, separatism and religious fundamentalism. This has generated counter-terrorist drives, as well as campaigns against Saudi-ization and pan-Islamization, also in the non-autonomous provinces such as the Hui regions of Gansu. The security forces in Xinjiang and Tibet are especially proactive in following Beijing's absolutist preoccupation with stability. The globalized platform of anti-terrorism and counter-radicalization are about reassurance as much as being a pretext for strikes. A system of comprehensive surveillance is in place in Xinjiang, via GPS tracking, DNA screening, face and voice recognition, cell phone and laptop searches, checkpoints and other regular securitization measures. Pre-emptive raids, mass internment and arrests have all swelled. A record 230,000 people were formally detained or sentenced to prison in 2017 and 2018 in XUAR,[49] driving even secular and integrated Muslims to dissent. Ilham Tohti, a professor at the Central Nationalities University, has been serving a life sentence since 2014 for his outspoken yet prudent concerns over abused minority rights. Yalqun Rozi, an editor in the Xinjiang Education Publishing House, received a fifteen-year jail term in 2018 for the charge of 'inciting subversion of state power' by including a historical photo of Ehmetjan Qasim, a communist founder of the East Turkestan Republic in

---

48 See for example Ilham Tohti, 'Why Have the Uyghurs Felt Defeated?', RFI, 6 July 2013, chinese.rfi .fr/node/132196.

49 Chris Buckley, 'China's Prisons Swell after Deluge of Arrests Engulfs Muslims', *New York Times*, 4 September 2019.

what was previously regarded in official account as the Three Districts Revolution in the late 1940s, in his edited textbooks. These are among a long list of targeted writers, translators, musicians, academics and scientists who are often state employees and take published state commitment and formal laws and policies too literally.

Outlawing complaints and closing access to public dialogue has worsened the situation by turning issue-specific discontent into broader, militant rebellions. Wang Lixiong describes a 'pressure cooker effect' of peaceful monks and Muslims being constrained to the point of potential explosion.[50] The 'de-extremification' campaign of 'anti-extremist ideological education' ran what authorities defined as vocational and legal training centres with armed guards.[51] Most 'students' were said to have graduated by the end of 2019, but by then hundreds of thousands of people were disappeared in these restricted facilities, fostering fear and resentment. The project's superficial effect of cutting down violent resistance is unlikely to last. In the TAR and surrounding Tibetan areas since 2009, at least 155 protesters have died from self-immolation, sustaining a continuous stream of suicide martyrs and a powerful moral narrative of unbearable injustice and desperate resistance. What is astutely depicted as 'Palestinization' rings tragically real for both regions, reflecting a self-fulfilling prophecy of hotbeds cultivated to produce deadly riots.[52] The simple truth of 'more oppression, more resistance' that both legitimized and explained the Communist Revolution is yet to be registered by China's frustrated and paranoid political class. Since the socialist, internationalist and anti-imperialist conception of the emancipation of all nationalities as both moral imperative and political wisdom is now long gone, and the state is stained by both capitalist greed and bureaucratic ignorance, reliance on suppression is justified by Han-centred Chinese nationalism. This

---

50 Wang Lixiong, 'Excerpts from My West China, Your East Turkestan – My View on the Kunming Incident', *China Change*, 3 March 2014, chinachange.org/2014/03/03/excerpts-from-my-west-china-your-east-turkestan-my-view-on-the-kunming-incident.

51 Austin Ramzy and Chris Buckley, ' "Absolutely No Mercy": Leaked Files Expose How China Organizes Mass Detentions of Muslims', *New York Times*, 16 November 2019; and Bethany Allen-Ebrahimian, 'Exposed: China's Operating Manuals for Mass Internment and Arrest by Algorithm', International Consortium of Investigative Journalists, 24 November 2019. Beijing responded to both these leaks in November 2019.

52 Wang Lixiong, cited in Joanne Finley, 'The Wang Lixiong Prophecy: Palestinization of Xinjiang and the Consequences of Chinese State Securitization of Religion', *Central Asian Survey* 38:1, 2019.

turn is symptomatic of a larger crisis in which the entire edifice of socialist fundamentals in China tremble.

Repairs are sought in a second generation of ethnic policies that explicitly advocates retracting ethnic recognition, regional autonomy and minority affirmative action. The borrowed notion of nationality, or *minzu*, is seen as politically unwise, even dangerous, for its conceptual affinity to nationhood. On a superficial level it is liable to promote minority nationalism and disunity by appealing to self-determination. The depoliticized term *zuqun*, or ethnicity, is considered more suitable in the official language of recognition, echoing China's imperial tradition of coexistence without modern institutional intervention. It is argued that ethnically specific territorial identities in the larger minority regions could encourage splitist demands or extrajudicial entitlements. Preferential policies under ethnic-regional administrations also have a cumulative 'reverse discrimination' effect that can adversely affect non-titular groups. The solution is de-ethnicization via the phasing out of existing arrangements, based on shared lives and knowledge that transcend exclusive identities and demarcations. To halt the perceived solidification of sub-state cultural nationalist and fundamentalist religious consciousness, China has continued to redress its socio-spatial unevenness and the gap between coast and interior, while 'promoting cross-group mixing, reforming minority cultures and making Mandarin mandatory in education'. It is considered desirable to dilute ethnic identities, build inclusive cultures and form a Chinese 'state-race'.[53] This idea of equal citizenship would like to distance itself from sinicization, yet in practice it amounts to a policy shift from the model of amalgamation to that of one way assimilation that strengthens Han ethnocentrism in the name of Chinese nationalism.[54]

If such a policy – already happening locally, from the reduction of extra points for minority students in university entrance exams to scrubbing Islamic signs from restaurants and cultural sites, and the current imposition of Mandarin as the main language of instruction in schools – were to

53 Ma Rong, 'The "Politicization" and "Culturization" of Ethnic Groups', *Chinese Sociology and Anthropology* 42: 4, Summer 2010: 31–45; James Leibold, 'Toward a Second Generation of Ethnic Policies?' *China Brief* 12:13, 6 July 2012; Mark Elliott, 'The Case of the Missing Indigene: Debate Over a "Second-Generation" Ethnic Policy', *The China Journal*, 73, 2015: 186–213.

54 James Leibold, 'Planting the Seed: Ethnic Policy in Xi Jinping's New Era of Cultural Nationalism', *China Brief* 19: 22, 31 December 2019.

be formally adopted, it would disastrously reverse magnificent historical achievements towards genuine communist universalism. This is not to say that the PRC system of ethnic-regional autonomy is perfect by design, or newer challenges are not grave enough to require policy adjustment. On the contrary, locally sensitive improvements in cultural autonomy and political representation on the one hand and measures to de-conflict and vanquish extremism on the other are both direly needed. Any reform, however, cannot succeed without the socialist foundation of equality and liberation being safeguarded; and the structural conditions of socio-economic empowerment and institutional semi-federalism remain pre-requisite. 'Undoing Lenin', as Christian Sorace put it, is a wrongheaded move comprising 'a departure from the political vision of the early Mao years' and offers no solution.[55] The regional policies that deviated from socialist recognition and egalitarianism are a moral disaster; right lessons must be drawn from the violent disintegration of the USSR and Yugoslavia.

Missing from the proposal is not only the basic rationale for the established frameworks, but also the participation in decision making by the minorities whose lives are at stake. Any policy approach that contradicts its own stated objectives would be self-destructive. Instead of further deserting the socialist contract between state and minority societies in new China, it needs to be reinstated and developed. Based on equality and autonomy, diversity in unity, like unity in diversity, is an unfinished project; favouring unity *over* diversity would end up achieving neither. Above all, it is not socialism but its distortion or devastation that has impaired central–local and ethnic perceptions. The former mass image of the beloved *jinzhumami* (PLA) as selfless chain breakers in Tibet contrasts startlingly with that of the feared armed police as invaders and oppressors for some in Xinjiang. With their habitual double standards the international human rights regimes grossly dismiss the communists' moral code and their capacity of organizing ethno-spaces, overlooking the riddle of why Beijing's policy crisis did not occur until the early 2000s. Here, critiques of a (self-)orientalizing rebranding of concepts such as *ethnicity*, *locality*, and *culture* are politically relevant only in the context of the breakup of communist unions and federal republics, and the ensuing wars and partitions. In the end, modernity versus autonomy is a false dilemma. China's majority and minority communities should all have their own

---

55 Sorace, 'Undoing Lenin'.

constitutionally enshrined rights and institutional means to develop on their own terms and in their own rhythms. All can succeed socioeconomically, culturally and politically, connected positively with national development, if they are provided with a democratic process of articulating desirable policy reforms.

The innovative formula *one country, two systems* is another test. As the departure from two systems, between socialism and capitalism, is largely completed by neoliberal market integration, this phrase rather too easily signals for many the distinction of autocracy versus freedom. Yet, the question is far more challenging politically; and there remain two economic systems, operating through different mechanisms and positioned differently in the international trading and financial institutional networks. The heightened foreign interference since 2014 has changed the balance or imbalance of power, but the future of Hong Kong and Taiwan is ultimately for the people in these regions to solve.

Concerning the Hong Kong Special Administrative Region (HKSAR) after the 1997 handover, the formula changed meaning not because of a central power encroaching on local affairs, but because the mainland is just as capitalistic, heavily relying on the ties between monopoly bureaucratic and private capital in both systems. Beijing's Liaison Office in Hong Kong made friends with business leaders and financiers rather than unions and social organizations. This line of state–business coalition has proven completely incapable of foreseeing or handling the huge demonstrations since 2014. The exploitative labour regimes and unequal social relations are evident in the city, in the awful housing situation, for instance, or the long hours suffered by manual and mental workers alike. These are just as real as what is singled out as 'the plunder of Hong Kong by local billionaires, rich mainland capitalists, and the PRC regime'.[56] The overarching contentions emerge from contradictions, from the autonomy and universal suffrage stipulated in the Basic Law (1990) to the short-lived draft of the Extradition Bill (2019) and the controversial National Security Law (2020),[57] and from incompatible identities as a colonial legacy and the mismanagement of the post-1997 era to the failures of what had been

---

56 Andrea Binder, 'Why China's Wealthy Elites Have So Much at Stake in Hong Kong', *Washington Post*, 21 August 2019.

57 See the full text of the Basic Law of the HKSAR, fmprc.gov.cn/mfa_eng/ljzg_665465/3566_665531/t23031.shtml; and 'Our Legal System' by the regional government's Department of Justice, 5 November 2020, doj.gov.hk/en/our_legal_system/index.html.

hailed as an exemplary legal system. Interestingly, as the Legislative Council has been dominated by business and property tycoons, segments of the economic elite joined the 2019 protest and forced the HKSAR government to remove the bill that included such penalties for 'offences against the law relating to bribery, corruption, secret commissions and breach of trust'.

Beijing's typically capitalist misconception ever since the 1984 Sino-British declaration is that preserving prosperity in Hong Kong would rely on pleasing its business circles. It is telling that 'pro-Beijing' and 'pro-business' are still interchangeable in local public communication, most ironically as 'colonial holdovers defined by the collusion of government and business'. As its inequality escalated, rising to a Gini coefficient of 0.539 in 2016, one of the highest in the world, Hong Kong became 'the sole case of a capitalist country that became more inegalitarian by joining a communist regime'.[58] The trend paralleled the one in the mainland. In August 2019 several global cities were subjected to scandalous demonstrations that involved Chinese students driving Ferraris and other luxury cars to support Beijing against the 'poor mobs' of Hong Kong. On 5 August a general strike called by the Hong Kong Confederation of Trade Unions brought the territory to a partial halt, although the older and larger Federation of Unions declined participation, citing its 'patriotic' stance and tradition of industrial actions against British colonialism. Looking away from pressing social issues – deindustrialization, financial oligarchy, inflated land value and sky-high housing prices, unemployment, dwindling wages, poor economic opportunities and inequalities of all kinds – that inevitably implicate both Beijing and the HKSAR government, Hong Kong's labour and intellectual lefts seem to be disabled by political confusions while workers and residents are bitterly divided.[59] No obvious socialist element can be identified in the student protesters' primary demands marred by a racialized rhetoric of democracy. Beyond all the destruction, a tragic mood persists: nearly a century ago, these were the very places (Guandong and Hong Kong) where the CCP organized the modern world's longest strike.

---

58 Thomas Piketty, *Capital and Ideology*, Cambridge, MA: Harvard University Press, 2019: 622.

59 Macabe Keliher, 'Neoliberal Hong Kong Is Our Future, Too', *Boston Review*, 9 September 2020.

All this raises the question of how Beijing can defend its identity as a sovereign socialist state in demand of patriotic loyalty, not just another self-interested colonial master. Hong Kong was rightly excluded from the 1961 UN Resolution on Decolonization because China had itself suffered colonialism. The Basic Law was depoliticized, since 'the idea was to de-colonize by ignoring politics in favour of capitalism.' In the words of Daniel Vukovich, 'it is not so much that China has re-colonized its stolen territory but that Hong Kong has never gone through a moment of decol-onization.'[60] Beijing has retained elements of an unpopular colonial system under the British, disappointing many who had celebrated their return to the motherland in 1997. The regional governance is then struc-turally unsound without a solid political consensus and institutional guarantee concerning Hong Kong's Chinese identity. This is comprised a challenge to the wisdom of the two systems policy and partly explains the protests of 2014 and 2019.

While these dilemmas bind Beijing's hands and feet, the 'free world' refuses to recognize that Chinese sovereignty is unnegotiable. The fact that freedom was taken away from Hong Kong by London is also conven-iently forgotten, but the scale of the demonstrations and toleration of violence draw natural comparisons with responses to the British Emer-gency Ordinance imposed in the 1960s. As a sort of 'colour revolution' loomed large, the White House and National Endowment for Democracy among others emerged into the limelight.[61] Focusing on the internal de-terminants of the protests, however, a younger generation of militants have grown in Hong Kong (and Taiwan), as those among Tibetans and Uyghurs. They renounce non-violence and the Chinese identity. A small number of them have vandalized the city and attacked people in the last few months of 2019, with neither clear goals nor basic political skills. Yet the rebellious youth drew extraordinary and extensive sympathy from the local population, which could have signalled 'a collective vote of no confi-dence in Beijing' and the HKSAR government.[62]

---

60 Daniel Vukovich, 'A City and a SAR on Fire: As If Everything and Nothing Changes', *Critical Asian Studies*, December 2019: 15.

61 Sara Flounders, 'Follow the Money Behind Hong Kong Protests', *Workers' World*, 16 August 2019; Wei Xinyan and Zhong Weiping, 'Who Is Behind Hong Kong Protests?' *China Daily*, 17 August 2019; 'Timeline: External Interference in Hong Kong', *China Daily*, 20 November 2019.

62 Chaohua Wang, 'Hong Kong v. Beijing', *London Review of Books*, 41:16, 15 August 2019.

Events in Hong Kong are significant for the mainland. As the cosmopolitan hub of finance and commerce with its own legal and monetary systems, Hong Kong has a unique economic status. It is a separate customs territory, tariff-free zone and offshore market for the yuan. It enables Chinese governments and firms to invest abroad and make foreign listings and transactions easily. It is China's primary station for inward and outward FDI; and it is also where capital flees to, both foreign gamblers and wealthy Chinese. The upswing of Shanghai, Shenzhen and other mainland ports cannot substitute for such a financial centre, one that is critical to China's economy and its global agenda. However, the two system structure also diminishes central control over Hong Kong's financial, monetary, taxation and judicial powers. Beijing has interfered at times of crisis, such as during a massive rescue operation in 2007 when the Hang Seng Index was under constant attacks by international capital and on the brink of meltdown. Under normal circumstances, however, its oversight is seriously constrained. It was not surprising to see the US Hong Kong Human Rights Act to revoke Hong Kong's special trading status passed by both houses in November 2019, and then for Trump to sign Hong Kong Autonomy Act in July 2020, also an economically motivated move to weaken a strategic competitor.

Politically too, what happens in Hong Kong has wider ramifications. Democracy came to the fore alongside issues of decolonization and capitalism. In 2007, the NPC granted direct elections to the HKSAR chief executive by 2017 and subsequently also to the Legislative Council; these would have transformed a colonial dictatorship into a locally adaptive and phased democratization. The proposal has been repeatedly rejected by the radical democrats. Some of them prefer to be British under the 'Hong Konger' banner, embracing an awkwardly racist sentiment against mainlanders. Yet their critique of the Sino-British negotiation and drafting of the Basic Law, which had very limited local input and little consultation among Hong Kong residents, was valid. The handover did not involve any democratic procedures, resembling many post-war examples of the retreat of empire. The 2020 National Security Law, legitimized by the PRC Constitution, was a replay of this top-down approach; its detailed clauses were declared even without the prior knowledge of the chief executive and her team.

Designed with Taiwan in mind, the one country, two systems formula tested in Hong Kong would be even less viable for a de facto independent

entity with an artificial yet ever stronger local ethno-national consciousness. As new Taiwanese nationalism, riding on democratization,
repudiates the Chinese identity, the Taiwan question has shifted ground:
no longer seen as a continuation of the Chinese civil war, it has become a
crucial piece in the game of Sino-US competition. Even for those who still
adhere to the idea of One China, it has become ever more difficult to
imagine any form of unification. Han Kuo-yu, former mayor of Gaoxiong
and briefly Taiwan's opposition presidential candidate from GMD for the
January 2020 general election, called for a return to the One China
consensus but emphasized that one country, two systems 'absolutely has
no market in Taiwan'. The stalemate of cross-Strait dialogue needs to be
overcome, but Beijing must realize that 'democracy and freedom are not
great scourges'.[63] The message, as protests in Hong Kong have brought
home, is that even extensive economic ties cannot be a guarantor of peace.
However, beneath the rhetoric of normative values, the movement for the
independence of Taiwan is yet to rid itself of the stigma of the Japanese
colonial legacy, as much as that of 'client nationalism' and Cold War
anti-communism. Its very dependence – politically, ideologically and
militarily – on American protection discredits the politics of separation.
Likewise, and more to the point, Beijing is also losing appeal by lagging
behind Taiwan, not only on political liberty but also on substantive social
policies. It has missed a potential opportunity, in other words, to take
advantage of having a socialist mainland compared to a breakaway martial
law regime in pursuit of unification.

By way of reiterating, a further clarification of terms applied is in order.
The PRC is a unitary multination state and semi-federal in its governmental structure. As such it can be conceived as a state-nation of equal
citizenship rather than a nation-state dominated by a singular or majority
national group. The latter has long been regarded among experts as an
inadequate model for the contemporary world. The Chinese translation
of 'nation' as *minzu* can be inaccurate if understood in the word's European originated meaning, since the collective identification with the
'Chinese *minzu*' is inherently multinational. Likewise, 'nationality', also
translated as *minzu*, may be out of favour today, but it connotes domestic
national or ethnic-religious identities within a unified state-nation, such

---

63 'Taiwan Opposition Candidate Calls for Return to One China Formula', Reuters
(Taipei), 14 November 2019.

as the integral Chinese (as opposed to Han) nation and people. To redeem the historical wrongs done to its national minorities, the communist state has conscientiously pursued ethnic-regional autonomy and affirmative action for social levelling, which, nevertheless, have been seriously eroded by the introduction of more assimilationist policies for over two decades.

Any correction must begin with a rigorous defence of the socialist initiatives still largely in place, highlighting two aligned factors: First, the accusation of 'colonialism' against the initial communist takeover of Xinjiang, Tibet, and other minority areas is misplaced. Not only did the revolution aim at the liberation of all and reject the nation-state model common to colonial modernity, constructing a novel political community enfolding both unity and diversity, it also carried out a social programme to achieve fair and equal recognition and inter- and intra-community solidarity. After all, Chinese socialism does not require a same cultural identification, and minority groups are by no means obliged to conform to the Han cultural traditions. Second, even the accelerated mutation of socialist universalism into capitalist nationalism through methods of homogenization is nowhere near to 'genocide', not in Xinjiang, nor anywhere else. Genocide doesn't go with poverty alleviation or other welfarist policies. The aforementioned evidence of faster minority population growth than the national average alone is self-explanatory. Concerning Xinjiang, between 2010 and 2018, the minorities grew in size from around 13 million to 15.86 million, in which the Uyghurs increased from 10.17 million to 12.7 million, or a 25 per cent jump. In the same period, the growth rate of Han people was 2 per cent.[64] The real point is that departing from socialism would only delegitimize the People's Republic as a multination state, destabilizing the minority attachment to it nurtured during decades of shared effort.

The central argument is that the revolutionary construction of the multinational, semi-federal PRC determined the nature of its self-defence, motivated not by nationalism but by socialism, with the ultimate aim of defeating capitalism and imperialism. Nationalism in China is thus defined and sustained by socialism: once the former overpowers the latter, that self-defence slips onto shaky ground. Deterioration of socialism,

---

64 The Xinjiang Academy of Social Sciences, 'A Research Report on Xinjiang's Demographic Question Hyped in the Foreign Media', 3 September 2020, tech.sina.com. cn/roll/2020-09-03/doc-iivhvpwy4663091.shtml.

then, means forgoing the original aim of national liberation and unification promised by the communist victory, thereby emptying nationalist
goals of their historically constructed and morally justified social
substance. Authoritarian capitalist integration would invalidate purely
nationalist assertions and strengthen centrifugal propensities more than
any foreign plot to dismantle China. Indiscriminate condemnation of
Beijing's Xinjiang policy exerts no real effect without a contextualized
analysis that differentiates between what is fading away and what is being
carried forward, or between the justice of communist commitment to
ethnic equality and autonomy translated into laws and policies, and the
injustice of capitalist homogenization imbuing majority assimilation. If
the communist baseline of 1949 is itself forsaken, the plan to 'Liberate
Taiwan', initially integral to the Communist Revolution, can no longer
appeal except as a purely nationalist goal. Contestation in Hong Kong is
ultimately not about local democracy, nor is it resolvable through the
demand of sovereignty alone. Rather than a choice between upholding or
demolishing the initial design, the nature of the *one country* and its system
matters. In the end, it all hinges on what develops on the mainland.
Without offering a socially and politically attractive alternative to authoritarian capitalism, China is fighting an uphill battle to contain separatist
forces. Only by keeping its laurels from liberation struggles can China be
guarded against a descent into an outlandish nationalist colonizer.

From women's liberation to reinventing feminism without socialism

The communists in China held the liberal and Marxist conviction of the
necessity of women's liberation. Marx and Engels in *The Holy Family*
affirmed Charles Fourier's idea that 'the change in a historical epoch can
always be determined by the progress of women towards freedom . . . The
degree of emancipation of women is the natural measure of general emancipation.'[65] But beyond theory, it was the extraordinary subordination and
suffering of women in traditional Chinese culture that helped motivate
and justified the revolution. In the sexual hierarchy, women were treated

---

65 Marx and Engels, *The Holy Family*, New York: International Publishers, 1975:
ch. 8, section 6.

as perpetual minors or inadequately human – in addition to experiencing class and other inequalities. In his 1927 report on the peasant movement, Mao famously called for the breaking of the 'four chains': political regime, clan patriarchy, superstition and the patriarchal family. The cause of women's liberation in China had been pioneered by educated republican revolutionaries, such as Qiu Jin and He Zhen, along with their male comrades.

The communists went many miles farther by engaging the 'woman-work' of consciousness raising and mass mobilization. In Ruijin 1934, 'citizens of the Chinese Soviet Republic' were declared equal 'without distinction of sex, religion or nationality'. The 'thorough emancipation of women' sought freedom from marriage: material support for women's independence from domestic bondage, as well as their public and political participation. Such cultural products as the 'white-haired girl' (who fled abuses by a landlord to survive on wild plants in the mountains before joining the revolution – a true story) and the 'red detachment of women' (who fought the white army in Hainan – also a true and legendary tale) promoted these values in popular culture of the bravery and beauty of revolutionary feminism. It took China over a century of reforms and revolutions to shatter many of the old forms of female oppression along with other fundamental social changes – a landed patriarchal structure, the fixed gender division of labour and the customary perception of women as an inferior class. The strenuous struggle by and for women, bound up with those for equality and justice across social arenas, is a significant dimension of communist revolution and its legacies.

Socialist modernization in the PRC continued to align socialism and feminism in a form of 'state feminism' – a term borrowed from the Nordic social democracies to indicate a women-friendly state obliged to equalize gender relations by legal and policy means. The communist government, through its 'transmission belt' infrastructure and particularly the All China Women's Federation (ACWF) with its local branches down to the villages and work units, eliminated foot-binding, child brides and the trafficking of women; it also outlawed forced widowhood chastity, arranged marriage without individual consent, domestic violence and workplace discrimination. The landmark Marriage Law (1950) set up a moral standard for the new society. A new version of this law was made in 1980 to ease divorce for the willing female partner, and again revised in 2001 to improve protection for women and children in a market environment where rich men were engaging in polygamy and other exploitative relationships. Women's participation in the workforce and other socially recognized activities and public life became the norm, as did the principles of equal pay for equal work, gender parity in educational opportunities, and medical services in female health and child care. Breaches of these principles even in the private sphere were met with government and community intervention, an approach that might be considered controversial but is nevertheless essential in a feminist state committed to women's protection – the public–private demarcation is in any case contextual. As organized workers, farmers and professionals with earnings and status largely comparable to their male compatriots, women in China enjoyed an unprecedented degree of economic autonomy, freedom and self-esteem. The profundity of civilizational advance represented by these changes cannot be exaggerated, as generally explained by Juliet Mitchell in *Women: The Longest Revolution*.[66]

Removing systematic and institutionalized male domination is one of the greatest achievements of Chinese communists. Vital to this undertaking is an ideology of empowering women. The goal of gender equality, still ideologically strong as a notion of justice in public culture, has survived the commercialization of values amid widening gaps between principle and reality, law and enforcement. The power of this ideology also helps explain why family planning was largely uncontroversial in urban China, and why legalizing gay rights have been relatively socially acceptable (starting with the decriminalization of homosexuality in 1997). As long as gender equality is upheld, women can fight and expect support from the government, ACWF and local teams, the courts, media and civil associations. Despite a drastic decline of both state feminism and social commitment towards equality in the marketplace since the 1990s, the PRC remains widely recognized as a model of women's liberation in the developing world. Amartya Sen is one of several commentators who have investigated how China, with its huge rural population and low average income, was able to achieve the levelling of life chances for women through female education, health care, employment and public participation.

Yet the guardian state has inbuilt limitations: it is simultaneously protective and repressive, liberating and intrusive. The one child policy

66 Juliet Mitchell, *Women: The Longest Revolution*, San Francisco, CA: Bay Area Radical Education Project, 1966. It includes a comment on the Chinese experience.

involved forced sterilization and abortion in rural areas, where it accommodated two children; subsequent research has shown that without such draconian methods both slower population growth and better gender balance could have been achieved. Mass participation from women themselves notwithstanding, national developmentalism and social paternalism overrode feminism. The institutionalization of pro-women provisions and the incorporation of women's organizations into governmental structures, conceived in statist rather than societal terms, amounted to a public patriarchy entailing dependency. This undermined the feminist commitment of the state itself, reflected in China's much poorer performance in the metrics of formal 'political representation and empowerment' than in other measurements of economic opportunity, educational attainment and health. Since losing the quota system implemented during the Cultural Revolution, which required one-third female representation in central and local government and legislature bodies, numbers of women in government have fallen to dismal levels. China's ranking in the annual UNDP's Gender Development Index dropped to number 86 out of 189 countries in 2017, and then in 2018 to number 103 of 149 countries – significantly down from 2006, when it was ranked 63 among 115 countries in the World Economic Forum's Global Gender Gap (GGG) Reports. Of the Central Committee's 205 current members, only eleven are female, while the 19th Politburo comprising twenty-five people includes only one woman and its standing committee is all male. The NPC fares better, with just under a quarter of its deputies being female, but in contrast to more egalitarian times very few women hold ministerial and provincial-level positions; factory and village heads are also mostly male. Women are more visible, however, among private entrepreneurs. The appalling underrepresentation of women in government is predictable, given the general repudiation of egalitarianism from these quarters.

State feminism had its own problems though. Mao's celebrated mantra that 'women can do whatever men can do' implied a hidden male standard for 'equality'. 'Equality through sameness', so to speak, promoted 'iron girls' and strict gender parity on the one hand and special care for the 'weaker sex' (during menstruation and pregnancy, for example) on the other, an approach that relied on a false epistemology of female physiological weakness. The theoretical dilemma of equality versus difference was resolved by ossifying the production and reproduction of knowledge about fixed gender roles; male supremacy was superficially rejected, but in practice men's work and physiology were standardized. Amid such biologically confined understandings of womanhood, any sexual difference, innate or adapted, appeared as obstacles rather than attributes to equality. Yet equality is required precisely because of the complex play of similarities and difference between the sexes as regards needs, desires, abilities and attainments, notwithstanding the technologies that have vastly increased human control over the body.

It might be accidental that 'gender' was not introduced into the Chinese language as socially determined sex roles until around 1993. This may have contributed to the socialist state's collusion in producing working women's 'double burden' of unpaid housework and child care. Although public dining and nursing helped to reduce that burden, domestic labour was not recognized as 'socially necessary' (in Marx's terminology), and therefore honorable and worthy of payment. Such labour tends to remain a female responsibility, and is now becoming more private and isolated across classes and regions. The persistence of gender divisions in labour everywhere is a great example of how the historically contingent can be unconsciously considered 'natural'. Even a state project could not eradicate it, and without further revolutionary changes in common culture, neither household technologies nor the equal sharing of housework will be able to transform this pattern. Still, the lost idea of socializing housework through public services, such as communal and work unit amenities, and the figuring of reproductive labour into the costs of production would make a difference, especially for women.

In the post-socialist transition, women have been losing ground. From the resumption of patriarchal relations and domestic violence to a consumerist construction of femininity in advertisements and TV shows, from private schools teaching codified female manners (*nvde*) and domestic service training classes denouncing equality between servants and their 'masters' to prostitution as a class-differentiated industry of both upscale clubs and shantytown hostels, there has been a sweeping downgrade of female existence. The transformation from a past where 'women held half the sky' in line with workers' pride and rights is staggering. Female enrolment in the nine-year compulsory education programme dropped sharply following rural depopulation, because there were fewer (and hence distant) schools; other factors included formalized teaching and testing, falling expectations and the return of gender discrimination. Nationally the rate of female illiteracy, around 15 per cent, has remained higher than that of males. With a rapidly aging population, falling birth rate and the world's most unbalanced sex ratio – more boys than girls at birth, a result of illegal selective abortions enabled by ultrasound tests – a multifaceted sociodemographic disaster is looming in China. A class implication of gender imbalance means that millions of poor rural males cannot find wives, hence the trafficking of women, even as an increasing number of urban female professionals are left single.

In the labour market, women are significantly disadvantaged. Given the difficulties they face in obtaining and retaining respectable jobs under the conditions of 'economic rationalization', and the additional pressure to succeed as a good wife and mother, women have returned to domestic confines in record numbers. Xi broke with the communist tradition to call on women to embrace their 'unique role' in the family and 'shoulder the responsibilities of taking care of the old and young, as well as educating the children'.[67] This contradicts the conviction of gender equality that is still popular in Chinese society. When the sexist children's song 'Mommy Don't Go to Work' was broadcast on a Central TV programme in 2019, it went viral, prompting a national outcry over sub-standard salaries for women and their subservience in the family. Once there was a belief in liberation through labour, and ten years into market transition the rate of female participation in China's workforce was still relatively high, at 73 per cent. By 2018, that figure had fallen to 61 per cent in an ILO estimation published by the World Bank. The average earnings of women slid down too, from nearly 80 per cent that of men in the late 1970s, to a low of 67 per cent in 2010; the rate has fluctuated since then. In a turnaround from the socialist position on workplace discrimination and the endorsement of pro-women court rulings, the state 'now looks the other way when employers, reluctant to cover costs related to maternity leave, openly pick men over women for hiring and promotions'.[68] Employers believe they are acting rationally in having women last hired and first fired, except in those trades where young women are seen as more cost efficient. Meanwhile, overtime, unsafe conditions and low wages are especially common among cheap female labour. These workers suffer a triply unfortunate identity, being simultaneously poor, female and of rural origin. Many are

---

67 Amy Qin, 'A Prosperous China Says "Men Preferred" and Women Lose', *New York Times*, 17 July 2019.

68 Qin, 'A Prosperous China'.

caught in a web of coercion, labour-related miseries and familial hardship.

In sum, market integration has had two effects on gender relations in China. On the one hand is weakened state and social commitment to equality, leading to some loss of protection for women; and on the other the opening up of new opportunities for individual careers and collective pursuits, hence a gain of more independent choices. Politically conscious feminists have joined officially sponsored programmes as well as connecting with non-governmental organizations. Women's studies has flourished across college courses and training classes through both rural and urban areas. A new feminist movement has developed via publications and translations, discussion and support groups, counselling centres, telephone hotlines, radio talks, oral history, art projects and many other endeavours. The core of the movement is constituted of dedicated scholars and professionals who have won popularity for their work at the grassroots level.

More in line with trends of cultural and identity politics, and often infused with a denial of class, younger activists often take a more liberal, individualistic approach. Rather than attending to market assaults on gender equality, they criticize state intervention, which they see as an imposition; meanwhile, their concerns are mostly middle class, holding little interest for female factory and service sector labourers. Following an earlier generation of mainly American critics, who made some valid criticisms of communists failing to defeat male chauvinism in their own ranks, new wave Chinese feminist claims that the male-dominated revolution conceded to patriarchy in its path to power while suppressing women's subjectivity, and that the top-down approach was undemocratic and unproductive. Each of these points can be countered, however. Revolutionary mobilization from above was apparently necessary, and was supported by extensive participation from below. A state power for women was needed because the structural opposition to women's liberation was sustained by the ideological, legal and coercive apparatuses of the old state. The PRC has had far more success in advancing the socioeconomic status of its female citizens than many others among both Third World countries and Asian capitalist democracies, an achievement that is clearly creditable to the egalitarianism once held dear by the revolutionaries. Decades of market incursion have still not wholly transformed the Chinese collective mind: it remains plain that the Confucian order was patriarchal, that imperialism was oppressive to all genders, and that modern feminist revolutions were needed to eradicate these traditions. The socialist state was both protective and empowering, although it could certainly have done more to overcome its contradictions.

The received metanarrative of women's liberation in China is well grounded. It is also all the more alluring at a time when inequalities are trespassing on social space. Old and new forces against women are a reminder of what has been hard won and what must be defended. Notably, while a youthful feminist revisionism is fashionable, many liberal feminists are also instinctively reluctant to cheer market values; in other words, the rightward drift of Chinese intellectual circles has been least apparent among the female contingent. It is hard to sell the total rejection of socialist feminism in a country where generations of women since the early twentieth century have themselves experienced revolution and liberation albeit alongside setbacks and disappointments. An obvious question, then, is why women's liberation as part and parcel of revolution and socialism should be attacked by feminists? Surely this is self-defeating and retards the endeavour of gender equality? What would be the better way forward?

Arguably, one fruit borne of the new feminist interrogation of state feminism is the delusion of equality as sameness. The (re)discovery of an authentic and essential female identity has prompted discourse around an ontological femininity that was once repressed. But such arguments seek to rehabilitate an oriental female image and related gender norms without harming women's social recognition, as though that were possible. Their politically charged starting point is that female agency was marginalized, if not crushed, by the nationalist and communist causes for which women's liberation was a means rather than the end. But can women be so severed from the nation and society at large? Did the independence of an oppressed people or the transformation of social relations generally have nothing to do with the female population? The conceptual separation between gender and class, or between women's liberation and proletarian emancipation, suggests that these ideas have different or even conflicting meanings.

To be sure, *liberation* is a contested concept, as is *equality*. Yet if women still desire to liberate themselves, can they achieve it without participating in the struggle to change society's structural conditions as a whole? Is gender equality really possible without inequalities being tackled across the political economy? Women might be treated as a special underclass, but their collective identity is plural and fluid. Poor women share more with their fellow males than with elite females. The fact that female migrant workers embody multiple disadvantaged positions is also a reminder that class analysis doesn't have to be gender blind. As the question of class encompasses other social divisions, nothing less than a socialist feminism can fulfil feminists' own objective of replacing old prejudices that reproduce not only gender but also class, ethnic, national and other inequalities. The women's movements in the global South are thus 'compelled by their localities to address the intersection of gender oppression with imperialist, racial, and class oppression'[69] This is why the Communist Revolution in China was consciously and inherently a women's revolution, integrating strands of socialism and feminism that have endured ever since. Given the modern consciousness of gender equality, does not a narrow, exclusive gender politics undermine and trivialize the feminist cause?

The cultural politics of difference and recognition is not necessarily one-sided, except where it slips into challenging the politics of equality as with some trends in middle-class feminism currently prevalent in China. Encouraged by and also kindling the neoliberal turn since the 1990s, this trend has trapped itself in a misconceived dichotomy between state and capital as between oppression and freedom. Detached from gendered class struggle, class-conscious feminist critiques and the traditional revolutionary women's movement, an essentialized identity politics embraces concrete commercialization and an abstract global modernity. The point is illustrated by the disjunction in China between a diminishing (though increasingly high-profile) elitist feminism and a labour politics that engages the mass of women workers.

This reinvented feminism could get back on track by widening feminist concerns to address where market reforms are failing women along with labour and national minorities. A synthesis of the best elements of state feminism and of anti-statist feminism might be attainable. The latter could contribute to redefining socialism by reviving its essence, in the form of the social. Although women are doubly confined to unsettled post-socialism and globalizing capitalism, imagining post-capitalist

---

69 Christina Gilmartin, *Engendering the Chinese Revolution: Radical Women, Communist Politics and Mass Movements in the 1920s*, Oakland, CA: University of California Press, 1995: 6.

possibilities in a path-dependent context of pro-women and pro-labour socialist legacies could begin with the social realm. This is where women's rights can be fought and support must be built, where female miseries and accomplishments can both assume public recognition, and where gendered socioeconomic structures and power relations can be contested and transformed. Such a strategy would also enable feminism to rise to demographic-ecological, political and cultural challenges, as feminism in both theory and practice can no longer be limited to questions of gender relations. Socialist feminism would engender universal implications. The *woman question* would transcend gender to engage with the *human condition*. Such a feminism is antithetical to both communist paternalism and middle-class disorientation. It fights for the liberation of all sexes. A political windfall could be that if people are equally limited in political freedom and participation in China, owing to the privileged legitimacy of gender equality in the communist tradition, feminism could lead the way in socialist struggles.

The return of class politics

None of the issues articulated in ethnic-regional, cultural-religious and gender perspectives can be resolved in isolation from their structural and class situations. Returning to this fundamental commonality, the primary category of the labouring classes (*laodong renmin*) as the main body of a sovereign people accentuates the question of subjectivity, agency and consciousness in China's transformed political and socioeconomic landscape. Although race, gender, ethnicity and other identities cannot be fully incorporated under *class*, a term that cannot be all-representative, it is also true that none of these categories can stand alone: they are all in flux and intersectional, cutting across and (re)configuring one another. Moreover, class does define the basic structure of social relations and conditions. Neither class determinism nor class denial is conceptually or empirically conceivable. In fact, sexism, strained ethnic relations, Islamophobia and racism have followed in the wake of the degradation of labour. The decline of respect and protection for minority cultures and women's equal rights is also synchronic with the burying of class language. Police oppression in response to labour unrest and minority protests is consistent. Social movements elsewhere hinge on class struggle in one way or another too. As Marx explains, workers are privileged as a revolutionary class 'which has a universal character because its sufferings are universal, and which does not claim a *particular redress* because the wrong which is done to it is not a *particular wrong* but *wrong in general*'.[70] This conviction of universal emancipation led by the working class is not dated in China, where numbers of industrial and service workers have swelled rather than shrunk. Broadly defined blue collar workers in the manufacturing sector alone are over 200 million strong, certainly the world's largest industrial labour contingent.[71]

One peculiarity of the PRC state is its position as supreme and effective arbiter, structurally, ideologically and communicatively, of class and social relations. Despite bureaucratic complicities, this state is autonomous with massive economic, political and cultural capital. Theoretically, the state is never neutral, and its autonomy is relative. But the reach of the communist state, through past struggle against class foes and its present erosion of class awareness, has determined the mutable nature of China's labour, gender and ethnic regimes, as well as its politics. The voided discourse of class – and along with it of exploitation, alienation, surplus value and so on – is nevertheless a vain attempt to conceal what is not concealable. If modernity requires state craft, and if the state is decisive for any socioeconomic system to survive antagonisms, then a functioning state must be in control of the compass of class. Class rule, in this sense of embodiment in state machinery and policy making of dominant class interests, colours or defines state power. Having retreated so much from its founding commitment, the regime puts its legitimacy on the line. Labour protests, ethnic riots, environmental disputes and other social discontents are localized, scattered, contained or crushed, but their political synergy is striking. The crisis of Chinese capitalism is simultaneously one of the PRC state. Mass incidents are not reminiscent of communist mass movements of the past, as the party leadership is not only absent but is also itself in question. Conspicuously, however, the language and framing of social resistance are sourced from the official ideology. Strikes, for example, 'are typically demonstrations in the name of the Chinese revolution not

---

70 Karl Marx, 'Contribution to the Critique of Hegel's Philosophy of Right', in Marx and Engels, *Selected Works in One Volume*, London: Lawrence & Wishart, 1968: 219.

71 Li Peilin and Cui Yan, 'The Structural Change of Social Strata and Its Socio-Economic Impact in China, 2008–2019', *Jiangsu Social Sciences* 4, 2020. 51–60.

protests against it. They contest capitalist norms and demand socialism.'[72]

Primary triggers of labour movements in the manufacturing sector since the 1990s, from mass layoffs and job precarity to inhumane conditions and general insecurity, have been extensively documented. In 2004, for example, the Japanese-owned Uniden, a Walmart supplier in Shenzhen, saw a sporadic yet determined strike that lasted five months. In 2010, striking workers at the Nanhai Honda motor plant in Foshan, Guangdong, demanded a pay rise based not on the minimal legal requirement but on what they believed to be fair. In an open letter they argued for economic justice: 'We know that this plant counts its profit in billions every year, and this is the fruit of our workers' hard labour.' Similar protests took place in several other Honda and Toyota auto parts supply factories in 2012–13. The largest strike in recent memory took place in 2014 and involved 40,000 workers in Dongguan, Guangdong, at the Yue Yuen complex that supplies Nike, Reebok and Adidas. Workers at a sister factory in Jiangxi acted in solidarity with their fellow shoemakers, and there was also support from workers in the China Operations arm of IBM in Shenzhen. The latest industrial actions have implicated many more multinationals, including Apple, Dell, Samsung, Flextronics International and Pepsi. Contractors in the retailing and construction industries tend to face even more unrest.

Workers are not free of capitalist exploitation and humiliation even in the state sector, as the market operates everywhere by the logic of profit. In July 2009, at Tonghua Iron and Steel, thousands of past and current workers protested against the provincial government's plan to privatize the company. They were accused by market liberals of having an SOE complex.[73] Workers at the Shenzhen Hengtong rubber factory also went on strike in 2013, prompted by the installation of surveillance cameras to spy on machine operators. As SOEs, much like POEs, are following the rule of capital, workers in both sectors are becoming more united. They are also better informed, connecting with one another through cell phones, text messages, microblogs and WeChat, and sometimes circumventing internet censorship. In April 2019, a group of workers suffering from silicosis signed a petition calling for the release of three labour rights

---

72 Vijav Prashad, 'The Chinese Ambition', News Click, 11 October 2018.
73 Press conference, 28 July 2009, unn.people.com.cn/GB/14780/21697/9732426.

activists who had offered them legal and material assistance. The wife of one of the three was also a feminist organizer.

The question, then, is whether there is an anti-capitalist proletarian agency in the making. Such a question may not resonate in the world's so-called post-industrial zones, but does in countries such as China where the real economy continues to absorb labour, despite scattered signs of deindustrialization as well as organizational and technological changes affecting labour processes and employment patterns. Should workers be expected to become the gravediggers of capitalism and eventually transcend class society? Can they develop a new social imaginary while forging a transformative political programme? From suicide (as at Foxconn) to collective action, from purely material demands to independent unionization, what do such developments signify? Are Chinese workers, after decades of holdups, finally on their way to conscious class struggle? Or rather is their movement at low tide, as the recent strike maps of China Labour Bulletin (CLB) seem to suggest? Having discussed workers' dilemmas resulting from the collision of state and capital, the riddle remains whether and how a defeated Chinese working class can remake itself. Leaving aside the unsettled theoretical question of whether class consciousness is imputed from within or injected from outside, it must be class struggle that engages the working class in its own making.

It is difficult to generalize over such different and complex situations across such a vast country, especially because of the gap between the class identification of a nominally communist party and the workers themselves – plus the absence of a political party capable of labour organization. If class consciousness is contingent on both ideological education and organized struggle, then by definition workers cannot be a 'class for itself' without a party of their own. The ruling CCP, however, is in fear of the labour movement from its own intimate experience of revolution and has pre-emptively proscribed the organizational, conceptual and terminological vehicles of such movements and class consciousness. The party is thus itself the biggest impediment to class renewal. The ACFTU has attempted top-down reforms, and local arbitration commissions have sometimes adopted conciliatory approaches and even won cases for workers. But local authorities often regard labour unrest as a menace to stability and have even resorted to force, including hiring thugs to disperse crowds. On 6 August 2019, the joint public security forces in a Shenzhen exercise openly used as their hypothetical enemies a group of workers holding placards demanding unpaid wages. An onsite WeChat commentator remarked that the government was not equivalently interested in target- ing financial tycoons who owed the nation billions of yuan in dodged taxes. Instead of 'masters of society' – a received self-identity of workers in new China, labour is now treated as low status, threatening and in need of taming. With its physical and discursive supremacy, the Chinese state in strong coalition with capital can manage to hold class politics at bay. Beyond this retreat from class, class power itself has been overturned in China. Losing even an imperfect workers' state is nothing less than a catastrophe for labour. No conscious class force is possible before the tri- angular relationship among labour, capital and state can be repoliticized for clarity to overcome the impasse.

A useful approach is to recognize the formation of a class against capital without making a dichotomy between class *for* itself and class *in* itself. Migrant labour movement in Guangdong, mainly outside institu- tional norms and official 'collective consultation' characterized by disengaging labour, shows that workers' agency is the impetus of class struggle in the face of formal unionism and authoritarianism.[74] An outstanding expression of class awakening can be read directly in workers' verses, such as those of Xu Lizhi, who wrote 'I swallowed a moon made of iron', before jumping to his death in 2014 at the age of just twenty-four:

> I swallowed an iron moon
> they called it a screw
> I swallowed industrial wastewater and unemployment forms
> bent over machines, our youth died young
> I swallowed labour, I swallowed poverty
> swallowed pedestrian bridges, swallowed this rusted-out life
> I can't swallow any more
> everything I've swallowed roils up in my throat
> I spread across my country
> a poem of shame.[75]

---

74 Tim Pringle, 'A Class Against Capital: Class and Collective Bargaining in Guang- dong', *Globalization* 14:2, 2017: 245–58.

75 Eleanor Goodman, ed., *A Verse of Us: Iron Moon – An Anthology of Chinese Worker Poetry*, New York: White Pine Press, 2017.

And 'On my deathbed':

> I want to take another look at the ocean,
> Behold the vastness of tears from half a lifetime
> I want to climb another mountain,
> Try to call back the soul that I've lost
> I want to touch the sky,
> Feel that blueness so light
> But unable to do any of these, I'm leaving the world . . .[76]

A line from an anonymous coal miner took an even sharper tone: 'We miners toil to dig out black coal, in the dark; darkness betrays the sun.'[77] And an earlier poem found on a factory dormitory wall was forthrightly political:

> We are a mass of *dagongzai* [young men who sell labour]
> Coming from the north, coming from the west
> At first we didn't know what *dagongzai* meant
> Now we know, toiling from the sunrise to the sunset
> Toiling with drops of blood and sweat
> Selling our labour to the boss, selling our bodies to the factory
> Do what they dictate to you, no negotiation, no bargaining, but obey
> Money is the magic, and what the capitalists bestow on you
> A commodity, a commodity.[78]

One thing that is preventing workers from politically organizing themselves is their atomized existence. The super-mobility of semi-proletarianized rural migrants constantly on the move leads to extremely fluid identities and collectives. Traditional socialization among people of the same regional origins and local dialects has diminished with the influx of heterogeneous migrants. Footloose between urban workplaces and rural homes, subsisting on quick-fix and precarious jobs, their collective and discrete spaces are not even consistently visible, especially

---

76 Chan, Selden and Pun, *Dying for an iPhone:* 190.

77 'Long Live the Miners', quoted in Pun Ngai, 'Miners in the Historical Tunnel: Back to the State or Forward to the Market?', *References* 18, 25 April 2014.

78 'Poetry on the Wall', anonymous, quoted in Pun, *Made in China*: 23.

in a vast informal economy. Such transient life paths are antithetical to the concentrated work and residential communities that are the classical settings of class formation. In addition, the digital generation squanders its attention on mobile phones and other individual and consumerist distractions. Perhaps a despondent elegy for what has been lost, such as the rustbelt of formerly commanding SOEs, in the market era China's mode of growth is better represented by casual construction and transport workers. The nationwide strike by long-distance truck drivers and haulage contractors in June 2018, for example, was unable to formulate any political demand other than higher hauling rates from an increasingly informalized industry dominated by app-based platforms and owned by private companies. China has witnessed an ever greater concentration of capital along with the fragmentation of labour: 'a generalized but segmented proletariat'.[79] This sheer power asymmetry is not being addressed by either the governments or the official trade unions.

One incident offers a microscopic illustration. In May 2018, workers of the Shenzhen Jasic Technology Company complained about their conditions to the local labour bureau. Rarely and remarkably, the official union branch encouraged self-unionization. Workers collected signatures in late June and July, petitioning for independent organizing. Their leaders were subsequently fired or detained, charged with 'gathering a crowd to disrupt public order', and there were over a hundred arrests. Some were put under house restrictions and surveillance, or subjected to security interrogations and assaults after release. CLB pointed out in a November plea for the detainees' immediate release that the protesters had done 'nothing more than demand workers' legal rights', and the case attracted much attention because students from elite universities came to the workers' aid. In early 2018 a group at Beijing University (Beida) launched a campaign for improving the conditions of service workers on campus; while studying *Capital*, a few also were inspired by the MeToo movement. Later, as though in belated answer to Mao's call for youth to walk a road that meets the workers, they formed the Jasic Worker Support Group and travelled to Shenzhen to join the workers on site. As the Marxist associations and Maoist reading groups spread among a young internet generation, they encounter closure orders and disciplinary punishments as well as police

---

79 Samir Amin, 'The New Imperialist Structure', *Monthly Review*, 71:3, July/August 2019: 38–9.

harassment. The suppression of Jasic mobilization in several urban centres 'is among the hardest . . . in contemporary Chinese history'. According to the administrations of Beida and Renmin University among others, these students were guilty of 'criminal activities' manipulated by 'black hands'. 2019 saw tighter control and further crackdowns, and six more students disappeared right before 1 May, the International Labour Day. A while later, in their public video confessions, even Yue Xin, a recent Beida graduate, ardent activist and highly respected student leader, appeared broken by emotional strain.[80]

Worker–student solidarity poses a daring challenge to a regime afraid of delegitimation and instability. Unlike Tiananmen in 1989 when the two protesting groups were clearly separate, this time they have begun to unite and have approached some sort of organizing strategy and class consciousness. Directly appealing to the twentieth-century communist tradition of intellectuals bending themselves into labour's cause, *New Left Review* carried an anonymous 'May Fourth Manifesto' in 2019, written from within an event where 'the Chinese working class [was] stepping onto the stage of history for the first time as an independent force'. This is historically inaccurate, given the raging workers' struggles throughout revolutionary China since the 1920s. But the 'Manifesto' did sharply discern, in the familiar language of the Cultural Revolution, 'a group of power-holding capitalist-roaders inside the Party': the 'bureaucratic bourgeois class' that subjugates society to the service of capital while criminalizing socialist dissent must be eradicated.[81]

In China, labour activists have insisted that their concerns are consistent with the party line. Workers and students take official rhetoric literally and speak within the boundary of state ideology. This brings us back to the thesis of rightful resistance by the subalterns, articulated and legitimized on the regime's own terms. To confront the discrepancies between

---

80 Among many reports, see Zhang Yueran, 'The Jasic Strike and the Future of the Chinese Labour Movement', 14 September 2018, chinoiresie.info/the-jasic-struggle-and-the-future-of-the-chinese-labour-movement; and 'Leninists in a Chinese Factory: Reflections on the Jasic Labour Organising Strategy', *Made in China* 2, 2020; Ivan Franceschini and Nicholas Loubere, eds, *Dog Days: Made in China Yearbook 2018*, Canberra: ANU Press, 2019: 26–75; L. Y. Au, 'The Jasic Struggle in China's Political Context', *New Politics* 17:2, Winter 2019; Jenny Chan, 'Jasic Workers Fight for Union Rights,' *New Politics* 17:2, Winter 2019; Yuan Yang, 'Inside China's Crackdown on Young Marxists', *FT Magazine*, 14 February 2019.

81 Young Pioneers, 'May Fourth Manifesto', *New Left Review* 116, May/July 2019: 1–3.

such terms and the reality is to push for what has been publicly pledged. While windows for even 'rightful' inputs have been ever fragile, the Chinese axiom of just rebellion continues to validate strikers, protesters and petitioners – and socialism rings truer with the opposition than with government. Still, state capacity of containing class struggle by both oppression and accommodation is not only about adaptability, but also a manifestation of the lasting moral pressure entrenched in the regime's former self, distancing the Chinese case from other capitalist countries.

Vacillating between a waning hope of empowerment and actual power-lessness, labour seems to be trying its last non-revolutionary resort: forcing the communist party and state to stick to its original legitimacy. Capitalist injustice and brutality cannot be socially desirable, and socialist values linger to sway policies. So long as the names of socialism and communism have symbolic power, Jodi Dean writes, they can 'touch the Real that ruptures them, keeping alive the possibility of its transformation'.[82] If class identities and alignment are liquid and open ended, the state–capital–labour dynamic would be where mass demands can be made and fermenting social power reinstated in defiance of systemic atomization and fragmentation. The tragic course of capitalism with Chinese characteristics must be reversed, despite or especially because of the conditions brought about by the information and technological revolution, automation and precarity. Chinese workers in all sectors engaging in defensive and offensive struggles and thereby their own class remaking still have a world to win.

---

82 Jodi Dean, 'Afterword' in Sorace et al., eds, *Afterlives*: 337–9.

7

From internationalism to neoglobalism

Since the 1990s, China has steadily deepened its voluntary integration into the system of global capitalism, changing its position in the world political economy in the process. This is a significant development, as the participation of China, with its giant, quality and hard-working labour force and vast market, has accelerated capital expansion and has helped to perpetuate the system globally. This effect of rescuing capitalism from its structural crisis is being paid for with the autonomy and socialist identity of the PRC, held since 1949, with vast human, social and environmental consequences. The short-lived post–Cold war relaxation of tension and the US distraction following 9/11 opened a small window for China to grow more integrated in the existing order of rules and institutions. The geopolitical barriers, however, as revealed in a unilateral and unlimited trade war as well as increasing US-led international pressures, lies in American determination to thwart any potential competitor. But what is the competition, and what is the nature of the prize? Are the competitors 'great powers', defined apolitically, or is it a matter of civilizational rivalries? Is the battle between opposing socioeconomic systems and growth models, or is there something ideological at stake, such as socialism versus capitalism, or, as many believe, democracy versus autocracy? Or is the struggle one of national interests against old and new imperialism, concerning security, welfare and a scramble for the planet's rapidly depleting resources? Might the contentions around globalization as we know it catalyse geopolitical conflict and cause social destruction, or could they potentially lead to a transnational movement for global equality and justice?

As noted, it should not be assumed that Chinese development must imitate the West. The supposedly normal pathway of capitalist modernization was blocked by foreign imperialism – which also explains the dual character of the Communist Revolution in China. Self-consciously a part of the long haul of a socialist world revolution, the communist victory decisively impacted the post-war realignment of international politics. In pursuit of economic self-reliance, revolutionary nationalism and Third Worldist internationalism, Maoist foreign policy aimed to establish a true global China in the 1950s and 1960s. In Chinese socialism, therefore, nationalism is premised on internationalism, and vice versa. Internationalism entailed two related concerns and policy dimensions: the liberation of exploited and oppressed peoples, both domestically and globally, bearing on internal ethnic relations as well as foreign affairs. Socialism is also tied to internationalism, as any corrosion of one would inexorably erode the other. This is evident in China's synchrony of ethnic conflicts at home and backlash abroad in recent years. To trace the convoluted trajectory of China in the world, both as part of the international communist movement and since its demise, we begin with a critical assessment of how the PRC lost its way amid the complex interactions and rivalries of socialism, nationalism and internationalism. Each underwent significant mutations through changing geopolitical and geoeconomic conditions.

Liberation nationalism and Third World internationalism

The capitalist mode of production and extraction is totalizing, as well as uneven. The Chinese socialist path can be seen as a torturous search for an alternative. New China set itself the task of development through both learning and leaping, in order to shake off its economic backwardness as fast and efficiently as possible both qualitatively and quantitatively (as specified in the 1958 General Line of Socialist Construction). This was possible above all because of the freedom China had earned through its epic revolution, breaking shackles both traditional and modern. Through intimate experience the Chinese people knew only too well how imperialist domination, extraction and sabotage would hinder poorer countries in their attempts to retain surpluses, perpetuating their anguish of underdevelopment.

Revolutionary nationalism was the source and condition of the PRC being fundamentally autonomous in its otherwise seriously constrained global position. The concept of a 'class nation' or a 'nation for itself' is a useful shorthand (as discussed in Chapter 1). Such a nation may acquire self-awareness of its class-like position in the capitalist system, and rise to change it. This explains how China, once hard to define within the European nation-state framework, could have emerged as an independent and powerful modern nation through its struggle for liberation and socioeconomic development. It is key here to distinguish between two categories of nationalism: that of the oppressed and that of the oppressor nations. To overturn its internationally 'classed' position, in stark contrast with crippled colonial modernity, the PRC born of national and social struggles had to seek international alliances for support and security while sustaining self-reliance as its foundational national policy. In other words, self-reliance could not be isolation, and China did develop important trade relations during its initial phase of import substitution. This double-class aspect to the Chinese revolution, both socially and nationally, is also antithetical to the bourgeois nationalism prevalent in Third World anticolonial and postcolonial endeavours.

Both class and nation are ingrained in the identity and nexus of a class-nation rooted in the capitalist materiality of uneven and compressed development, amid tensions between domestic class conflicts and anti-imperialist foreign relations. As yet, the Communist Revolution in China pursued national and social liberation simultaneously, where internal class relations had to be readjusted in accordance with more pressing nationalist demands. At times, the party's 'united front' partially suppressed class interests. Similar approaches were adopted to bring around or neutralize and mutualize the upper class within ethnic minorities. This was reassembled as the strategic starting point for Third World solidarity in Chinese socialist foreign policy. The PRC state was then able to chart such compatibility in bridging class-based communist internationalism and nation-based Third Worldism, where the success of a united front hinged on carefully steered class struggle. Politically and ideologically consistent, the dual-natured Chinese revolution prepared the ground for the new regime's diplomatic crusade to renounce all the unequal treaties imposed on China in the past and to reshape regional and global geopolitics and power relations.

As 'socialism in one country' is untenable, both by definition and in practice, Chinese communists had no illusions, and declared that 'the people who have triumphed in their revolution should help those still struggling for liberation. This is our internationalist duty.' It was world imperialism that rendered it impossible for 'a genuine people's revolution in any country' to win and consolidate victory 'without various forms of help from the international revolutionary forces'.[1] China thus went out of its way to provide support and aid to its socialist neighbours; to communist guerrillas in Southeast Asia and Palestine; to Arab and African nationalists; to North American socialists, civil rights activists and black liberation fighters; and to economic projects in many developing countries. Mao's April 1968 statement reiterated the Marxist position that 'racial discrimination in the United States is a product of the colonialist and imperialist system . . . [which] will surely come to its end with the complete emancipation of the Black people.'[2] These actions were an attempt to replicate class struggle internationally and produce an united front, rather than simply to export revolution, and were predicated on self-defence as much as on moral duty. The East was indeed 'red and black' in the long history of communist internationalism since the International Workingmen's Association.[3] Over 50,000 Chinese fought the multinational Whites during the civil war following the Russian Revolution. It was reported from the frontline in 1918 that

> the revolution has made a miracle as the Chinese workers take arms to organize internationalist troops. They are devoted to the socialist cause because under their yellow skin red blood flows and brave hearts beat together with the world proletariat . . .[4]

1 Mao, 'Talk with African Friends', 8 August 1963, *Quotations from Mao*, Beijing: Foreign Language Press, 1966: 178, and 'On the People's Democratic Dictatorship', 30 June 1949, *Selected Works IV*.

2 Mao, 'A New Storm Against Imperialism', *Peking Review*, 19 April 1968: 5–6.

3 Robeson Taj Frazier, *The East is Black*, Durham and London: Duke University Press, 2014.

4 *Arm the People*, 5 September 1918.

Workers from China either returned home to take part in the ongoing Chinese revolution or joined revolutionary struggles in their adopted countries. Their loyalty and courage as International Brigade volunteers in the Spanish Civil War is just one of many examples.[5]

By the same logic, China drew support and assistance from comrades and friends abroad throughout its arduous journey of revolution. Norman Bethune, the Canadian medical doctor who died on duty in the communist Eighth Route Army in Shanxi, deeply moved generations of Chinese people. Mao's commemorative article about him, written ninety years ago in the spirit of world revolution, remains popular. It argued for the necessity of common struggle among the global proletariat and (semi-)colonial peoples, and pledged that proletarian unity was the only way to overthrow imperialism and to liberate nations and peoples: 'This is our internationalism, the internationalism with which we oppose both narrow nationalism and narrow patriotism.'[6] In the same spirit many others travelled to share the Chinese struggle. That class nations of the world should unite, as in the Chinese national anthem – *Arise! All who refuse to be slaves!* – was determined by the global power of transnational counterrevolution, in line with classical proletarian internationalism. In search of an internationalist coalition, the socialist countries and Third World were natural allies. Like China, most poor nations found no passage to independent capitalist development from imperialism's creation of peripheries. Beyond decolonization, an escape had to be blazed from the structural impasse of a globe entangled in unending poverty and conflict.

China was a major player in the first Afro-Asian conference in Bandung in 1955. Based on the 'five principles of peaceful coexistence' previously codified between China and India on trade and communication in the Tibetan region, a 'ten-point declaration' was signed by the participants on national sovereignty and integrity, equality of all races and nations, and non-intervention in international affairs. Zhou Enlai, the PRC premier, skilfully secured a popular front–style platform, despite such anti-communist voices as Nasserite nationalism, which

---

5 For a summary, see Gary Jones, 'The Chinese Volunteers Who Fought in the Spanish Civil War', *South China Morning Post Magazine*, 15 July 2016, scmp.com/magazines/post-magazine/long-reads/article/1989792/chinese-volunteers-who-fought-spanish-civil-war.

6 Mao, 'In Memory of Norman Bethune', 21 December 1939, *Selected Works II*: 337–8.

shielded the brutal suppression of the Egyptian communist movement. China had to perform a difficult balancing act in the region, given its contradictory goals of supporting the Communist Parties, building a united front with the nationalist regimes, and minimally protecting the ethnic Chinese, mostly as business elites, especially in Southeast Asia. One example was Beijing's ambivalence towards events in Indonesia in 1965, standing idly by when hundreds of thousands of accused 'communists' were massacred. With Bandung as a precursor, Yugoslavia, India and Egypt initiated the Non-Aligned Movement (NAM) in 1961 as an autonomous force in a superficially bipolar world. The more radical phase of the movement followed the 1959 Cuban Revolution. Later, in his speech of 1965 at the Second Economic Seminar of Afro-Asian Solidarity held in Ben Bella's Algeria, Che Guevara identified Cuba, like China, as 'an underdeveloped country as well as one that is building socialism'.[7] When the Tricontinental was founded in Havana in 1966, Third Worldism became almost synonymous with Third World socialism. Although initially supportive of this development, China's growing enmity with the Soviet Union and hence the Warsaw Pact countries, as well as Tito's 'revisionism', increasingly led it to treat the NAM as a rival. In the aftermath of an unexpected border war forced on China in 1962, with India pursuing a Forward Defence policy when secular internationalism shattered on both sides, a Sino-Indian discord in Jakarta 1965 aborted a preparatory conference for a second Bandung.

Although this alienated some of its allies and split the Bandung nations along the way, China had otherwise been steadfast in supporting oppressed peoples in their struggles – through a string of progressive events, from Congolese independence to the Algerian revolution. Mao used the occasion of the anti-US protests in Panama in 1964 to call for a 'broadest united front' of 'the peoples of the socialist camp, of Asia, Africa and Latin America, of every continent of the world, of all the countries in love with peace and all the countries suffering from aggression, control, intervention and bullying from the US' to counter imperialist war policies.[8] Meanwhile, China maintained its aid

---

7 Che Guevara, 'Speech at the Afro-Asian Conference in Algeria', 24 February 1965, *Che Guevara Reader: Writings on Politics and Revolution*, New Delhi: LeftWord Books, 2004.

8 'The Chinese People Firmly Support Patriotic Struggles for Justice by the Panama People', *People's Daily*, 12 January 1964.

operations and friendship diplomacy through gratis funds, interest-free loans and direct construction projects alongside its service and training programmes for transferring expertise and technologies. The TAZARA, designed and financed by China in the late 1960s and early 1970s to connect cities in Tanzania and Zambia, was the single longest railway in sub-Saharan Africa. Although China took the initiative in 1961 to repay its debt to the Soviet Union accumulated since the Korean war (eventually refusing an offer of repayment extension) and cleared it by 1965, it kept a much larger foreign aid programme. 'Considerably more altruistic than its peers', according to John Knight, China spent between 5 per cent and 7 per cent of its budget on foreign aid in the early 1970s, compared to 1.5 per cent by the US, 0.9 per cent by the USSR, and 0.7 per cent by the UK.[9] The PRC's international conduct on this front was highly appreciated as a visible and feasible alternative to the prevailing relations between the first and Third World, poisoned by condescension as well as unequal and exploitative exchanges.

Serious distortions had already set in, however, with the Maoist strategy and rhetoric of 'anti-hegemony'. Not exactly replacing traditional Marxist class analysis, China's rejection of the 'camp analysis' of Soviet communism versus US-led capitalism did result in prioritizing nationalism over socialism. The French-originated Three Worlds theory had now been rearticulated in Mao's mapping: the first world was comprised of the US and USSR; the second, the middle elements of Europe, Japan, Canada and Australia; and the third, all of Asia (except Japan), Africa and Latin America. This broad area of the Third World, constituting majority territories and populations as a global countryside, was home to popular resistance that would surround and eventually seize the hegemonic cities comprising the two superpowers. Identifying itself with the Third World rather than the East Bloc, China still defended its own vision of socialism in opposition to what it deemed a betrayal by the Soviet leaders, from Stalin's statism to Khrushchev's revisionism. Indeed, with its own revolutionary path to national ascendance conditioned on liberation from imperialist chains, China's historical experience was more intimately relevant to Third World countries. Beijing was then better positioned than Moscow to impact Non-Aligned

---

9 John Knight, 'Review of Julia Lovell, *Maoism: A Global History*', H-Socialisms, H-Net Reviews, March 2020, h-net.org/reviews/showrev.php?id=54885.

circles: 'That the Chinese communists resisted the idea that the darker nations should be divided into spheres of influence of the two powers made it a principled ally of the third world.' It was not the Soviet version of Three Worlds theory, 'with its partial truths and opportunistic twists', that seized most radical imaginations. Rather, the contingency of anti-communism mostly assuming an anti-Soviet form, as well as the youthful radicalism and Third Worldism of the 1960s, enabled the Chinese perspective to gain 'the widest global currency' and true prestige.[10]

The notion of the Third World was variously criticized for its shifting theoretical grounds, contradictory ramifications and mystified rhetoric. From a Marxist point of view, it also displaced class and social emancipation in its bourgeois nationalist connotations by focusing on the nationalist states more than internationalist social movements. Meanwhile, the undertheorized concept of 'social imperialism' (borrowed from Lenin's *Imperialism: The Highest Stage of Capitalism*, which was written in a very different context), used to describe Soviet hegemony, seemed erratic or sectarian. Disregarding Lenin's original meaning, the CCP adopted the label, paired with 'social fascism', to condemn the 1968 Soviet crackdown in Prague, among other interventions considered illegitimate by the Chinese, in addition to what were perceived as Moscow's chauvinistic impositions on China since the late 1950s. By the 1970s, the fall of the multi-versioned theory itself along with the world it once denoted had become inevitable. The idea of a global alliance against capitalism and imperialism as the Third Worldist project, an international political opposition, gave way to the economic primacy of 'emerging markets' and a thriving development discourse. Decolonization could not live up to its aspiration of reshaping an unjust world for popular democracy and global equality. Stuck in poverty and dependency, many countries under weak bourgeois or strong patrimonial regimes were also susceptible to military coups and communal strife. The east wind had subsided: an age of revolution and liberation was over.

---

10 Vijay Prashad, *The Darker Nations: A People's History of the Third World*, New York: The New Press: 37; Aijaz Ahmad, *In Theory: Classes, Nations, Literatures*, London: Verso, 1992: 306.

Losing the world? China's global repositioning

The rigidity in opposing the Soviet line had grave consequences for the international communist movement and the Third World. China's foreign policy became confusing and at times outright detrimental to local progressive forces and to socialism more generally. The seeds of fracture between the two parties had been sown in the 1920s, over strategies for the Chinese revolution. But it was not until after the 20th Congress of the Communist Party of the Soviet Union (CPSU) in 1956 that fraternity between the two states collapsed. Despite their historical grievances over Stalin's distrust, the Chinese were shocked and angered by Khrushchev's secret speech and subsequent de-Stalinization. Mao refused the military cooperation proposed by Khrushchev, which he considered to be 'big party jingoism' towards China as a dependent junior partner. China shelled Kinmen in August 1958 as a signal of solidarity with the Iraqi revolution against US interference in the Middle East during the Lebanon crisis, but failed to forewarn the Soviets. By 1960 as the Sino-Soviet bilateral relationship had soured, the Soviet Union broke the compact and contracts, withdrew aid and recalled its scientific and technical advisors. They deserted unfinished industrial and defence projects, taking with them blueprints and key equipment. The loss of aid was substantial: despite technically being a loan, with interest payable, it had been duly appreciated. In losing a valuable coalition while simultaneously gaining a powerful enemy, China's foreign environment worsened to the extent that Beijing, amid threats of imminent attack, had to prepare for war. In 1964 China began to build its Third Front industries, moving over two thousand enterprises to remote mountain areas, including nuclear and military research and manufacturing institutions. The Maoist strategy, later summarized as 'digging deep tunnels, storing grain everywhere, and never seeking hegemony', might be hugely wasteful but was believed necessary in these international conjunctions. In the long run and countering coastal bias, it also laid the foundation in parts of China's hinterland for today's Developing the West and BRI projects.

Without getting into the theoretical debate between the two fiercely opposed ideological stances, it will suffice to mention here two *People's Daily* editorials published in 1956 on 'the historical experiences of the proletarian dictatorship'. Mostly in the form of open letters, the CCP published a sequel of 'Long Live Leninism' in 1960 and 'Suggestions on the General Line of the International Communist Movement' in 1963, followed by nine foundational commentaries in reply to the CPSU leadership (1963–4). These critiques – of the post-Stalinist doctrine of 'peaceful' coexistence and competition with the capitalist camp, and of the party and state of the 'whole people' rather than the working classes – were of real theoretical significance, especially in light of the CCP's own belated turn to such a change in the 1990s. The Chinese argument focused on three central questions: the nature of imperialism; war and peace; and relationships among the communist parties.[11] The Soviet position was regarded as a deviation from the Marxist basics of class and revolution: internally prone to a 'capitalist restoration', and externally a betrayal from the internationalist cause of world revolution. By rejecting the Third Way of Nasser and the like endorsed by the Soviet line, the CCP represented the more militant wing of international anti-capitalism, embracing armed national liberation. It also promoted a wider global alliance of workers and peasant masses, as well as intellectual and pro-fessional progressives, against the Cold War order. The disputes between the two parties were indeed over principles.

Practical realities, however, are always more complex. On the one hand, at the first Afro-Asian–Latin American people's solidarity confer-ence in Havana 1966, Wu Xueqian, the lead Chinese delegate, challenged the Soviets. He asked why they had discouraged wars of national liber-ation, and collaborated with the US in the UN by voting to send troops to suppress the Congolese people and by agreeing with the unjust reso-lution on the Dominican ceasefire, while also tolerating South Rhodesian racism. Why had they sat with the representatives of Taiwan, South Korea and South Vietnam to discuss the founding of the Asian Develop-ment Bank? Why had they demanded Soviet–Chinese joint action in Vietnam while attacking China's due effort? And why had they also offered a 'guarantee' of no war in the West, which enabled the US to transfer troops to South Vietnam and elsewhere?[12] These were serious charges. On the other hand, the internationalist commitment in Soviet

---

11 Wu Lengxi, *Ten Years of Debate: 1956–66: Memoir of the Sino-Soviet Relationship*, Beijing: Central Documentary Press, 2013: 312.

12 George Yu, 'China's Failure in Africa', *Asian Survey* 6:8, August 1966: 461–8, 468.

foreign policy seemed to be reviving from years of passivity. The legacy of October, if with zigzags, was seen as 'gradually redeemed rather than irretrievably abandoned.' The agitated third world 'occasioned a substantial and visible exercise of Soviet military power in support of them.'[13] The USSR supplied heavy armaments and specialists to the Vietnamese fighting the US, and provided airlift and equipment to the Cuban forces in Angola and Ethiopia when South Africa intervened (backed by the US, China and Zaire). It directly deployed troops in Afghanistan (however disastrous the outcome) and dispatched aid teams for the Sandinistas in Nicaragua and elsewhere in the Third World jungles. Although the concept of proletarian internationalism has been relegated in revisionist theories, the Soviet state furnished some indispensable assistance to the Third World. 'Even where there was no Soviet military involvement as such, states allied to the USSR or revolutionary movements in conflict with the West were in some measure protected.'[14] Again, such involvement by the Soviet Union was not merely ideological but was also a question of direct security as well as a desire to counterbalance Chinese influence.

Meanwhile, dictated by the enemies of social imperialism, China's own foreign policy became blurry and self-contradictory, and ended up buttressing certain anti-communist dictatorships and reactionary forces. In 1968–9, while having rebuffed American olive branch when the Chinese were deeply involved, with both weapons and field troops, in Vietnam fighting the US invasion, China started to contemplate manoeuvring between the two superpowers. It sided with Pakistan against Bangladeshi independence and sent emergency aid to Sri Lanka in 1971 to put down the left-wing insurgency of the Lanka Samaja Party. It praised the Greek military junta in 1972 and welcomed Gaafar Nimeiry of Sudan to Beijing after the regime massacred the Sudanese communists in the same year. It quickly recognized the 1973 coup in Chile and expelled the Chilean ambassador to China, who refused to comply with Augusto Pinochet. China also accepted a counterrevolutionary coalition against the popular Angolan government that had just emerged from a

---

13 Perry Anderson, *Spectrum*, London: Verso, 2005: 285; Piero Gleijeses, *Conflicting Missions. Havana, Washington and Africa, 1959-1976*, Chapel Hill: University of North Carolina Press, 2002.

14 Ralph Miliband, *Class War Conservatism*, London: Verso, 2015: 266.

long war against Portuguese colonialism. Later it opposed the Afghan communists as well, along with the US, Iran and Pakistan. This shocking record shows the slip into an indiscriminately anti-hegemonic project and how it poisoned the potential for an alternative world order. The passage from socialist and Third Worldist internationalism to an inconsistent, unprincipled nationalist standpoint might have been situationally justifiable as a temporary measure. It was nevertheless ultimately destructive.

This preoccupation with the hegemony of global politics led to China's categorical miscalculations on Soviet power and the East Bloc as a whole, preventing any prospect of a unified anti-imperialist alliance among communist and nationalist states. Khrushchev's ruthless ideological blunder and opportunistic foreign policies – adventurism followed by surrenderism during the Cuban Missile Crisis, for example – and his chauvinistic attitude towards the Chinese and smaller communist parties certainly did not help. He once even used the phrase 'yellow peril'. Mao, too, sometimes forewent international communist considerations and allowed nationalistic sentiment to override Chinese foreign affairs. Yet in its 1956 letter to the CPSU, the CCP presented the dispute as 'internal', since 'the basic contradiction of the era' was defined as the one between imperialism and socialism. In 1960, the need for all-inclusive solidarity was emphasized 'in the fundamental interest of the Chinese people as well as the peoples throughout the world'. Mao vowed that 'the two big socialist countries must unite'.[15] However, it looks as though the mishandling of 'contradictions among the people' that occurred inside China had spread internationally, with internal disagreements among the communist parties escalating into 'contradictions between enemies'. For all its faults and failures, the USSR had functioned as a powerful brake on imperialist war and money machines. This can be fully appreciated only in retrospect: the disappearance of a union of socialist republics in 1991 was of great social and geopolitical significance, amounting to 'an unmitigated catastrophe'.[16] Even if the CPSU was not on the right side at different phases of its dispute with the CCP, the Soviet state was

---

15 Wu, *Ten Years of Debate*: 54, 151, 157.

16 Eric Hobsbawm, *Age of Extremes*, quoted in Anderson, *Spectrum*: 313; Wallerstain, 'What Cold War in Asia? An Interpretative Essay', in Zheng Yangwen, Hong Liu and Michael Szonyi, eds, *The Cold War in Asia: The Battle for Hearts and Minds*, Leiden: Brill, 2010: 23–4.

in the end 'not subject to the logic of imperialism'.[17] Both parties, in their own way, compromised a common cause, by submitting to the Cold War logic of détente or nuclear 'balance of terror' and inflicting fatal damages on international communism and progressive movements in both core and peripheral capitalist regions.

The USSR and PRC had each played a critical part in curbing the Atlantic powers, while sharing responsibilities for the end of both the international communist movement and the Third World. The geopolitical difficulties between the two destroyed their own socialist and internationalist assets. If China's position was particularly painful, that is because it also belonged to the Third World and had been baptized through revolutionary national liberation. Moreover, while the Soviet state evolved into a managerial gatekeeper of the status quo, China's Cultural Revolution was a doomed attempt at shifting the communist project out of the orbit of bureaucratic statism. These differences made the alienation of the PRC from so many of its socialist and Third World fellow travellers all the more lamentable. A precious episode of 'unity of the coloured peoples' was so transitory that it had hardly made any lasting historical change.

Ultimately, it was the communist ruling parties' failure either to present a coherent model of social transformation or to consistently support decolonization and development that botched the prospect of Bandung and NAM. There was also structural constraint on the socialist states, which were geopolitically limited in their support for popular struggles in other countries and had to tolerate forms of anti-socialism. The USSR from time to time watched with folded arms when dictators cracked down on labour activists and the military's counterinsurgency campaigns wiped out leftist rebels. Widely seen as ultra-radical, China also largely steered clear of exporting revolution. It was the toxic wrangling around the Sino-Soviet split that was most obstructive to building mass struggles across the continents, eventually demoralizing and exhausting the hope and energy of postcolonial regeneration. Breaking away from their former metropolitan masters, poor countries inevitably became divided, competing for economic and political favours between China and the Soviet Union. Local communists, often the backbone of social change, were forced to fight factional battles between Maoist and

---

17 Miliband, *Class War Conservatism*: 255.

other Marxist variants, with dividing parties everywhere in 'an ever more accelerated disintegration of the internationalism of the classical communist movement'.[18] Having drifted away from internationalism, socialism and Third Worldism went down together.

The passing of an era of raging popular struggles also predicted the fall of the socialist camp, with infighting among communist states accelerating this descent. An earlier row between Yugoslavia and the USSR, subsequently involving Romania and Albania, became unremarkable in light of Sino-Soviet border clash at the Ussuri River in 1969. It was a small skirmish militarily, but marked a political watershed. In a spiral of escalation, successive belligerents from Vietnam in Cambodia to China in Vietnam tore the comrades and brothers apart, with the exception of Cuba, which stood alone as an outstanding icon of internationalism. China's 1979 war of 'punishing' Vietnam was a military and emotional nightmare, but worst of all a blatant gift to Washington, a statement of its changing attitude towards the US and its desire to draw economic aid from the West. Previously Zhou Enlai, representing the Chinese leadership, had repeatedly confirmed his country's commitment to the Vietnamese party and people, and China was indeed Vietnam's major comrade in arms. Had Zhou lived to see the disaster of 1979 he would have been mortified. China's heavy casualties should be a hard lesson that it must never strike anywhere without moral support from the locals. Such wars were perhaps rooted in 'bureaucratic nationalism', the culprit in intra-communist relationships faced with capitalist crusades ever since 1917, as compared with an ever more united world of global capitalism.[19] They betrayed the logical belief that socialist national security can only be safeguarded by an internationalist approach.

Retracing China's strategic realignment and how it might have contributed to the Cold War capitalist victory, one important clarification is in order. China's diplomatic opening began with the Maoist Three World strategy aimed at containing the Soviet threat and bringing China out of its geopolitical predicament. China could then negotiate on an equal footing with the West and Japan for a political and economic turnaround. Beijing took a permanent seat on the United Nations

---

18 Wallerstain, 'What Cold War in Asia?': 24.

19 Perry Anderson, 'Internationalism: A Breviary', *New Left Review* 14, March/April 2002: 10.

Security Council in 1971, for which it was hugely indebted to the newly independent countries across a drastically enlarged UN platform. Mao famously acknowledged China's appreciation of 'our Third World brothers'. The next sequence of events, from President Nixon's visit to China in 1972 when the US urgently needed to find a way out of Vietnam, to the renormalization of China's diplomatic relations with Canada, Japan, Australia and others, and eventually also with the US, constituted a breakthrough in the structural establishment of international relations. Ever since the young communist regime had founded itself in the height of the Cold War, the Chinese had emerged unrepentant from each interaction. Despite mistakes and setbacks, China and the Third World enjoyed a real measure of soft power during this period, which has not been surpassed. It was the only time when the Chinese could accurately and confidently claim, in a popular phrase, that 'our friends are all over the world'.

China's rapprochement with the US remains controversial. It is crucial to differentiate between the Maoist anti-hegemonic balancing acts against the narrow logic of the Cold War and the post-Mao project of global integration, beginning with Deng's invasion of Vietnam to court the US. The former was indeed a hard blow to radical forces, especially to revolutionary insurgents in Southeast Asia, but it is nevertheless crucial to recognize the two distinct phases. Mao initially did not respond to US entreaties and China didn't give in an inch on where it stood for concerning Indochina or Korea, let alone Taiwan.[20] Even after the submit, the Chinese side stated clearly in the 1972 Shanghai Communiqué that 'wherever there is oppression, there is resistance. Countries want independence, nations want liberation and the people want revolution – this has become the irresistible trend of history.' Mao is known to have penned these words. Beijing also declared that 'China will never be a superpower and it opposes hegemony and power politics of any kind . . . It firmly supports the struggles of all the oppressed people and nations for freedom and liberation.' After all, China did not sign a treaty with the US against the Soviet Union, nor did it seek hegemonic power: the world Mao envisioned was free of hegemons. He told the Ministry of Foreign Affairs right after Nixon's visit to 'let him manage his small triangle [the US, Soviet Union and China], and we

---

20 Westad, *The Cold War*: 408–12.

should carry on our big one [Asia, Africa and Latin America]'.[21] China renormalized its diplomatic relations with both the US and USSR in line with 'independence and autonomy', as affirmed at the 12th Party Congress in 1982.

If revolutionary China sought to work its way out of a nearly impossible geopolitical milieu of encirclement, and tactically accepted the American gesture of conciliation conditional on bilateral equality, the reformist regime drifted rightward and made fundamental concessions. If the Maoist endeavour was to disrupt a bipolar world order by playing on antagnisms between the superpowers, today's policy of global integration has largely given up on resistance, trying wishfully to appease capitalist rule makers. These opposing lines are grounded on China's reimagined self-positioning on the world stage: from socialism to 'socialism with Chinese characteristics'; form the internationalism of uniting the world's class nations to a globalism of capital expansion and resource extraction; from independence to subordination; and, in historical terms, from revolution to counterrevolution. If Mao occasionally deviated from socialist and internationalist principles, his generation nevertheless remained true to communist goals. Their successors became cynical about ideology and have stopped using the word 'internationalism'. But the lost international is a foil to China's new ambition that blends seemingly depoliticized nationalism and globalism, all subject to the power of capital.

National rejuvenation and neoglobalism: Dreams and impediments

As the tradition of communist revolution and socialist internationalism has faded into a distant past, China's repositioning towards a collaborative relationship with the US as a 'G2' is illusory. These are two highly asymmetrical economies, in a highly unequal trade and financial relationship: the US has benefited enormously from the cheap and ample supply of Chinese goods and labour, and from its market as well as its (effectively nominal) dollar reserves. The illusion fades in the case

---

21 Jun Sheng, 'No Return to Sino-US Relations?' CWZG.CN, 5 March 2020, mp.weixin.qq.com/s/TqG0RAQTY1zoKU4VBTAADQ.

of the Chinese technology company ZTE, where Roscoe Howard, of Troutman Sanders LLP, was stationed as US attorney for a ten-year term, by forced agreement. He was granted the right to oversee all the corporation's business decisions and activities, with his expanses paid by the Chinese. This unilateral imposition embodies the reality of the G2. The choice of the reformers to focus exclusively on one of the potential-ities Mao opened but did not intend for China – that of joining the global capitalist system – allowed the US to become the sole global hegemon after the Cold War and assisted it in overwhelming the East. The irony is that now, with its globally unchallenged economic and military supremacy, the US has begun a pivot to China. Contentions between the two are bound to intensify, regardless of what Beijing is willing to accept from its senior partner.

The transformation of communist China from its position of outside challenger to that of rule-taking collaborator in the international divi-sion of labour, as well as its transformation into a growth centre of global accumulation, marked just another world-historical defeat for socialism, no less than that of the collapse of the Soviet Union. Politi-cally, as a newcomer and subordinate in the system, the world's most populous country can no longer be identified with global rallies for renewed anti-capitalism. This alters the intricate national and transna-tional interactions of today's world. Revolutionary nationalism, necessarily encompassing socialist internationalism, is being replaced by national developmentalism through global market integration. If socialism has to be internationalist because capitalism is global, as are anti-socialist forces, then abandoning socialism amounts to a departure from internationalism. The nature of nationalism within China then changes accordingly, from revolutionary to conservative politics, although the centrality of state capacity in economic nationalism remains common sense. Abandoning communist nationalist and inter-nationalist traditions and subscribing to a globalizing dream of 'great rejuvenation of the Chinese nation' are two sides of the same coin. Chinese nationalism today embraces globalization at both elite and popular levels, with significant support from a young and expanding middle class and the emerging internet generation. Not always in unison, official and popular nationalist sentiments share an air of voluntarism as well as a fusion of authoritarianism and populism – however reductionist these terms might be. China has entered uncharted waters as an alternately submissive and reluctant participant in the global system, while shoring up that same system in practice.

China's determination to benefit from global market integration entails reconciling the conflicting interests of domestic, comprador and foreign capital. Under the neoglobalist worldview, further economic move of 'going out' is made a necessity which has served to obliterate the last element of Maoist internationalism. After decades of taking a pragmatic, low-profile gesture, China has begun to seek a central place on the global stage. Engaging in proactive diplomacy and extensive foreign adventures, Xi declared that the Chinese approach to solving problems facing mankind, from poverty and conflict to eco-crises, are universally applicable. His 'new era' in search of 'common destiny for the human community' espouses a peculiar nationalism that champions globalization and free trade. Yet the deals imposed on China by Washington to preserve the American advantage, or the West's policy on agricultural subsidies alone, should have taught Chinese leaders long ago about these myths they hold dear. Sheer monopoly and other forms of market disparity are manifest every-where, not least in the fact of China being widely open without reciprocity from the US or Europe. Chinese optimism contradicts the law of capitalism, and China's own subordination.

If globalism 1.0 of China's first reform decade was meant to utilize foreign capital, managerial skills and technologies to advance an auton-omous national economy, then it has since been outdone. Continuing the trend of deep integration since the turn of the new century, globalism 2.0 is a fundamental reversal of the prior self-reliance. It requires *shengai*, or a deepening of the reform, pushing towards further globalization that has encompassed a restructuring of state firms and banks, commodifi-cation of land, and the loosening of financial regulations on private monopolies. Bearing Xi's own name, this rebranded globalism features two related drives. One is an upgraded dependence on market expan-sion particularly due to China's current overcapacity and excess capital; the other is its ever greater reliance on foreign supply of resources – in everything from energy to cereals. Both these features have entailed the exploitation of labour and raw materials. As trade and other disputes have unfolded between China and other nations, unavoidable questions have arisen as to just how much leverage the country can really have. It appears that foreign market dependency has undermined national self-determination and defence, especially in an age of financial volatility and cyber insecurity.

Borrowing the image of the ancient Silk Road by land and sea, the mega-idea of the BRI was set to create new overland economic corridors and maritime trade routes, physically connecting over a hundred countries, 70 per cent of the world's population, and three-quarters of the globe's energy reserves via railroads, highways, electric grids, mines, pipelines, dams and ports. Tapping into desired development of countries, China would use its financial, infrastructural, manufacturing and technological capacities to offer deals around the world. In particular, Eurasian integration was hoped to involve Western Europe as well as the Mekong basins, the Gulf, the Indian Ocean and Oceanic nations, and to link Africa and South America more closely. Featuring colossal explorative investments and grand infrastructural projects, the initiative has been hyped as defining China's future development, spurring growth in its western hinterland and industrial rustbelt as well. It would address issue of internal east–west relations while enhancing regional cooperative networks. It also has a social dimension, as it would export goods, entrepreneurship and technologies along with schools, medical facilities, poverty alleviation programmes, agricultural cooperatives and pollution treatment plants. It has pledged to honour UN global climate and sustainable development goals by promoting cost-effective and low-carbon methods for a 'green belt and road'. The scale of this scheme, hedged with more than $1 trillion, is unparalleled. Funds are accrued from the new Silk Road Infrastructure Fund and Asian Infrastructure Investment Bank (AIIB), along with older banks to offer interest-free as well as commercial loans. The Export-Import Bank of China (EIBC), for example, is a policy bank designated to provide concessional loans and preferential export buyers' credits. Promising to reform development finance for the developing world, these banks focus on South-to-South bilateral partnerships.

Yet, in the years since the BRI was proposed, many problems have surfaced. On the lending side, labour relations through onsite workers and local unions and officials challenged Chinese investors and managers representing central and provincial state capital, and increasingly also private capital. A labour regime permitting poor conditions and abusive management was being transplanted abroad, customarily ignoring locally legalized labour standards. Some sub-contracted and even undocumented workers from China worked without any legal representation or protection. Local labour protests have not been uncommon in Chinese-owned factories in some African and Southeast Asian countries. Corruption, waste and fraud have been rife. The heavily subsidized cargo to Europe has occasionally moved empty containers. Certain going-out projects had nothing to do with development, such as the construction of around fifty casinos in Cambodia. Many others entailed high greenhouse gas emissions, including more than sixty coal-fired power stations. Chinese investments generally lacked transparency and routinely involved bribes and brokerages to the ruling elites of authoritarian states, as frequently reported in Central Asia. Above all, the BRI deals are made between states and rulers, mostly without touching on the local relations of domination and resistance.

From the receiving side, the record so far seems mixed, with successes in some cases and resentment in others. The latter, apart from incidents derived from unexpected local conflicts, focused on government indebtedness, and hence the prospect of dependency, local resource extraction and pollution-related hazards, as well as lost job opportunities when large number of workers were brought in from China. Unrest abounded as seen in new ports in Kazakhstan, Pakistan, and Tanzania; railways and especially high-speed rail in Malaysia, Indonesia and Saudi Arabia; gold mines and a logistics centre in Kyrgyzstan; coal plants in Bangladesh and Kenya; hydropower dams in Nepal and Myanmar; and other controversial ventures in Ethiopia, Congo, Ecuador, Mexico and elsewhere. Quite a few agreements and ongoing projects, involving hundreds of millions of dollars, were later cancelled or suspended. Doubts and discontentments in Central Asia were reinforced by tensions in Xinjiang.

Facing severe pushback, from complaints about sovereignty or financial and environmental sustainability to rioting, the BRI appears precarious in the absence of an internationalist commitment, stronger preparation and the full backing of security assurance. China is a net exporter of capital and assets and the world's top creditor, but its income is barely mid-level: it is thoroughly compromising its own financial health. Its foreign lending rose from being negligible in 2000 to reach over $700 billion in 2019, more than twice as much as the World Bank and IMF combined.[22] Yet the debt issue remains unaddressed despite the

---

22 'A New Study Tracks the Surge in Chinese Loans to Poor Countries', *The Economist*, 13 July 2019.

need for recapitalization against excessive lending, as though only a shrinking current account deficit could slow these highly risky greenfield investments. Moreover, China's supposed foreign strategic partners in finance, some with direct ties to their own governments, are permitted to take large numbers of shares as well as voting rights in the Chinese financial institutions. The June 2019 research report from the Ministry of Commerce admitted that American investors to China's financial sector had earned $32.6 billion by the end of 2017. If this figure is added to the country's dollar reserve and the level of Chinese investment in the US, that number rockets to $1.37 trillion.

According to China's lending practice, state commercial banks observe a normal annual interest rate of between 2 per cent and 5 per cent for fifteen to twenty years on loans, often containing a grace period of five to seven years. These terms are not necessarily more favourable than other lenders, but beyond the One China principle (of Taiwan being a part of China) there is no attachment of fiscal or environmental disciplines, as in the International Monetary Fund (IMF) model of conditionality. Poor countries risk repayment difficulties with default liabilities, and Chinese loans to sixty-eight such countries, already heavily indebted, doubled in the four years through the end of 2018, to make up about one-fifth of their outstanding debt.[23] When Sri Lanka found itself unable to repay its $1.5 billion loans for the infrastructural work in Hambantota in December 2017, the port was formally handed to two Chinese state companies under China Merchants Port Holdings as the project's majority shareholder on a ninety-nine-year lease. Although this deal was not about clearing debt to EIBC but to obtain needed cash for a national bailout, such events put China on the moral defensive and, not surprisingly, Mahinda Rajapaksa, the newly elected Sri Lankan president, would like to retake the port. Similarly, in May 2018 prime minister Mahathir Mohamad announced that Malaysia was to renegotiate the terms of its East Coast Rail Link as a major BRI project; and in April 2020 Tanzanian president John Magufuli cancelled a Chinese loan worth $10 billion for port construction, as well as the ninety-nine years of uninterrupted lease signed by his predecessor. The star China-Pakistan Economic Corridor

---

23 Yufan Huang and Deborah Brautigam, 'Putting a Dollar Amount on China's Loans to the Developing World', *Diplomat*, 24 June 2020; 'China Doubles Loans to 68 Nations, Further Tightening Grip', *Nikkei Asian Review*, 6 August 2020.

port of Gwadar is heavily burdened as well by around $800 million in loans plus import obligations from China worth up to $2.2 billion by the time of its completion. Following the common BRI model – build, operate, transfer – the port would be run for forty years by Chinese operators who would take 91 per cent of any profit, as well as 85 per cent of the income of the surrounding free zone. Africa has accumulated more than $150 billion in debt from China since 2000.

Meanwhile, allegations of China's 'debt-trap diplomacy' or 'asset seizures' can be refuted by another aspect of the story. A recent research finds that between 2000 and 2019, Chinese lenders restructured or refinanced dozens of individual African loans without any attempt to take advantage of countries in debt distress.[24] The fact that debt relief can happen without formal renegotiations when China unilaterally forgives debt in part or in full, 'even when there are few signs of financial stress on the part of the borrower', shows the overriding importance of political or geostrategic objectives.[25] It also signals the remnants of the noble tradition of Chinese socialism and Third Worldism, as seen in the legend of China in Africa. In summer 2020, in the face of the Covid-19 pandemic, Beijing has forgiven its interest-free loans to Africa and has so far agreed to delay repayments that are due. Outbound state capital, now less than half of Chinese total FDI stock, still goes to under-resourced rich countries and has behaved differently from private capital, pursuing longer-term local economic, as much as social, development. But without remaking the rules, investment is increasingly all about market, profit and resources: it is ever harder to distinguish Chinese transnational practices from those of other lenders, and China is deep in the game of global exploration and accumulation. Even without colonial character of outsourcing in search of super-profits from cheap land and labour, 'China's relations and contracts in Asia and Africa are capitalist'.[26]

24 Kevin Acker, Deborah Brautigam, and Yufan Huang, 'Debt Relief with Chinese Characteristics', China Africa Research Initiative, John Hopkins University, Working Paper 39, June 2020: 3.

25 Patrick Mendisand and Joey Wang, 'Washington's Blue Dot Network (BDN): Missing the Mark on its Counter-China Strategy', China-US Focus, 18 December 2019.

26 Joseph Ball, 'China: Victim of Imperialism not Perpetrator', 30 December 2019, josephballcommunist.wordpress.com/2019/12/30/china-victim-of-imperialism-not -perpetrator.

Could the BRI potentially be transformed into an unambiguously socialist and internationalist undertaking? Before we can answer this question, another must first be considered: can China itself be truly socialist? By skipping this question about the China model itself, it is argued that the outflow of Chinese FDI is not motivated by exploitation of labour and the search for economic surplus in poorer nations. In comparison with the neoliberal pattern of financialization, China has a key advantage in its real economy. Practising intra-regional local currency convertibility in fund allocation can also be a step towards the internationalization of the yuan, which would weaken the dollar hegemony and stimulate an international framework in defiance of financial imperialism. As such, sidelining the regimes of financial monopoly and speculative capital, the BRI could win China influence in the institutions of global governance, and among such regional groupings as the Shanghai Cooperation Organisation (created in 2011 to boost economic and security cooperation among China, Russia and the Central Asian states) and ASEAN Plus Three (the Association of Southeast Asian Nations plus China, Japan, and Korea, despite tensions over the disputed South China Sea Islands, fishing rights, Chinese dams upstream damaging the Mekong ecosystem and so on). The Chinese economy and its overseas expansion are viewed to 'have exhibited elements of both submission and resistance, where capitalism is not a dominant tendency'.[27] Local national media in China has lavished praise on this as a 'socialist' super plan, and gained some solid domestic support. Even otherwise sharp-eyed critics of neoliberalism have been lured by such notions as 'growth for all', 'a shared future of prosperity' and 'a human community of common destiny'. They imagine that aligning the BRI with locally beneficial development across the globe, especially in the global South, can nurture cooperation and interdependence on the path to some grand alternative to neoliberal globalization.

There are a number of controversial issues, however. National development, as opposed to dependent development, once a primary aspiration in the postcolonial world, remains a real concern. The Chinese economy has been stimulated as much as entrapped by the global system, and is

---

27 Lu Di, 'Has China "Going Out" Suppressed Global Development?', Observer Net, guancha.cn/ludi/2016_12_22_385467.shtml?web; Zhang Wenmu, 'The Three Changes of Postwar Global Political Structure and the Emergence of Historical "Breaking Point"', *World Socialism Studies* 1–3, 2017.

thus itself partially dependent. By operating in China for the world market, profit-driven multinationals (factoring in Chinese GDP) dwindle the state's fiscal and monetary tools of macro management. This mode of diminished autonomy is unsustainable. Just as pressing is the social concern around exploitation and inequality. Chinese FDI, when rigorous public supervision is missing at both the dispensing and receiving ends, and especially with private investment, does in fact involve the unbridled drive for profit. Conspicuously absent from the debate around BRI is a basic class analysis on international relations. For example, the positional statement of the AIIB reads that its managerial policies 'must remain flexible regarding labour and environmental standards' so as to be compatible with 'the limited financial capacity of less affluent countries'.[28] Using the same excuse, China is strongly against including labour protection clauses in any bilateral trade agreement. Its ambassador to Canada blatantly dismissed the Canadian pro-labour Progressive Trade Agenda as having no place in free trade.[29]

China's global quest for resources became an economic necessity before the official promotion of 'globality, connectivity, equality, sharing and commonality'. For many countries, this is questionable from a standpoint of national and environmental self-protection, and is certainly sensitive in terms of realpolitik. China has been the world's largest oil importer since 2014, and the top buyer in the international energy and mineral (futures) markets. Chinese demand immediately and considerably affects prices and stocks. Its foreign investment and acquisition attempts intensify global scrambles. China's appetite for foodstuffs also facilitates multinational agribusiness to supersede subsistence farming in one place after another. Deforestation to aid cattle farming and the cultivation of soybeans and other commercial crops for Chinese consumption is imperilling the Brazilian Amazon. The charge against China of neo- or sub-imperialism is not all undeserved, and questions of profit and financial blunders are about political choice. From a Marxist perspective, capital in search of new resources and markets defines inter-imperialist rivalry and entails capitalism's

---

28 Zheng Xinye, 'The AIIB Must Buck Financing Trends to Improve the Fortunes of Nations along the Belt and Road', *The Economist* online (originally published in *Beijing Review*), 2017, chinafocus.economist.com/index.php/blazing-a-new-trail.

29 Radio Canada International, 10 April 2018, chinascope.org/archives/14838.

inherent crises. The test here is simply to observe the direction of capital flows and whether any substantial surplus is sucked out from recipients of FDI, or whether foreign investments are beneficial for local development. Can Chinese investment foster the hitherto unachieved ability of surplus retention while enhancing native development and improving welfare for the locals? Is there a real possibility that China's global engagements could structurally modify capitalist globalism?

The intertwining problems of indebtedness/dependency, exploitation/inequality, displacement/dispossession, and environment/resource extraction are only the most palpable among many. Their global expansion runs counter to the stated objectives of the BRI. In the economic background is China's gigantic stimulus package in response to the 2008 financial crisis that was triggered by the US subprime meltdown, and which has greatly aggravated debt-financed built environment and overcapacity in an infrastructural revolution. An antidote to neoliberal financialization and capital speculation, China had the highest investment growth rate as well as the highest investment share of GDP in history.[30] However, as the land and ecosystem of community after community have been wiped out by construction, the national economy has also been exposed to mounting government debt and the threat of the bubble bursting. China has seen its debt-to-GDP ratio balloon to 306 per cent (from around 130 per cent in 1999 and 200 per cent in 2009), and this, alongside the policies of the US, has driven the soaring global debt.[31] The BRI replicates this pattern on a transnational scale. Capitalized by both state and private as well as multinational investors, and operated overseas, the participating Chinese firms and their mostly private subcontractors binding to the logic of capital cannot be an answer to the quandary of economic imbalances, home and abroad.

The argument, then, is that China must solve its own problems before it can offer the world anything appealing. Hyper-globalism cannot be a diversion from difficulties at home. In the end, China must remould its growth towards a more humanly and environmentally sound social model, on which any real success of its global ambition will depend. That

---

30 Matthew Klein and Michael Pettis, *Trade Wars Are Class Wars: How Rising Inequality Distorts the Global Economy and Threatens International Peace*, New Haven: Yale University Press, 2020: 114–19.

31 Data from the Institute of International Finance. See Umesh Desai, 'Blowout Response to China Global Bonds Offering', *Asia Times*, 14 November 2019.

is, whether China can refashion globalization would be determined by what kind of society it is building for itself. To date, the image of the Chinese dream has been tarnished by class and social contradictions, and the neoglobalism attached to it is highly dubious. How these scenarios will play out in the long run is a matter of imagination, politics and chance.

Illusions of reinventing tradition: Confucian universalism meets realpolitik

President Xi's 'Chinese solution' and 'Chinese wisdom' have been elaborated by Jiang Shigong, a prominent legal scholar and government advisor, who claims that his programme is 'not about adding Chinese characteristics to an already defined "socialist framework." Rather, it uses China's lived experience to explore and define what, in the final analysis, "socialism" is.' This definition is to be 'universally recognized throughout the entire world'. For supporters, such poise has a great deal to do with the depth of China's cultural heritage. In a way, the mainstream Chinese outlook is always worldly and universalist. The premodern Sinosphere of East Asia, for example, was 'a universal system of diversity within unity, capable of absorbing different peoples, cultures and religious beliefs'. To promote such an inclusive civilization is 'the greatest historical mission of the Chinese people in the Xi Jinping era'.[32]

The ancient Confucian concept of *Tianxia* is often expropriated in this discourse, it means 'all under heaven' – a spatial cosmology of grand amalgamation and great harmony. This political order stems from a moral ruling by the mandate of heaven, a spatially differentiated and ritually relational system which otherwise recognizes no stable inner and outer boundaries. The constant internalization of the external produces a boundless realm of *wuwai* – literally nobody and nothing is excluded. As Zhao Tingyang explains, if the Greek polis developed state politics, 'all-under-heaven invented world politics'. The latter, as 'an ontology of coexistence' and a worldview of 'compatible universalism', is a superior

---

32 Jiang Shigong, 'Philosophy and History: Interpreting the "Xi Jinping Era" Through Xi's Report to the 19th National Congress of the CCP', *Open Times* 1, 2018: 11–31. See also David Ownby and Timothy Cheek's introduction to Jiang's text in Reading the China Dream, 2018, readingthechinadream.com/jiang-shigong-philosophy-and-history.html.

philosophy for global convergence that transcends the Kantian universe of perpetual peace.[33] China's modern revolutionaries did utilize this notion without its primeval baggage to indicate their internationalism, and could do so because the Chinese had not been agents of colonization. The empire was handicapped at the time of European expansion, and what was once a virtue became a curse. The imperial expansion of China, nearly doubling in size under Qing rule, was mainly a process of unarmed pacification through conciliations and liaisons. 'In sharp contrast to the European powers and their colonial-settler descendants, China did not seek to construct an overseas empire.'[34]

Aware of the flaws inherent in trendy civilizational discourse, Wang Hui cites China's historically socialist, internationalist and Third Worldist moments and offers a more politically conscious, if idealistic, elucidation. The old *Tianxia* notions of discernment – distinguishing the barbaric (*yi*) from the civilized (*xia*) – and acculturation have no place in the new perspective; but neither does the ossified capitalist system of nation states and their international relations. By envisaging a Chinese past for the global future in a malleable 'supra-state' and 'supra-civilization of civilizations', in place of the coercion and conflict of modern homogenization, the BRI could 're-establish mutually respective social relations' of communicative global intersubjectivity, combining valued traditions with modern socialism. Highlighted in Wang's radical interpretation of a 'world historical' BRI is the idea of connectivity. *If* – a big if – the project could remain uninfected by expansionist motives and methods, and look past the 'political philistinism' of economic pursuits in order to spread neoliberal growth, it could open a path for more participation, communication and sharing based on autonomy and equality. China could then seize the opportunity to end the Cold War legacy of US–Japan maritime dominance in the region and eventually 'recreate civilization' to the benefit of everyone. Methodologically, as overlapping temporalities are integrated into non-static spatial categorizations to invent world politics anew, the familiar panorama of geographically or culturally based identity politics will give way to the political subjectivity intrinsic to universal

---

33 Zhao Tingyang, 'All-Under-Heaven and Methodological Relationism', in Fred Dallmayr and Zhao Tingyang, eds, *Contemporary Chinese Political Thought: Debates and Perspectives*, Frankfort: University Press of Kentucky, 2012: 46–51, 62–5.

34 Peter Nolan, 'Imperial Archipelagos: China, Western Colonialism and the Law of the Sea', *New Left Review* 80, March/April 2013: 80.

emancipation.[35] This argument for the blending of a traditional mandate and a new blueprint in a spatial revolution, which would enable China to avoid repeating the catastrophes of colonialism and imperialism, has sent intellectual repercussions across the left. Carrying forward the positive legacies of its former self, the PRC could catalyse global renewal to counter capitalist hegemony. Such is an attractive project for the Chinese leadership to redirect globalization and South–South cooperation in a post-capitalist fashion. A rising China, engaging the world peacefully and constructively, would help foster equality among nations.[36]

Couched in an essentially apolitical narrative of searching for a cure for global ills, this is largely a matter of Chinese left's self-projection. For one thing, a repressive hierarchy characterized China's premodern social norms as well as the Sinocentric regional order. Equality existed, but only in the demands of peasant uprisings and utopian social thinking. Confucianism, with its doctrines of rigid social hierarchy and oppression of women, is hopelessly reactionary and obsolete. It was, after all, an ideology of the old ruling class. Even modernized, Confucian revivalism is no soft power able to compete with the global ideology of liberal democracy. The revolutionary idea of legitimate rebellion is suppressed in a carefully selective state-sanctioned discourse. China's rich cultural traditions beyond Confucianism, nature-friendly meditation and market management devices alike, might be usefully reappropriated or creatively transformed; and its deep history can be a source of framing a (self-)critical standpoint towards standard modernity. Yet the resources derived from its twentieth-century revolutionary movements are far more relevant and powerful. Bizarre scenes of party secretaries conducting ceremonies where they kneel to a statue of Confucius at an ancestral temple or educational campus are a sure sign of ideological bankruptcy. It is also politically escapist – or defeatist or devious – that a communist party should have found it necessary to have recourse to an ancient saint.

---

35 Wang Hui, 'Civilization Between the Pacific and Atlantic', part I and II, *Economic Herald* 2015, 8: 10-21 and 9: 14-18, and 'The Taiwan Question in the Great Change of Contemporary Chinese History', *Beijing Cultural Review* 1, 2015: 55-7; Yang Beichen, '"Asia" as a New Issue of World History: Wang Hui on "Asia as Method" Again', *Film Art Magazine* 4, 2019.

36 Xu Jinyu, 'The Geopolitical Economy of China's One Belt One Road: Inclusive *Tianxia* or Exceptional Space?', *Open Times* 2, 2017, opentimes.cn/Abstract/2341.html; He Guimei, 'How Has Traditional Culture become a "Consensus" among Different Social Forces in China', *Chinese Social Sciences Today*, 28 January 2016.

Another problem lies in the wishful and erroneous portrayal of Chinese tradition as uniformly benevolent and ascendant, disavowing its Han-centrism and obsession with order. The romanticization of Tianxia can never rival pragmatic liberal or realist theories of great power politics, and leading Chinese scholars have unintentionally done a thorough job in deconstructing internationalism by precluding the national and thereby also the international, rendering it conceptually void. Predictably, class is also analytically annulled. For Jiang, a classless cultural nation like China is only tangible in 'its indigenous, national nature, its authentic Chinese nature, rather than in the Party's class nature'. China's contribution to humanity will also 'prove that the great revival of the Chinese people is not nationalistic, but cosmopolitan'.[37] This crude conflation of Confucianism and communism involves a head-on collision with the basics of Marxism and glorifies China's imperial and conservative inheritance at the expense of its revolutionary transformation. In the depoliticized language of universal harmony, anti-capitalism is substituted for the striving for global supremacy, and the struggle between socialism and capitalism converts to shifting centres of economic gravity. Such a seemingly culturalist perspective serves a political purpose in that it debars self-scrutiny and criticism. The debate is further complicated by the fact that globalization is internal to China, that the country has engaged itself globally, that participating capital in the BRI is no longer limited to Chinese FDI and that this capital is inadequately regulated by public institutions. It is necessary to be clear that the two conceptual agendas are incompatible: civilizational versus the (inter)national; cultural magnetism versus class and universal liberation. Efforts at reconciling them result in discarding socialist internationalism.

Such incompatibilities are not a matter of mere intellectual politics, but have direct geostrategic consequences. The question of China going out is inevitably one of realpolitik. Using a bookishly un-self-conscious interpretation of neoglobalism as a dual strategy for development and security, it is assumed to transcend geopolitics – both a delusion and a self-defeating promise to the world. As such, the BRI and the thinking behind it are entirely toothless. The fact that China is consuming resources worldwide mostly through bilateral deals is enough to doom

---

37 Jiang, 'Philosophy and History'.

its local reception, notwithstanding those projects that are locally beneficial and hence welcomed. As Chinese traditionalism also goes global,
geopolitical realities sharply rebuff the fantasy of it being anything like
'the art of co-existing through transforming hostility into hospitality'.[38]
While the current global order is dominated by a ruthless industrial-
financial-military complex via the long arms of the judiciary, intelligence,
ideology and media, utopian Tianxia-ism denounces frontiers and force.
In this confidence in a completely open China, one requisite that has
been conspicuously neglected is the ability of state power to achieve any
national goals at the global level. In this sense, the Westphalian system
cannot be corrected by a civilizational reconfiguration. Indeed, many
national boundaries have been arbitrarily drawn as legacies of imperialism, but since the world is neither flat nor borderless, the whole BRI
plan appears ill prepared, self-deceptive and practically defenceless.

Believing in its destined 'marriage' to the US, as loudly announced by
more than one heavyweight politician in Beijing, China overlooks the
residues of Cold War anti-Chinese propaganda as much as it ignores the
West's new fear of the rival power as an enemy of democracy and
freedom. Regardless of its own intentions and efforts towards collaboration and convergence, China has redrawn and expanded the map of
global economics and politics. Its current assertive and proactive diplomacy constitutes a challenge to the Atlantic conception of order.
Ultimately, the logic of capitalist global rivalry points towards war and
conflict. The core powers, once eager to bring China into their remit of
market and realignment, have awaken to the 'China threat'. Washington
leads the way by reaffirming the US pivot to Asia. Typically, Henry
Paulson, former US secretary of the Treasury, remarked that by a
growing consensus China is viewed 'not just as a strategic challenge to
the United States but as a country whose rise has come at America's
expense'. He also specifically targeted the digital Silk Road that could
export Chinese cyber sabotage and other adversarial incursions into the
US and allies.[39] A *New York Times* editorial advised that 'given its

---

38 Zhao Tingyang, 'Can this Ancient Chinese Philosophy Save Us from Global
Chaos?', *Washington Post*, 7 February 2018.
39 'Remarks by Henry M. Paulson, Jr., on the United States and China at a Crossroads', Paulson Institute, 6 November 2018, paulsoninstitute.org/news/2018/11/06/
statement-by-henry-m-paulson-jr-on-the-united-states-and-china-at-a-crossroads;
and 'Remarks by Henry M. Paulson, Jr., on the Risks of an "Economic Iron Curtain"',

economic, military and technological trajectory, together with its authoritarian model, China, not Russia, represents by far the greater challenge to American objectives over the long term'.[40] Washington thus needs 'a new grand strategy' to contain China 'rather than continuing to assist its ascendancy'.[41] Secretary of State Mike Pompeo shifted away from Washington's neutrality on disputes in the South China Sea, and on 13 July 2020 he denounced China's 'completely unlawful' maritime claims. The White House has broken its 1972 One China commitment by twice sending senior envoys to Taiwan in the summer of 2020. If the silky package of BRI has mitigated anti-China sensitivities here and there, and if a lack of allies prevents China from engaging in proxy wars in surrounding regions, things can change. The clear consensus across political parties and spectrums in the US, above all, is that 'a decades-old policy of peaceful engagement with China directly has given way to an era of confrontation and conflict'.[42]

For profits and rents to be globally clutched, as in the preceding centuries of colonialism and imperialism, military backing is required. The monopoly finance capital of late imperialism has reinvented surplus extraction through outsourcing and the control of global value chains by multinationals. Indeed, imperialism and militarism are inseparable, with wars as a hallmark of their accord. For the existing powers, a rising economy of China's size is hard to swallow. In particular, it threatens what Bruce Cumings has called 'American pacificism', the strategy that has defined regional relations since the Cold War. The US cannot toler-ate any strategic rival, let alone one ruled by a communist party, powered by modern industries and deemed aggressive in its hi-tech espionage of the West. Even if China really has no problem with American hegem-ony, and the two countries' businesses are intertwined, Chinese development and security objectives defy the US-Euro-Japanese defined and defended geopolitical and geoeconomic balances. US trade and financial wars aiming at sabotaging Chinese technological advances and

Paulson Institute, 27 February 2019, paulsoninstitute.org/press_release/remarks-by-henry-m-paulson-jr-on-the-risks-of-an-economic-iron-curtain.

40 *New York Times*, 21 July 2019.

41 Robert Blackwill and Ashley Tellis, 'Revising US Grand Strategy Toward China', Special Report 72, Council on Foreign Relations, New York, March 2015: 4.

42 Liz Moyer, 'Engaging China, or Confront It? What's the Right Approach Now?' *New York Times*, 11 November 2019.

industrial policies have a following in a largely compliant international community. Washington won't hesitate to resort to force whenever expedient, as demonstrated by the NATO bombing of the Chinese embassy in Belgrade in 1999, among other provocations. The fact that more than half of China's imports and exports pass through waterways under the control of the US Navy alone jeopardizes the Chinese economic lifeline.

The grim reality is plain: there is no parity between China and the US, militarily, geopolitically or indeed in any other aspect of power. It is not this imbalance per se that is at stake, but a straightforward mismatch between Chinese dreams and American realism. Tensions have risen in the East and South China Seas, the Himalayas and the Korean Peninsula, among other spots under US influence. The notion of Chinese defence as a string of pearls in the Indian Ocean or a nine-dash line in the South China Sea has entailed the construction of artificial islands with military facilities, which similarly engage other coastal parties leaning to US protection and fiercely contested. In 2016, the Permanent Court of Arbitration ruled in favour of the Philippines against China over maritime territories, but contentions there, along with the Sino-Japanese dispute over the Diaoyu (Senkaku) Islands, continue to drag on. The Chinese hope for 'strategic mutual trust' among its neighbours remains intangible. Under the Pentagon's encirclement of China, missiles have been deployed in a ring from Okinawa through Taiwan to the Spratly Islands, accelerating a (nuclear) arms race. Taiwan is also a critical actor in all this. Zhang Wenmu, one of the foremost Chinese strategists, has argued for a shift in national security from defending the nation's territorial integrity to achieving global status. But even as he suggested that Beijing extend its control to reach the east sea line of Taiwan while China gets ready for its 'peaceful return' so that 'China's effective security border is drawn at the deep water of the west Pacific', Washington made another $2.2 billion arms sale to Taipei in July 2019, and announced a further $7 billion expenditure on advanced military equipment in September 2020.[43] Given the steep military asymmetry between the two countries, Chinese globalism 2.0, at its most

---

43 Zhang Wenmu, 'State Security Understood in a Perspective of Totality and Dynamic Equilibrium', 81.cn, 15 April 2019; 'The Yangtze and National Defence', part I, II and III, *China Engineering Consulting*, 2018, 5: 55–61, 6: 37–43, 7: 48–53.

adventurous, is either illusory or reckless. This is not only a question of the realpolitik of national interest and big power rivalries, but also, and more relevant to long-term socialist goals, whether and how a global China – still undefined – might withstand capitalist expansionism, including its own.

Returning to the question of socialist versus Confucian universalism, the convergence and divergence between China and global capitalism cannot be adequately understood by either the economic law of market standardization or by the cultural logic of national characteristics. To say that nothing is destiny or preordained by economics or culture is to recognize the primacy of politics, best illuminated by the synchronous singularity as much as the universality of the Chinese Communist Revolution. Any conception of cultural China is politically constructed, and to be defined only by the common historical experiences and liberation movements of a diversely constituted Chinese people. Confucianism or any other cultural tradition is not universally Chinese. Only socialism can offer an universalist alternative to capitalist integration. If culturalist approaches are to be of any value, they must repoliticize the problems and dangers of the current geoeconomic and geopolitical situations in a self-reflexive manner. The ideas of shared sovereignty or soft borders, for example, might be worth contemplating for a future people-to-people diplomacy, and pragmatic cooperation might then facilitate ecologically responsible co-exploitation of oil, fish and other resources in disputed territories. Imperialist demands, such as freedom of navigation by the US and provocative military manoeuvres involving more countries, remain great obstacles.

Lost in accumulation? Reconstructing the national and international

So far, the developmentalist core of neoglobal exposition has largely been left unquestioned. Growth has been taken for granted as an intrinsic right and a fundamental need for the developing world. But this is a flaw of the Chinese plan, and contradicts many of its promises. China's eager market integration, to the extent of being itself a driving force for global neoliberalization, has negated the transformative role it could have otherwise played. Regarding economic gains alone, it is a truism that China is both a beneficiary and victim of globalization; the issue is whether other countries would be able to repeat the more positive aspect of this path, given the increasing unsustainability of growth. The paradoxes born from the challenges of Chinese growth have bred both more openness and dependency, national pride and foreign-worshiping, political flexibility and autocracy. By prescribing free markets, the CCP has been remade as an unlikely champion of neoliberalism and globalism. The gulf between its revised 'socialist' ideology and the unambiguously capitalist policies it has pursued is confounding, as are its nationalist-cum-globalist postures. These paradoxes perpetuate an ever more personalized and bureaucratized state machinery, leaving little scope for a coherent socialist position.

As argued above, any answer to the question of whether the BRI could be a grand socialist scheme would ultimately depend on how well China can address its own existential dilemmas. If it sits among the most unequal societies in the world, how could it pursue equality abroad? If over-accumulation in China is attributable to the under-consumption of its own underpaid workers, following a management model of multi-level subcontracting, how could it form a different labour regime abroad? And if China depends considerably on the global market, while also encouraging the commodification of its rural commons by private investment, how could it help poorer countries and their local communities to evade foreign dependency and communal dissolution? Would its own exports and constructions not undercut local industrial capabilities? The answers to these questions are already visible: protective tariffs are lifted and state companies privatised; the labour market is liberalized to take in jobs outsourced on poor terms and conditions; many other mechanisms for imposing the newer international division of labour are becoming established.

The point then is not so much about any potential Chinese imperialism - and it would be a mistake to liken a China not using coercive force, or taking monopoly profit, or seeking political domination in host countries to the old colonial or neo-imperialist powers anyway - as whether China's growth model, if transplantable at all, is locally beneficial. In other words, the logical continuity between domestic and foreign policies means that the character of China going global is determined by the nature of its national model. The farther it is away from socialism domestically, the more possible it can become imperialist abroad. John

Hobson believed that overproduction and underemployment in a 'false economy' led to scuffles for foreign markets and hence imperialism. The solution lay in transferring income from the possessing to the working classes in the home markets.[44] It makes good sense that the accumulation of China's political and socioeconomic contradictions cannot be resolved by blame-shifting anywhere. China has to amend its own domestic imbalances of polarization, overinvestment and excessive debt. Apparently, for example, to secure national food supply is not to replace subsistence farming with the global agricultural value chain, nor to acquire land and contract farming in foreign countries. The way to resist imperialism is certainly not to make oneself imperialist.

Even if China's neoglobalist position seeks no substantial reordering of domestic and international class and power relations, the so-called rise of China is one commanding factor of our times. Ironically, the resilience of capitalism is nowhere better manifest than in the ongoing transformation of the PRC, where aspects of development have become humanly, socially and eco-environmentally indefensible. If the People's Republic, on losing its founding distinctions and commitments, is merely becoming another great power – or one of the *lieqiang* (a common reference to imperialist powers in the revolutionary terminology), or more likely a conformist sub-power – it will continue to be exploited and harassed by greater powers, as well as becoming internally explosive. Moreover, if China's domestic needs remain broadly unfulfilled – and particularly in the perpetuation of massive low-income households, and the absence of free education beyond nine years and healthcare for all – and if the economic, financial and technological foundations of China are not yet strong enough to fend off foreign dependency or external shocks, are there not more urgent and less risky ways of managing the economy than the strategy of ploughing massive investment and operations into overseas ventures? The fact, for instance, that many innovation-aspired and risk-taking enterprises are underfunded or at the brink of insolvency, or that wage areas and social insecurity are widely persistent in the informal sector and even among rural school teachers on the county government payrolls, illustrates this strange phenomenon of vastly exporting 'surplus capital'. The recent

---

44 John Hobson, *Imperialism: A Study*, New York: James Pott & Co., 1902: Part I, chapter IV.

scaling back of some BRI spending commitments could perhaps be an opportunity to strategically shift investment priorities, away from superficial international competition or globally buying support and back to domestic social needs. Only advances towards socialism at home could offer China a stable foundation for its global adventures that might become fruitful in the direction of socialist internationalism. Again, China cannot reshape the world before it starts to correct its own missteps.

The retreat of the PRC state is an indication of the extent to which its initial goal of providing a socialist and internationalist alternative has been diluted, and it is also a causal factor in this dilution. The theoretical indivisibility and dense connections between socialism and internationalism can be seen in China's simultaneous departure from both domestic socialist policies and internationalist ones. The neoglobalist approach that replaced these policies has been criticized for its generally pro-US stance in the UN Security Council, and indifference to global anti-capitalist/imperialist forums and movements, as well as to regional liberation struggles such as in the Middle East and Latin America. China's lost world of the social and the international, also shown in its indifference to the popular struggles around the World Social Forum slogan that 'another world is possible', is nevertheless vital for the country's own renewal. While the ideology of capitalist superiority and teleology might seem somehow proven by market transitions, the system is continuing to cause multifold devastation. Given that socialism and internationalism are mutually embedded and committed, nationalism must be checked by socialism and internationalism. A sounder position for China, both morally and strategically, would be to stand in solidarity with a reconstructed global southern front and win back trust and support regionally and globally, with a long-term aim of overcoming capitalism as the only viable path towards justice and peace.

PART FOUR
Socialism, the Spectre

8

The impasse of ideological defeatism

As noted, a standard Marxist criticism of the CCP attacks its petty bourgeois character: the founders of the party were intellectuals while the revolution took the form of a land-centred peasant struggle. But the Chinese revolution for both national and social liberation was intended to pave the way for socialism. In that sense, the party was proletarian in nature, in strictly Marxian terms. The Chinese communists were conscious modernizers, and socialist modernity in China aimed to encompass political and social power, socioeconomic development and cultural transformation. As such, the revolutionary alternative was not essentially about any national characteristic but addressed the universality of socialism as emancipation. It was to be a political project of defeating capitalism, rather than a cultural one of competing with the West, as exemplified in the sinicization of Marxism. Conceptually then the socialist revolution is at once singular and universal; and does not in any sense represent just another variant that pluralizes modernity or the global. Despite being structurally confined to the parameters of the capitalist epoch, and having now also largely abandoned its anti-capitalist ambition, a combination of organizational continuity and ideological break is most instructive for understanding the party today.

The signification of *culture* in China can be as broad as the 'way of life' (from Raymond Williams's definition to Chinese traditionalism and revolutionary communism alike) and as specific as Maoist ideological struggle or Gramscian hegemony and counterhegemony. The Frankfurt

School's critiques are also resonant in a cultural landscape swept by the commodification of values as well as digitized consumption. Remarkably, China has never ceased to be a politically searching and engaged community: people discuss and argue passionately through all kinds of media. They do so in the midst of fervent consumerism and political cynicism on the one hand and a monotonous *lingua franca* of propaganda and repression on the other, under various censorships, not only of state but also of IT-financial capital which has achieved significant power over information flow and public opinion. The irony is that the government's preferential policies are what have nurtured such companies in the hitherto guarded content and media communication industry, only to undercut its own political and ideological autonomy. The relevant debates are representative of liberal politicization in response to official depoliticization, and socialist repoliticization against both state-led and anti-state capitalism. Concerning the nature of the Chinese regime and society today, is there a China model? How is the meaning of political reform, supposedly lagging behind economic reform, contested? What kind of cultural politics is needed and feasible for change? Where is the party's theoretical work oriented? Such questions defy any notion that there is a predestined natural evolution for a 'new era of socialism with Chinese characteristics'.

'Farewell to revolution?'

In urban China, the 1980s is known as a decade of 'cultural fever' and 'neo-enlightenment'; these terms refer to a flourishing of 'scar literature' or stories of the wounded, 'misty poetry' about perplexed youth or lost individuality, the production of avant-garde artworks and the excitement over the new mantra of 'boundless reading without forbidden areas'. While public discussions of socialism, humanism, democracy, the purpose of socialist production and so on have receded since the late 1970s, critical and creative energy salvaged from a closed and stifling monoculture was not just liberating, it was explosive. There were big translation projects to introduce Western schools of thought, from liberal humanism to ideas about market rationality. Alongside the official reformist discourse of de-radicalization and de-ideologization, influential scholars were engaged in rethinking radicalism and criticizing ultra-leftism as 'social feudalism' or 'feudal despotism'. In the vanguard of this post–Cultural Revolution agitation, culture became a fifth or political modernization – the other four being industrial, agricultural, military and scientific/technological – as advocated by the 1978 Democracy Wall Movement. This movement was initiated in Beijing, spreading briefly to other cities, and ended by Deng Xiaoping calling to uphold socialism and the CCP leadership, known as the Four Cardinal Principles. Ideologically directed public discourse, as Mao stressed, always led the way for any revolution or counterrevolution. A social Darwinist flavour present in offerings such as *River Elegy*, a popular TV show that celebrated the Western outward-facing 'blue' (ocean) civilizations over the Chinese inward-facing 'yellow' (land) one, helps to show how such discourses functioned. The cultural products of neo-enlightenment shared a common penchant for oriental orientalism that was uncritical of the West and of modernity.

Riding on the reformist wave among a population exhausted by economic austerity and political turbulence, and also echoing the intellectual revolts in the Communist Bloc, the philosopher Li Zehou borrowed from distinguished American scholars such as Joseph Levenson and Benjamin Schwartz to revisit the Communist Revolution in China. He reframed the tradition–modernity binary in the Chinese context and argued that revolutionary radicalism since the May Fourth was the 'mistake of the century', as the impulse for national salvation was allowed to overwhelm cultural enlightenment. Moreover, as the Communist Revolution had to root itself in the backward rural bases and peasant population, a designated modern undertaking was inadvertently corrupted by the premodern propensities of feudalism and despotism. These unfortunate circumstances then hindered the spread of liberal thoughts and hence of modernization in China.[1] He and his followers sought to remedy this with a paradigm shift, away from the thinking and metanarrative of revolution. One obvious error here, however, is the false separation of what were inseparable– the national and social dimensions of the revolution – and another is the lack of historical awareness about the absence of an alternative to such a revolution, and about its foundational achievements. Failure to

---

1 Li Zehou, 'The Double Variation of Enlightenment and National Salvation', *On the History of Chinese Thoughts*, Beijing: Dongfang Publishing House, 1987.

understand the counterrevolution is just as problematic: the rediscovered 'golden Nanjing decade' of 1927–37, for example, disregarded the fascist GMD rule. Meanwhile some politically leftist advocates of a new enlightenment developed an interest in the intellectual dissent and cultural conservatism of Carl Schmitt and Leo Strauss. Among them Gan Yang wrote an influential essay on the predicament of contemporary liberalism, in which he criticized 'aristocratic liberty' from the point of view of 'mass democracy'.[2] Even in such a corrective effort, the Maoist conception and practice of 'people's democracy' were safely avoided.

The debate over the 'farewell to revolution' – as it was subsequently dubbed – was prominent as China ended its revolutionary century with the party's embrace of a post-socialist transformation. Many changes in the 1990s were already germinating in the cultural movements of the 1980s. This bold counterrevolutionary assertion was reinforced by a revisionist historiography that departed from serious scholarship to include selective evidence and personal memoirs that posed as history. Attempts to rewrite history aimed to reverse the established verdicts in order to discredit the fundamental justice of the revolution. Among these multi-pronged claims, for instance, were the lamented 'premature death' of late Qing westernization and destruction of a 'civic society' by the revolutionary violence that followed. Likewise, the CCP was alleged to have taken advantage of the Japanese invasion to strengthen itself instead of fighting the enemy. The accusation that inner-party purges since the early Soviet period, in the Red Army, through Yan'an, and in the run up to the Cultural Revolution and the extremes of the latter itself, is not factually unfounded but prejudiced against the main truth about the Chinese revolution as a whole. Now the landlords appeared innocent and more enlightened than the peasants, republican China more civic and progressive than the PRC, and the GMD a better fit for making China modern – with Taiwan's economic success and democratization held up as proof. The argument went so far as to praise imperialism for having done some good, such as the American use of Chinese 1900 indemnity money to found hospitals and universities. Even more startling, the civil wars in China were described not as class struggle but rather as senseless acts of violent self-harm: 'Chinese killing Chinese'. A newly awakened brand of feminism joined the crusade, objecting to a revolution hitherto

---

2 Gan Yang, 'Liberalism: Aristocratic or Popular?', *Dushu* 1, 1999: 85–94.

believed to have championed women's liberation: the revolution's female participants had been sacrificed for a male-dominated cause in which national and class interests took priority over gender relations.

The demonization of revolutionary socialism was of course itself ideologically motivated. While the party's 1981 resolution was not directly challenged, China moved to reshuffle its official ideology, restructure the country's media outlets and revise the school curriculum and textbooks. Here was another post–Cold War attack on great social revolutions: its mantra, precisely the opposite of Barrington Moore's classical liberal consensus, proposed that negating the revolutionary legacies would be an entry ticket to the liberal democratic end of history. The Chinese version was especially vicious though, if only because the Communist Revolution in China was especially protracted, arduous and costly, and the manifestation of its extraordinary idealism and heroism impossible to erase. Belatedly touting a Cold War mentality, the revisionist theories disseminated from the Central Party School and other elite institutions flourished alongside real and fabricated horror stories. The fundamentals and complexities of China's long revolution were disregarded, and the narratives attacking and mocking the revolution contradicted the popular understanding and sentiments, emphasizing the decisive differences between old and new China. The landmark of the 1949 revolution that had involved a quarter of humanity continued to enjoy mass popularity. In fact, without a consensual recognition of the basic legitimacy and historicity of the revolution and its valiant struggle to power, there is no way for its mistakes and failures to also be examined and criticized; nor can the conditions from which another revolution could arise be prevented.

While it is often asked, counterfactually, whether the revolution was necessary in light of its costs, any answer would have to begin with the presence or absence of choice. As far as modernization is concerned, it remains plain that in the capitalist peripheries national independence and state capacity are required for development. Again, revolution was a result, not a cause, of underdevelopment. It was indeed not until the PRC consolidated its sovereignty that the country could effectively pursue growth and could choose between self-reliance and negotiating foreign trade, investment and technological transfers. Meaningful comparative benchmarks for evaluating progress and retrenchment in the PRC thus cannot be taken from mature capitalist democracies. Such comparisons should rather focus on China's own past and on similar cases in the (former) Communist Bloc and Third World. The lack of thorough land reform in many parts of the latter, for example, explains major developmental hurdles. The truthful approach is simply that a fair judgement can be reached only with the moral obligation 'to weigh the costs of revolution against the costs of going without revolution'.[3]

No less important is the culture of revolution and the revolution's cultural impact. Defying the post–Cold War aura of ideological anti-communism, and notwithstanding its costs and tragedies, the Chinese revolution remains a culturally powerful force. Alongside its structural and military fronts, the revolution had a significant following among the educated and saw a sequence of profound cultural and intellectual transformations, not least through its programme of arts for the people and the party's relentless rectification campaigns. For Mao, a genuine revolution is necessarily and simultaneously cultural and discursive: 'Concerning its spirituality', revolutionary culture in China 'has exceeded that of the entire capitalist world' – exemplified by the cultural fighter Lu Xun's integrity in representing 'the most precious quality' of an oppressed people. Revolution is understood in terms of everyday representation, structurally as much as symbolically. Mao also famously spoke at the 1942 Yan'an Forum, describing struggle for the liberation of the Chinese people on the 'fronts of the pen and of the gun' and affirming that a 'cultural army' was 'absolutely indispensable'.[4] Mao was Gramscian, or Gramsci was Maoist, in their shared commitment to cultural politics.

The complicated legacies of this tradition are magnificent sources of both critical reflection and innovation. The conviction in the sovereignty of a multiethnic nation and people, the dignity and the wellbeing of labour, the duty of serving the people and the ideologies of equality, solidarity and popular wisdom are constitutive of the common socialist culture. This culture can incorporate certain treasured aspects of tradition, such as the idea of people as a foundation (*minben*) of state power and the unity of nature and humans, as well as the best liberal values of freedom and liberation. It was after all the Chinese revolution that

---

3 Meisner, 'The Significance of the Chinese Revolution': 12.

4 Mao, 'The Bankruptcy of the Idealist Conception of History', *Selected Works*, Vol. 4, Beijing: People's Publishing House, 1960, and 'Talks at the Yan'an Forum on Literature and Arts', May 1942, *Selected Works of Mao*, Vol. 3, Oxford/New York, Pergamon Press, 1965: 69.

changed the ethos or spiritual presence (*jingshen mianmao*) of China, once known as the sick man of Asia, and afforded it a modern identity, with national pride and an international standing. A sense of loss among ordinary people in the reform era's everyday experience of vanished workers' clubs or 'cultural palaces' throughout urban China as well as once widespread rural cultural stations can be understood only in this context, in tandem with the present challenges and social discontent. There is a poignant and bewildering distance between the enduring red classics of revolutionary literature, socialist cinema, music and artworks, and the newer subaltern culture of migrant workers, with their intellectual supporters on the one hand and the official rhetoric of 'never forgetting our original aspiration' (*buwang chuxin*) on the other. These are different genres, marking different political and symbolic orders, and representing different motions of political aesthetics and cultural politics, insofar as actual socioeconomic policies tell a different story.

The market transition has also been a cultural one, mirroring the fall of a socialist hegemony. It is commonly acknowledged that de-radicalization in China, when long-held political beliefs collapsed, produced an ideological vacuum and spiritual crisis. Apathy and hedonism replaced so-called totalitarian utopianism. The former idealistic zeal was rechannelled into hysterical consumerism and the fetishization of money. Neoliberal values are gaining ground through a money-centred public discourse. Michael Sandel, on an international lecture tour arguing for upholding moral values against unlimited market forces, found that 'in the US and China, there are strong voices who will challenge the whole idea of there being any limits'.[5] Rather than the enhanced freedom of choice that market romanticists promised, the commodification of public culture and human values has transformed people into enslaved and atomized market players. Privatization and its aura of possessive individualism have prevailed over collective solidarity and social support. It was inevitably a polarizing process, one that made people the tools or enemies of one another, fracturing the tissue of society while fostering loneliness and disorientation. Social dissonance and alienation led to a general identity crisis and a moral decay. This, as noted, has explained much of the spectacular upsurge in religious and quasi-religious movements, in defiance of communist atheism. Disorganized

---

5 'Lunch with the FT: Michael Sandel', *Financial Times*, 5 April 2013.

rural China has also seen the spread of superstition, gambling, backward customs and other symptoms of cultural decline. Marx's moral lyric is germane:

> *Religious* suffering is, at one and the same time, the *expression* of real suffering and a *protest* against real suffering. Religion is the sigh of the oppressed creature, the heart of a heartless world, and the soul of soulless conditions.[6]

As Chinese society has grown economically with marked material gains for the majority of the population, it has been dwarfed culturally. It is ever more senselessly consumerist, possessively individualistic, bureaucratized and hierarchical; and ever less guarded against polarization, dishonesty and conformism. If capitalism was imposed from above and outside, that imposition, to quote Michael Burawoy on Russia, comprised 'the life and death costs' from the workers' point of view.[7]

Yet China's labour movement is scattered and weak. Workers' political incapacity cannot be explained by repression alone; its impairments are multifaceted, stemming particularly from the opaque features of the state with its baffling ideology and language of socialism. One repercussion of a vanished 'leading working class' and worker–peasant alliance is the isolation and fragility of green, gender and other solidarity movements. Under the circumstances, only a renaissance of a class vocabulary without the baggage of its past excesses, both officially and popularly spoken, could regenerate a new politics for counterhegemonic struggle. One small example is *New Workers' Literature*, a magazine created in 2018 by a workers' reading and writing group based in the Beijing Home of Workers in the Pi village on the city's eastern suburb. With support from its wide networks, including some scholars, it has published writings by (self-)educated workers. Its chief editor, Fan Yusu, writes after her day job. The magazine set up an email address for submissions, and has drawn energetic participation as well as a sizable readership. A new workers' culture, rooted in their intimate experiences, somewhat echoes

---

6 Marx, 'A contribution to the Critique of Hegel's Philosophy of Right', 1843, marxists.org/archive/marx/works/1843/critique-hpr/intro.htm.

7 Michael Burawoy, 'Working in the Tracks of State Socialism', *Capital and Class* 98, 2009: 34, 62.

the tradition of Left Literature and can be a signpost of class making or remaking. But unlike the revolutionary past, they are missing the party leadership in political education and cultural production as a vital dimension of class struggle.

At first the revolutionary state tried and failed to prevent a new ruling class from emerging. Then the post-socialist state negated much of its revolutionary and socialist inheritance. The contradictions embodied in these developments have been seemingly dissolved by the CCP disavowing its old self while 'rationalizing' China's political economy, social policies and global position. It is not so much the capitalist triumphalism that is astounding, but rather the wild attacks on anything once communist, as though the experiences of fully one-third of the world's population have been nothing but endless victimhood and are ultimately worthless. Paradoxically, the highly ideological perception about brainwashing under communism is construed as genuinely objective, sustaining outdated Cold War preoccupations. Portrayals of a despotic, fanatical and murderous Mao era not only in English and other languages but also and especially in Chinese have surpassed even the worst anti-communist propaganda. Globally, even on the left, reflections on historical communism often begin with the words, 'although it has failed', leading to the instant dismissal of any socialist argument. Relevant debates in China are terminated with the swift reminder of the Great Leap or the Cultural Revolution and their victims: two disastrous episodes that can disarm even the revolution's most rigorous defenders on sight. The fear of a return to past torments and chaos nurtures a propensity for the status quo, whatever its problems. Although views on all sides depend on the specific master narratives, it is the defence of socialism that is often accused of being ideological.

China's revolutionaries and socialists were keenly aware of their errors and limitations, long before the revisionist mobilization. They took responsibility for the misadventure of 1958 and its catastrophic effect on people's lives, as seen in policy corrections both at the time and subsequently. Impractical targets for production were amended, and Mao intervened in the autumn of 1958 and spring of 1959 against ultraleftism. The difference between the two kinds of critics in the debate on history is that socialists oppose the wholesale negation of their endeavour, and uphold the principles and possibility of socialist advance. For them, the failed Leap cannot be used to deny the necessity, fruits and potentials of socialist transformation and collective farming. Any failure was not predestined because systemic self-destruction is not in the nature of socialist construction. Reckless voluntarism and adventurism notwithstanding, the people's communal system enabled internal capital and labour accumulation, contributing decisively to both industrialization and rudimentary rural welfare. It has generally been compared favourably to forced collectivization in the Soviet Union. Furthermore, the Leap was meant to decentralize and democratize the economy, and to transform the countryside into locally autonomous moral communities, so as to avoid the savage proletarianization and urbanization that had characterized earlier industrial capitalism – as they affect so many people in China today. The seemingly irrational campaign was intrinsically rational, then, with a utopian, egalitarian and emancipatory character. Its failures should not obscure its basic policy goals of securing food and other public provisions, building bottom-up participation in rapid social changes and finding a way to 'break superstition and liberate the mind' – a party slogan at the time. A more realistic managerial structure of three-level ownership based on a productive team was adopted after learning hard lessons, demonstrating a systemic ability to self-correct.

The larger picture remains convincing that the PRC had really achieved a leap before market reform on every key index of human development – from reduction of abject poverty and infant mortality, to rapid increase in life expectancy and improvement in living conditions – than other poor countries in the same period.[8] Even the devastating famine of 1959–60 does not counteract these achievements (needless to say that there was no deliberate starvation or genocide, despite the claims of some influential literature).[9] It was plain, as serious economists, demographers and historians agree (including Amartya Sen's famous thesis of press freedom for famine aversion), that apart from infantile grassroots radicalism, it was bureaucratic blindness due to communication blockages that prevented a misled central government from acting to prevent the disaster. Natural calamities on 40 per cent of China's

---

8 Relevant statistics are provided in Chapter 2. See also Jean Dreze and Amartya Sen, *India: Development and Participation*, Oxford: Oxford University Press, 2002: chs 3 and 4; Amartya Sen, 'Quality of Life: India vs China', *New York Review of Books*, 12 May 2011.

9 See book reviews from the left and right alike. For example, James Scott, 'Tyranny of the Ladle', *London Review of Books* 34:23, 6 December 2012; Jonathan Mirsky, 'Chairman Mao Devours His Foes', *Spectator*, 30 April 2016.

farmland, including prolonged drought, unprecedented floods and hail-storms in the meteorological records of three difficult years, also played their part, along with systemic and human errors. In comparison with the Soviet path, Perry Anderson has rightly noted: 'wildly voluntarist though it was, the GLF . . . was never intended as an attack on the peasantry, or any part of it.' By the same token, no comparable alienation of the peasantry ensured.[10] It was indeed phenomenal that no revolt occurred during this famine, despite a strong Chinese tradition of peasant rebellions against grain seizure; and it was obviously not due to police ferocity amid sprinkled border patrols. Meanwhile, nowhere was the reach of the communist power carrying with it inertia of the moral appeal of the revolution could be more revealing than the willful policies of the Leap. 'Only a government that had been built from the countryside and had the self-confidence of popular support could have been strong enough to cause a disaster of such magnitude.'[11]

Emerging research challenges dubious figures based on inaccurate census data and computational errors during the chaotic process of implementing the new household registration system. For example, experts privately doubted the 1953 census data at the time on the ground that it was conducted unscientifically and registered 'an unbelievable [population] increase of some 30 per cent in the period 1947–1953'. This in turn rendered the 'worthless' claim that 17 million or many more people were 'missing' in the famine years based on a population base of 600 million.[12] Likewise, the numbers first released by the NSB in 1983 show that China's death rate dropped from 2 per cent in 1949 to 1.08 per cent in 1957. Such a dramatic fall in just eight years is highly unlikely. By another estimation the same downward curve is even more dramatic as from 3.8 per cent to around 1.81 per cent, which again is demographically impossible.[13] Yet these unsubstantiated 1957 data were used as the baseline for calculating subsequent deaths. The

10 Anderson, 'Two Revolutions': 67.

11 Brantly Womack, 'In Search of Democracy: Public Authority and Popular Power in China,' in Womack, ed., *Contemporary Chinese Politics in Historical Perspective*, Cambridge: Cambridge University Press, 1991: 75.

12 Wim Wertheim, 'Wild Swans and Mao's Agrarian Strategy', *China Review*, Aug 1995; Ping-ti Ho, *Studies on the Population of China, 1368–1953*, Cambridge, MA: Harvard University Press 1959: ch. 5.

13 Judith Banister, *China's Changing Population*, Stanford: Stanford University Press, 1987: 80.

methods used to gather information at the time were also problematic, failing to include the extraordinary population movements back and forth between rural and urban areas around 1956–62, which again distorted book keeping. Large discrepancies in the population statistics are now shown to have been caused by the belated addition of millions of deaths that had previously gone unreported (motivated partly by food rationing), as well as duplicated registrations (of those who moved into cities as industrial labour) being remedially cancelled through the streamlining the records in the period 1960–4.[14]

Whatever the actual toll, the politics of number crunching in famine research has replaced the empirical question – 'how many perished and why?' – with 'how did the communist regime kill tens of millions among its own people?' With an anti-communist famine industry racing for body counts, the fatalities were inflated by taking figures from some of the worst affected counties and multiplying for all the other administrative units at the same level, or by tacitly equating starvation-related deaths with all types of unnatural deaths, among other questionable methods. Once the numbers reached 80 million, Mao could be declared a greater mass murderer than both Hitler and Stalin.

The issue here is not the numbers. Hard evidence – statistics, archival documentation, raw experiences and the like – is just as manipulable and subject to interpretation to fit preconceived (and, in this case, emotionally charged) positions. The famine, whether it cost the lives of several million or tens of millions, deeply harmed people's livelihood and will always be unforgivable by socialism's own standards, and the policy blunder responsible for it is absolutely indefensible. At stake is rather how to dissect as objectively as possible the rights and wrongs of a system facing adverse conditions. Aside from ideologically motivated data fabrication, even neutral observers tend to overlook the context or the historical perspective of what Mike Davis called 'imperialist famines'.[15]

14 Sun Jingxian, 'Population Change during China's "Three Years of Hardship" (1959–1961)', Contemporary Chinese Political Economy and Strategic Relations 2:1, April 2016: 453–500; Yang Songlin, Truth Must be Told, Haikou, Nanhai Publisher, 2013; Cheng Enfu and Zhan Zhihua, 'A Study of Unnatural Death during the Difficult Three Year Period in China, 1959–61', Science & Society 82:2, April 2018: 171–202; Li Chengrui, 'New Developments in Research on the Population Changes during the Difficult Three Year Period', Internal Drafts of Social Sciences of China 1, 2014: 107–111.

15 Mike Davis, Late Victorian Holocausts: El Niño Famines and the Making of the Third World, London: Verso, 2001: part IV.

Famine is no stranger to histories the world over, including old China known as 'land of famine'. The Chinese mortality trend in the twentieth century, for example, is consistently complicated by higher rates before 1949 than after, even taking into account the worst year of 1960. Comparison with other staggering cases, such as that of the Raj between 1896 and 1900 when more than 10 million people died in avoidable famines out of a population of a little more than one-third of China's in 1960, puts the case in perspective. Even in the post-independent democratic India, during the years of good harvest and in the favourable conditions of abundant foreign aid and general peace, malnutrition, starvation and destitution persisted for the masses of lower-caste Indians, especially women and children. As Jean Dreze and Amartya Sen recognize, even if the 30 million Chinese toll was the case, 'India seems to manage to fill its cupboard with more skeletons every eight years than China put there in its years of shame'.[16] The lack of social progress 'has led to human suffering and loss of life, not through mighty disasters like in China but through the quiet, continuous suffering of the 40 per cent of the population who are in absolute poverty'.[17]

On the basis of similar vertical and horizontal comparisons, Utsa Patnaik asks why India was not seen as experiencing a famine after independence, since its food output per capita remained consistently less than that of China's. To be sure, output is not the same as availability, given regional, class and other disparities, and the factors of pricing, supply, entitlement and distribution. But concerning 'lost births' which allowed experts to numerate a population decline attributable to the Leap in more than 60 million, Patnaik reveals the operation of 'ideological statistics.' It is bizarre how a procedure that calculates excess deaths by estimating normal fertility rates – allowing death to add up before birth – was utilized only in the Chinese case, when it 'does not seem to have been ever applied . . . before, and never applied in contexts other than China'.[18] This peculiar methodology has resulted in some wild

16 Jean Dreze and Amartya Sen, *Hunger and Public Action*, Oxford: Oxford University Press, 1990: ch. 11.

17 Georg Sorensen, *Democracy and Democratization: Processes and Prospects in a Changing World*, Boulder, CO: Westview, 2007: ch. 5.

18 Utsa Patnaik, 'On Famine and Measuring "Famine Deaths"', in Sujata Patel, Jasodhara Bagchi and Krishna Raj, eds, *Thinking Social Science in India: Essays in Honor of Alice Thorner*, London: Sage, 2002: 53, 64–5; 'Ideological Statistics: Inflated Death

exaggerations, regardless of whether it has been replicated elsewhere since. Once again, imperialist atrocities should be kept in mind to avoid historical whitewashing, not to elude any due responsibility of the communist regime but rather to locate it squarely. This clarification is important because global and peripheral capitalism continues to trap large populations in prolonged food shortages or insecurity and poverty in the midst of unparalleled accumulation of wealth.

The Cultural Revolution – or 'ten years of holocaust' as it is referred to in the post-Maoist official documents – is the other killing point in debates on the revolution. Even more than the Great Leap, this is a polarizing event even half a century on. Against the standard evaluation, there is a small and distinctive literature that shows how the Cultural Revolution, after an unruly first couple of years, stimulated political, economic, sociocultural and scientific advances. It was a period of horrifying persecutions, as much as it was an upsurge of self-reliant productive and innovative capacity and democratic participation functioning to cultivate the subjectivity of the popular classes. It was also seen as an experimental decade of egalitarianism that enriched peasant lives. Rather than demonizing Mao and taking China as beginning to modernize only in his wake, Richard Kraus indicates that 'the CR was violent, yet it was also a source of inspiration and social experiment', and that Mao was denounced so as to 'justify some of the nastiness that accompanied the turn to market reforms'.[19] Gao Mobo argues that the established account of the Cultural Revolution ignores the experiences of many times more people, particularly those less privileged, than the tales of persecuted cadres and intellectuals in a movement against bureaucratic alienation. The discourse that focuses on brutalities and sorrows is biased towards urban and eventually privileged voices. Popular nostalgia for the Mao era testifies to the fact that the desire for social equality cannot be erased.[20] While the Cultural Revolution is deeply divisive, causing conflicting emotions in many, there should be

Rates of China's Famine, the Russian One Ignored', socialisteconomist.com/2018/11/ideological-statistics-inflated-death.html.

19 Kraus, *The Cultural Revolution*: xiii, 63–83. For relevant statistics see Carl Riskin, *China's Political Economy: The Quest for Development Since 1949*, Oxford: Oxford University Press, 1987; Naughton, *The Chinese Economy*: ch. 3.

20 Mobo Gao, *The Battle for China's Past: Mao and the Cultural Revolution*, London: Pluto, 2008: chs 1 and 9.

no fear of open debate regarding its constructions and destructions. The Communist Revolution did have a dark side, and involved huge costs and personal injuries. It was an experience full of profound contradictions, 'of both great successes and spectacular failures, and both in abundant measure'.[21] Seeking historical truth is the only way to arrive at a broadest possible social consensus.

Beyond these débacles, the deeper story, at once high-minded and painfully difficult, is crying out to be retold. While true defenders of revolutionary and socialist legacies cannot be unprincipled apologists, and neither can they harbour the intention nor the possibility of restoring the Maoist past, the answer to the question of whether the revolution was necessary can be answered resoundingly in the affirmative. As discussed in the previous chapters, its achievements are clear and compelling. The modern PRC has left behind the ruins of foreign domination, unending wars, widespread poverty and many forms of social injustice; the revolutionary aspiration towards liberation also sowed the seeds of popular democracy. The ultimate justice of the Chinese revolution lies in the necessity of transforming national and social conditions to the point where violent revolutionary transformations are no longer inevitable.

Debating the China model

The intellectual campaign of 'farewell to revolution' was consequential, part and parcel of the post–Cultural Revolution reordering of ideology and politics. A new dictatorial market order, however, would end up sharpening rather than solving the contradictions of the Maoist political economy in the following decades, while generating new post-socialist problems and crises. It is neither coherent nor stable. Rather than as merely transitory, however, this transition involving interactions and indeed intertwining of state, market and society, and their translocal and transnational intervening agencies, needs to be recognized in its own right. It is hybrid and embodies both path-dependent and path-breaking developments. Is there then a distinct Chinese model – and if so, does it represent an alternative to

---

21 Meisner, 'The Deradicalization of Chinese Socialism': 352.

capitalism? The debate over the Washington versus Beijing consensus is so limited that projected differences quickly diminished. The question of whether a rising China can be a contender for supremacy from within the global system remains unanswered. If the word 'model' can be rejected on the ground that what happens in China is unlikely to be replicable elsewhere, it might nevertheless be useful for us to look into the specificities of a national experience that does not easily conform to existing theoretical benchmarks.

What explains China's economic miracle since 1978 – an average growth rate of 9.5 per cent between 1979 and 2018, 'doubl[ing] the size of its economy in real terms every eight years'?[22] With a (nominal) GDP per capita of around $9,580 in 2019, China was in seventieth place in the IMF and World Bank rankings. Its share of the global economy based on purchasing power parity went from 2.2 per cent in 1980 to 19.7 per cent in 2019, despite a slowing trend since 2013. However flawed might be the methods to measure and calculate GDP, these numbers are indicative of growth, though not necessarily of 'success' – taking into account the price paid for them. Given 'large-scale capital investment (financed by large domestic savings and foreign investment) and rapid productivity growth',[23] China is physically transformed. Its networked high-speed rail, newly built Hong Kong–Zhuhai–Macau Bridge (the longest of its kind in the world, yet scantly used so far – its wastefulness not untypical in the context of an infrastructural revolution), and the BeiDou Satellite Navigation System are just a few of its recent unparallelled accomplishments.

Two interlinked sets of explanations emerge: the Keynesian model of central and local government creating institutional incentives, injected with elements of economic nationalism while stressing state capacity and facilitation; and the neoclassical comparative advantage of international trade enabled by marketization and privatization, highlighting market functions and globalization. Both explanations are compatible with an investment-driven growth model. Concerning foreign investment crucial to both theses, it should be noted that upon the national agenda of opening, one-third of 'foreign' capital was from Taiwan, Hong

22 US Congressional Research Service, 'China's Economic Rise: History, Trends, Challenges, and Implications for the United States', updated 25 June 2019: 5–6; IMF Datamapper, docs.google.com/spreadsheets/d/1y41WVbvc-GDJ54yN6NtW-o9Ir-W0cPNIHg18J_srCzY/edit#gid=0.

23 Congressional Research Service, 'China's Economic Rise'.

Kong and the Chinese diaspora. And the timing couldn't be better, as international industrial capital was looking for new markets, with an incipient IT revolution hastening spillovers in an expanding global economy. China is now the world's largest trader and the second-largest receiver of FDI (after the US at $73 billion in the first half of 2019) as well as capital exporter.[24] This position comes with many costs and risks, but its ability to seize international opportunities is not accidental. Why did global capital flow into China at such a scale? The common response focuses on China's cheap labour and lack of independent unionization – and hence its weak bargaining power. But other, more important causal factors must be found, because workers were even cheaper and unions much weaker in many other countries.

The importance of FDI in a China as 'workshop of the world' has decreased, allowing a second factor to underpin the real economy – an explosion of domestic demand after decades of policy priority of accumulation over consumption and internal capitalization. Between 1990 and 2015, boosted by innovation and technological upgrading, total labour productivity in China grew by an average of 9.2 per cent annually (peaking at 13.7 per cent in 2007).[25] Side by side with domestic capital becoming dominant, in an investment-led growth that defied global financialization, China's productive (re)investment in fixed assets for capital formation, infrastructure across sectors and research and development has maintained a rate as high as 40 per cent throughout the past two to three decades.[26] This was possible chiefly due to the persistence of long-term strategic planning (or *guihua*, to be distinguished from *jihua* in the old command economy), macro, micro, and local subplans alike, enabling mobilization and allocation of resources to serve national priorities amid ad hoc disruptions by profit-driven and rent-seeking deals. Meanwhile, 'imports of capital goods and intermediate inputs required to climb the technological ladder' rendered China's export-oriented path simultaneously 'a particularly effective version of import-substituting industrialization'. A huge surplus on its current

24 UNCTAD's Investment Trends Monitor, October 2019, unctad.org/en/PublicationsLibrary/diaeiainf2019d2_en.pdf.

25 Lu Di, 'The Question of Productivity in China's Economic Development', *Bao Ma*, 19 September 2019.

26 Dic Lo, 'Developing or Under-Developing? Implications of China's "Going out" for Late Development', SOAS Department of Economics Working Paper 198, July 2016.

account and foreign exchange reserves also endowed remaining SOEs with seamless state loans and subsidies. This 'organized capitalism' provided 'the greatest possible incentives to non-financial corporate producers and exporters' with 'cheap land, world-class infrastructure, low taxes and cut-rate energy prices, as well as cheap credit'.[27] Government support allowing firms to gain a global market share and become internationally competitive, moreover, is selectively though substantially available in the private sector as well. Huawei received 'as much as $75 billion in tax breaks, financing and cheap resources';[28] formally private, it has an employee shareholding structure. The Chinese photovoltaic (PV) industry survived deadly European anti-dumping actions while still emerging as a global leader in both wind and solar capacity, because the Big Four state banks rallied behind it. Central and local state banks are in turn taken care of by state asset management companies at times of need to deal with their non-performing loans.

The internal, socialist pre-reform preparations are neglected in mainstream perceptions but are vital. The revolution had first liberated the nation and its productive forces, and positive developments in the reform era still relied on the socialist foundation of state capacity, financial autonomy, capital and labour accumulation, and public investment in human and physical infrastructures. Again, poverty is not attributable to socialism and antipoverty is not attributable to market reforms. Development and public welfare have consistently featured in Chinese policies since 1949. And it is not cheap labour (a complicit concept yet to be eradicated) but an educated, healthy and disciplined workforce that offers China a formidable advantage over most other developing nations. Supporting the workforce was the socialist state. It aimed for leaps in GNP (as opposed to GDP that includes also the value of the products of foreign and transnational companies) and to transform an agrarian economy into a complete industrial system of heavy, light and energy industries as well as transportation and other infrastructure. This process of construction required enormous accumulation not only of capital but also of labour, hence constant productive (re)investment.

---

27 Victor Shih, 'China's Credit Conundrum', interview by Robert Brenner, *New Left Review* 115, January/February 2019: 59–61.

28 Chuin-wei Yap, 'State Support Helped Fuel Huawei's Global Rise', *Wall Street Journal*, 25 December 2019.

Indeed, the Maoist model of labour or human capital accumulation is a valuable theoretical contribution to development economics. Regarding the extent of this strategic pursuit, based on a study of the Jiangsu province as a growth pole in the 1970s, Chris Bramall argues that 'a Chinese economic take-off, diffusing out of the Yangtze Delta, would have occurred even without post-1978 policy change'.[29] His study also suggests that development can be more balanced and less costly than the kind of market fundamentalism China subsequently practised. Indeed, China had already made itself into an industrial powerhouse before marketization: its industrial output grew by an average of 12.3 per cent a year in 1952–65, and 10.2 per cent in 1965–78, 'significantly outpacing Japan during the same period'.[30]

Obviously the 'new economic growth theory' of endogenous dynamism is not new to China, and external stimuli had to be internally adapted anyway. Globalist and localist perspectives can both claim partial truths. Their blending in the Chinese experience can seem contradictory with the boosting of growth, something that challenges existing economic models and known categorizations of social formation. Consider, among other contradictions: an extraordinarily huge market without compatible demands at home; a high investment rate that outstrips any other country and sustains a real economy while also overheating it into bubbles (incentivized by a pro-capital 'GDPism' since the 1990s); parallel privatization and state intervention or state-directed privatization; a massive push for clean and renewable power by the world's largest energy consumer sustaining a high level of carbon emissions (though China's per capita emissions by metric tonne, including those produced by multinationals for export, are less half those of the US); oscillations between decentralization and recentralization due to central coordination being ignored or fragmented; coexistence of experimental flexible policies and involuted bureaucratic formalism, and of neoliberal and Keynesian tools. The contrast between domestic vulnerability and foreign policy boldness, as between an autocratic political order and libertarian economic policies, is just as stunning. Tensions and rivalries between and among these features contribute to an impasse

---

29 Chris Bramall, 'A Late Maoist Industrial Revolution? Economic Growth in Jiangsu Province 1966–1978', *China Quarterly* 240, December 2019: 1039.

30 Andreas, *Disenfranchised*: 162.

of superficial overcapacity. Unbridled competition, enormous waste, runaway debt piling and capital flight all undermine stable and effective monetary policy and public financing. This is a bifurcated model geared towards more comprehensive neoliberalization.

The *shengai* policy of deepening reforms emboldened financial market integration. Capital controls are loosened, above all, so that foreign banks can operate in China and hold over 50 per cent of local bank stock, allowing the exchange rate of Chinese currency to fluctuate. Weakening sovereign control over the capital account threatened the nation's autonomous macro management and economic security. Moreover, China missed a chance to alter the global operation of financial capitalism: 'Remaining out opens room for a possible construction of alternative independent regional systems with the perspective of creating better conditions for the advancement of an alternative non-hegemonic globalization.'[31] It has now gone so far down this path that the option to step back is no longer available. Its integration into the orbit of 'dollar imperialism' – as 'a part of the very *modus operandi* of capitalism' today – continues apace.[32] What is waning is a popularly mandated national capacity conditional on an independent, secure, sustainable and need-driven economy, on which surplus retention and public wellbeing also depend. Ultimately, socialism distinguishes itself from capitalism by free producers, as opposed to commodified labour, producing for need rather than profit.

In the end, the erosion of the groundwork for socialism can go a long way towards explaining the immense costs of growth in the post-reform period. China's official self-identity as a polity undergoing primary stage socialism is open to elaboration by its intellectual transcribers. This positioning, in the now formal reference to Xi's new era, is defined by the CCP leadership: an economic system of macro-strategic planning, resource allocation and mainstay SOEs, with welfare-minded public policies. The question though is not only whether these attributes still hold after a period of deepened reform, but also if they are in themselves necessarily and distinctively socialist. They lack the essential

---

31 Samir Amin, 'Financial Globalization: Should China Move In?', Defend Democracy Press, 14 August 2018, defenddemocracy.press/22137-2.

32 Utsa Patnaik and Prabhat Patnaik, *A Theory of Imperialism*, New York: Columbia University Press, 2017: ch. 8.

component of class and social power and socially transformative movements towards higher stage socialism. If, as argued, the nature of state sector depends on that of the state itself and measurable by whether it is fundamentally driven by profit or social needs, then ownership pluralization and demutualization only discredit the sector's supposedly socialist identity. A recent incident illustrates the fallacy: hundreds of shareholders of state owned Guizhou Maotai, a highly profitable liquor maker which had transferred a small portion of its equities to the provincial SASAC, planned to file a class action lawsuit against the company making 'donations' to local government projects.[33]

It is perhaps plausible to argue, from a historical materialist standpoint, that generating wealth can be fundamentally legitimate, when it has transformed the material lives of one-fifth of humanity for the better. Moreover, the PRC government has pledged to green the country along its BRI reaches towards an 'ecological civilization'. The two centenary goals set for China are also politically remarkable: to build a fully fledged *xiaokang* or moderately prosperous society (measured by doubling the 2010 per capita income while eliminating poverty) by 2021, the hundredth anniversary of the party; and to achieve a 'strong, democratic, civilized, harmonious and modern socialist nation' by 2049, the hundredth anniversary of the PRC. Both slogans – 'national rejuvenation' and 'common human destiny' – reflect these projects.

The current conditions in China, however, even by the party's critically compromised interpretation, cannot meet the minimal requirements of socialism. On full display are ruthless accumulation, exploitative production relations, a privatized economy infused by foreign capital (accounting for more than two-thirds of GDP and 80 per cent of waged employment), and the degraded labour and subaltern masses suffering appalling conditions and extreme inequality. What else can better define the collapse of socialism or capitalist degeneration? From the vantage point of China's position in relation to global capitalism, the message of the Chinese political class that champions free trade and globalization cannot be clearer. It is about compliance with the Atlantic-cum-global order within epochal parameters, albeit with elements of rivalry. This positioning,

---

33 Shen Xinyue and Timmy Shen, 'Moutai Shareholders to Sue Distiller for $120m Government Donations', Caixin, 11 December 2020, asia.nikkei.com/Spotlight/Caixin/Moutai-shareholders-to-sue-distiller-for-120m-government-donations.

moreover, vastly favours international capital and ultimately prolongs the system in crisis due to China's market size, pro-capital structure and rule-obeying commitments. It has for years depressed the values of labour and goods in the global value chain, hurting workers and development in other regions of the world as well. That China is geared towards deeper globalization, even at the price of its own exploitation and subordination, also divides the country and makes its overseas engagements risky. The political implications are just as disturbing – recall Marx's warning against counterrevolution in newly converted capitalist regimes.[34] With no decisive reorientation in sight, China continues to lose its original substance and distinction as a people's republic. Seeing growth in China as not simply capitalist but Smithian; or it is still 'submissive-cum-resistant' vis-à-vis the systemic dynamics of global capitalism miss the crux of the matter: whether any socialist alternative can be on offer since the market transition has validated exploitation and inequality under the repressive power of capital – private as well as bureaucratic, domestic as well as transnational.[35]

This can be further clarified through an examination of China's much celebrated poverty alleviation project. Hyper growth has indeed impressively reduced abject poverty, benefiting over 700 million people, the vast majority of the world's total figure in poverty alleviation. Continuing from the gains of the first half of the 1980s, the number of people below the official poverty line fell dramatically from nearly 100 million in 2012 to 5.51 million by the end of 2019.[36] The poverty occurrence rate in the same period also went from 10.2 per cent to 0.6 per cent – what the *People's Daily* called 'a great victory of socialism and of humanity'.[37] There was also a laudable campaign of 'targeted poverty alleviation', pushing to 'accurately' identify and aid the rural poor. Transferred payment from richer to poorer regions have amounted to nearly half of the country's total revenue in recent years. Central and local

---

34 Marx, 'To Engels', 8 August 1858, *Collected Works of Marx and Engels*, Vol. 40: 345–6.

35 Arrighi, *Adam Smith in Beijing*; Lo, 'Developing or Under-Developing?': 12.

36 The PRC official line for absolute poverty is $324 a year per capita annual income, as compared with the World Bank's $700 (in constant 2010 values) for the middle income countries.

37 Huang Yuli, 'China's Last War Against Absolute Poverty', *People's Daily*, 12 March 2020. The government's minimal benchmark for security subsidies in 2018 was about $700 per person per annum.

governments devote themselves to complete the rural 'three networks': roads, water, electricity – and in many places the internet too. Children's vaccination and nine-year education are compulsory by law. The affordable housing programmes have relocated 150 million people from quasi-slums or areas deemed naturally uninhabitable. Millions of local officials, the foot-soldiers of policy implementation, are tasked with helping poor families. Eradicating poverty is an extremely important commitment and China's efforts are unparalleled in human history, proving that the goal of ending poverty on earth, debated since the industrial revolution, is achievable.

When looked at more closely, however, several issues come to light. First, the problem of poverty is not merely economic. It is endured by policy protected exploitation and polarization, and cannot be outrooted without another economic restructuring. The narrowly conceived anti-poverty campaign carried out as a top down government charity project for people to receive aid or basic living allowance (*dibao*) is therefore not specifically socialist. The poor are more expected to be grateful than recognized as their own agents with universal social right. Second, the assumed linear positive correlation between growth and poverty reduction is not questioned. Yet, not only has growth simultaneously produced both billionaires and new poor, it is also seriously offset by grave human and environmental costs which disproportionately harm the poor, urban and rural. Pollution and industrial or occupation-induced diseases are one example; migrant workers' hardships of displacement, precarity and insecurity, is another. In the freezing winter of 2017–18, Beijing drove out tens of thousands of migrant workers from its outskirts. Treated as an underclass or 'low-end population' (*diduan renkou* – though the shamefaced municipal officials denied that they had used that language) unfit for urban gentrification, they were a disposable commodity despite their indispensable contribution to the economy and everyday life of the capital. Urban poverty itself is yet to engage policymaking, and the whole project is bound to continue.

Third, unlike the socialist vision of self-managed, productively and culturally shriving communities, the project is seen as part of, and relying on, deepening marketization. The negative social consequences of market forces, especially in basic public utilities and services, are disregarded. The anti-poverty method drawn up alongside the campaign for 'rural revitalization' focuses on external investment, infrastructural standardization, and commercialization of local productive factors. Invaluable local eco-diversity, knowledge, subsistence resources and preferences are frequently disregarded. In one typical example, the regional party secretary of Guangxi published a report in *Qiushi*, the party's flagship journal, emphasizing 'featured agriculture' of commercial crops, animal breeding, 'ecotourism' and cross-border trade.[38] Instead of investing in public good provision, local governments in poor regions have spent massively on superfluous administrators, office buildings and tourist sites. Fourth, education and healthcare are not priorities. For example, government acceptance criteria on poverty eradication have not included school enrolment. China 'has failed to invest enough in its single most important asset: its people'; and it has 'one of the lowest levels of education of any nation' – 12.5 per cent of its labour force has a college education, and about 30 per cent is educated to high school level or above (2015 data).[39] Finally, the programme is also used as a tool of stability maintenance in general and the main route towards ethnic peace in particular, without first addressing non-poverty-related causes of tension, such as forms of cultural oppression. In Xinjiang, poverty alleviation cadres of both Han and minority origins have been dispatched to live in Muslim homes. To a lesser extent in Tibet as well, locals are trained to work at faraway factories in areas unfamiliar to them, though only on a voluntary basis. Yet what is hard but very common elsewhere in China, migrant working frustrates people locally and is exploited by foreign critics as an ethnically specific form of imposition.

Above all, both in reality and the official statistics, the recurring poverty caused by structural deficiencies keep reproducing poverty. The market reforms of education, healthcare and pensions have created 'three new great mountains' (as opposed to the old ones, 'imperialism, feudalism and bureaucratic capitalism' in the revolution's terminology) in the popular discourse. The grand issue of unaffordability, from housing to care or marriage, is a persistent source of social insecurity, and hence poverty. China's latest rounds of medical reform are all guided by market incentives and are confined to paid insurance rather

---

38 Lu Xinshe, 'Research Notes on Targeted Poverty Alleviation', *Qiushi* 9, 2019, qstheory.cn/dukan/qs/2019-05/01/c_1124440787.htm.

39 Scott Rozelle and Natalie Hell, *Invisible China: How the Urban-Rural Divide Threatens China's Rise*, Chicago: University of Chicago Press, 2020: 5.

than free public medicine with universal coverage, retreating from the socialist practice in the past though it was only at a rudimentary level and focusing on prevention. Now a serious illness can easily bring a whole family into destitution, and the sick and poor often avoid seeking hospital treatment. Attending primary school is a daily struggle in some rural areas, especially for girls and children stranded by family difficulties. The expectation of governmental and communal public provision, previously taken for granted in the PRC, is fading. The logic at work today is that the market transition must legitimate itself by repudiating this basic socialist commitment.

It is clear that neither poverty alleviation nor SOEs are by themselves necessarily socialist. Needed social and industrial policies, and more generally a strong public sector and schemes for public provision, are not unfamiliar to welfare capitalism. For that matter, the West too has written off debt for poor countries from time to time. In fact, essential utilities such as water are partially privatized in China but not in some core capitalist countries. China's financial sector is less protected than most free market economies. Unlike in China, free healthcare and education are maintained in a number of former communist states, not to mention the amazing Cuban model of social services and medical internationalism. Having escaped the acute transitional contraction characteristic of post-communism, the transformation of Chinese political economy has turned out to be far more radical in the long run. It is not the *minsheng* policies as such that are lost in China – the materially 'beautiful life' is prioritized under Xi – but what has been abandoned is the once powerful aspiration towards classlessness, the abolition of exploitation and the nurturing of self-realization. Anti-poverty does not define socialism; freedom and equality do. To be sure, Maoist society was never fully free and equal. But there is a striking contrast between the former egalitarian cultural politics and today's market perversions of globalism and developmentalism. In an interview of 1991, Fidel Castro marvelled that the objective of socialism suddenly seemed to be understood only as an improvement in living standards. 'To me,' he said, 'socialism is a total change in the life of the people and the establishment of new values and a new culture.'[40] Indeed, as soon as equality was pitted against efficiency, and consumer choice replaced freedom,

---

40 Quoted in Prashad, *Red Star*: 130.

inequalities – class, gender, ethnic, regional, sectoral – and subjugation
became ideologically justifiable.

Moreover, it is officially admitted that poverty (and wealth) are overwhelmingly inherited.[41] The vanishing of equality as a common culture
or public belief is one of the most regrettable 'Chinese characteristics'.
Writing on inequality in contemporary China 'between communism
and plutocracy', Thomas Piketty observed, more conservatively than
some of his Chinese counterparts, that the richest 1 per cent own 30 per
cent of national wealth, and the richest 10 per cent own 67 per cent,
while the bottom 50 per cent own just 6.4 per cent. Between 1995 and
2015, 'China has gone from a level lower than that observed in Sweden
to a level approaching that of the United States.' Worse, China's Gini
coefficient could be as high as 0.65, since there is neither progressive
taxation for the wealthy nor inheritance tax. This is a matter of political
choice and ideology.[42] In May 2020, Premier Li Keqiang revealed that
the monthly income of 600 million people was less than 1,000 yuan
(about $140). The number is supported by the delineated data, showing
that 220 million, mostly in the rural interior, received even less than 500
yuan ($72). The high-earning group comprising about 7.84 million
people, measured by a monthly income of over 30,000 yuan or around
$4,286, constituted only 0.05 per cent of the PRC population.[43]

Dismantling many of its hard-earned successes, China has become
one of the world's most unequal societies, where frantic luxury spending
sits side by side with poverty and insecurity-induced underconsumption. The latter is another word for overcapacity, when the proportion of
labour income, as roughly indicated as gross household income,
decreases in relation to national accumulation. This disparity, both in
terms of poverty and a high savings rate, has also been behind the BRI
drive. For decades China's growing productivity was not matched by an

----

41 Feng Hua, 'Some Poor People Move from Temporary to Cross-Generational
Poverty', 23 January 2015, finance.people.com.cn/n/2015/0123/c1004-26435980.html.

42 Thomas Piketty, 'On Inequality in China', Le Monde, 14 February 2017; Tom
Clark, 'Thomas Piketty's Capital Idea', Prospect, 28 February 2020.

43 Zhou Tianyong, 'Imbalance of Insufficient Demand of Domestic Consumption
and Industrial Productive Overcapacity', Xinlang Finance and Economy, 23 June 2020;
Yang Yiyong quoted in the party journal report 'Investigative Report on Polarization in
Big Cities', Biweekly Review 22, 2009, and published online in May and June 2020; Wan
Haiyuan and Meng Fanqiang, 'Where Are these 600 Million People?', Caixin Global, 3
June 2020, opinion.caixin.com/2020-06-03/101562409.html.

equivalent increase in wages and disposable income. 'The net effect was that the household share of GDP contracted ... to possibly the lowest we've ever seen in history.'[44] The 2019 figures – household income and consumption relative to national GDP at 43.42 per cent and 30.29 per cent respectively – are significantly lower than the world averages of 55–65 per cent and 50–60 per cent correspondingly. In particular, the total income of registered rural residents (780 million, including 230 million migrant workers) accounted for only 16 per cent of the GDP.[45] As usual, the *People's Daily* carried a happy-ending report on 23 July 2020: a coalminer in Shaanxi who had earned 'as much as' over 10,000 *yuan* a year (about $150 a month) had returned to his village and become a fungus producer. Incidentally, this is also a reminder that miners in new China were once among the most respected and best treated industrial workers, enjoying higher salaries and better food supplies, taking artificial sunbathing daily after work and visiting workers' sanatoriums on the seaside or mountain retreats regularly for health maintenance. As the groundwork for a post-liberation moral economy as well as some remarkable socioeconomic gains of early reform have been thoroughly eroded, systemic imbalances destabilize any model that China claims. Extreme inequality alone makes a mockery of China's socialist self-identity. Systematically engineered neoliberal mutation has also further distanced political and economic elites in the upper echelons of governmental and legislative bodies from the labouring masses. Such distance can easily be measured by the prevalence of office status fetishism, arbitrary exercise of power and a pandemic of corruption. Positioning itself as destined for globalization, China is also ever more vulnerable to exogenous shocks of financial meltdown and eco-disasters.

The balance sheet is in the end a tangle of contradictions. As Michael Mann put it:

Never have modern industries and urban infrastructures grown so fast, never have people moved out of poverty so fast, but never have both inequality and corruption grown so fast, and never have workers

---

44 Adam Tooze, 'Trade Wars Are Class Wars', interview with Michael Pettis and Matthew Klein, 13 June 2020, phenomenalworld.org/interviews/trade-wars-are-class-wars.
45 Zhou, 'Imbalance of Insufficient Demand.'

or peasants, formerly theoretical masters of the state, been treated so ruthlessly.[46]

One can well add more specifics. Never have the old lived so long, but never have the medical resources been allocated so unfairly and work-related injuries and deaths such as pneumoconiosis so perpetually neglected. Never has the higher education system expanded so much (60 per cent of high school students can now attend university, up from 20 per cent in 1980), but never have so many children of migrant workers, a whole generation, grown up practically parentless and incapable of completing nine years of schooling. A more contentious change is the cultural and moral decline, of which shocking indicators are the number of patients with depression (mostly left untreated) and rate of suicide. A 2016 Beijing University study revealed that 100 million people were suffering from depression in China; and, according to a Beijing Health Bureau spokesman, 'our nation has one of the highest rates of suicide in the world' (22.23 per 100,000 people in 2011) before it was brought down.[47]

Returning to the rival explanations for China's growth, beyond an investment-led model ensuing credit and asset bubbles, either indigenously sourced or FDI and neoliberalization enhanced, can the Chinese experience be conceptualized in terms of socialism versus capitalism – both themselves in flux? Without subscribing to an oversimplified demarcation, again it is a wishful thinking to take the Soviet NEP as an analogy for the Chinese reform. The NEP was a temporary retreat, while reform in China has over the decades forged ahead in its own right. Although the present regime retains features resembling a socialist state, it is losing the last defence of a socialist political economy, even if public land and capital control still linger. Any alternative China forges would still be open to shaping and reshaping. Phrases such as 'market Stalinism', 'Hayekian communism', 'autocratic capitalism' or 'bureaupreneurship' might sound paradoxical while tensions grow, they capture some mechanism of fast growth facilitated by a post-socialist state

46 Michael Mann, *The Sources of Social Power, Vol. 4*: 236.

47 'China's Suicide Rate "Among Highest in World"', *Medical Xpress*, 8 September 2011; CRIENGLISH news, '100 Million People Suffer Depression in China', *China Daily*, 28 November 2016; Liu Chang, 'The Silent Cries of China's Depressed Netizens', Sixth Tone, 10 September 2019, sixthtone.com/news/1004543/the-silent-cries-of-chinas-depressed-netizens.

committed to market integration.[48] The Chinese governing and social system is not monolithic, either functionally or in its perspective. In all events, however, it is both a challenge and threat to liberal capitalism. The point is that any articulation of a China model, if at all useful, would not be descriptively socialist as far as it goes. Whether socialism can remain a normative idea for and in China will depend on the socialists regaining the upper hand and struggling against the tide while engaging the labour and social movements locally, as well as globally.

Political reform: Whose legality? What democracy?

The puzzling nature of the PRC state and its political economy is vulnerable to contentious politics. Chinese society has been torn apart not only by socioeconomic and political inequalities but also by an ideological tug of war. The established legitimacy of reform and opening delegitimizes any critical questioning of the policy direction. Splits in public opinion are also no longer clearly identifiable with such labels as left and right. Paradoxically, the intensity of debates has proved that there remains a resilient public space, despite tight restrictions on the flow of information and free expression, aided by digital control and mass surveillance. Against the backdrop of a broken social consensus, the consistent call for political reform is perceived by liberal intellectuals as a solution to the mismatch between China's economic opening and political closing, or between market radicalism and political conservatism. That China's largely liberalized economy appears to have remained politically straightjacketed without a corresponding political overhaul is presumed a fundamental problem, and the remedy is imagined only as some kind of Perestroika. This fails to appreciate that the market transition and neoliberal policies have been imposed via state tyranny: they are perfectly compatible.

At stake, then, is the very meaning of *political reform*, starting with the legalization needed to produce a market economy and involving legally binding transactions and significant foreign participation. Legal reform in China was introduced with the help of scholars and lawyers from the

---

48 Branko Milanovic, 'Hayekian Communism', 24 September 2018, glineq.blogspot.com/2018/09/hayekian-communism.html.

West: inspired by both liberal (US) and authoritarian (Singapore) capitalist paradigms, the doctrine held that a mature market is to be founded on clarified private property. The party has engaged constitutional amendments accordingly since 1988, legitimizing unlimited growth of the private sector. Drafts of China's first property law (2007) had been rejected during rounds of public reading and drew several oppositional petitions calling for the dominance of public property to be upheld.[49] Yet what appeared to be an anachronistic consciousness of the 'inviolability of private property' belatedly travelled to the East to impact on China's new legal stipulations. By then SOEs – seen as having suffered soft budget constraints, incentive deficiency and all kinds of issues around the 'tragedy of the commons' – had been significantly transformed. Public ownership in general was deemed a drag on market competitiveness, damaging to a rational economy and freedom, and unreformable. 'It is time to let go of this vain hope once and for all', called János Kornai, a guru of privatization in formerly communist zones, in 1991.[50] In 2004, the PRC constitution enshrined an article to render legally acquired private wealth and inheritance 'inviolable'. Not even major capitalist states as diverse as the US and India use such a language; a comparable German clause is conditional on associated social obligations.[51] When privatization dominated the transitional economies, most European social democracies did not give up on their state sectors, even amid intense assaults on the welfare state. The Canadian Charter excludes property rights by a landmark Supreme Court ruling.[52] Tensions between property and democracy seem to be eased with the priority of democracy: capitalism has to rein in property to remain minimally welfarist and democratic.

The rule of law is commonly accepted as a valid goal in China, partly because of past lawlessness but also in light of the present ills of a legal and

49 Eva Cheng, 'Wrangle over Law To Legitimize China's Looted State Property', *Green Left*, 18 January 2007.

50 'Problems of Communism', Special Materials Section, US Information Agency, 31 December 1991: 4.

51 Cui Zhiyuan, 'A Comparative Study of the Relationship between Property Right and Constitution', lecture at the legal studies forum, Renmin University, March 2003, wyzxwk.com/Article/jiangtang/2010/12/4810.html.

52 Ha-Joon Chang, 'State-Owned Enterprise Reform', UN Department for Economic and Social Affairs, United Nations DESA, New York, 2007: 6–7, 12–13; Alexander Alvaro, 'Why Property Rights Were Excluded from the Canadian Charter of Rights and Freedom', *Canadian Journal of Political Science* 24:2, June 1991: 326–7.

penal system often abused from within and without. But legality and judicial independence as such cannot be sufficient. The class nature of the post-reform legal system is attested to by the extent to which it fails tens of millions of workers, especially in the informal sector. Their legal rights, such as those for a forty-hour work week and minimum wages paid on schedule, are poorly protected. Many lack the contracts that would legally have to be presented in any labour dispute. In an exceedingly flexible market, salaries and occasionally even identity cards can be withheld by the 'bosses' – another restored referent or symbol of old society. In particular, 'labour's impotence within enterprises means that potentially prolabor laws and collective agreements frequently go unenforced.'[53] The subordination of atomized workers to capital was exemplified by the fierce contention over the 2006 draft labour law. In the face of threatened withdrawal of investment from the American and European Union Chambers of Commerce and the US-China Business Council that was representing a lobby of multinational companies, including General Electric and Google among others, the Chinese government reduced channels of contractual bargaining and 'scaled back protections for employees and sharply curtailed the role of unions' from the drafted version. Microsoft's director of human resources in China told *Businessweek* that 'we have enough investment at stake that we can usually get someone to listen to us if we are passionate about an issue.'[54] As the game was played under rich nations' rules, the Chinese legal system complied.

When workers are tried for disrupting stability after rallying over labour conditions or a controversial managerial decision, and when leaders of villagers protesting over losing illegally seized collective land are arrested and charged with corruption, it is not the legal procedures that are at issue but the morality of the law. Which laws are upheld? What judiciary and in whose interest? Moreover, legality is also a means of containing contentious politics, defusing distress and thwarting the ferment of insurgency. Independent workers' organization, a hallmark of the Cultural Revolution, must be supressed. The clause in the PRC constitution (Article 45) granting freedom to strike was removed in 1983; any strike or protest since can be legally designated as disturbing

---

53 Friedman, *Insurgency Trap*: 5.

54 Brendan Smith, Tim Costello and Jeremy Brecher, 'Undue Influence', Common-Dreams, 3 April 2007, commondreams.org/views/2007/04/03/undue-influence.

public order or inciting instability. The legal channels under a state–capital coalition fundamentally limit labour-friendly settlements. Lin Zulian, the village leader in the Wukan stand-off in Guangdong against illegal sales of collective land pointed out that none of the responses proposed by the provincial arbitrators – dialogue, bargaining or suing – would resolve the issue. Protecting the farmers and farmland is the responsibility of the government.[55] Legal formalism poses a dilemma for fragmented labour: the philistine framing of labour disputes as a matter of individual legal rights reflects a socialist state stripped of class power. However imperfect the socialist state had been, its replacement by a legal state pretending to be apolitical must result in toleration of the suffering of labourers. The gap between ideational legal rationality and the enduring appeal of fundamental social justice is telling. The myth of a dilemma between freedom and security has informed a redefinition of the social contract and disavowal of state paternalism, leading to social deprivation in terms of both security and freedom.

Political reform, envisioned by a politically conscious economic elite with a foot in public institutions and policy making, seeks to legitimize and thereby secure what has been privately seized and will continue to transfer public wealth into private hands. Fully corroborated privatization would provide assurance for such transfers and outlaw any possibility of de-privatization, which would also be in the interest of international capital and its local arms. Such a process is described in popular Chinese as 'capitalization of power and empowerment of capital'. A peculiar interpretation of civil society works in the same way, as a chimera of normative framing. Class and social conflict or sheer asymmetrical power relations are disguised by an assumed state–society antagonism. However, the ideological purchase of an all-virtuous civil society, both conditional and constitutive of democracy, is self-deceptive. In a state-led market transition, the rich and powerful can enjoy freewheeling civic autonomy and private yet institutionalized privileges. This situation renders so-called political reform anti-democratic and locally suspicious or unacceptable. If it is the moral imperative of the people's collective sovereignty and their capacity as lawmakers that fundamentally defines democracy and legality, then neither the official agenda of depoliticized rule of law nor the fetishized pretence of

---

55 Yang Jiang, 'Lin Xulian: Restoring a Real Wukan', *Xinmin Weekly* 682:11, 2012: 36.

competitive party politics can answer the real social demands in China. The political and social rights of the labouring classes bestowed by the communist revolution are neither vanished nor dispensable in mass consciousness. The socialist democratic presupposition about the moral foundation of law holds and is the only true impulse for China to democratize. That is, political reform, including legal justice and due process, cannot be endorsed separately from substantial *social* justice.

Since neoliberalism's coming of age during the 1990s in China, in a one way traffic of globalization without a competing communist world, it is questionable whether popularly desirable political change and truly democratic citizenship could make ground in the marketplace of inequalities and political indifference that has held sway. A transgenerational nostalgia for national self-reliance and an honest, mass-inclined government has gained some momentum. But the glory of the people, lost in the transformation of socialism, is yet to recover its rightful appeal. Where this to happen, there would be the potential for socially and politically innovative outcomes – not through another revolution, and beyond formal democracy. Bringing the people back in, however, threatens the status quo; and the more resistant the social forces, the more ferocious is the response of the new order. It must crush any opposition, dissolve critics and pacify unrest. It is for this inherent struggle, rather than the parochialism and condescension of an imported set of assumptions, that democracy makes concrete and pressing sense in today's China. With its own unfinished project of people's democracy, China has an indigenous resource on which to draw. Maoism was an experiment in 'intimate governance', an attempt to dismantle the divide between leaders and the led. As a normative goal, it 'did not eradicate ruling class entitlements and arrogance but delegitimized them and opened them up to public scrutiny'.[56] Is this still the case as seen from within? There have been notable efforts at local levels for government to be more transparent and responsive through grassroots elections, public consultancy and online feedback channels, and can be further informed by the evocative socialist traditions of popular participation, supervision and self-government. Democracy is by definition endogenous, and can proceed only in accordance with *this people's* yearnings and judgements.

---

56 Christian Sorace, 'Metrics of Exceptionality, Simulated Intimacy', *Critical Inquiry* 46:3, Spring 2020: 555.

The kind of structural legal and political reforms that liberals advocate for in China – matching the economic global integration to a political order – would only enhance the private concentration of power, wealth and resources, and continue to conceal or obscure the basic reality of a bureaucracy–capital coalition. As Maurice Meisner posited: 'Any serious impetus for democratic change will more likely come from the victims, not the beneficiaries, of state-sponsored capitalism.'[57] To unpack the meaning of democracy in an equivocal liberal discourse of constitutionalism and legality is to refuse complacency and stand by the socialist principles: democracy and freedom for the subalterns, labour and common people. For procedural legality and electoral democracy to make any sense in China, as opposed to in countries without revolutionary experience, they will have to be morally and socially substantiated.

A party without theory

The problem is that as the Chinese revolution has degenerated, the banners of freedom and democracy have been taken by or, more precisely, given up to bourgeois ideology and liberal capitalism. The Cultural Revolution failed to beat bureaucratization, and instead provoked a horrendous revenge: today power is defended for its own sake, bureaucracy having formed an alliance with capital and repressive social management. The enemies of socialism righteously condemned totalitarianism in their Cold War interfusion, as the lack of secured liberties makes even what Lenin referred to as 'sham bourgeois democracy' desirable. His theoretical proposition that a socialist democracy would be 'a hundred times more democratic' is yet to be materialized. In China, the revolutionary aspiration of constructing a people's democracy was aborted decades ago. The Dengist interpretation of socialism was narrowly economic, focusing on 'common prosperity', and then moved away from that keyword *common* as well. In the context of the infamous cat theory (whatever its colour a cat who can catch mice is a good cat) against ideological contention over isms, and promotions for those who got rich first, the reformers denounced mass line democracy but intended no

---

57 Maurice Meisner, 'Capitalism, Communism, and Democracy in China: A Review Essay', *Progressive* 71:11, 2007: 41.

democratic substitute. The tendency to idealize Maoism, not only among the poor but also increasingly among the educated urban youth, is not without good reason: it is a gesture of protest against old and new forms of inequality and injustice. Yet the idea and practice of labour participating in management and state affairs or the mass supervision of officials and policies drawn from the Paris Commune model are simply intangible in the present political ecology.

One of the theories implicitly supporting the official discourse is that China (like most other East Asian nations) is culturally and rightfully illiberal, and that there is nothing lamentable in collectivism cum conformity. This theory seems to mistake the political for the cultural. Too often politically unconscious, the imperialist stain of liberalism is overlooked – the violent introduction of liberal imperialism to China was what blocked liberal development at the country's threshold to modernity. A powerful argument of New Democracy was precisely that as the capitalist path had been foreclosed the revolution would pave the way for socialism. It would be too little to argue that China must be understood on its own terms – the same is true for all societies, even in an age of global communication and interdependence. Any Sinocentric insistence on Chinese exceptionalism would only confirm the validity and superiority of the supposedly normal and universal, based on capitalist-centric experiences. Essentialist dichotomies conceal what really matters – socialism – to which national characteristics are subordinate. There is indeed no single solution or paradigm as liberal capitalism propagates, but any rational and viable alternative must not be illiberal or anti-democratic. Yet, even if it is at times necessarily resistant in its interaction with the global system, the Chinese ruling order has in effect submitted itself to the neoliberal transmutation of both socialism and liberalism.

This situation follows the post–Cultural Revolution logic of renouncing grand democracy without delineating its complex legacies. Giving up altogether on a socialist interpretative capacity for democratic governance, the reformist move to de-ideologize was itself highly ideological. It specifically targeted a socialist opposition to market opening, clearing the ground for reformist policies while hardening the dogma that granted absolute priority to growth. The new hegemony of developmentalism then delegitimized criticisms of its political and social consequences. This post-Mao moment of a single minded advocacy of the forces of production anticipated another discursive round of the end of ideology and of history globally, in reconfiguring the post–Cold War landscape. Domestically, China began a process of dismantling the shared sense of fundamental rights and wrongs after 1949, recasting social consciousness to the extent that a standard rebuff to any criticism of the present – 'Do you then want to return to the days of Cultural Revolution?' – would instantly ruin a conversation. The utopianism and high-intensity politics of mass democracy are gone, replaced with fervent consumerism, and alternating political passion and apathy. Social trust and solidarity are down, overpowered by selfish individualism or polarity amid ideologically charged beliefs. The heavily censored social media is nevertheless vibrant but also gradually catalysing a mingled culture of materialism and patriotism, aided by such inventive applications as a 'social credit system' and others – a likely objective for the leadership. The rule of 'no arguing' has been escalated to 'no wilful commenting' on top-level designs and decisions, for party members and common citizens alike, effecting social disempowerment in favour of personal loyalty. Socialism is less relevant than regime preservation; and with an intense air of insecurity, dissenting voices must be stifled to ensure central control over crucial narratives of power.

In this suppression of public discussions about China's direction, the reform has deviated from its original intent of socialist self-improvement and has simultaneously lost the mechanism of self-correction. Any social engineering of the magnitude of the Chinese reform would need strategy and policy checks to ensure success. The mistiness of the other side of the river being crossed by touching the stones is attributable to prolonged avoidance of clarifying a socialist vision, leading to increasing returns on a derailed reform path. Along the way, the CCP has forsaken its precious tradition of party building through democratic centralism, criticism and self-criticism, and cadres receiving education and supervision from the masses. The absence of line struggle, the party's lifeline and mechanism for self-correction that had required theoretical exploration and open debate, forfeited the whole communist political culture and its construction of subjectivity. This inner-party vitality is where the CCP once markedly differed from its ossified and stagnant counterparts under Stalinism. The conservative turn of Chinese politics in the aftermath of the Cultural Revolution similarly produced political opportunism and social philistinism, changing the party's colour as much as its character – a depoliticized and de-theorized state party, in Wang Hui's analysis, subject to the bureaucratic order.[58] The Maoist intuition has once more been proven right: *no arguing, no party; and no debate, no renewal.*

After an initial attempt at theorizing a socialist market economy by China's Marxist economists, formal ideological reproduction became thinner still over time. Its interpretation of Marxism sounded more decorative than real; and the distortion is best illustrated by the word *buke*, literally 'making up a missed lesson' (of capitalist development). This rhetoric thrived in the 1980s and has since taken root in the minds of market reformers: China mistakenly skipped a necessary historical stage (a linear notion of history falsely ascribed to Marx), which explains the failure of its socialist adventures. Rather than openly embracing capitalism in direct violation of the socialist codes, the slippery language of a primary-stage socialism leaves room for the capitalist stage to be taken as prerequisite. Backtracking in order to gain the material basis deemed necessary for socialist development then functioned to justify a pro-capital agenda in Marxist terms. The 1945 CCP programme of New Democracy became recurrent for the same purpose: it was initially premised on the parameters of a socialist state as guarantor, with the political, legal and regulative instruments to fend off capitalist corrosions – as practised in the first few years of the PRC. But the interplay between state and market fell into a war of euphemisms as soon as the market tools were redeemed to dictate the course. An early episode of revisiting the 'Asiatic mode of production' (AMP), sparked by the Chinese translation of an otherwise little-known Italian publication by Umberto Melotti, titled *Marx and the Third World*, is revealing.[59] It was an instant hit in Beijing's intellectual circles in 1981, as the reformers seeking a breakthrough found its critique of 'bureaucratic collectivism' straightforwardly useful. At issue was not the validity of AMP or 'oriental despotism' as such, but their symbolic contemporary inference. The orthodox stage theory aided reorientation through a deformed Marxism, making capitalist development ideologically acceptable in the long shadow of Chinese socialism. Accordingly, Marxism was re-devised to validate staunchly anti-Marxist theories and policies. The reformist

---

58 Wang Hui, *The End of the Revolution: China and the Limits of Modernity*, London: Verso, 2011: 7-9.

59 Umberto Melotti, *Marx and the Third World* (1972), London: Macmillan, 1977 (Chinese translation: Beijing: Shangwu Publishing House, 1981).

party, thoroughly bureaucratized, corrupt and equipped for technological social control, disowned its ideological distinction.

The reinterpretation of China's relationship with capitalism was thus
pivotal for subsequent ideological contentions. These were limited from
the beginning, to allow for customization of the notion of 'socialism
with Chinese characteristics'. It is now a plastic basket in which anything
fits; even capitalist teleology and institutionalization can be naturalized
when the party's monopoly is an end in itself. Although China's basic
economic system is officially defined as a 'mixed economy dominated
by public ownership', the party is also 'unwaveringly committed to the
development of both public and private economies'. As such, the exploitation and polarization inherent to market liberalization are natural
and tolerable, while formal party and government statements simply
avoid these notions along with the whole Marxist language of class,
surplus value and the abolition of private property. The *buke* theory
was a serious departure from what was central to the theoretical foundation of Chinese communist revolution – that socialist development
is conditioned on the revolutionary creation of new relations of production rather than any material basis prepared for by prior capitalist
development. The historical impossibility of liberal and independent
national capitalism in colonial and semi-colonial societies in the era of
imperialism was used to explain the Chinese Communist Revolution.
With a small and fragile national bourgeoisie, under the combined
pressures of foreign capital as well as bureaucratic compradorism and
landlordism, and with much of the nation's wealth and autonomy
stolen, where could China begin its own primitive accumulation for
industrialization? It was never given a chance to refuse any such
golden opportunity, as claimed in the revisionist historiography. The
Chinese Marxist counterfactual argument that imperialism was a fatal
interruption of indigenous developments in most parts of the Third
World is a political one.

An immediate yet unanswered logical hurdle of this pseudo-Marxist
theory points to the fallacy of capitalist means serving socialist ends. If
capitalism in an effectively post-socialist society can succeed, why
should it then be expected to prepare for its own demise? Conversely, if
it is destined to fail, what could possibly rationalize its necessity? And
why would socialism matter if it is unable to achieve greater forces of
production than its capitalist competitors? This last question was behind

some Maoist policy controversies as well as the conventional belief in central planning. It deserves probing in relation to the assumption that development is intrinsically desirable. Rather material affluence as such might well be questionable; and the style of living by the rich cannot be rationally emulated by others. Marx praised unprecedented productive capacity of revolutionary capitalism but also warned of its perils and harms on labour, both short and long term, as reengaged in a growing body of eco-Marxist works. In light of nature's revenge alone, the claim of capitalist universality and indispensability has already been proven wrong. Chinese developmentalism also borne its own responsibilities.

Pseudo-Marxist ideological re-articulations reflect market pragmatism and the collapse of political theory. The latter marks an inexcusable decline from the party's uniquely strong intellectual tradition of standing against both dogmatic and revisionist Marxisms. Jiang Zemin's Three Represents ratified at the 2002 party congress opened the communist party to private entrepreneurs as agents of 'the most advanced productive force'. They were regarded as 'advanced elements in the newly arisen social strata' sharing 'fundamental interests' with labour. Formally speaking, such a notion is unconstitutional, given the enshrined postulation of a leading working class. But in an astonishing twist, supporters found it was 'successfully avoiding the crisis of representation that would occur if the party were only to represent the interests of workers and peasants'.[60] Apparently, this was a highly political move of re-legitimation, based on a very different conception of the regime and its power base.

Private businesspeople have since entered the party just as the party members have entered into private business. They have also become party branch secretaries, representatives of various trade associations, and deputies to the national and local people's congresses and consultative conferences. The 2013 CASS (Chinese Academy of Social Sciences) annual Blue Book revealed that one-third of China's virtual capitalists were organizationally communists; of those owning more than 100 million yuan (about $16 million), 53 per cent were party members. Seven multibillionaires attended the eighteenth party congress in 2012. Among the country's super-rich, with a collective family net worth of $221 billion, 160 were identified as party

---

60 Jiang, 'Philosophy and History': 17.

representatives, NPC deputies or members of the CPPCC. The NPC
'may boast more very rich members than any other such body on
earth'.[61] A record 415 billionaires controlled a combined wealth of $1.7
trillion by July 2020.[62] This scale of both private accumulation and its
infiltration in political power have continued to fortify 'capitalism with
Chinese characteristics', while the party keeps 'painting its lips red', in
the words of Huang Jisu, playwright of *Che Guevara* which drew a huge
Chinese audience in 2000.[63]

The Hu Jintao administration promoted scientific and people-centred
development and social harmony, in a remedial effort to redress the
social problems that intensified during the 1990s. One popular policy
was the removal of the agricultural tax and most other rural levies
around the year 2006. The investment in scientific development could
have been used to halt the frenzy of urbanization and developmentalism, but it remained abstract, as though the economy was running all by
itself. Xi Jinping has inherited from his predecessors the focus on livelihoods, but has injected strong elements of personal authority and
nationalism. The quest for national rejuvenation rather than the socialist rectification of accumulated inequality and injustice features in his
new era. The Marxism he peddles is just as slanted, typified by the 2017
nineteenth party congress identification of the Chinese system's 'principal contradiction' with that 'between inadequate development and
people's ever-growing demand for a good life'. Fairly *minsheng* oriented,
this diagnosis is nevertheless an outright evasion of the relations of
production, hence of a structural perspective on class and the power of
capital. This seemingly apolitical statement instrumentalizes the rhetoric of socialism for economic modernization, concealing real social and
political contradictions. It blindly or wilfully endorses vulgar developmentalist biases, as though issues of food and water insecurity, land
and industrial pollution, resource depletion and eco-environmental
degradation, and multiple rifts of state and society are not all severe
enough.

61 James Areddy and James Grimaldi, 'Defying Mao', *Wall Street Journal*, 26 December 2012.

62 Narayanan Somasundaram, 'Chinese Billionaires' Wealth Soars 41 per cent in
Post-Lockdown Resurgence', NikkeAsia, 7 October 2020.

63 Huang Jisu, 'The Two Legacies of the Chinese Revolution', 17 September 2015,
zhurengong.net/index.php?m=content&c=index&a=show&catid=46&id=172.

Yet politics is emphasized in Xi's guideline, and his definition of socialism is about power retention. In a July 2020 article in *Qiushi*, he declared that 'the most essential feature of socialism with Chinese characteristics is the leadership of the CCP'. More specifically, this means 'above all, insisting on the authority of the party centre and its centralized and unified leadership'.[64] For the first time, democratic centralism had been cut in half in a formal party document. What a misinterpretation of Marxism and socialism this is, that can mute the language of class, subdue class struggle, absolutize the power at the very top without either ensuring its class position and representative validity or respecting party members' right to speak. The working class has been deprived of what is in theory its own party leadership, and the two are far from organically connected as in the revolutionary past. Precisely in light of this vulnerability of labour and the disoriented lifeworld as a whole, no faithful Marxist could evade class analysis. Obviously, since class is a conceptual vehicle for workers to organize and agitate while overcoming their atomization and powerlessness, it finds no place in a ruling ideology obsessed with maintaining institutional power. Nor can it fall into an internationalist category in a foreign policy strategy immersed in neoglobalism. China is increasingly on a lonely path of its all-out global market integration, tailing the neoliberal phase of globalization which since 2008 has entered an endgame.

Xi's thought also leans towards a revivalism of tradition – something else that belies its Marxist label. With assistance from establishment intellectuals, he highlights Chinese civilizational uniqueness, enticing ruling methods rather than common heritages. One of the authoritative expositions of this thought stresses a single narrative that blends Marxism and Confucianism – a century after the May Fourth Movement that opposed both imperialism from abroad and Confucianism at home, and as such was a precursor of the Communist Revolution. The line of thinking here is not one that, as Timothy Cheek and David Ownby point out, seeks to 'help the people rise up – workers of the world seeking to lose their chains will have to look elsewhere'.[65]

---

64 Xi Jinping, 'The Most Essential Feature of Socialism with Chinese Characteristics Is the Leadership of the CCP', *People's Daily*, 16 July 2020.

65 Timothy Cheek and David Ownby, 'Make China Marxist Again', *Dissent*, 65:4, Fall 2018: 71–7.

Interestingly, the use of traditionalism has to be cautious in what it emphasizes: the (moral) right to rebel against tyranny, central to the Confucian mandate of heaven two millennia before the French *Declaration of the Rights of Man*, is negated both for its post–Cultural Revolution baggage and for the sake of absolute stability. As the party forgoes its original ideological commitment as well as its wartime tradition of the mass line, much of what was culturally overhauled by the revolution is being restored, and much of what was culturally imagined about the socialist new person and new world is abandoned.

The notion that Xi's ideological ambition and leadership style resemble Mao's is mistaken. The distance between their respective worldviews, visions, policy commitments and personal temperaments could not be greater. Their conceptual modes and theoretical outlooks differ, too; and they also speak to and act on very different historical conditions. After all, Mao was a revolutionary, a rebel of his own making and an astute strategist who would 'never forget class struggle' and always believed in the creative potential of the masses. His theorization of the mass line is a seminal contribution to both Marxism and contemporary politics. Like Marx or Gramsci, he also cherished independent and critical thinking, and the innate ability of everyone to be a philosopher and collectively self-governing. Defying the personality cult, something that he must take the bulk of responsibility for, as a dialectical thinker Mao consistently deplored dictation by one voice (*yiyantang*) and insisted on self-criticism. He was also of the view that willingness to work with dissenters should be a required quality of 'worthy successors to the revolutionary cause'.[66] Xi takes the opposite position: the fact that he feels the need to concentrate power in his own hands and take decisions personally may signal an intense power struggle at the top. But it has also resulted in willful policy making and difficulty correcting mistakes. Infallibility is double edged. Meanwhile, the party is deprived of theory, and its confusing ideological stance echoes the collision between its nominal identity and its actual policies, which are guided by illusions

---

66 'Not only must they unite with those who agree with them, they must also be good at uniting with those who disagree and even with those who formerly opposed them and have since been proved wrong in practice . . . they must be imbued with the spirit of self-criticism and have the courage to correct mistakes and shortcomings in their work.' Mao, quoted in 'On Khrushchev's Phony Communism and Its Historical Lessons for the World', *People's Daily*, 14 July 1964.

about global capitalism. The defeatist Marxists' self-deception about the inescapability of capitalism is one form; the promoted self-confidence in the present course, oblivious to its dangers, is another. The capitalist world is no longer reciprocal, recovering from its own fantasy about a liberalizing China. The Chinese dream is facing ever more determined and concerted external challenges.

The dialectic of hegemony and cultural politics

Losing one of its most precious sources of strength, the party suffers from the poverty of theory, this being both a cause and symptom of its crisis of representation. The party has otherwise retained a formidable organizational and mobilizational capability. No longer a conscious proletarian vanguard and aloof from or inimical to working-class consciousness contingent on the rhythm of class struggle, the class identity of party rule and party–mass relations in general poses a question that is difficult to answer. Since the CCP is no ordinary political party in electoral competition with others, and is itself the state power, it is undercut by China's voluntary submission to global capitalism. This has recklessly impinged on national autonomy and social cohesion. The global repositioning of the PRC has allowed the overhaul of its socioeconomic system without overturning its ruling order, as happened in the former Communist Bloc. Apparently, this so-called regime durability in China involves profound adaptations of the regime itself, disproving *communist* as an undifferentiated label: there are resounding ideological and policy distinctions between pre-reform and post-reform, and between the first reform decade and subsequent ones. The puzzle of the CCP staying in power in a post-communist age certainly cannot be tautologically reduced to the idea that it has simply outlived its day. The party's powerful record is magnificent as much as contradictory, and the problem does not stop at theory – it is about history: socialism, emptied or perverted, and class rule, defeated, are persistent and crying out for rehabilitation.

That the CCP has retained power, even without a distinctively communist ideology, makes a huge difference. It is this party monopoly that has enabled the formation of a post-socialist bureaucratic-neoliberal state. State–market interdependence and bureaucratic neoliberalization, in particular, epitomize the dualism of socialist remnants and capitalist novelties, making the Chinese state iconoclastic midwife to some of the twenty-first century's world-shattering changes. Given China's contested hybridity and its evolution from a rebellious variant of state socialism to an unprecedented variant of capitalism, any updated conceptualization must be differentiated from the known models of rentier capitalism, patrimonial capitalism, crony capitalism and so on. The term state capitalism, most commonly applied, can mean anything, as it signals nothing about important differences among such states, between various phases of a trajectory of individual cases, or between divergent development possibilities. China's present and future are open to experimental practice and historical judgement. Discernible though is the alliance of state and capital, and this is where China's liberal opinion leaders are at fault, by directing public discontent towards the state alone, and acquitting capital. The market utopians simultaneously condemn state intervention and demand government enforcement of privatization and financial liberalization. As such, the state is never their real target since neoliberalism has to be embodied in state policies, especially where such policies are resisted by a public culture still permeated by certain socialist values.

The culture of the transmuted PRC state has been underwritten by a few factors. First, this state follows the 'only hard truth' of growth. Unlike the historically laden impulse of catching up or overcoming the anguish and stigma of economic backwardness wherever socialist revolutions took place, market-driven developmentalism is a pure ideology. The standard narrative of China's national economy falling to the brink of collapse by the end of Cultural Revolution was never empirically proven, but the fiction is being fortified as conventional legitimating sources are drained.[67] Second, resembling the nineteenth-century reformist language of wealth and power, nationalism is another central piece of ideology hailed as the China dream. The state is taming the future and enshrining the revolutionary past, Rebecca Karl observes, 'as if it had been fought to secure the victory of national capitalism'.[68] At

---

67 Sets of essential pre-reform economic statistics can be found in Zhou Enlai's 'Government Work Report', 13 January 1975, and in the 1981 CCP Resolution on History, regarded as largely reliable by development economists and economic historians.

68 Rebecca Karl, *China's Revolutions in the Modern World: A Brief Interpretative History*, London: Verso, 2020: 207.

times youthful nationalist sentiments can flood both the official and non-official media, as a generation that has grown up in an ascendant China comes to resent Western arrogance and double standards. Patriotism infused by ethnocentric chauvinism also feeds local tribalist or splittist tendencies. Without socialist and internationalist ordinance, both sides can be self-destructive. Nationalist ideology, clinching a neoglobalist imaginary and embracing not only capitalist integration but also a global China, is especially prone to power and resource chasing and geopolitical clashes. The era of revolutionary nationalism and internationalism is long gone; myths around Chinese homogeneity, ascendancy, military formidability and entitlement to superpower status dangerously lead the way.

A third pillar of state culture is a seemingly irresistible propensity to 'grant unity' (*dayitong*), an obsession with monist authority and non-negotiable unitary control. This is probably a multi-millenarian tradition since the Qin unification. Regardless of repeated upheavals and divisions, unity or unification must be preserved at all cost as an intrinsic virtue and defining feature of the great state itself, however fluid or transcendental the Chinese entity and its spatial boundaries have been.[69] The post-Mao leaders have all been allergic to any suggestion of chaos, and their fear of disorder results in an inability to perceive a dynamic social balance and buttresses oppressive state apparatuses today. Generally, order is indeed a scarce resource among countries in poverty and conflict, but superficial and short-term stability has little public value. Police forces have been deployed to control not only violent protesters but also peaceful petitioners and dissidents, and indeed idealist students, from Tiananmen to Jasic. The maintenance of stability takes the largest slice of government expenditure, and its growth has outpaced that of national defence in the last decade, when the total sum exceeded 'the combined budgets for healthcare, diplomacy and financial oversight'. More is now also spent on state surveillance as a much feared component of dystopian digital capitalism. In the face of social tensions and governing quandaries, the state's most effective trope is preventing cultural revolutionary-style anarchy. Denying free speech and association is in line with the primacy of stability as a proxy for public consensus.

---

69 Brook, 'Great State'.

The nature of the politico-economic and socio-cultural changes unfolding in China is yet to be determined. Until key political divisions and class alignment within and without the party are settled, preliminary questions concerning friends and enemies cannot be answered. In comparison with the revolutionary twentieth century, not only is the extent of bureaucratic capital controlling the means and surpluses of production nearly impossible to quantify given muddled ownership and property relations, the oscillating ideological stance of the CCP is also confounding. Having avoided formally denouncing its constitution, the party tries to reconcile pro-*minsheng* and pro-capital policies, while in the transition from a post-revolutionary to a post-socialist state redrawing class and every other line in domestic and foreign policy making. That the fostering of a private and financialized IT industry and its media networks has undermined the party's own cultural hegemony is a case in point. Obviously, the influential idea that automation and digitization dissolve the old public–private distinction is unconvincing, and the free flow of information cannot by itself be communist in terms of knowledge commons.[70] In such a tangled condition of cultural politics, the concept of post-socialism is deliberate. It is to indicate the structural conditions predicated on a post-capitalist logic since the prior socialist experience is premised on the negation of capitalism.[71] This is paradoxical: the linguistic and conceptual inference of post-socialism instantaneously designates both the death and survival of a passing era. While the prefix is mostly a negative signifier, the positive references of socialism in connection with an epic, yet enormously complicated historical movement transform the connotations of *post-socialism*. Socialism remains prescriptive when emerging opportunities can be seized.

The social reproduction of cultural hegemony both nationally and transnationally is synchronic with that of the structural conditions. The objectification or routinization of this hegemonic agenda kindles a conformist public sphere, adverse to class consciousness and popular struggle. It is the dominant cultural capital that keeps reinforcing

---

70 Michael Hardt, 'The Common in Communism', *Rethinking Marxism* 22:3, 2010: 346–56.

71 Arif Dirlik, 'Postsocialism? Reflections on "Socialism with Chinese Characteristics"', in Dirlik and Meisner, eds, *Marxism and the Chinese Experience*: 377–8.

alienated labour. It 'relentlessly adapts its subjects to existing social relations, deadening their energies and abilities to imagine any other and better order of the world'.[72] As authoritarian capitalism degrades labour while cultivating uniformity, however, it also engenders anti-pathy and opposition. Because of the surviving socialist moral standards, by which government decisions and policies are still socially gauged, Chinese subalterns, while suffering everywhere, still have a strong sense of entitlement and can still defend their constitutionally and legally recognized rights. 'Extremely brutal forms of exploitation of laborers exist in China'; but 'the Chinese working classes know how to fight and have confidence in themselves. There is no submissive atti-tude as seen elsewhere' in Third World capitalism.[73] If this sounds overly optimistic, given that political dilemmas and state repression have debilitated Chinese labour subjectivity as well, some collective memory and latent energy are indeed there. Moreover, a wholesale capitalist transition is utopian and has offered no solution to many of the problems created during the transition. Capitalism with Chinese characteristics aggregative of global systematic impasses might be manageable only by some more realistic, post-capitalist and hence transformative approaches.

To see China's socialist path dependency as having not entirely evaporated is to recognize contradictions within the party and state themselves, as well as the lasting egalitarian and democratic initiatives in society at large. Obviously, the Chinese resources here are far more tenacious and richer than the Polanyian double movement of social self-protection. Without such resources bolstering social pressures, the transition could have been even more calamitous. If the socialist end is to trade with the mere preservation of the regime, the 'social state' designed to serve the people could plunge into 'social fascism'. Recall-ing Marx, his objection to social oppression is equally important: not only must *state*-ism not be mistaken for *social*-ism, but the notion of the social is not immune to tyrannical or xenophobic perversions. His edifying warning is that the free association of the future must not exist

---

72 Perry Anderson, *The H-Word: The Peripeteia of Hegemony*, London: Verso, 2017: 152.

73 Samir Amin, *The Long Revolutions of the Global South: Toward a New Anti-Imperialist International*, New York: Monthly Review Press, 2019: 340, 344.

at the expense of its members, who must remain free producers: 'One must above all avoid setting "the society" up again as an abstraction opposed to the individual.'[74] This is where socialism and liberalism in their true forms converge; and why the significance of people's democracy trialled in Chinese socialism ought to be critically appreciated. This is also where the social must be defended from right-wing populist abuses that conceal social class and power relations in a binary anti-state rhetoric.

For one thing, the unintended outcomes of the Great Leap and the Cultural Revolution need to be contextualized in their specific circumstances; and for another, these events were not what the Chinese socialist enterprise was all about. They did fall into disarray, but the larger landscape of successful development since 1949 is indisputable. One does not need to look further than India – comparable to China in size and starting point – to see what difference a thoroughgoing social revolution can make for the lives of common people. The fact that both the national population and life expectancy nearly doubled in the first three decades of the PRC speaks for itself. The post-Mao crusaders for socialism have invoked symbolic power to forge a prevalent narrative of a dark pre-reform history. Any breakthrough in cultural politics will have to begin with rejecting the discursive habitus of this fictitious history. The pretext of failed historical communism in general, and Chinese socialism in particular, should be refuted. E. H. Carr's commentary on Soviet history is certainly fairer: 'The danger is not that we shall draw a veil over the enormous blots on the record of the Revolution, over the cost in human suffering, over the crimes committed in its name. The danger is that we shall be tempted to forget altogether, and to pass over in silence, its immense achievements.'[75] The same could be said, perhaps still more fittingly, of the Chinese case where the battle is not yet over.

Fragile and discrete resistance in China is attributable to ideological and policy contradictions, and hence to confusions over statecraft. The Communist Party, nominal rather than authentic after the

---

74 Marx, 'Economic and Philosophical Manuscripts', (1844), in T. B. Bottomore, ed., *Karl Marx: Early Writings*, New York: McGraw-Hill, 1963: 117.

75 E. H. Carr, 'The Russian Revolution and the West', *New Left Review* 111, September/October 1979: 25.

radicalization of reform since the 1990s, has broken a once organized working class and fragmented society and its common culture. It is significant that degraded and dispossessed labour and other socially or culturally aggrieved groups, as well as segments within the political elite, opposed the transition to authoritarian capitalism yet have not contemplated a revolution. The socialist critics in China reject old-fashioned revolutionary upheaval, not primarily because of any objective obstacle, from the repressive and ideological state apparatus to the party's coercive and non-coercive hegemonic reach and stabilizing functions; nor is it merely about an objection to undue violence. It is because in their eyes the regime has not exhausted its greatest credibility from the revolutionary and socialist past. Moreover, they must confront the anti-communist 'revolutionaries' at the same time.

That is, as China's capitalist integration is far from conclusive, the socialist task is to mount pressure on the party and state power, to the extent of reappropriating it from within the system hampered by paramount contradictions, unblocking or reopening the passage to socialism. This would be a renewed historical project and revolutionary in essence. 'Politics in command', a powerful idiom of Maoism, still resonates: it calls for class and line struggle, party rebuilding and democratic institutionalization, mass line and social movements. The recaptured party must then (to borrow from Gramsci) clarify its relationship with the popular state on the one hand, and its class positioning on the other. With great foresight and the intricacies of the Russian Revolution in mind, Gramsci from his prison cell in Turin made an intriguing analysis pertinent to a very distant time: the proletarian political party is 'the first cell containing the germs of collective will which are striving to become universal and total'. But when such a party is 'no longer recognized as the proper expression of their class', a crisis of opposition would arise between the 'represented and representatives'. Particularly, as the party bureaucrats turn themselves into 'the most dangerously habitual and conservative force . . . standing by itself and feeling independent from the masses, the party ends by becoming anachronistic.'[76] Having rather accurately tracked such a journey, except that it has also gone further by subsuming the state through

---

76 Antonio Gramsci, *The Modern Prince and Other Writings*, New York: International Publishers, 1959: 137, 174–5.

depoliticizing its own ideology in the managerial terms of governance, the CCP's most spectacular failure is ideological.

Neither neoglobalism nor neo-traditionalism, both centred in developmentalist national rejuvenation, is faithful to the Marxist outlook and commitment to class and universal emancipation. Facing a presumed new cold war, the party is still full of illusions about globalization under the dominant global teleology of capitalism. Any 'modern prince' missioned to accomplish the transition to socialism is yet to be reborn, but organization is indispensable for reforming the reform. What Alain Badiou among others imagined – emancipatory struggles as 'a politics without party' or a 'post-party' politics[77] – cannot be a winning strategy for the Chinese socialists in their post-revolutionary as well as post-socialist conditions. 'Crowds', as Jodi Dean insists, must be organized into conscious class forces.[78] It is not subalternity as such, but common awareness and determination to change it form the collective subjectivity of a transformative politics. Precisely because the CCP is no longer ideologically and organizationally communist, the making and remaking of the historical subject from below would involve the same process as party reconstruction. Only a Gramscian 'war of position' for a radically democratic counterhegemonic bloc could reverse the course of neoliberal capitalist authoritarianism and imperialism. This prospect is not inconceivable.

Historically, the CCP has taken with it the labouring classes and their allies into various situations, and proven capable of self-corrective adaptability. Its future will depend on the ongoing hegemonic struggles within the system. The uniquely valuable resources of equality and liberation rooted in the Chinese revolution and socialism could be an extraordinary advantage, and China's greatest reserve of soft power. Otherwise, 'repoliticization is meaningless' if not combined with the 'gradual assumption of responsibility by workers in the management of society at all levels'.[79] An example is the new united front requirement of a party branch to be located in all sizable private firms, as though leaving the basic state–capital alliance intact and without workers' participation, this would not merely instrumentalize the party for capital

---

77 Badiou, 'The Cultural Revolution'.
78 Jodi Dean, *Crowds and Party*, London: Verso, 2016.
79 Amin, *The Long Revolution of the Global South*: 349.

control over labour and management. Instead, the re-accentuated politics is to be measured and contested by depicting and overcoming contradictions between socialism and Chinese characteristics. Here a chronic legitimacy crisis cannot remain hidden for long, if the regime keeps moving away from its own ranks and traditional supporters. And since legitimation is to a crucial extent a function of ideological and discursive power, it must be fought for against the false politics of preserving power for power's sake.

To regain socialist persuasion in China as elsewhere, is to re-engage culture and win battles for ideas, and thereby for class and popular agency. As Yuezhi Zhao noted, 'oppositions against neoliberal developments continue to surface at every turn of the reform process in politics and ideology'.[80] Essential to this counterhegemonic struggle is an alternative economic vision. Indeterminacy of transitional economies is laid bare in China, demonstrating how decisive political and cultural infrastructures are for a socialist market. Such a vision is especially challenging for a post-capitalist knowledge economy and society. The imagination and theorization of a socialist political economy superior to the capitalist mode and relations of production and the market as we know it have been a constant undercurrent in the reform era. There have also been numerous experiments with 'market socialism' at all levels, some governmental and others spontaneous, and even failed ones can be valuable for enhanced future practices. These have yet to be discussed more extensively; let it suffice here to stress that whether socialism is attainable in the long run lies in the economic sphere, or the ability of socialists to envision and leap over the threshold of what Lenin referred to as an 'extremely difficult task', an 'epoch-making undertaking' of 'completing the foundations of socialist economy'.[81] There will be retreats and defeats; and the inertia patterned on capitalist and pre-capitalist path dependency can be enormous. But accumulated crises could also catalyse change. Such an opportunity would be indicated by a viable socioeconomic programme of democratic planning, needs oriented allocation of resources, unalienated labour and protected

---

80 Yuezhi Zhao, *Communication in China: Political Economy, Power, and Conflict*, Lanham, MD: Rowman and Littlefield, 2008: 8.

81 Quoted in Slavoj Žižek, *First As Tragedy, Then As Farce*, London: Verso, 2009: 44–5.

eco-environment ready for experimentation. Labour and the population at large would by then also have been prepared through a long war of position for an alternative: what once seemed impossible can become unpreventable.

Epilogue

This is the last struggle

This book is a critical analysis of the Communist Revolution, socialist development and post-socialist transformation in China, a trajectory best understood through the country's changing position vis-à-vis global capitalism. Where revolutionary China was a rebel that broke free from the global system, reformist China has made itself an economic beneficiary, for the time being, by participating in it. That enormously costly project of market integration seems to have reached its limit, as China is now perceived as a vicious competitor to the existing global rule makers and must be stopped. Yet all the same, post-socialist transition in China has proven unsustainable, and the first sign of reorientation emerged from the CCP's October 2020 Central Committee meeting, against the overwhelmingly intricate internal and external background of a global pandemic, an all-round trade, technological and fiscal war waged by the US, and freshly entangled difficulties at home. Although the Chinese economy is recovering even as economic contraction has been worsening globally, what matters is not the resumption of an exhausted or gridlocked old order, but how to open up a new path.[1] Arundhati Roy was right when she wrote, 'in the midst of this terrible despair' the pandemic 'offers us a chance to rethink the doomsday

---

1 According to the most recent IMF report, global growth is projected at minus 4.4 per cent in 2020 and plus 5.2 per cent in 2021 – of which 60 per cent would be China's contribution. IMF, 'Crisis and Opportunities: New Finance and New Economy in a New Situation', 24 October 2020, imf.org/en/News/Articles/2020/10/24/sp102420-crisis-and-opportunities-new-finance-and-new-economy-in-a-new-situation.

machine we have built for ourselves. Nothing could be worse than a return to normality.' Instead, humans should 'break with the past and imagine their world anew'.[2] Indeed, a rare consensus emerged among those who dare to imagine an alternative future: that in fact there is no normality to return to, which is certainly true for China.

Fighting coronavirus

The year 2020, *gengzi* in the Chinese sexagenary cycle, has seen massive crises, starting with the outbreak of Covid-19 in Wuhan. This has been a punitive test of the government's leadership, public health system and social solidarity, as well as state capacity in a world context. China, along with a few smaller countries, has so far come out a winner in the contest. Ian Johnson, writer and veteran *New York Times* correspondent who was among those critical reporters expelled from China in March, produced a testimony from personal experience. He encountered a flyer distributor in his residential building in Beijing a few days after Wuhan had gone into lockdown which lasted from 23 January to 8 April 2020 and other cities had declared a public health emergency. The flyer, written by the Beijing municipal government in eight languages, was one of the many means along with official websites and social media accounts to disseminate the latest, most authoritative information about the virus, as well as advice on basic precautions to be taken. It also listed over 100 hospitals designated to handle fever in Greater Beijing. 'The manager was diligent,' wrote Johnson. 'She checked with me about my neighbours [away for the Chinese New Year] . . . and asked me if I had a mask. After a few minutes she cheerfully left to carry on with her rounds' to make sure that everyone was well informed. This housing manager turned out to be among the mass of regular foot soldiers in China's combat against the virus, who worked tirelessly in much more severe situations around the country over the next few months. In particular,

> compliance in China was overwhelmingly voluntary. Beijing's streets were empty not because people were forced to stay home (as was the case in Italy and Spain) but because they mostly accepted the

---

2 Arundhati Roy, 'The Pandemic Is a Portal', *Financial Times*, 3 April 2020.

leadership's message. The result is that China, the pandemic's epicenter, a country of 1.4 billion people, has had 4,634 deaths – a seventh of Spain's, an eighth of Italy's, a ninth of Britain's, and less than a fortieth of the US's.[3]

Martin Wolf of the *Financial Times* stressed that just as China was successful in 'bringing the disease under control in Hubei', so it helped to halt the spread across the country.[4] There was never a pan-Chinese outbreak. According to a speech at an October 2020 international medical conference by Dr Zhang Wenhong, a sober and trusted professional voice and leader of the Shanghai coronavirus expert group, this success in almost eradicating the disease in China over two months is unknown 'in the history of human pandemic management'. This speedy control among so large a national population also meant substantial mitigation of the serious side-effect where health systems overwhelmed by one ailment led to delays or unavailability of care for others.

How has China done it? Whatever criticisms we may have of the many draconian measures imposed – to the extent that villages were often 'barricaded like medieval fortresses, and housing compounds run as if under martial law', clear government directives and effective social physical distancing 'became standard procedure around the world'.[5] No doubt major mistakes were made in Wuhan, from dismissing the alarms by doctors towards the end of 2019 and delays in enacting the national early warning system built after SARS 2002, to permitting a public banquet of 40,000 families in mid-January. There was also a gathering of thousands of deputies for the provincial and municipal 'two sessions' at around the same time, even as certain urgent work on public information about disease control was suspended. But after initial confusion and panic when hospitals in Wuhan were overwhelmed, the central government moved decisively in late January with a national programme of elimination, identifying and admitting all the patients into hospitals for free treatment, and prevention, making all the

---

3 Ian Johnson, 'How Did China Beat Its Covid Crisis?', *New York Review of Books*, 8 October 2020.

4 Martin Wolf, 'The Tragedy of Two Failing Superpowers', *Financial Times*, 31 March 2020.

5 Wolf, 'The Tragedy'.

confirmed and suspicious cases subject to immediate quarantine. Many observers have noted the effectiveness of the Chinese science-based strategy in breaking the chain of infection: strictly enforced lockdowns of the megacity and large areas surrounding it, involving more than 50 million people; fast and comprehensive testing, tracking and treating every patient; complete quarantine procedures; use of traditional medicine; simple messaging; and strong, extensive logistical networks for supply and delivery. The government has maintained 'accurate prevention and control' in the 'new normal' since mid-2020. All this relies on sophisticated organization, efficient central–local and local–local coordination, and broad cooperation at the grassroots level of neighbourhood committees and community networks. The Chinese system has worked to save lives.

Three key factors can be highlighted. First, government determination and state capacity were vital in crisis management. Putting people first, ahead of economic priorities, rather than 'totalitarian management' seen by some critics, was the essence of China's strategy for the pandemic, even if ultimately the two goals converge. People especially appreciate it when they see the residual party tradition of acting on the hardest tasks. Of the 496 health workers and volunteers who died on the frontline as of 29 April 2020, 328 were party members. It has also been crucial to maintain state control over basic physical and financial infrastructures, hence the macro efficiency of emergency planning, and investment and resource allocation – an argument in support of the fortification of SOEs. In mobilizing public and social resources, over 200 medical teams of more than 42,000 medics, with ample equipment, were dispatched to Hubei from other cities; large new hospitals were built in days; convention and sport centres and student dormitories were remodelled into makeshift hospitals to host and treat less serious patients; ventilators, protective suits, masks and so on were massively produced on a wartime schedule. Importantly, China has also managed to send doctors and medical supplies to a number of other countries, and pledged that 'Chinese vaccines will be made a global public good.'[6] Second, social mobilization reminiscent of the revolutionary mass line has remained necessary and effective in these circumstances. Once again, ordinary people, including dedicated cadres, community

---

6 Xi Jinping, speech at the World Health Assembly, 18 May 2020.

workers and countless volunteers, have shown extraordinary energy, self-discipline and self-sacrifice at a time of crisis. Third, rural China demonstrated its strategic importance in sustaining agrarian production, receiving returned migrants from their suspended urban jobs, self-organizing to guard villages and stop contagion, and securing grain and vegetable supplies to cities under siege. The 2020 harvest was not affected by the multiple natural disasters of the year. While urban employment declined by 6 per cent, about 26.4 million people, in the first quarter of 2020 due to lockdowns, many of these were migrant workers who returned to their rural homes where they still hold land rights and have families to rely on. As such, villages acted as a shock absorber.

All these factors – state economic and organizational capacity, mass mobilization and cooperative self-initiatives and discipline, and the absorptive rural backstop – are legacies of revolution and socialism. The explanation for China's success is thus found not in 'Asian values', but in enduring socialist traditions. It is also worth remembering the huge supplies and donations shipped to China from a dozen countries, involving normal trade as well as humanitarian aid, as well as huge contributions from overseas Chinese and foreign volunteers. The notion of shared humanity makes concrete sense in the pandemic.

Reassessing China's global position

Coming out of this sudden, unprecedented public health crisis, the PRC has found itself in an unfamiliar or indeed hostile foreign environment, the most difficult since 1989. Globally, the pandemic has widened and deepened existing tensions and generated new crises. Confronted with a US-led smear campaign against China, Beijing can no longer delay a reassessment of its place in the world, and must reposition itself accordingly so as to navigate out of the quandary it faces. Is it really an era of 'peace and development' after the one of 'war and revolution' depicted by the reformers' Maoist predecessors, as they have long perceived it? Or is it something quite different?

The one sure thing that is often neglected in China's reformist worldview is imperialism, regarding which Lenin's familiar theory on monopolistic, financialized, capital-exporting, and territorially aggressive features for superprofit remains highly relevant. Paul Sweezy's *Monopoly Capital* (1966) posited that the tendency of rising surplus in the ever more concentrated and oligopolistic mode of capitalist production would replace that of the 'falling rate of profit' characteristic of a more competitive capitalism, which explained how the newer markets could speed up accumulation and prolong capitalist lifespan. Information and other technological revolutions have reshaped production and consumption as much as exploitation. Varieties of collaboration notwithstanding, tensions are growing between national sovereignty and multinationals, productive and financial capitals, formal and informal economies, permanent and precarious workforces, and so on. FDI-stimulated manufacturing hubs in the global South contrast with the increasingly deindustrialized global North and its speculative and volatile stock and money markets. This malformed North–South interdependence, with a parasitic Northern class enabled by financialization and internet transactions extracting profits and rents from the South, globalizes domestic class polarization and is inherently unstable.[7] Clearly, imperialist law also strongly inclines towards technological monopolies and the shielding of a rentier oligarchy and states from any competition. Its function though relies on local regimes. Critiques of imperialism wouldn't be effective without touching on its local collaborative power.

This neoliberal hyperglobalization has not only seen an accelerated accumulation in the core but has also had a major impact on labour in its (semi-)peripheries. The contradiction appears no longer confined to one between (domestic and foreign) capital and labour, but also among labour, as though countries at the receiving end of FDI and their workers producing for the world market are responsible for outsourced real economy, depressed wages and job losses in the more advanced economies. As labour's misery in trade surplus countries is correlated with collateral damages in trade-deficit ones, trade wars are indeed class wars.[8] Making labour cheap as a comparative advantage in the global labour arbitrage hurts labour everywhere, above all domestically. This is

---

7 Samir Amin, 'The Surplus in Monopoly Capitalism and the Imperialist Rent', *Monthly Review* 64:3, 2012: 78–85; John Smith, 'Imperialism in the Twenty-First Century', *Monthly Review*, 67:3, 2015: 82–97.

8 Matthew Klein and Michael Pettis, *Trade Wars Are Class Wars*.

a basic factor of international trade conflicts and class politics. While debate over industrial policy has returned to haunt the US, which has never really abandoned such a policy in preserving its economic and technological supremacy, China has paid a terrible price for its participation in the reconfiguration of global capital, and that only reinforces existing power relations: partial dependency, extreme inequalities, labour deprivation, environmental degradation – imposed from outside but duly internalized. The fact that the US has taken advantage of low-cost goods made in China and of China's outsized foreign reserve holding in US bonds – both untenable – can be viewed as either success or failure from each state's standpoint. On the Chinese side, a more self-reflective evaluation is, among the many negative effects of neoliberalization, about a loss of thirty years of China's own industrial software due to strategically short-sighted and opportunistic policies. Unequal exchange that continues to see the core capitalist powers chasing profitability and extracting surpluses abroad warrants both economic nationalism and labour internationalism. Any tension between the two needs to be registered as a protest against imperialism and globalization-fuelled polarization.

Regardless of the great disparity between the two powers, China's ascendancy is obviously incompatible with the current global order, which underlines the reasons for the pursuit of the new cold war, so called, waged by the US and its allies since the late 2010s. There is no replica of high Cold War, however, and the US-led global order is absolutely unrivalled. The present rivalry is missing the essential factor of two socioeconomic and political-ideological systems – socialism versus capitalism. China's intended integration into multilateral global capitalism, rather than surpassing it (while inadvertently challenging the US hegemony), makes all the difference. Such a cold war can at most be a rhetorical shorthand, a warning of dangers, without a real alternative. When the aggressive containment of China is favoured by an otherwise divided American political class, the only option China has is to self-reposition, re-identifying itself with the working and oppressed peoples internationally. It has never been so urgent to counter imperialism and the drums of war.

Issues with long-term strategy

One unintended consequence of the external pressures imposed on the PRC has been the bursting of its illusions, forcing it to seek a path-breaking alternative. As the Chinese economy rebounds and export upsurges, its role in the now racked global supply chain becomes a burning question when growing trade protectionism looms, with embargos, sanctions and the desertion of foreign capital. As one of the world's foremost manufacturers and trading partners for many countries, has China prepared for a decoupling with the US, and is it able to cope with any serious fallout? Although its foreign trade dependency rate had already declined markedly before the pandemic (from about 65 per cent in 2006 to 32 per cent in 2019), could China survive a US-initiated separation, sometimes misperceived as deglobalization? What a historical irony that China and the US have swapped positions: contrary to the 'delinking' in resisting capitalist global scramble of the remaining local commons long proposed on the left, now it is China, reluctant to give up its G2 illusion, that champions for continuous globalization.

China has responded with a plan of national and transnational 'dual circulation' and high quality development based on new or renewable energy. It has vowed to achieve more technological autonomy, with an emphasis on science and education, and 'new infrastructural construction' hailed as a part of the fourth industrial revolution, that will move toward a networked 'intelligence economy and society'. Its hi-tech sectors are making growth qualitatively rather than quantitatively defined. The proposal for dual circulation has been promised on a domestic market augmented by growing internal demand. Such a market, it is hoped, will nurture self-reliance at a higher level and overcome the signature capitalist crisis of overproduction caused by mass underconsumption (though not officially admitted in these terms), previously managed by an export-led economic model. Earlier in 2020 the government had already announced its intention to move forward on the banning of exports of strategic substances and technologies to foreign companies. But an air of reluctance also abounds. The *People's Daily* has repeatedly stated that 'neither the general tendency of globalization nor China's own open policy will change.' Foreign investors are promised to see widening preferential treatment, such as in land use at 70 per cent of the lowest national industrial land pricing.[9] Experts advised that dual circulation should be understood as a concept of mutual reinforcement between its two components; and some prefer to interpret it as just another detour to removing capital account control and completing land marketization.

The abuses of the US nevertheless seem to have served as a wake-up call for the country to restore an independent development agenda that could somewhat resemble the massive achievements of the programme of 'science for the people' under high socialism. Now there is really a chance for a new set of policies capable of managing economic rebalancing at long last, even moving China out of the cheap labour zone in the global market altogether. Most importantly, the December 2020 politburo meeting acknowledged for the first time in decades the need to curb monopoly and forestall unruly capital expansion. Taking *xiaokang* or moderate prosperity as the point of departure,[10] and retracing *Made in China 2025* in the party's new *2035 Vision*, the 'two century goals' are not beyond reach in economic terms. These ambitions, however, are ultimately about competing with other powers within the system rather than overcoming capitalism.

Moreover, the proposed changes are far from breaching the growth-centred framework, and are surprisingly unaware of their environmental implications in spite of the 'clear waters and green mountains' rhetoric. Neither are structural obstacles – such as an increasingly mixed public sector, loosened capital control, labour precarity and exploitation, and marketized public services – specifically addressed. Obviously, without the radical reduction of household educational and healthcare costs and large rural and urban low-income groups, boosting domestic demands could be wishful thinking. Unlike many countries, China's (post-)Covid stimulus package (in the same pattern of scanty financial aid to flood victims in the summer) focus on the resumption of infrastructure, entrepreneurship and innovation, rather than flat emergency cash

---

9 Xinhua News, 'China Issus New Policies to Attract Foreign Capital', *People's Daily*, 30 December 2020.

10 The government announced in November 2020 that all of China's 832 impoverished counties (defined by more than 2 per cent of the given population of a county makes less than 4,000 yuan or around $600 per year) had done away with absolute poverty.

transfers. The government has neither repeated the 2008–9 programme with its lasting complications of economic bubbles nor addressed the exceedingly unequal redistributive and public provision systems. The idea of market stimulus is in any case, by definition, short sighted.

While the long-debated thesis around universal basic income (UBI) has entered the government agenda in some countries, it exerts no influence on Beijing, even temporarily. Yet the idea, even with many sceptics, could be useful for the wellbeing of the vast Chinese population, among which nobody should ever be 'surplus' or disposable. This is so not only because of the immediate pressure on employment due to automation and relocation-induced industrial labour redundancy (8 million 2020 university graduates alone are struggling to find fitting jobs), even though massive new roles are also being constantly created, in addition to the enormous demand from improving and expanding human infrastructure. It is also because the two important local traditions of a social moral economy and a public culture of collective volunteerism would lessen barriers to designing and implementing a UBI scheme. Although work and life have begun to be reconceived and reorganized towards discarding both 'bullshit jobs' and 'jobless classes' in a post-capitalist realm of freedom,[11] and notwithstanding valid criticisms of UBI from the left, the Chinese socialists are yet to envision anything like a social dividend underpinning full activity without full employment. Legalizing shortened workweeks could also be both socially and environmentally beneficial, if the legal 40 hour week can first be implemented. The government has nevertheless taken a positive step that large industrial and financial SOEs have been instructed since 2017 to contribute a standard 10 per cent of their total equity to the national pension and social security funds. Belatedly, some sort of wealth and inheritance taxes are also being contemplated. Since universal provision of basic income, also as a universal right, if not presumes, then can certainly more securely relies on a public sector dominated by socialized investment free of the threats of capital strike and flight,

11 David Graeber, *Bullshit Jobs: A Theory*, New York: Simon & Schuster, 2018; Philippe Van Parijis, 'A Revolution in Class Theory', in Wright, *The Debate on Classes*: ch. 6; Cui Zhiyuan, 'Founding a Permanent Trust Fund of the Chinese People', interview in *Shanghai Securities News*, 3 March 2008, and 'Basic Income as a Component of Liberal Socialism', *Experimentalist Governance* 121, 11 July 2016.

and for equal sharing of its earnings among all citizens, than mere taxation, this proposal is antithetical to privatization.

A regrettable omission from China's post-Covid plan is the health system. Despite 'healthy China' being a stated policy goal, the system has been in a deadlock of endless rounds of wrong-headed reforms, which have resulted in profit-driven public hospitals and privatized pharmaceutic companies notorious for expensive or even unsafe drugs. During the pandemic, the government was able to provide free treatment to all coronavirus patients from late January 2020. This emergency practice could have been directly translated into a programme towards equal and universal free care as the only solution to the two serious popular concerns: unaffordability and health inequality. The hindrance is not financial but political, as attested by what China could achieve through rudimentary yet free public care and preventive medicine, when it was many times poorer; and many people reasonably expected such hindrances to be brushed away after the crisis.

The socialist experience of eliminating smallpox and snail fever (schistosomiasis), and effectively controlling other pestilences, is legendary. It featured a low-cost, comprehensive public network involving state investment in a three-layered health protection system of county hospitals, township medical centres and village clinics, as well as urban medical professionals taking turns to work in rural areas and train the locals, plus an army of community clinics and barefoot doctors. Mass immunization and basic care along with general improvements in sanitation and nutrition also greatly helped treating and restricting infectious diseases. The well-known story of fighting snail fever has been recognized in several WHO reports. In Mao's 1958 poem celebrating the defeat of the disease in the most infected regions, 'Farewell to the God of Plague', the verse about '6 hundred million marvellous Chinese all being equal to Yao and Shun' (the ancient sage kings) is still a popular aspiration. That victory on the health front, among others, explains how life expectancy could nearly have doubled between 1949 and the late 1970s. In fact, schistosomiasis made a return after decollectivization and the loss of organized communal defence. The lesson is clear: healthcare is a realm for public management rather than market calculation. China's 'new infrastructures', highlighted in the fourteenth five-year plan, could have rebuilt public medicine with universal coverage, beginning by extending the emergency practice into a new norm. Instead, nominally socialist China continues to allow itself to lag behind both former communist states and capitalist social democracies in this crucial public welfare area.

National financial independence and stability is another key battle-ground. In addition to strengthening capital account control and preventing more defaults (which triggered money market distresses in late 2020), the regulation of private monopolies and shadow banking is essential. The government has taken steps to clear up the mess of smaller high-leverage peer-to-peer lending, but stopped short of reining in private finance more decisively. The Alibaba empire, its payment system and the (usury-like) microloan and online banking subsidiaries, and the Ant Financial Services group informally affiliated to it, have even made their stakeholders, through public offering, government financial institutions as large as the National Social Security Fund and China Investment Corporation (sovereign wealth fund). In July 2020, the group's private placement of shares was valued at more than $45 billion. Sovereign state credit was thereby granted to shore up private oligarchs, including foreign investors holding half of the shares. An element of tech fetishism played a part in this, but financial innovation in e-commerce, like those innovative bank derivatives which led to the 2008 global meltdown, can be hazardous. It has nothing to do with hard technology, but is merely about the big-data enhanced process of big profitmaking. That China pioneered such internet trading and financ-ing, drawing daily transactions by 800 million people, is hardly something to celebrate. The annual 11 November e-buying sprees, tril-lions of dollars' worth (without generating proportional tax income for the public) is exemplary of the unrestrained consumerism, hedonism and market absurdity; which also encourages a demeaning gendered pattern of coercive consumption.

The CEOs of Alibaba and Ant were summoned to an interview by the central regulators, and their planned dual listing in Shanghai and Hong Kong (set to be the biggest stock debut in history) was postponed in early November 2020, followed also by an antitrust investigation in December. Many wonder how this came so late, and what kind of hidden interests were involved, implicating the regulatory regime itself. The CEOs of big private financial and IT companies do not only top the lists of China's and the world's billionaires, but are also prominent 'peo-ple's deputies' to the NPC and local congresses or members of the national and provincial political consultative conferences. They have bought some control over the media and hence certain discursive power as well, to help lobbying the government and gain support and protection for their business model of digitizing the infrastructure of a monopolistic and financialized information capitalism. This is a large case to show how international and fictitious capital can spectacularly augment not only through traditional forms of exploitation, property speculation and financial gambling, but also private internet enclosures, big data control and transnational e-commerce. It also shows how the IT-enhanced tendency towards socialization of knowledge production may not change the relations of production in their totality. The new managerial mode under private capital and (intellectual) property rights regimes tends to tolerate fake news and disinformation rather than open source for equal access.

Digitization in everyday Chinese life has seen a ruthlessly expanding and competitive platform economy brutalizing its intensely exploited gig labour. Delivery workers went on several cross-provincial strikes in the autumn of 2020, over unbearable automatically programmed timetables and wage arrears. In this context, the belated central interventions in the name of constraining capital could be a sign that the public authorities are finally moving to rein in private financiers and unruly markets, and along with it the toxic level of family and government indebtedness, which has mounted from debt-funded investment and spending. Such private monopolies contradict the intrinsically public and socialized disposition of platforms, shielded by a mass culture of commodity fetishism and advertisement-led desires and consumption.

Another oversight has been in the country's rural strategy. The new five-year plan does stress national self-sufficient of grain and food security, autonomy in seeds, R&D for smart agriculture and further greening by increasing forest coverage, as well as raising household income and the integrated development of primary, secondary and tertiary industries in the rural areas. But little attention is paid to the essential agency of peasant subjectivity and a socialist moral economy of rural communities in terms of overall national and social security. Central policy continues to prioritize 'industrialization, urbanization and agricultural modernization', without addressing the serious issues of village collectives losing leverage over land, or agrocapital undercutting organic farming and peasant commons.[12] Yet one outstanding feature in China's response to the pandemic is the position of the countryside as the lifeline in crisis management and disaster relief – as the country navigates turbulent waters, the depth and resourcefulness of its rural rearguard is again strategically significant. Rural China, with its boundless potential, is vital for the nation's food and general protection, not to mention for the benefits of a less energy-intensive living against a backdrop of the modern urban/industrial civilization-induced global warming. Precisely because science and technology are transforming agriculture, wider productive activities and village life with it, policy thinking needs to be aware of the open possibilities. The trend should be geared towards the vision of communal socialism: an organic eco-agriculture, rural reorganization of diversified works and of life, free provision of universal healthcare and quality schooling (that alone would demand huge human capital investment, known as creating jobs), so as to consolidate rather than weaken rural China. Only then can the whole country become safer, greener, healthier, and also better cultivated and connected through stronger knowledge commons and faster communication.

Defining a critical socialist stance

In China, the Marxist socialists have sought a reorientation. They are cornered by ambiguities, not least in identifying friends and enemies in class terms. They face the stark ideological and policy contradictions of the PRC state and society, intensified imperialist aggression towards China, and the wide divisions of a fragmented left. In a repressive and ever narrower political and discursive space – for both left and right, and especially labour activism – the socialists have to endure doubts and be extremely cautious not to overlook any chance of anti-capitalist change from within the system's core, while preventing their own criticisms from being confused with, or exploited by, right-wing China bashing. These constraints could limit their analyses, mute their voices and halt their influence at a time when, as Arif Dirlik wrote thirty years ago, 'the major casualty of postsocialsim is the concept of socialism

---

12 Li Keqiang, *People's Daily*, 4 November 2020.

itself'.[13] The situation of Chinese socialists abroad is especially difficult. They are reluctant to criticize China not because of a nationalist sentiment as such, but because of an obligation to demarcate themselves clearly from anti-socialist attacks on China. Yet precisely because of their unyielding defense of the principles of the Communist Revolution, their position inevitably contradicts much of the official one.

What socialist critics have since endeavoured to carry through is this very synchrony of socialism and criticism (regarding China's departure from socialism). To do so they must reclaim the fundamental justice and historicity of revolutionary and socialist practice, and reappropriate socialist language credibly and meaningfully. They must also re-engage in the ultimate struggle between socialism and capitalism, one that was blocked by the failure of the Cultural Revolution, which, in turn and paradoxically, facilitated a process of making China an agent of capitalist globalization.

Such a critical stance towards the party line is often challenged by the fact that the regime retains substantial support, and not only because there is no viable alternative. Among a series of sizable surveys conducted in mainland China in the 2010s, the popularity of the central state (as compared with local governments) is consistent. According to a Harvard study of recent polls on citizens' perception of government performance between 2003 and 2016, 'across the board, satisfaction levels have risen'.[14] While such surveys may not be free from refusal bias or sampling limitation, and history shows us that popular support does not automatically vindicate any regime, it is socialist critiques invoking a kind of line struggle that have helped push and could continue to push policies leftward. The latter could entail recovering and buttressing the CCP's original power base. As argued here, the regime's resilience can be explained by a combination of historical revolutionary legitimacy, the legitimizing effect of improved *minsheng* and enhanced national standing. But the phenomenal public approval does also sharpen the question concerning hegemony itself, or the 'educative and formative role of the State'. This state is capable of assimilating society 'into a total and

---

13 Dirlik, 'Postsocialism?': 363.

14 Edward Cunningham, Tony Saich and Jessie Turiel, 'Understanding CCP Resilience: Surveying Chinese Public Opinion Through Time', Ash Center for Democratic Governance and Innovation, July 2020.

molecular (individual) transformation of ways of thinking and acting'; hence the struggle over collective political will.[15] In the midst of a materialist culture saturated with market values, socialist counterhegemony is a long revolution to recuperate social solidarity with labour, the poor and marginalized, and the toiling masses of the world. The socialist subject is made and can be remade.

This struggle is thus waged on a triple front simultaneously, against i) capitalist and cold war anti-communism; ii) unchecked Chinese nationalism (differentiated from earlier revolutionary nationalism) that betrays the socialist cause of class emancipation and class-based internationalism; and iii) compromised international leftism sitting on the fence between the US and the PRC, as though the two countries are politically equivalent. Can a warmonger with troops stationed and combating abroad and warships navigated often thousands of miles away from home, and a road and plant builder abroad, even if self-motivated, really be equitable? Putting aside the common foe of the right, a critical socialist left distinguishes itself, first, from the standpoint that maintains an unconditional defence of China and its pro-capitalist outlook and characteristics, and second, from a leftist eclecticism and its refusal to condemn imperialist and racist provocations against China. Neutrality can be complacency. These distinctions allow the socialists the scope to maintain their principled position.

Being steadfastly critical of a China drifting to the right in the past three decades beneath the party's confusing rhetoric, the constructive internal socialist opposition insists on categorical differences between the social characters of pre- and post-reform and further between the first and subsequent reform decades (discussed in Chapter 2). This insistence is not merely about historical accuracy or intellectual honesty, but is essentially a pathway to source the overlapping experiences of Chinese transformations to deal with today's challenges. Socialism in the prevalent perspective never really existed, or was no more than a doomed and parenthetical episode. But that is fiction, not history. An especially pressing question is that without the socialist values of freedom, equality, fraternity and democracy being substantively reclaimed in its mainland political economy, public institutions and

---

15 Gramsci, in Hoare and Nowell Smith, eds, *Selections from the Prison Notebooks*: 242, 267.

social-cultural policies, on what ground can China pursue unification and justify its minority policies and global projects? The answer to imperialist and racist bullying and interference thus lies not only in the country's determined opposition to unilateralism and militarism, but also and mainly its own strengths and international support. China must refuse to play dangerous war games with the US concerning cross-Strait relations. Taiwan is a political question and can be resolved politically; only dialogue can lead to any form of a democratically legitimate union, conditioned on peace.

Critical socialism is premised on seeing history as an open contour. A conviction underlining this book is that the developmental juncture at which China has arrived was neither unavoidable nor natural, as China's Hayekists argue; and it is not unchangeable either. The possibility of a fundamental transformation of late capitalism is not closed. Development is always multilinear, sanctioning paths not (yet) taken and invoking asynchronous temporalities. Since the capitalist promise offers no solutions to local and global predicaments and the system keeps inflicting cataclysms upon society and nature, and since capitalism with Chinese characteristics is not only aggregative of global systematic damages and risks but also reinforces local problems, that path is neither rational nor viable. To unblock China's stalled transition to socialism, or, more accurately, to reverse its transition to capitalism (though the complex and contending trends may not be definable purely in these terms), is not to subscribe to a teleology of any predestined outcome. There is nevertheless an advantage in China to be appreciated: that socialist transition began earlier and endured for a sustained period of time with some lasting effects; and that socialism has never vanished, but is rather a stubborn negating force cutting into the processes of capitalist construction and destruction. Moreover, while one of the main tragedies of the communist revolutions is that they failed to establish a truly democratic state form, a failure primarily attributable to the overwhelming power of counterrevolution, the legacies of China's experimental revolutionary and socialist democracy can be viewed from the local lens of desires and knowledge, in contrast with state adaptation to market dictatorship in an authoritarian neoliberal era.

Without another violent revolution, the tenacity or fragility of the CCP would be at once contingent on and decisive for the next stage of China's protracted post-socialism and potential reorientation. If the optimism is not groundless regarding a degree of 'the internal solidity of the polity and the potential revolutionary protagonism of its people' in China,[16] and if the socialist energy released by fighting the pandemic can mount, then the PRC may have a chance to lead the way – a long way – in socializing the means and factors of production, and in decommodifying society and founding democratic socioeconomic management. After all, socialist China has had extensive experience with a modern moral economy of rural and urban commons geared towards the dignity and wellbeing of labour and the people. That the aspiration of socialism is still popularly alive is a case in point.

In a bridgeable distance from the Marxist students committed to the working class, there has also emerged a new generation of socialists who have been engaged in vibrant online forums debating the issues of the day. One example is Bilibili (the B Site), although the majority of its 170 million followers may not yet be consciously political; at the same time the growth of independent thinking and social participation has been noticeable. More widely, there are tens of millions of idealistic 'millennials as volunteers' devoted to 'nonconfrontational' public good activism.[17] Young professionals and activists are working in community regeneration, antipoverty projects, rural reconstruction (mixing wartime communist and reformist practices), social care, tech support, charity services and much else. They are not constitutive of a civil society in an antagonistic relationship with the state, but new agents of change, belonging to 2 million registered civil organizations and many more informal networks frequently collaborating with local government, Communist Youth League and Women's Federation branches. Any viable pathway to empowering a transformative politics requiring joined labour and social struggles, however, is still murky under a regime in fear of tracing its original class basis.

---

16 John Bellamy Foster, 'China 2020: An Introduction', *Monthly Review* online, 1 October 2020.

17 Jing Wang, *The Other Digital China: Nonconfrontational Activism on the Social Web*, Cambridge, MA: Harvard University Press, 2020: 142.

'This is the last struggle, unite for tomorrow.'

As the Chinese saying goes, crisis also signals opportunity; it can potentially spark real change. Yet, just as likely, the momentum gained for a socialist countermove after China's resounding first-stage success in controlling the virus could slip away. Taking into account the entire socialist groundwork behind it, recall Marx's sense of urgency about rescuing the Russian Mir for a communist transition: 'The finest chance that history has ever offered to a nation' not to 'undergo all the fatal vicissitudes of the capitalist system' could be missed quickly.[18] For China to seize the moment, it must above all continue to combat the pandemic in a likely second wave, and beyond its borders. It must share coronavirus research information and vaccines regardless of intellectual property or profit considerations, commit quality medical equipment supplies to others and cancel debt for poor and stranded countries. These can be first steps away from neoglobalism while also enforcing other collective efforts at a halt to arms race and climate crisis.

The strategic task is thus to discard the ideology of developmentism or growth-centrism, also noting the contribution to ecological devastation by multinationals operating on Chinese land. China has indeed promoted green consciousness, led exploration of wind and solar power, and begun to construct special ecological zones. But it is also the world's largest emitter, and its soaring carbon emissions account for 28 per cent of the global total. It faces the paradox of having to cling to coal-fired power plants in order to be more energy self-reliant, before clean energy can dominate and old energy-intensive industries shrink. In 2020 the government issued five times more business licences for coalmining than it did in 2019. Rather than divesting fossil fuels, most new projects are still based in them.[19] Under the 2015 Paris climate accord, China's emissions would peak around 2030; in September 2020 the official commitment was extended to reaching carbon neutrality by 2060. Without fundamentally remaking the infrastructural state,

---

18 Marx, 'To the Editor of the Otecestvenniye Zapisky' (1877), *Collected Works of Karl Marx and Frederick Engels*: 199.

19 Tim Daiss, 'China Reverts to Its Dirty Coal Ways', *Asia Times*, 8 July 2020.

however, these could end up vain pledges. More fundamentally, the plan of 'green financing' through a carbon trade market, with a newly set up national green development fund of 88.5 billion yuan, is ambiguous yet delusive, insofar as the colossal plenary crisis cannot be solved within the framework of capitalist market mechanisms. While negotiations between rich and poor countries over emission caps and credits would never settle fairly and effectively, fundamental contradictions between carbon neutrality and unending growth continue to trap China. 'Given the need to maximize growth, employment, and consumerism, China's leaders find they have no choice but to let the polluters pollute.'[20] This applies to many BRI projects as well, which amplify flaws of a domestic pattern.

Ultimate, carbon politics has to be post-capitalist to break the short-sighted mismanagement of climate change under market dictation. It is really time that the fetishization of growth, and along with it standardized modernization and frenetic consumerism, is renounced, even in China and the global South, where nations and peoples have every right to develop. At issue is not the relinquishment of a legitimate right, nor merely the hard constraint of ecological finality (imagine the environmental consequences of social middling by expanding the already hugely wasteful models of consumption). Rather, this is about becoming free from developmentalist alienation as well as the immediate harms of eco-degradation, pollution and depletion of essential resources imposed on everybody everywhere.

The inherent logic of developmentalism, as of capitalism itself, is the endless accumulation of capital and a distorted market demand severed from any socially rational and proportionate needs. Its intrinsic polarizing tendency reproduces commercial homogeneity as much as social disparities, and cannot be a sustainable solution to poverty either. Climate struggle is also class war, as the world's richest 1 per cent live lavishly and generate emissions double those of the entire poorest half of the human population – China's population has a large part in both demographics.[21] Subordinating human needs to the market and its

---

20 Richard Smith, 'The CCP is an Environmental Catastrophe', *Foreign Policy*, 27 July 2020.

21 Fiona Harvey, 'World's Richest 1 Per Cent Cause Double CO_2 Emissions of Poorest 50 Per Cent, Says Oxfam', *Guardian*, 20 September 2020.

commodity fetishism also entails social-psychological victimization, as illustrated by the way in which even leisure pursuits rely on money and commercial facilities, and participate in a culture of competitive consumerist fantasies. The rhythm of capital directs market actors. In China, the mode of unbridled consumerism exploded when investments flooded in, for 'maximum absorption of exponentially increasing volumes of capital in forms of consumerism that had the shortest possible turnover time'.[22] In fact, if an economy deemed healthy must be maintained by cycles of needless production (from ghost towns to exclusive luxuries) and excessive consumption (fashion-chasing upgrades of possessions among many examples), does that not mean that the doctrinal fundamentals around demand and supply in received theories of economics are questionable?

Contradictions between the logic of capital and our finite earth are not manageable within a system that thrives on billions of people paying for it with their livelihood. These contradictions also disrupt the world's food chain, driving the planet into a multifaceted catastrophe. A different mode of production must reconfigure capital and replace unsustainable growth from overproduction in coexistence with class-divided overconsumption and underconsumption. China needs another liberation of the mind to pursue an alternative, flouting the chimera of capitalist universality and the modern standardization of industrialism, urbanism and private property supremacy. The option of de-growth, beginning with halting urbanization and neoliberal globalization, has never been so pressing. And again, such a reverse course with China in the lead, thanks to its incomplete global integration, is not unthinkable under mounting geo-ecological pressures on coordinated actions of countries. At stake is the impasse of ecological annihilation and barbaric horrors – hunger, conflict, extreme climate conditions, and masses of refugees on a planetary scale, and the stark choice of 'socialism or barbarism' more urgently than ever before. The post-pandemic moment provides China with an impetus to take the hypothesis of ecosocialism as ambitiously and realistically as it can in order to conceive of a very different future.

---

22 David Harvey, 'Anti-Capitalist Politics in the Time of Covid-19', *Jacobin*, 20 March 2020.

Dialectic of revolution and counterrevolution

The Communist Revolution in China changed the fate of the Chinese people and redrew the map of the modern world. Chinese socialism underwent major detours, resisting Stalinist statism while battling global capitalism with its hot, cold and other wars, even threat of nuclear attacks. The market transition of 1978 promised a socialist fine-tuning and had broad consensus before it unexpectedly entered a radical phase after the long 1980s, leading to the overhaul of party ideology, economic structure and consequently class and social relations, as well as foreign policy. As socialism is overwhelmed by a developmentalist nationalism, the previous equilibrium of a dialectic triad of socialism, nationalism and development has broken down since the 1990s.[23] On the other hand, the near eradication of abject poverty is the biggest transformation of its kind the world has ever seen – here again, dependency theory's zero-sum thesis has to bend to account for the Chinese case, although the various brakes now put on it by the capitalist core economies and indeed capitalist ecological destruction also reconfirm the limit on catching up.

On the scale of modernity and history, this trajectory can be clarified in a double narrative of revolution and counterrevolution. The Communist Revolution in China began with a new bourgeois democratic phase, in an agrarian semi-colonial society (to defeat imperialism and feudal landlordism before capitalism). Its subsequent socialist development under the PRC state was then twice jeopardized: first by the failed continuous revolution of Maoist attempts to overcome bureaucratization; and next by the accomplished market reforms under Dengist regimes. The latter ended the revolution and normalized the state in which the ruling CCP no longer assumed a revolutionary organization. Granted the perspective of the socialist transition as a 'very long historical period', as Mao put it, the 1960s represented the first interruption, an abortive revolution within the revolution; the period from the 1990s onwards constituted another interruption, this time counterrevolutionary in the sense that neoliberal development turned against much of what '1949' had stood for. If the 2012 Chongqing clampdown only temporarily appeared as the last milestone in the Chinese path of

---

23 Lin Chun, *The Transformation of Chinese Socialism*: 60–74.

negating socialism because of an element of power struggle, then the 2018 suppression of Jasic workers and their student supporters was an unambiguous indication of the completion of a great reversal. The original intention of both communist revolutionaries and socialist reformers was negated, though *not* irreversibly, contrary to the baffling official discourse.

Strategically, this double narrative can be read as a dialectical shift between revolution's victory and defeat. Wang Hui circumstantiates these terms in their subjects' persistent effort to act on the weak links of counterrevolution while redefining revolution itself, for the real measure of failure 'is not the failure as such but whether the logic of struggle continues.'[24] Confronted with the monumental retreat from socialism and emancipation in China, not substantially different from the ruined zones of historical communism, unrepentant socialists must first resolve if they will not change the will to change, breaking despair and impasses across the horizon. They may well begin with urging an open debate on the nature of today's Chinese state and society, in which the concept of class will return as compass to stimulate political renewal. This is premised on the converging signs of a new turning point. The looming scale of the party's post-pandemic agendas is significant, to the extent that with a big dose of self-critical soul searching, China can take back the torch of socialism and become an epoch-changing power.

The function of historical indeterminacy and contingency is such that intensified external anti-China forces have aggregated important internal changes. The party's proposals are cautious, but one visible gesture is its plenum communiqué, which indicates the need of enlarging and consolidating SOEs (more than just state capital), self-reliant technological capacity, urban–rural integrated social security and climate change actions. However limited, some steps are already taken, from halting private monopolization to backing off from land privatization. Apparently, new American cold warriors are doing China a great service by compelling its leadership to stop wavering and to furnish a rejuvenation of its socialist ambitions. This enticement turns out to be necessary to smash any lingering illusions about win-win capitalism and the neoliberal utopia. Rather than making even more steep concessions,

---

24 Wang Hui, 'Revolutionary Personality and the Philosophy of Victory', *Beijing Cultural Review*, April 2020, sohu.com/a/390048255_115479.

it is in the fundamental interests of the Chinese people to be more independent from a system that draws their sweat to keep itself going. China could catalyse a spatial revolution in the world economy, with wider implications given its current economic gravity. For such a counter-transformation to happen, the party's emerging shift needs to be developed and deserves a positive response from the left. A popular subject of transformative and emancipatory politics will detect and craft openings from history's artificial closures constructively. This reaccentuated politics would in both cognition and practice cohere the century-long socialist struggle in China that has never ceased, even only as an undercurrent.

Marx's famous passage makes concrete sense for contemporary socialist struggles and is worth reading again. The proletarian revolutions would

> consistently engage in self-criticism, and in repeated interruptions of their own course. They return to what has apparently been accomplished in order to begin the task again; with merciless thoroughness they mock the inadequate, weak and wretched aspects of their first attempts; they seem to throw their opponent to the ground only to see him draw strength from the earth and rise again before them, more colossal than ever; they shrink back again and again before the immensity of their own goals, until the situation is created in which any retreat is impossible, and the conditions themselves cry out: hic Rhodus, hic salta! Here is the rose, dance here![25]

A hundred years ago, the small group of communist representatives, who secretly gathered in the French concession in Shanghai to formally found the CCP, escaped police pursuit by conducting the last day of their congress in a humble boat on the suburban South Lake in Jiaxing. Later this site of the red boat became a tourist attraction. How a tiny party, facing formidable obstacles and ready to go through fire and water, grew to make the world's largest modern social revolution is something epically awesome. Nothing can be more tragic if those many millions who joined the revolution and sacrificed their youth and lives

---

25 Karl Marx, *The 18th Brumaire of Louis Bonaparte* (1852), New York: Mondial, 2005: 62.

on its arduous path are forgotten in a gilded age of materialism and cynicism. As Pun Ngai laments, capitalist surges are allowed to destroy revolution and its 'fruits of socialist goals including economic equality, human emancipation and people's democracy, which the vanguard of revolution shed its blood to achieve'. When the revolution was hysterically denounced and dismantled, blood was shed in vain.[26] Refusing surrender, the socialists, by asking themselves if the 'immensity of their own goals' remain true a century after the birth of the CCP, and if the manifold human and natural disasters of capitalist globalization have not reached the point at which 'any retreat is impossible', must reclaim the revolution's original ideal. If the centennial commemoration of the party will not slip into a self-congratulating and formalistic farce, it can facilitate critical scrutiny and political regeneration. In the dialectic of revolution and counterrevolution, the spectre of socialism persists in haunting us.

---

26 Pun Ngai, 'Chinese Communism Revisited: Still a Class Perspective, But Why?', in Alex Taek-Gwang and Slavoj Zizek, eds, *The Idea of Communism*, Vol. 3, London: Verso, 2016: 42.

Index

Finley, Joanne, 201
Fishman, Ted, 20
Flounders, Sara, 206
Foster, John Bellamy, 336
Fourier, Charles, 210
Franceschini, Ivan, 174, 226
Frank, Gunder, 8
Frazier, Robeson Taj, 231
Friedman, Edward, 34, 106
Friedman, Eli, 175
Fukuyama, Francis, 4, 73
Furet, François, 111

Gan Yang, 50, 270
Gao Liang, 141, 148
Gao Mobo, 280
Garside, Roger, 42
Gellner, Ernest, 12
George, Henry, 130, 138
Gerschenkron, Alexander, 152
Gerth, Hans, 11
Gilmartin, Christina, 218
Gindin, Sam, 20
Gleijeses, Piero, 238
Goldstein, Melvyn, 192
Goodman, David, 77
Goodman, Eleanor, 224
Graeber, David, 328
Gramsci, Antonio, 13, 111, 130, 179, 315
Gries, P. H., 194
Grimaldi, James, 305
Gu, Hallie, 134
Guevara, Che, 110, 233, 306
Guizhou Maotai, 287
Guo Liyan, 150
Gurley, John, 34

Ha-Joon Chang, 296
Han Changfu, 130
Han Jun, 134
Hao Peng, 146
Hardt, Michael, 167, 180, 312
Harvey, David, 8, 17, 21, 44, 120, 339
Hassard, John, 143, 144
He Guimei, 255
He Xuefeng, 133, 184
He Zhen, 211
Heberer, Thomas, 189
Hegel, G. W. F., 220, 274
Heilmann, Sebastian, 58
Hell, Natalie, 290
Heller, Agnes, 82
Hershatter, Gail, 179
Hillman, Ben, 199
Hinton, William, 164
Ho Chi Minh, 110
Ho, Peter, 131
Hoare, Quintin, 13, 179
Hobsbawm, Eric, 180, 239
Hobson, John, 261, 262
Honda, Nanhai, 221
Hong Liu, 239
Hornby, Lucy, 151
Howard, Roscoe, 244
Hu Bangding, 87
Hu Feng, 40
Hu Jintao, 44, 306
Hu Yaobang, 43
Huang Jisu, 306
Huang Qifan, 130
Huang Shudong, 149
Huang Xiaohu, 129
Huang Yanpei, 72